Corporate Social Responsibility

Madhumita Chatterji

Director
Acharya Bangalore Business School
Bengaluru

OXFORD
UNIVERSITY PRESS

YMCA Library Building, Jai Singh Road, New Delhi 110001

Oxford University Press is a department of the University of Oxford.
It furthers the University's objective of excellence in research, scholarship,
and education by publishing worldwide in

Oxford   New York
Auckland Cape Town Dar es Salaam Hong Kong Karachi
Kuala Lumpur Madrid Melbourne Mexico City Nairobi
New Delhi Shanghai Taipei Toronto

With offices in
Argentina Austria Brazil Chile Czech Republic France Greece
Guatemala Hungary Italy Japan Poland Portugal Singapore
South Korea Switzerland Thailand Turkey Ukraine Vietnam

Oxford is a registered trade mark of Oxford University Press
in the UK and in certain other countries.

Published in India
by Oxford University Press

© Oxford University Press 2011

The moral rights of the authors have been asserted.

Database right Oxford University Press (maker)

First published 2011

All rights reserved. No part of this publication may be reproduced,
stored in a retrieval system, or transmitted, in any form or by any means,
without the prior permission in writing of Oxford University Press,
or as expressly permitted by law, or under terms agreed with the appropriate
reprographics rights organization. Enquiries concerning reproduction
outside the scope of the above should be sent to the Rights Department,
Oxford University Press, at the address above.

You must not circulate this book in any other binding or cover
and you must impose this same condition on any acquirer.

Third-party website addresses mentioned in this book are provided by
Oxford University Press in good faith and for information only.
Oxford University Press disclaims any responsibility for the material contained therein.

ISBN-13: 978-0-19-806983-6
ISBN-10: 0-19-806983-9

Typeset in Baskerville
by Jojy Philip
Printed and bound in India at Repro India Ltd., Mumbai
and published by Oxford University Press
YMCA Library Building, Jai Singh Road, New Delhi 110001

*To my partner in life
for being a constant source of strength and inspiration*

*And to my children
for keeping dreams alive*

Preface

With the present-day demands of globalization, free-market competition, diverse workforce, and increasing technological complexity, organizations are facing new challenges in trying to cope with the social and environmental impacts of such demands. The power and influence of business in society is greater than ever before because business makes major contributions to every society by creating goods and services, generating employment, contributing to the national exchequer, and driving economic development. Companies have to go beyond bottom-line analysis to ensure that social, environmental, and economical considerations are integrated and synthesized in the decision-making processes at different levels. As organizational values and decisions stem from the individuals who operate them, there is a need to inculcate wisdom in the managers to help them realize the human values that are inherent in them.

The orientation towards sustainable value in terms of human, social, environmental, and economic capital is at the crux of corporate social responsibility (CSR). Although CSR, as a concept, still defies a single definition, there is a universal acceptance of the ideology and that it refers to business engagement that creates economic value for itself while meeting social, ethical, legal, and public expectations. Thus, CSR is the management of a company's impact on its stakeholders, the environment, and the community in which it operates and is more than just a philanthropic activity for some charitable causes.

Today, CSR has attracted public attention and has received global resonance, as the risks associated with unbridled growth are becoming realities. As the demands on business to be accountable are constantly becoming more complex and challenging, CSR provides the means to understand and appreciate these challenges more clearly. The writing of this book has coincided with the phenomena of worldwide economic recession, the BP oil spill, the Satyam debacle, the Google controversy, the exposure of the inhuman and unethical approaches to the Bhopal gas tragedy, the IPL cricket scam, the scams behind Commonwealth Games, and many such episodes, which have amply justified the original idea to endeavour to create an awareness among the youth about the importance of CSR.

The book provides the knowledge and skills to understand modern societies in a more systematic way and thus encourage the emergence of a symbiotic socio-economic structure that can advance our ability to address real-life situations and concerns.

ABOUT THE BOOK

Corporate Social Responsibility has been designed to capture the urgent and immediate need of social responsibility at all levels—national and international. Its purpose is to increase manifestations of CSR practices through increased awareness and motivation. The unique feature of the book is the blending of human values and practical ethics through simple models to explain how organizations can use CSR to become globally competitive and locally effective.

This book explores the core concepts of corporate responsibility and explains them through numerous examples, mini cases, exhibits, and case studies. It discusses CSR practices of Indian and global companies such as Hindustan Unilever Limited (HUL), ITC, Philips, Satyam, Tata Group, Poti Port in Georgia, GlaxoSmithKline, and Nestlé.

This book will be useful to management students studying strategy, ethics, and corporate governance and will also aid professionals in understanding that CSR is not philanthropy and that corporations have to move beyond the financial bottom line to the social and environmental bottom line.

PEDAGOGICAL FEATURES

The various pedagogical features of the text are
- Learning objectives before each chapter highlight major learning insights
- Mini cases and examples provided in the chapters have an Indian context to make the subject matter interesting and relevant
- Key terms introduced in each chapter are defined at the end
- End-chapter exercises such as critical review questions will enable students to reflect on various issues
- Each chapter has research questions and project assignments to facilitate experiential learning, information gathering, and analysis
- References are provided in each chapter for advanced learners

COVERAGE AND STRUCTURE

The book is divided into ten chapters and each one captures the different facets of CSR.

In Chapter 1, Understanding Corporate Social Responsibility, a brief description of the concept of modern business is given. It then provides a brief history of CSR to show that the values inherent in humans have always tried, through various means, to achieve welfare for society. A section on the history of CSR in India has been incorporated to make the topic relevant to

Indian students, who most often are provided a general overview that is skewed towards the practices in developed countries.

In Chapter 2, Evolution of Company and CSR, the concept of corporation is elaborated and a brief history of the development of the corporation is provided. The topic of corporate governance is introduced in this chapter to showcase the importance of governance in running large business entities. The governance structure highlights the responsibilities that business entities have towards various stakeholders and how responsibility and ethics are not exclusive to earning profit.

Chapter 3, Stakeholder Theory, introduces the most important aspect of CSR, an understanding of the stakeholders of business. The chapter gives an insight into the relationship that various stakeholders share with business. It is necessary to understand the impact of the stakeholder relationship on business because often they are very subtle and if ignored can injure business in the long run and make recovery impossible. The stakeholder concept brings to the forefront the importance of values and ethics in business.

Chapter 4, Role of Various Institutions in CSR, portrays business demands, along with the institutional environments with special reference to government, not-for-profits and nongovernmental organizations, the media, and academics. The attempt is to show that CSR is integral to the development process of society and the major institutions of the civil society have an indisputable role to play to enhance the understanding of CSR.

In Chapter 5, Creating CSR Framework, the relevance of culture is explored in detail to explain the significant role local customs play in the design and implementation of CSR practices. It discusses different methods to implement CSR practices and examines the processes of integrating CSR into the strategic framework of organizations. The chapter highlights that CSR perception and delivery have to take into account both global and local practices to be competitive and sustainable.

Chapter 6, Framework for Rating Corporate Social Responsibility, provides the framework that can be designed to put CSR into practice and is aimed at creating an understanding of the importance of CSR reporting. It explores conscientious organizations as not new ventures but value-driven companies that define a core set of values and rely on these values in making all strategic decisions. For corporations, ethical attitude and sustainable success are achieved by striking a balance between the bottom line on one side, and the interest of the employees and the community at large on the other.

Chapter 7, Sustainability and Its Challenges, describes how any form of governance, whether socialistic or capitalistic, has to have a human face in order to achieve sustainability. The different means of measuring sustainability show how it is perceived differently by different stakeholders and organization as a whole and therefore, efforts to ensure sustainability often go in vain.

Chapter 8, The Indian Saga, provides an insight into CSR practices prevalent in India. It offers a brief historical perspective of economic development in India as the background to the development of organizations and their growth. Illustrations of present practices of CSR have been given to encourage learning about the creation of CSR framework by organizations.

Chapter 9, Global CSR, provides a thematic representation of the global scenario. It is observed that designing a 'one-fit-for-all CSR model' is not easy. To present a glimpse into the diversity of the socio-economic as well as the political realities of different countries and their ethical practices, four countries (US, UK, New Zealand, and Indonesia) from four different continents and at different levels of economic development have been portrayed. This helps in understanding the ground realities that organizations should appreciate and realize the long-term perspective that needs to be woven in their CSR strategies.

Chapter 10, The Road Ahead, provides an optimistic, yet a realistic future. Organizations will have to be visionaries who can promote that ethical attitude and sustainable success that is achieved by striking a balance between the bottom line and the interest of the employees and the community at large.

ACKNOWLEDGEMENTS

This book is a tribute to the common man who has shown the real human spirit in any crisis. I owe an intellectual debt to all the brilliant Indian and foreign thinkers and writers on the subject of CSR. This book would not have been possible without the support of the many friends and family members who sincerely believed in and shared ideas about CSR.

A few deserve special thanks. I would be failing in my duty if I do not acknowledge the support provided by Mr Anant G. Nadkarni, Vice President – Group Corporate Sustainability, Tata Council for Community Initiatives (TCCI), who shared the Tata group CSR initiative details and framework. In fact, the reporting framework designed for the Tata companies, with TCCI spearheading the activities, has been showcased in the book to inspire every corporate to undertake CSR activities. The Tata ideology of improving the quality of life of the people concerned has helped the group to create a sustainable value in terms of human, social, natural, and economic capital. TCCI is ever willing to give a helping hand to any institution interested in gaining a firsthand understanding of CSR with an objective of designing a CSR framework and can be reached at tcci@tata.com.

I am grateful to Mr R. Ravikularaman of the CSR team of Suzlon for extending help and support and providing details about the Suzlon CSR programme. Ms Swati Ramanathan and Mr Ramesh Ramanathan as well as the Janaagraha team deserve special thanks for sharing their ideas and initiatives. I must also convey my gratitude to Prof. L. Ramakrishna who willingly contributed his valuable inputs in the area of sustainability with special reference to Philips. My sincere thanks to Dr Nitha Palakshappa and Dr Gabriel Eweje, who generously contributed to the section dealing with Global CSR. Two of my students—Anindita Banerji and Bidish Chatterjee—deserve appreciation for their efforts in preparing case studies. Two individuals who have always guided and encouraged all my endeavours are Dr Rupa Padaki and Dr Vijay Padaki and I must convey my sincere thanks to them. Each one's support has enriched the book by adding varied perspectives.

My husband, Dr S.K. Chatterji, deserves special mention for being there whenever needed and for patiently enduring the tribulations of authorship as he nurtured my early thoughts and goaded me into writing my second book. My son Siddhartha and daughter Sukrita were my sounding board as they brought in the perspective of the new generation and showed remarkable understanding.

I am grateful to the Institute of Finance and International Management (IFIM Business School) for providing me the opportunity to pursue research and allowing intellectual freedom, which bred a spirit of innovation and enquiry. The encouragement provided to faculty to participate in various national and international conferences certainly added to my learning and understanding.

I am very grateful to all those anonymous reviewers who helped to add value to the book by their timely and important suggestions. The last word of acknowledgement goes to the extraordinary cooperation extended by the entire editorial team from Oxford University Press, which deserves a heartfelt gratitude from me. Their human touch in dealing with every aspect of the publication is indeed praiseworthy. Without their continued guidance and support, this book would never have seen the light of day.

Madhumita Chatterji

Contents

Preface   v

1. Understanding Corporate Social Responsibility   1

Introduction   1
What Is Business?   3
　Development of business   4
Dimensions and Importance of CSR   5
Definitions of CSR   8
　Analysis of various viewpoints and related definitions   8
　Economic perspective   9
　Common good   10
　CSR as a continuum   10
Understanding CSR   12
　Responsibility   12
　Accountability   14
　Sustainability   15
　Social contract   16
History of CSR in India   18
　Role of the state   18
　Impact of religion   19
　Emergence of the merchant Class   21
　Merchant charity and CSR   22
　Importance of education   23
　Important business categories   24
　Seeds of modern CSR   24
　First industrial corporations   25
Conclusion   26
Case Study 1: CSR in Hindustan Unilever Limited   31
Case Study 2: CSR in ITC   33

2. Evolution of Company and CSR   37

Introduction   37
Seeds of Early Corporations   38
Development of Modern Corporations   39
　The incorporation of a company   41
Governance and Management of Company   43
Theories of Corporate Governance   44
　Agency theory   44
　Stewardship theory   46
　Shareholder versus stakeholder theory   48
　Transaction cost theory   49
　The sociological theory   50
Importance of CSR in Corporate Governance   50
　Leadership Crisis   52
　Relation between values and skills   53
　The Social Impact   54
Conclusion   57
Case Study: The Satyam Odyssey   61
Annexure: An Overview of Important Corporate Governance Committees   72

3. Stakeholder Theory   82

Introduction   82
Taxonomy of Stakeholders   84
Stakeholder Relationship   85
　Stockholders   85
　Employees   86
　Suppliers   86

Customers/consumers 87
Competitors 88
Government 88
Society and community 89
Impacts and Dilemmas of Business 89
   Intangible aspects of the stakeholder approach 92
   Balancing emotional quotient and intelligence quotient 92
   Importance of ethics 93
   The tussle between means and ends 94
   Combining tangible gains with intangible satisfaction 94
   Holistic growth 95
Stakeholder Trade-offs 96
Conclusion 98
Case Study: CSR in the Tata Group 103

4. **Role of Various Institutions in CSR 117**

Introduction 117
Role of Government 117
   Different markets 118
Role of NGOs and Not-for-Profit Organizations 128
Role of Educational Institutions 134
Role of the Media 138
Conclusion 139
Case Study: Janaagraha Centre for Citizenship and Democracy 143
Annexure: Recommendations on Accountability, Transparency, Governance, and Trust 146

5. **Creating CSR Framework 147**

Introduction 147
Relevance of History and Culture 147
Creation of Strategy 148
   Risk analysis 149
   Building trust 150
   Subliminal impact of history 150

Corporate ideology and history 150
Appreciating culture 152
Governance and culture 154
Apprehensions of societies 154
True nationalism 155
Creating a Framework for CSR 156
   Creation of a corporate culture 156
   Three-level implementation framework 157
   Inner corporate ideology 157
   Micro-level integration by the firm 159
   Macro-level integration by the government 159
   Integration of CSR at the operation and process level 160
   Intermediate national ideology 163
   Statutory regulations 163
   Danger of stereotyping 164
   Outer global ideology 166
Creating an Implementation Framework 166
Conclusion 173
Case Study: The Poti Port in Georgia 178

6. **Framework for Rating Corporate Social Responsibility 185**

Introduction 185
Understanding CSR Ratings 185
Available Accepted Rating Frameworks 186
   Global reporting initiative 186
   Specialized securities indexes 188
   Regulatory bodies and stock exchanges 189
Structure of BITC's CR Index 192
   Rating criteria and basic structure of the rating process 194
Experts in Responsible Investment Solutions 194

Sustainable Investment Research
International 195
Infosys Sustainability Solution 196
Tata Group's CSR Rating Framework 197
Assessment Process 198
Identifying Parameters for Indexing
Tata CSR 201
Philips—Framework for CSR Rating
Related to Environmental
Reporting 203
    Green products 204
    Green innovations 206
    Collection and recycling 207
Conclusion 208
Annexure: *Report on Environmental Reporting* 211

7. **Sustainability and Its Challenges** 225

Introduction 225
Capitalism 229
Humanizing Capitalism 230
Sustainability 233
    Brundtland Report 235
Integrating CSR in Organizations—
Guidelines to Effective Change 238
    ISO and CSR 238
    Triple bottom line 245
    Importance 242
    Triple loop learning 245
Conclusion 248
Case Study: *GlaxoSmithKline—CSR through Innovation and Research* 256
Annexure 1: *Agenda 21* 261
Annexure 2: *UN Millennium Declaration* 261

8. **The Indian Saga** 265

Introduction 265
Post-independent India 266

Models chosen to revive the
economy 267
Emergence of the private sector 267
Reforms and their impacts 267
The Grim Reality 269
Government Initiatives 270
Challenges 275
    Community development and
empowerment 275
Conclusion 276
Case Study: *Case of TCCI—Developing the CSR Framework* 279

9. **Global CSR** 285

Introduction 285
Multinational Companies 286
    Differences in CSR practice 287
    Challenges of multinationals 288
Country-specific CSR Initiatives 288
    The US 289
    The UK 296
    Indonesia 301
    New Zealand 311
Conclusion 318
Case Study: *Suzlon Foundation* 323

10. **The Road Ahead** 327

Introduction 327
Dynamics of the Modern Business
World 330
    Optimistic view of CSR 331
    Pessimistic view of CSR 332
Future Trends in CSR 332
The Awakened Stakeholder 336
The Public-Private Partnership 337
Conclusion 341
Case Study: *The CSR Practices of Nestlé* 343

Index 346

Understanding Corporate Social Responsibility

INTRODUCTION

The word organization is a combination of two words, *organic* and *ization*. If both the words are combined, then we get the concept of bringing a process to life. Organizations are nothing but living systems that interact both internally and externally. They are made up of two aspects: the human aspect and the technical aspect. The differentiation between the human and the technical aspect is based on the fact that technology by itself does not have a thinking mind and therefore cannot take decisions. In reality, even the technical aspect is actually driven by the human mind. Hence, it is the human aspect that decides the purpose of the organization and the means of achieving that purpose with the help of technology. As generally understood, the purpose of business is to earn money for the shareholders or stockholders and to provide products and services to the customers. Achieving the purpose obviously requires certain processes, with technical support, which includes machinery, engineering, and other technical know-how like information technology, ergonomics, safety, and maintenance, etc., which have to be put in place to achieve success. These processes are known as the functional areas of business and in the simplest form include (1) market research to understand the needs of society or the consumer, (2) finance to allocate funds to all the related activities of business, (3) production and operations to source raw materials, design products or services, produce them, and send them to the market, (4) sales and marketing to advertise, manage supply chain, distribute, and finally reach the customer, and (5) human resources to take care of the employees who are involved in all the above processes.

The processes are not simple because every activity needs to be planned well and will have a number of sub-activities that must be focussed upon for success. Since our aim is not to go into the details of the technical and functional aspects of business, it suffices

LEARNING OBJECTIVES

After studying this chapter, you will be able to
- Understand organizations as living systems and assess their purpose
- Get an overview of the concept of modern business
- Get a glimpse of the history of CSR, specifically in India
- Define CSR as a concept
- Analyse the different dimensions of CSR

here to understand that while achieving the purpose, business impacts the socio-economic as well as the political structure of a nation. With globalization, these impacts have grown by leaps and bounds and are no longer limited by the geographical boundaries of a nation (the subsequent chapters provide more details on this). The simplified concept of management is diagrammatically represented in Fig. 1.1.

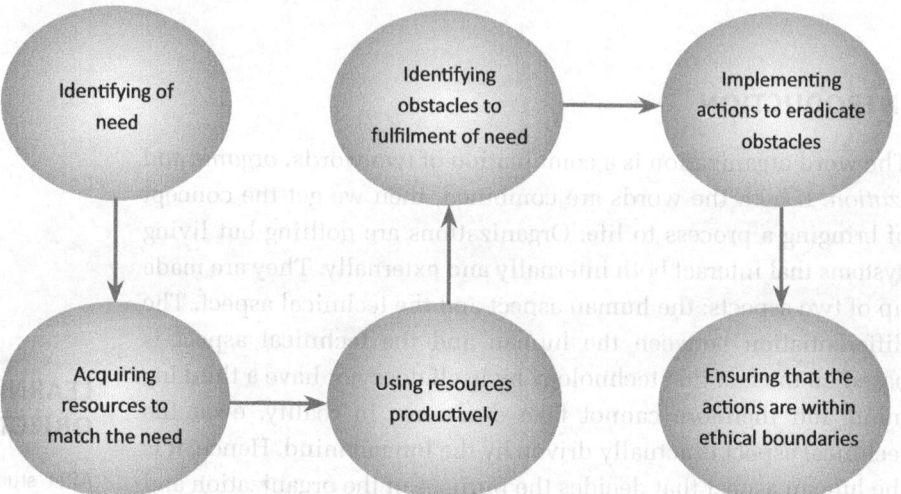

Figure 1.1 The concept of management in organizations

This entire process requires the 'right' human intervention for it to succeed because if we analyse it closely, we will find that at every step a moral question has to be answered. For example:

- Are we, as managers, assessing the present needs and prioritizing them, or are we creating new needs as a successful business venture?
- Whose needs are we catering to?
- Are any sections or groups getting marginalized in the process?
- What is the level of satisfaction and dissatisfaction in the process?

Only human beings are gifted with the power of discriminating between what is moral and immoral. Therefore, each of us plays an important role in finding the right answers to the above questions.

From time immemorial, one of man's greatest endeavours has been the search for happiness and satisfaction, and it is not possible to achieve either by a mere mental process or through literary thought. Unfortunately, more often than not, this search for comfort and contentment has been misled by selfishness, brutality, unkindness, and dishonesty. These unethical activities have been glorified by creating new management jargons such as ambition, the search for identity, and the survival of the fittest. Naturally, this has helped to justify any corporate sin as long as profits have been earned. The reason for this may be that expertise in ethics requires a long-term commitment. Today's living mantra of Anything Anywhere Anytime is encouraged by a market-driven economy, which believes in earning profits by catering to the wants and needs (which very often are created by the business itself) of the customer as quickly as possible by any means, moral or immoral. This glorification of consumerism (continuously creating new wants and needs and providing complementary products and services to cater to them) by the business world in the name of progress often overlooks the means of achieving profit, and unethical short-cuts that harm society, the economy, and the environment are favoured. The question that arises then is, 'What *is* business?'

WHAT IS BUSINESS?

In common parlance, any activity related to buying, selling, and trade is considered business. However, for our understanding, we shall look at a more precise understanding of the term.

Business relates to any activity that creates utility for either the masses or the classes, and to command a price for these utilities, the demand has to be more than the supply. This, in economics, is called the demand–supply gap and business can manipulate this gap in various ways to earn profit. The free-market economy is supposed to reduce this gap and offer enough choice to consumers by encouraging free entry and free exit to organizations operating in the market. In reality, even the free market has its own limitations with cartelling (companies coming together and fixing the price of the product in the market), niche marketing, lack of true information, patents, and other forms of privileges used by business to earn profits (for more details see Chapter 3).

There are four major types of utility creation.

Form utility Here utility is added by converting the input (usually raw materials) into output by changing the form. For example, iron is converted into steel, which is then converted into car. Here, at every stage, we find that value is being added to the original raw input.

Place utility Here any good, service, or person, is transported to a different destination and value is added as a consequence. For example, exotic goods and services, or travel destinations, which command a premium price.

Time utility This relates to any value addition that happens as a result of time factor, i.e., production happens at a particular time but consumption and/or usage is and/or can be deferred. For example, seasonal fruits and vegetables are kept in cold storage and sent to the market during off-season as well.

Knowledge utility This relates to developments in the field of advanced learning, research, technology growth, innovation, etc., which have led to the enhancement of economic activities and commanded a price for the activities (tangible or intangible) related to these fields. For example, information technology (IT), IT-enabled services (ITES), advertising, communication, etc.

In simple economic terms, we can divide business activities into the following sectors:
- Primary sector   – Agriculture
- Secondary sector – Industry
- Tertiary sector – Services

Under these main sectors, we have indirect productive sectors like infrastructure, education, health, communication, financial sector, IT, and other forms of economic ventures.

Development of Business

History is witness to the phenomenon that any form of business and production needs a marketplace for exchange. In ancient times, marketplaces probably developed at the borders of different human settlements. Groups of people in each settlement produced or grew products that would be of value to another group, as skills and resources differed in different regions. Archaeologists have discovered extensive trade networks belonging to as early as 3500 BC in Mesopotamia. The fabled trade of the Orient (especially India, China, and Persia) and the Mediterranean are well known. Trade was the foundation on which European countries like England, Spain, Portugal, France, and the Netherlands built their mighty political and mercantile empires. This clearly proves the pervasive influence of business.

The great trading companies were the first business enterprises. Business activities got organized into three major categories—sole trading concern, partnership firms, and joint-stock companies (both private limited and public limited)—depending on resources, business development plans, promoters, etc. For the purpose of this book, we shall limit ourselves to mainly public limited companies, though references to other forms of business would be made wherever necessary.

The most commonly used term for a business enterprise is the word company. Company can be defined as an association of persons coming together voluntarily to pursue a certain economic activity with the motive to make profit. The Indian Companies Act allows pursuance of non-economic activities like arts, science, sports, etc. also to be registered as companies. By the Indian Companies Act 1956, Section 3(1)(i), 'a "company" means a company formed and registered under this Act or an existing company ... registered under any of the previous company law.' 'Like any juristic person, a company is legally an entity apart from its members, capable of rights and duties of its own, and endowed with the potential of perpetual succession' (Hahlo and Trebilock 1977). By incorporation under the Act, the company is vested with a distinct legal persona and exists independent of its members. The process of incorporation includes filing with the Registrar of Companies to get a certificate to commence business (see Chapter 2 for incorporation details).

The relationship of the company beyond the legal existence to the socio-economic scenario is well summarized by Berle (1959). According to him, the 'company' is not merely a legal institution. It is rather a legal device for the attainment of any social or economic end and to a large extent, this is done publicly and by being socially responsible. It is, therefore, a combined political, social, economic, and legal institution. This brings us to the concept of corporate social responsibility (CSR) as corporations derive wealth from society, create wealth for society, and earn profit by dealing with the wealth for society. Thus, in the larger perspective, it is society that actually gives permission to business to operate in society and earn money. This obviously demands that the business world pays for this permission by a legitimate sharing of the wealth it is earning from society by sharing it with society.

Since CSR is a responsibility that corporations have to fulfil, first we shall understand the dimensions of business behaviour and the importance of the concept for the business world, which includes all corporations, before we analyse the various definitions that have been offered on CSR.

DIMENSIONS AND IMPORTANCE OF CSR

The dimensions of corporate behaviour encompass those activities of the corporate that ensure responsible and just behaviour towards society. There are four major dimensions of corporate behaviour:

1. Setting boundaries of learning, accountability, and responsiveness
2. Building activities that form the basis of learning
3. Creating measures that validate and make knowledge effective, and so form the basis for decision-making and action
4. Institutionalizing (making it an integral part of the corporate strategy and system) trust in ways that create a virtuous circle of practice and further engagements with stakeholders.

Values are, therefore, essential to the organizational function and dynamics. This is the reason CSR has received such importance in management studies. The human aspect (as explained in the Introduction) of any organization is its core asset, as they are the data generators as well as the data users. Organizations are nothing but the collective consciousness of all the members contributing to its activities. This human operator (individual) of the organization is certainly more important than the objective result because the result is achieved by what the individual does. Chakraborty (1995) sums up this aspect succinctly when he says, 'Is the human being for industry-technology or is industry-technology for the human being?' Here, we encounter the importance of the phenomenon of CSR, which is about business taking into account their total impact on society and the natural environment.

Businesses have to align their profitable opportunities with their social identities and underline values of corporate responsibility. The world is increasingly undergoing rapid development. More powerful and enabling technologies are constantly being created. Life and its choices are becoming more complex. These necessitate that we radically alter our view of ourselves and the world and our functioning as beings in order to ensure sustainable development. The present situation is one of bewilderment and confusion about the ways in which the corporate world has exercised its size and power, and at what cost and result.

However, we cannot deny the extraordinary ability of business activities to bring economic prosperity to those communities that need it most. Corporations have also helped to develop and apply technologies that are most likely to offset the destructive impacts of unrestrained growth. Therefore, even the harshest critics or committed enemies of the corporate world would not like to destroy business activities. The corporate community's universal influence makes it very unlikely that society can wish it away.

Therefore, the need is to 'system engineer', which deals with finding specific solutions, appropriate to the surrounding culture and environment. The need is to transform instead of just trying to constrain and tame or offer general standard solutions that may not be implementable in every situation (this idea would be further discussed in the chapter on models of CSR).

The above aspect is more relevant today because of the massive and rapid changes that are occurring around us. Modern economy is marked by three underlying dynamics. The first is the speed of change as a technological phenomenon as well as in spheres of social and personal activities. The second characteristic of this new economic growth is the increased importance of knowledge, innovation, and communication. A notable feature of the knowledge economy is the growing importance of intangible assets, such as intellectual capital, skills, research and development, brand relationships, and reputation. The third characteristic of this recent economic development is shifting closeness, which puts diversity at centre stage, because it brings people from different spheres (cultural, regional, skills and knowledge related, gender related, etc.) together. The workspace is increasingly reflecting the extraordinary spread of communities from which expertise is being drawn (Zadek 2001). The impact of these factors leads to increasing distribution of core activities within the company and the country in which the company is situated, as well as beyond national boundaries. This requires the establishment of values, leading to an increase in trust and integrity among the physically dispersed staff.

Therefore, the prerequisite is that the relationship between business and society be built on the basis of trust so that the culture of policing business activities is minimized. The hard reality at the end of the day is that we will survive only if everyone can operate with a sense of self-esteem and faith. If trust is lost, then we will no longer have an organization (the living force as explained in the Introduction) but automation, without a soul and a heart.

With increasing democratization of politics, economics also needs to be democratized, which means wealth has to be shared and equal opportunities should be available to all without discrimination. As in political democracy, power is seen as a force by the people, of the people, and for the people. Similarly, economic progress should also be distributed as a product of a force by the people, of the people, and for the people. This is where the responsibility of the corporate world becomes pronounced. With more liberalization, corporates have begun to enjoy more freedom with responsibility. Real freedom can be enjoyed only when one respects others' freedom responsibly. Therefore, the modern 'free market' has to stay 'within the boundary' for everyone to enjoy the benefits.

CSR provides this framework of boundary for the free market to operate responsibly. However, CSR also appears to be the most misunderstood. Corporates are still struggling to give a formal structure to their CSR programmes. Social responsibility has been variously described as a vague and ill-defined concept (Preston and Post 1975). They opine that 'in the face of large number of different, and not always consistent, usages, we restrict our own use of the term social responsibility to refer only to a vague and highly generalized sense of social concern that appears to underlie a wide variety of ad hoc managerial policies and practices. Most of these attitudes and activities are well-intentioned and even beneficent; few are patently harmful. They lack, however, any coherent relationship to the managerial unit's internal activities or its fundamental linkage with its host environment.'

According to Votaw (1973, p. 11), social responsibility is a concept with a variety of definitions. To quote him, 'the term is a brilliant one; it means something, but not always the same thing, to everybody. To some it conveys the idea of legal responsibility or liability; to others, it means socially responsible *behaviour* in an ethical sense; to still others, the meaning transmitted is that of "responsible for", in a causal mode; many simply equate it with a charitable contribution; some take it to mean socially conscious; many of those who embrace it most fervently see it as a mere synonym for "legitimacy", in the context of "belonging" or being proper or valid; a few see it as a sort of fiduciary duty imposing higher standards of behaviour on businessmen than on citizens at large.' Similar thoughts have been expressed in definitions like 'it is a concept lacking theoretical integration and empirical verification' (DeFillipi 1982; Post 1978); and a concept susceptible to subjective and value-laden judgements (Aupperle et al., 1983). Let us take a closer look at the definitions and understand why it is so difficult to explain or to arrive at a consensus.

DEFINITIONS OF CSR

The World Business Council for Sustainable Development (WBCSD) defined CSR as 'the continuing commitment of business to behave ethically and contribute to economic development while improving the quality of life of their workforce and their families as well as of the local community, and society at large.' In an interview, Björn Stigson, president of WBCSD said, 'There is no universal definition of CSR because the concept is always being redefined to serve changing needs and times. It is up to each company individually to define the values and principles it stands for, its "magnetic north" (like the mechanical compass which always shows the magnetic north, similarly the values and principles are the internal compass of a company that help the company to stay steadfast on their ethical journey) as we call it in the WBCSD. The companies that do not manage their social issues in the same way they manage other strategic business issues will not stay in business long term' (excerpt from WBCSD).

CSR can also be defined as 'bringing corporate behaviour up to a level where it is congruent with the prevailing social norms, values, and expectations of performance' (Sethi 1975).

Business can never ignore the fact that profit is a proactive part of its economic perspective. Therefore, there cannot be any argument against profit. The only concern is the process of earning profit and its distribution, which relates to the concept of CSR. This aspect has been viewed differently by different authors and they have emerged as definitions. Some prominent viewpoints are given below.

Analysis of Various Viewpoints and Related Definitions

Milton Friedman (1970) made the historic statement that 'there is one and only one social responsibility of business—to use its resources and engage in activities designed to increase its profits, so long as it stays within the rules of the game, which is to say, engages in open and free competition without deception and fraud.' This has been used by business houses as the solution to justify every activity. His argument of social responsibility is based on the 'legal recognition view,' which asserts that 'the corporation is an autonomous entity

... owned and run by freely constituted group ... It is not a creation of society' (DeGeorge 1990). However, when implemented, certain shortcomings of this thought are obvious. They are: First, this argument does not take into account that there can be a lack of moral virtues among the practitioners of business. Second, it assumes that there will always be a well-ordered civil society in which business will operate. The third concern is that the idea gives the processes of production and distribution less importance than exchange, and hence the actual free market with free entry and free exit and equal sharing of information does not come into existence. Like Friedman, Levitt also believes that society is committed to radical pluralism (multiple vested interests) and this social, economic, and political pluralism can be best sustained when 'functional groups' do not encroach on each other's province of business. He says, business ... like a good war ... should be fought gallantly, daringly, and above all not morally' (Levitt 1983).

Economic Perspective

The economic perspective has been justified through neo-classical economics, which endorses that the greatest social satisfaction (borrowed from utilitarian ethics) occurs when individuals are free to pursue their self-interest. Therefore, as explained by Hirshman (1981) and endorsed by Vogel (1991) and March (1992), it views self-interest and other interest as mutually beneficial. However, the business world with its multifarious activities and a growing awareness that government alone cannot bear responsibility, has given birth to thoughts that look beyond economic gains. This has led to the development of the duty/responsibility perspective, which highlights benevolence and duty-based morality (Etzioni 1988; Hausman 1992), and it is believed that this aspect can no longer be ignored by business. Duty has been classified on the basis of rights and justice. The individual, on one hand, has the right to protect the entitlement which fundamentally relates to the idea of protection from harm and, on the other hand, the right to extension of entitlements (Velasquez 2005).

The neo-classical theory answers this need of the duty, rights, and justice by accepting that there are public policies, ethical traditions, and laws that restrain self-interest and will deter individuals from behaving selfishly, irresponsibly, or in an unjustified manner. Lindblom (1977) divided these restraints into 'authority and persuasion'. The idea was further supported and developed to encompass all means that society uses to provide direction to business to achieve socio-cultural values (Chamberlain 1973, 1977; Buchholz 1982, 1985; Frederick 1986; Steidlmeier 1987; and others). However, the rights and duty aspect centre around the respect for what Kant describes as 'moral personhood of others' (Velasquez 2005; Freeman and Gilbert 1988; Donaldson 1989; Boatright 1993).

Common Good

Keith Davis (1960), an early analyst of social responsibility, said, 'social responsibility is applied (means is already taken into account) in any situation, if it influences a businessman's decision even partially.' According to his analysis, the mere consideration of social needs/wants/desires by the organization decision-maker is sufficient to be considered as corporate social responsibility. Frederick (1960) gives a lengthy but not very clear understanding of corporate responsibility by highlighting the common good. According to him, it is a requirement that business 'oversee the operation of an economic system that fulfils the expectations of the public. And this means in turn that the means of production should be employed in such a way that production and distribution would enhance total socio-economic welfare ... resources are utilized for broad social needs and not simply the narrowly circumscribed interest of private persons and firms.' In his later book, written in 1978, he highlighted the lack of clarity for operationalizing such a concept by raising four key issues:

1. The extremely vague content of CSR
2. The institutional mechanisms through which this concept is to be put in operation
3. Difficulty in understanding tradeoffs between economic and social costs and goals
4. Difficulty in defining the moral underpinnings of CSR

According to Hopkins (1998), CSR is concerned with treating the stakeholders of the firm ethically or in a socially responsible manner. The aim of social responsibility is to create higher standards of living, while preserving the profitability of the corporation.

CSR as a Continuum

An ardent promoter of CSR, Simon Zadek (2001) has viewed the development of CSR in terms of three generations: The first generation showed that companies can be responsible in ways that do not interfere with commercial success. During this phase, the most prominent changes would include adoption of a strategic approach to philanthropy, expansion of the geographic focus of the corporate, and evolving of measurement tools. The second generation is focussing on CSR as an integral part of long-term business strategy (Schendel and Hofer 1979). The third generation of CSR is expected to make a significant contribution to address issues such as poverty, exclusion, and environmental degradation. This will involve both partnerships with civil society and changes in public policy (Zadek 2001).

Archie B. Carroll (1979) defines social responsibility as a four-stage continuum. According to him, beyond economic and legal responsibilities lie ethical responsibilities, which are 'additional behaviours and activities that are not necessarily codified into law but nevertheless are expected of business by society's members.' Carroll did not see a tradeoff between the economic and the social goals of the company. He introduced a model where economic, ethical, legal, and discretionary goals are integrated. Further, he went on to outline a 'corporate social performance' (CSP) framework, which includes the philosophy of social responsiveness, the social issues involved, and social and economic responsibilities.

Various scholars have tried to find an integrated fundamental model to define and explain the subject as it involves data from divergent fields like economics, politics, sociology, history, psychology, anthropology, philosophy, law, etc. For example, Jones (1983) says one has to incorporate the central premises of the field, reflect on appropriate methodologies, and guide the further development of theory in the field by enhancing explanatory and predictive power. Fitch (1976) advocated, 'CSR is the serious attempt to solve social problems caused wholly or in part by the corporation' (p. 38). When this fails to happen, the firm's licence to operate (i.e., their legitimacy) may fall into question. In his work, the problem concept is operationally defined and social problems are distinguished from non-social problems. A method of social problem solution, based on the principles of applied behaviour analysis, is demonstrated using an industrial accident reduction example. In 1982, Arlow and Gannon made a bold effort to connect and link corporate social and economic performance to organizational structure. They examined corporate social responsiveness, including its relationship to economic performance. Their research suggests the use of a contingency approach to social responsiveness, based on factors such as organizational size, relevance of a social issue, and industry characteristics. According to them, the relationship between social responsiveness and economic performance is inconclusive. Perceptions of CSR have been dealt by Boal and Peery (1985).

Bowie (1991) analyses the issue of motivation and intentionality in CSR. 'With respect to the duty to help solve social problems, should that duty be taken on because by doing so profits may be increased, or because it is a moral responsibility to do so?' He cites economist Robert Frank (1988): 'You can't adopt altruism as a strategy like "honesty is the best policy" and gain the advantages of altruism ... For the model to work, satisfaction from doing the right thing must not be premised on the fact that material gains may later follow; rather it must be intrinsic to the act itself.' Bowie contends that 'my ideal business partner is someone who doesn't merely adopt altruism because it pays but adopts it because he or she is committed to it. She or he is not an opportunist because opportunism is wrong.' Therefore, he says, 'it is in the interest of business to adopt an extended view of CSR that includes a duty to help solve social problems. If business adopts that duty because it thinks it will benefit, its actions will be viewed cynically. Moreover, because an improved labour force is a public good for business, the only real reason for an individual firm to help solve social problems is altruistic. Thus, employees and other corporate stakeholders have a good reason to believe that corporate attempts to solve social problems are altruistic.'

If all the above definitions and arguments with their strengths and weaknesses are combined together, then the definition of CSR can be summed up as: CSR is a management concept where good business is not only seen as maximization of shareholder value but also of stakeholder value. It is about the management of a company's impact on its stakeholders, the environment, and the community in which it operates. It is more than just a philanthropic activity for some charitable causes. It is about the integrity with which a company governs itself, how it fulfils its mission, the values it has, what it wants to stand for, and how it engages with transparency. Here, the corporations have to move beyond the financial bottom-line to the social and environmental bottom line.

Keeping in mind the differences of viewpoint, it is important to highlight the factors that need to be adhered to by the business world for a better understanding of social responsibility.

UNDERSTANDING CSR

It is important to understand that CSR goes beyond philanthropy, though that may be its beginning. It has to take into account integrity and accountability in the long-run process of sustainability. For a better understanding of this concept, it has been divided into four broad aspects of CSR:
- Responsibility
- Accountability
- Sustainability
- Social contract

Responsibility

Clarkson (1995) has tried to differentiate between responsibility, responsiveness, and performance. He has argued that a fundamental problem in the field of business and society has been the notable absence of definitions of corporate social performance (CSP), corporate social responsibility (CSR), and corporate social responsiveness (CSR2), and the lack of consensus about the meaning of these terms from an operational or managerial viewpoint. He emphasizes that CSP can be analysed more effectively by using a framework based on the management of a corporation's relationships with its stakeholders than by using CSR models and methodologies. This, he believes, is a better way of understanding because corporations are the nexus of a complex web of stakeholder relationships.

Therefore, corporations manage relationships with specific stakeholder groups rather than with society at large. The crux of the problem stems from the meaning of the word 'social' and how it links to everyday business activities. In fact, Clarkson (1995) defines society as 'a level of analysis that is more inclusive, more ambiguous, and further up the ladder of abstraction than a corporation itself.' In the same vein, William Frederick (1994) has taken the concept of CSR to a higher level by discussing about corporate responsiveness. According to him, corporate social responsiveness 'refers to the capacity of a corporation to respond to social pressures.'

From the creativity view of history, there is a need for new forms of creativity and innovation in the era of globalization to deal with the challenges that corporations face while pursuing profits. From the liberation view of history, we learn the lessons of empowerment, and the fall of the fittest view indicates the need for continuous innovation and a better understanding of the change process (Sharma 2005). Ethically accepted corporate activity and profit-making are not mutually exclusive (not opposed to each other). Sustainable growth and success demands ethicality in the process of dealing with stakeholders.

As analysis of history shows three distinct approaches to understand the relationship between the victor and the victim. These are: domination, exploitation, and oppression (Fig. 1.2). This can also be extended to the business world, because when selfish means of earning profit is practised by the business world, then society becomes the victim of domination, exploitation, and oppression. However, this way of earning profit is not sustainable in the long run, as it leads to both economic depletion of resources and social upheavals as a result of exploitation. The result of such degradation and exploitation would impact the business that is promoting it, so future avenues of earning profit would not be available. Therefore, mutual respect and sharing of benefits would lead to a continuous flow of profits through better productivity based on trust.

We have to create a framework that meets the requirements of internal uniformity and operational stability. Often, CSR has been challenged on the grounds of relativity, which means that what may be considered right by one may be considered wrong by another. Arriving at a consensus for CSR checklists may not be easy. There will be the perennial and inevitable disagreements on 'cause and effect' in the development process, as every organization has its own perspectives and perceptions regarding service to society. This needs to be innovatively handled because there are certain universal values that are acceptable to all and are collectively known as human rights. Therefore, in a cross-cultural scenario that is riddled with diversity, issues have to be prioritized, keeping the human aspect of compassion and justice in the forefront. This

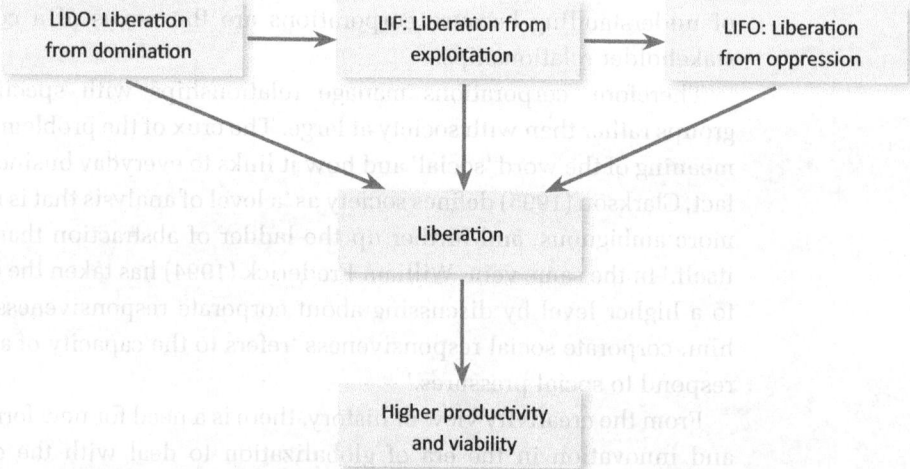

Adapted from Subhash Sharma, 'A Brief History of History: Some Models of History and Lessons for Leadership and Management', *Journal of Human Values* 11:2 (2005).

Figure 1.2 The relationship between victor and victim

concept is certainly not new. Every age in history has tried to find a symbiotic relationship between the economic man and the social man.

Accountability

The easiest way to understand the different levels of accountability is to adhere to the report on Social Responsibilities of Business Corporations issued by the Committee for Economic Development (CED) in 1971. The CED was initiated in 1942 to address national priorities that promote sustained economic growth and development to benefit all Americans. CED is a non-profit, non-partisan, business-led public policy organization. It conducts in-depth research on major economic and social issues, and provides suggestions on the implementation of its recommendations by the public and private sectors. Members include about 200 senior corporate executives and university leaders who provide the body important academic and practitioners' view on research and outreach efforts to meet the changing socio-economic scenario. However, one should remember while complying with the framework that the report does not take into account the legal responsibilities and therefore precaution should be taken not to ignore the legal aspects.

The report consists of the following three concentric circles.

Inner Circle

The inner circle includes the clear-cut basic responsibilities for the efficient execution of the economic function—products, jobs, and economic growth. For example, for a product such as an automobile, a number of people get employed to help in the production, and economic growth happens because of better means of communication, growth of ancillary (related) industries that cater to the main vehicle producing company, and various other factors like export, import, and similar economic activities.

Intermediate Circle

The intermediate circle encompasses responsibility to exercise this economic function with sensitive awareness of changing social values and priorities; for example, with respect to environmental conservation, hiring and relations with employees, more rigorous expectations of customers for information, fair treatment, and protection from injury.

Outer Circle

The outer circle outlines newly emerging and still amorphous responsibilities that business should assume to become more broadly involved in actively improving the social environment. Society is beginning to turn to corporations for help with major social problems such as poverty and urban blight. This is not so much because the public considers business singularly responsible for creating these problems but because it feels large corporations possess considerable resources and skills that could make a critical difference in solving these problems.

CSR includes integrity and accountability because it demands knowledge that goes beyond the traditional framework of business understanding, i.e., profit-making and bottom line. It brings business face to face with the pertinent questions regarding sustainable and value-added development in the political and socio-economic environment. CSR is rewarding as it provides us with knowledge and skills for doing business by understanding modern societies in a more systematic way.

Sustainability

Sustainability places an extended set of expectations on business. Such issues as layoffs, plant closures, product quality, financial frauds, or industrial pollution demand the consideration of a diverse and complex range of systemic solutions. Businesses have the resources and expertise to create systems that have at least the potential to contribute to sustainable and humane development. Therefore, CSR requires not only techniques and performance metrics for achievements but also revolution in the way that companies think and act.

The reason CSR has to promote beyond philanthropy is because familiarity with unethical practices often makes society extremely tolerant and insensitive. Business, with its set of professionals, can see the dangers of lack of perception due to familiarity with unethical activities. Therefore, business also understands that often there is a reduction in the level of self-control on the part of society in keeping a watch on the harmful activities in the environment. Now the responsibility lies with business either to be extra vigilant to ward off catastrophes or take advantage of the not-so-alert situation to pursue unethical activities. There is an urgent need to encourage integrity and ethics to rein in greed, corruption, crime, communal disharmony, and terrorism.

The objectives of a company's CSR governance must be clearly defined with respect to its different stakeholders. The business environment will always be in a continuous state of flux due to the influence of socio-economic and political changes in the micro (locality, region, and state) and the macro (country and world) level. Therefore, CSR needs a strategy that needs to uphold the ethical standards. The design, communication, and implementation within the organization and society should be geared for support and motivation of all stakeholders.

Legal and ethical principles of business are outcomes of the chosen behaviour of individuals who could be the principal (owner) or agent (managers) acting on behalf of the organization. Therefore, the action of the principal or the agents in either business or government must stand the test of morality if their actions have to be enforced under the law. Total business relationship with its various stakeholders is a concept that would embrace both legal and ethical obligations and contractual rights and duties. More often than not, there will be ethical conflicts in serving the different constituents of business, not only because of the conflicting interests of different constituents but also due to the differences in understanding the purpose of business. This dilemma of differences can be solved by following CSR in its true spirit.

Social Contract

CSR is related to the social contract between the business and the society in which it operates. At any one time in any one society, there is a set of generally accepted relationships, obligations, and duties between the major institutions and the people. Philosophers and political theorists have called this set of common understandings 'the social contract' (Steiner and George 1972).

If we take this understanding further, we find that at any point of time the accepted relationships, obligations, and duties differ between and within society, and therefore business practitioners prefer to either ignore or criticise the concept of CSR as only theory based. However, when business professionals were surveyed even a decade ago, nearly 81 per cent of 248 executives believed that wealth maximization and social involvement were not contradictory concepts (Edmonds and Hand 1976). This thought is further corroborated by the twin surveys conducted by McKinsey in 2007 (*The McKinsey Quarterly*,

2007), which reveal that 84 per cent of executives and 89 per cent of consumers believe that corporate obligations to shareholders must be balanced by contribution to the broader public good; for example, providing good jobs (jobs that ensure sustainable livelihood), making philanthropic donations, and going beyond legal requirements to minimize pollution and other negative effects of business activities. The consensus for engagement (business engaging in socially relevant activities) is widespread, ranging from 75 per cent in China to 90 per cent in India among executives, and from 86 per cent in India to 91 per cent in the UK among consumers.

Business has responded in a very fragmented manner to the demands of responsibility by enacting labour laws, employee welfare programmes, consumer satisfaction policies, environmental protection activities, etc. But there is no collective long-term impact on the community and therefore it has become imperative to consolidate the concept of CSR and fit it into an overall plan.

It is interesting to note that certain themes have evolved about how business can relate to ethical behaviour. According to Robin and Erie (1989), 'business activities that have a foreseeable and potentially serious impact on individuals ought to be regulated by the values of deontological (related to rules and regulations) reasoning.'

'For all business actions that do not have foreseeable serious consequences for individuals, the arguments of utilitarianism (greatest good for the greatest number) seem appropriate within capitalistic democracies.'

'... For the level of performance, Aristotle's *Virtue Ethics* describing the "golden mean" i.e., neither excessiveness nor deficiency in performance is suggested.' This relates to earning profit by ensuring that neither is CSR emphasized so excessively that profit suffers, nor is CSR totally ignored and profit is earned by exploitation.

For social responsibility, 'the image of an average family using central values to solve family problems provides a benchmark for developing values within a business organization.'

Though business has the bigger responsibility of going beyond philanthropy, we must also keep in mind that each stakeholder also has reciprocal duties with others and the consuming community also has the obligation to make the tradeoff between cost and sustainability and integrity. Different stakeholders also cannot be driven by their selfish interests alone because each stakeholder has an important role to play and one cannot be destroyed for the benefit of the other. Just as business needs to do just tradeoff between stakeholders based on priority and sustainability, stakeholders also have to understand that at times one has to give up one's interest for the benefit of all. This reciprocal relationship between business and society is shown in Fig. 1.3.

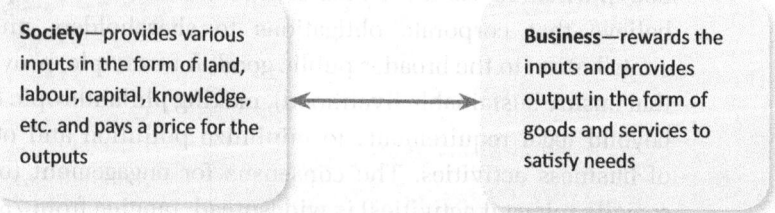

Figure 1.3 The reciprocal relationship between society and business

HISTORY OF CSR IN INDIA

The history of CSR can be traced back to the description of the aim of the state found in ancient Indian literature. Observations in the Vedas suggest that peace, order, security, and justice were regarded as the fundamental aims of the state. Chandogya Upanishad (V.11.5) records that religion was to be promoted, morality was to be encouraged, and education was to be patronized. All-round welfare of the public was clearly regarded as the chief aim of the state during the Vedic and Upanishadic ages. These relate to periods as old as c.1000 BC and c.600 BC.

Literatures on politics describe the promotion of *dharma* (moral law), *artha* (wealth), and *kama* (pleasure) as the aims of the state (Altekar 1977). The state was to promote *dharma* by fostering a feeling of piety and religiousness, by encouraging virtue and morality, and by patronizing social institutions like hospitals, feeding houses for the poor, as well as promoting literature and sciences. *Artha* was procured by encouraging trade, industry, and agriculture. Fresh land was brought under cultivation, and dams and canals were built to reduce dependence on rain. Rules were formulated for systematic and extensive working of mines. *Kama* was ensured through establishment of peace and order. Individuals could enjoy life undisturbed and pursue finer arts and aesthetic culture. Ancient policymakers were thus fully committed to the ideal perfect development of the individual, which culminated in the full development of society.

Role of the State

The activities of the state, as envisaged by the *Mahabharata* and the *Arthasastra*, relate to all the aspects of human life: social, economic, and religious. The idea that state was a necessary evil was refuted and even the laissez-faire theory that the activity of the state should be reduced to the bare minimum of maintaining law and order was not advocated popularly. The state was to administer in a manner that encompassed society as a whole. Thus, the activities included establishing piety, morality, and righteousness, by encouraging learning, education, and art. The state delivered public welfare by maintaining rest houses, charity halls, and hospitals to provide relief during distress situations like floods and famines. The state ensured increased productivity in agriculture by acquiring fresh land, and by building dams and canals. It is interesting to note that the state was encouraged to see that the population was evenly distributed and for this, fresh lands were often colonized and developed, so that there was not over-dependence on one place and development was well spread out by enriching resources like forests, mines, etc., along with agriculture. Thus, the state played a proactive part in helping trade and industry and ensuring that common citizens did not suffer from capitalistic greed and selfishness. The state regulated vices like gambling and drinking by appointing officers to supervise these institutions.

Extreme precaution was taken that individual liberty did not suffer in this embracing of welfare activities. This was achieved through a balance between bureaucracy and independent institutions like trade guilds and *Sramana* or *Brahmana* assemblies, which were local in nature. In these assemblies, people had the upper voice, meaning they were not state-controlled and had the autonomy to take independent decisions. Decentralization was carried out by empowering the village *panchayats* (council), city councils, and trade guilds. In periods of economic instability, guilds took over decision-making and governance roles at local levels (adapted from Altekar 1977, pp. 58–63).

Ancient Indians understood and appreciated the idea of collaboration and felt that the state could reconcile conflicting interests if its bureaucracy worked in close cooperation with well-established popular bodies. During the Maurya (c.300 BC) and Gupta (c.500 AD) periods, this collaborative, socially responsible process worked extremely well and India experienced its golden era of political strength and socio-economic harmony and stability. This portrays the continuity of social responsibility, which can be traced from the BC (before Christ) era to the AD (after the birth of Christ) period in history as an ideology in ancient India.

Impact of Religion

Religion played a major role in encouraging charity. Hindu scriptures highlighted the concept of using wealth for granting charity, performing sacrifices, and discharging debts. The best gift was the gift of spiritual knowledge and the lowest that which satisfied the basic physical needs of human beings. Therefore, most Hindu merchants made generous gifts to temples, monasteries, and conglomerates of religious practitioners like priests and monks. To encourage secular learning, scholarships were instituted by the merchant families and educational institutions were set up. Other forms of gifts included land, cattle, food, etc. The founder administered all endowments, whether small or big. This thought of giving evolved into the final philosophy of *Lokasangraha* (universal brotherhood) and *Sarvabhutahita* (welfare of all beings) found in the sacred book of the Hindus—the Gita.

Jainism also encouraged charity and many hospitals, rest houses, and libraries were constructed from their endowments. Since the Jain religion strictly prohibited any kind of violence and cruelty, Jains normally provided charity to all races and creeds as part of the practice of compassion for all living beings.

Islam popularized Zakat, i.e., a certain percentage of the acquired wealth and profit should be dedicated for the purpose of charity. Building mosques with attached educational institutions was a common form of charity.

Christianity was made popular by the Jesuits who visited India during the Mughal rule, and was entrenched as a religion when Great Britain colonized India. The tenet of giving was central to Christian teachings as well. In fact Christians were told 'let thy right hand not know what thy left hand gives', signifying the importance of giving but not for publicity. In Christianity also, wealth was considered as a trust and therefore, distribution of wealth was also about doing justice to society, not just compassion. Christianity highlighted the importance of giving time and personal service for the welfare of others, and that encouraged great humanitarian activities by the followers of the religion.

The Parsi community in India drew its strength from their religion, Zoroastrianism. The religion, in a way, preached a middle path by neither glorifying poverty nor wealth. It was more about self-development through self-help and hard work. Prosperity was to be shared through works of beneficence and public well-being.

Charity was, by and large, motivated by religion and spirituality. However, at times practice faltered in terms of strict adherence to the religious tenets because self-interest drove charity. This is visible when we find that very often charity was linked to business interest and practices. Studies by Rudner (1995) and Bayly (1983) have clearly shown that religious giving was often linked to social creditworthiness and this in itself was self-reinforcing and self-fulfilling. Quotes like 'the social consequences of Sangha (Jain religious brotherhood) are many. On the one hand, prestige is acquired by the Sanghapati (head of the Sangha) and financial reputation is earned through spending large sums of money, which begets investment and credit facilities, which in turn lead to expansion of business' by Singhi (1991) highlights the underlying business agenda in charity. This encouraged the practice of combining charity with the bottom line of business.

Often, merchants who had endowed temples with charity used the temple grants to increase their business. As trustees of endowments, they came to occupy important social positions and respect, which further enhanced their business. Historical sources verify that various means of religious gifting were used as mechanisms by merchants and mercantile communities to penetrate into new localities and create respectable social identities, which helped them entrench their authority over commercial enterprises (Rudner 1995). Religious grants were supplemented with individual secular spending, like building wells, rest houses, and commissioning relief work at times of peril to gain social status by merchants.

Emergence of the Merchant Class

The emergence of reform movements like Buddhism and Jainism, which later became independent religions, gave an extraordinary fillip to trade and business. These religions emphasized non-violence and therefore those who embraced it chose to follow trade as a profession because it helped them maintain the tenet of non-violence. This was so because in the social system then prevalent, there was a movement against Brahmanic hegemony. The Kshatriyas were the warrior class, the Vaisyas tilled the land, which injured living organisms when land was cultivated, and the Sudras performed menial labour. The merchants practised frugality, honesty, and believed in individual responsibility. These qualities were supported by religious and spiritual teachings and the merchants came to be highly respected in the community. They donated wealth for social causes like setting up educational institutions, hospitals, gardens, charity homes, orphanages, etc. They were renowned for their charity, which also helped them gain social status.

History records eminent merchant families like Virji Vora of Surat, Shantidas Jawahari of Ahmedabad in Western India, Jagatseth of Murshidabad in East India, and Malaya at Pulicat in South India. Similar merchant guilds like those that flourished in ancient India can be traced in medieval India as well. A businessman was called *shreshthi*, which later changed to *seth* or *sethi*. The wealthiest businessman was also selected as the *nagarseth* who took care of the city's needs as a modern day mayor does.

With the establishment of British rule in India, there was a change in the position of the merchant families. The British brought modern banking and uniform currency system, which affected the merchant bankers and money lenders. Though business flourished because of improvement in transportation, irrigation, communication, etc., traditional business families could not keep pace with the changes. Families who migrated from pure trade as business to industries became the next famous group of businessmen.

The Indian merchant community consisted of various religious and regional groups. Some of the famous communities were the Marwaris, Khatris, Chettiars, and Parsis. These communities utilized the opportunities that the British provided by either becoming intermediaries, working in the East India Company, or becoming contractors and brokers. Most of them had strong community ties and helped needy members of the community. Among these communities, it was only the Parsis who embraced western education and western culture (adapted from Sunder 2000).

Though the merchant community was heterogeneous, there was an underlying bond of unity based on commercial solidarity (Rudner 1995). The communities collaborated at different levels of common interest, like religion, supplying credit, marketing, etc. They actively participated in social reforms and ensured the growth of social welfare.

Merchant Charity and CSR

Merchant gifting was a strategic ploy in gaining political influence and smoothening relations with rulers whose origin was outside the community, city, or country. In return, the donors were credited with honours by the rulers, which enhanced their prestige and added to their creditworthiness, and thus improved business. During the British rule, gifts to buy favours with the rulers took the form of philanthropy, since a different moral code precluded personal gifts.

Merchant charity can be studied under four broad headings—religious, secular, individual, and collective. Religious grants were made, as the name suggests, to any activity of religious significance and was not limited to any geographical boundary. Merchants often donated to religious institutions beyond their homelands. Secular charity included donations and grants to activities like development in infrastructure, education, arts and culture, and public welfare, etc. There are references to individual merchant charity and even of a number of merchants coming together in a group and offering collective grants and donations.

Perhaps the earliest religious endowments can be traced to the Buddhist era, when land was donated for building stupas, or financial help was given to build them and monastic institutions like the Sangha was also given financial support by devout merchants. Similar activities were followed by Hindu merchants for their religious communities and temples. Merchants often went beyond their geographical boundaries and donated to famous religious institutions. Some notable examples are the Travadi family, a wealthy family of Brahmin bankers, who built a big temple in Surat and many others across India. The leading banking family of Surat—the Chakawala family—built a temple of Shiva in a nearby village and also donated huge sums to Vaisnavite (followers of Lord Vishnu) deities elsewhere. The well-known family of jeweller Manekchand Jhaveri, who belonged to the Jain community, built rest houses for pilgrims and hostels for Jain students in Surat, Bombay (now called Mumbai), Kohlapur, and other places where Jains traded and worshipped.

Merchant families kept a portion of their profit to use for charitable purposes. Individual grants were made in areas of public welfare, like feeding the poor, building roads, rest houses, wells, providing relief during natural calamities like floods and famine, setting up schools and colleges, and giving alms. Rich merchants often helped their less well-to-do colleagues with financial support because of strong community ties that were ingrained in every community. Communal institutions like hostels were usually built to cater to members of the same community. Animal homes were also provided for as an extension of *ahimsa* (non-violence) as a religious mandate.

It is also evident that merchants collectively supervised charitable activities for the benefit of the common population. The Buddhist Jatakas record incidents of collective charities organized through the collection of various rates and taxes, which were used for public benefit.

Similar instances can be traced back to the nineteenth century, when businessmen like jewellers and grain dealers came together in an effort to help their city by collecting cesses (taxes). Hindu and Muslim merchants often helped in the upkeep of each other's shrines through donations (Haynes 1987). Although the usual help was extended mainly to members of the same community or caste, it was not unnatural to find grants being given for the development of entire villages and cities, especially during times of calamities.

Importance of Education

Education was considered one of the most important needs of society and substantial grants were made to promote it through granting land free, building the institution, providing free hostel facilities, etc. An interesting quote elaborates this point further: 'Respect for learning has always been the redeeming feature of the East ... The most unscrupulous chief, the avaricious moneylender, and even the freebooter vied with the small moneylender in making peace with his conscience by founding schools and rewarding the learned. There was not a mosque, a temple, or a dharamsala that had not a school attached to it to which the youth flocked for religious education. There were few wealthy men who did not engage a maulvi, a pandit, or a guru to teach their sons, and along with them the sons of their friends and dependents. There was not a single villager who did not take pride in devoting a portion of his produce to a respected teacher' (Sunder 2000). Thus, we see that social work has always been one of the driving forces for business, whether meeting urgent needs or long-term commitment for social well-being.

Important Business Categories

With the establishment of the British hegemony, the urban economy of India threw up two distinct classes of business categories. One was dominated by the typical westernized expatriate businessmen who usually concentrated on running mines, plantations, or indulging in export-import trade. Businesses were controlled by small groups or managing agencies like Shaw Wallace, Andrew Yule, and Dunlop, to name a few.

Indian business houses drew capital from the 'bazaar economy', consisting of the local bankers, money lenders, wholesale merchants, and others. This new group was not the extension of the earlier mentioned merchant families. They belonged to the same community, but to new families who had made fortunes in opium, indigo, cotton, land, and banking. Some of them had extended beyond the confines of India and forged ties with businesses in other countries. Some famous communities that ventured beyond India to do business were Parsis with China, Chettiars with Burma, and Bhatias, Khojas, and Memons with the Middle East and East Africa. Others had become brokers (the Banias of Calcutta and Dubashes of Madras) to the European agency houses (Majumdar et al. 1995).

There was an intellectual movement in India at this juncture. This new intelligentsia drew its impetus from the introduction of English education, which helped in the growth of liberal ideas, and scientific and technological learning was encouraged. A critical outlook on the past and new aspirations for the future marked the new awakening. The pioneer and true representative of the new spirit of the age was eminent social reformer Raja Ram Mohan Roy, whose English biographer remarks that the Raja 'presents a most instructive and inspiring study for the new India of which he is the type and the pioneer ... He embodies the new spirit ... its freedom of enquiry, its thirst for science, its large human sympathy, its pure and sifted ethics, along with its reverent but not uncritical regard for the past and prudent ... disinclination towards revolt' (Majumdar et al. 1995).

Seeds of Modern CSR

Indians quickly built on their potential by embracing new technology and business opportunities that were beneficial to Indian society. Charitable activities were still on traditional lines, like donating to educational and religious institutions. However, with the spread of western education, as represented by Raja Ram Mohan Roy, a perceptible change was noticed in the process of charitable investment. Now the shift was towards more inclusive philanthropy, based on the equality of all human beings. Christian missionaries, with their humanitarian approach, played a significant role in bringing about this change. The political awakening in India, on the lines of democratic and secular understanding of freedom, helped in creating an atmosphere of social justice, equality, individual freedom, and universal brotherhood. The state helped by awarding status to individuals engaged in philanthropy.

There was a realization that the development of society depended on public enlightenment. Therefore, education was the most popular and favourite field for donations. Public health was also a concern that received charitable help as health facilities were very poor. Endowments to build libraries, meeting halls, parks, and gardens are also recorded. Indian culture was encouraged through theatre, dance, and music. The Parsi community was more proactive in providing basic needs like housing and sanitation than the other philanthropists. Agriculture and rural development still did not receive the attention they should have.

According to Rudner (1995), personal interest was a major driver in the philanthropy of that age: 'Religious gifting and secular philanthropy—far from constituting irrational expenditures for other worldly ends—were investments in the conditions that made worldly commerce possible.' (This means that philanthropy was not limited to only religious charities for spiritual fulfilment but also added to actual material gains and profits in economic terms.) Philanthropy in this period suffered from the stigma of traditionalism, but it cannot be denied that it prepared the ground for future institutional reforms.

First Industrial Corporations

There were momentous changes in the Indian business firmament with the establishment of industrial houses and expansion of the entrepreneurial base. The freedom movement united the efforts of all members of society and there were major shifts in philanthropic activity geared towards achieving independence. Mahatma Gandhi's call for trusteeship, which promoted the idea of voluntary renouncement of part of the wealth by the business community for the good of the community, and also acting as trustee of that wealth to ensure proper and fair implementation, appealed to the business community. Gandhi clearly emphasized that trusteeship was neither charity nor philanthropy—it was to be a way of life. 'The art of amassing riches becomes a degrading and despicable art, if it is not accompanied by the nobler art of how to spend wealth usefully. Let not possession of wealth be synonymous with degradation, vice, and profligacy' (Venkatsubbiah 1997).

The combined effects of political and socio-economic factors led to the development of large-scale philanthropy, and famous families like Tata, Birla, Shri Ram, Godrej, Dalpatbhai Lalbhai, Singhania, Modi, Murugappa Chettiar, Kuppuswamy Naidu, Mafatlal, Mahindras, and others became the backbone of India's economic strength. To this day, these families are the pride of India.

Slowly, the dawn of the era of social responsibility was being acknowledged by business. The government also moved from closed economy to open economy policies. The enlightened educated business leaders realized that government alone cannot be held responsible for development and therefore a movement towards social responsibility emerged. An important change was the industry acceptance of social responsibility as part of the management of the enterprise itself.

There was a visible movement towards the rural sectors and the poor communities living at the edge of urban industrialized sectors. However, the pace was slow, as there was scepticism about the lack of knowledge in various sectors and an amorphous understanding of social responsibility. The good news is that steps had been taken and there was going to be no looking back. Smaller groups also decided to join the established business houses in their mission towards CSR.

CONCLUSION

Thus, we see that CSR is not a modern discovery and certainly not a discovery that can be credited to the economically developed countries of today. The basic question is: is economic development a prerequisite for CSR or does economic development follow CSR? The answer is not simple because CSR involves a number of stakeholders with unique demands of their own. The uniqueness of the demands stems from the fact that each actor in the socio-economic scenario is a product of the scenario and also shapes the scenario. Therefore, CSR needs to be part of the DNA of an organization for the organization to understand this dilemma and institutionalize the concept. This requires that the organization be driven not only by rules and regulations, but also by idealism. This stakeholder concept and the processes needed to institutionalize the CSR process will become more comprehensible in the chapters that follow.

Two examples of modern CSR efforts of organizations are given at the end of this chapter to show the tremendous growth and acceptance of the concept among the industrial and business community.

SUMMARY

The basic dimensions of corporate behaviour require value judgement and only human beings are gifted with the power of discriminating between what is moral and immoral. The human aspect of any organization is its core asset, as people are the data generators as well as the data users. Corporates are still struggling to give a formal structure to their CSR programme. CSR goes beyond philanthropy and has to take into account integrity and accountability. The analysis of the concept of stakeholder is important to implement sustainable, value-added development.

> Business relates to any economic or non-economic activity that adds utility to the masses or classes and is traded and commands a price. The history of CSR can be traced from the ancient policymakers who were fully committed to the ideal that perfect development of the individual culminated in the full development of society. There were momentous changes with the establishment of industrial houses and the expansion of the entrepreneurial base.

KEY TERMS

Accountability Responsible for one's action.
Amorphous Unstructured or vague.
Business Any activity that creates utility either for the masses or the classes.
Organization Business institution.
Philanthropy Charity or generosity.
Responsibility Dutiful.
Social contract Agreement between business (state) and society (population) for mutual advantage.
Sustainability Support growth over a long period.
Urban blight Suffering caused due to development and modernization (urbanization).

EXERCISES

Concept Review Questions

1. What do you understand by the term 'corporate social responsibility'? Justify your answer.
2. Why should CSR look beyond the concept of philanthropy?
3. Explain the importance of the human aspect in an organization.
4. Briefly trace the history of CSR in India.

Critical Thinking Questions

1. Why is CSR considered an important management concept today?
2. How do companies ensure that business and CSR are not mutually opposed to each other?

Research Question

Explain the concept of trusteeship promoted by Mahatma Gandhi.

Project

Visit any company of your choice and analyse whether their CSR practices are limited to philanthropy and bottom line, or relates to responsibility, accountability, sustainability, and social contract.

REFERENCES

Altekar, A.S. (1977), *State and Government in Ancient India*, Motilal Banarsidas Publishers, Delhi, pp. 48–74.

Arlow, P. and M.J. Gannon (1982), 'Social Responsiveness, Corporate Structure, and Economic Performance', *Academy of Management Review*, vol. 7, issue no. 2, pp. 235–241.

Aupperle, E. Kenneth, Archie B. Carroll, and John D. Hatfield, 'Instrument Development and Application in Corporate Social Responsibility', *Academy of Management Proceedings*, August 1983, pp. 369–373.

Bayly, Charles (1983), *Rulers, Townsmen and Bazaars—North Indian Society in the Age of British Expansion 1770–1870*, Cambridge University Press, Cambridge.

Berle, A.A. Jr. (1959), in Foreword to *The Corporation in Modern Society* by E.S. Mason, Harvard University Press, Cambridge.

Boal, K.B. and N. Peery (1985), 'The Cognitive Structure of Corporate Social Responsibility', *Journal of Management*, vol. 11, issue no. 3, pp. 71–82.

Boatright, J.R. (2003), *Ethics and the Conduct of Business*, Pearson Education, Delhi.

Bowie, Norman (1991), 'New Directions in Corporate Social Responsibility,' *Business Horizon* vol. 34, issue no. 4, pp. 56–65.

Buchholz, R.A. (1982), *Business Environment and Public Policy*, Prentice Hall, Englewood Cliffs, NJ.

——— (1985), *Essentials of Public Policy for Management*, Prentice Hall, Englewood Cliffs, NJ.

Carroll, Archie B. (1979), 'A Three Dimensional Conceptual Model of Corporate Performance,' *Academy of Management Review*, vol. 4, issue no. 4, pp. 497–505.

Chakraborty, S.K. (1995), *Human Values for Managers*, Oxford University Press, New Delhi, p. 161.

Chamberlain, N. (1973), *The Place of Business in America's Future—A Study in Social Values*, Basic Books, New York.

——— (1977), *Remaking American Values*, Basic Books, New York.

Clarkson, M.B.E. (1995), 'A stakeholder framework for analyzing and evaluating corporate social performance', *Academy of Management Review*, vol. 20, issue no. 1, 1995, pp. 92–117.

Committee for Economic Development (1971), *Social Responsibilities of Business Corporations*, CED, New York, p. 15.

Cowell, E.B. and R.A. Neil (2002), *Jatakas*, 6 vols, PTS (Pali Text Society), New Delhi.

Davis, K. (1960), 'Can Business Afford to Ignore Social Responsibilities?' *California Management Review*, Spring, vol. 2, issue no. 3, 1960, pp. 70–76.

DeFillipi, R.J. (1982), 'Conceptual Framework and Strategies for Corporate Social Involvement Research', in L.E. Preston (ed.) *Research in Corporate Social Performance and Policy*, JAI Press, Greenwich, Connecticut, no. 4.

DeGeorge, Richard (1990), *Business Ethics*, 3/e, MacMillan, New York.

Donald, P. Robin and R. Erie Reidenbach (1989), *Business Ethics—Where Profits Meet Value Systems*, Prentice Hall, Englewood Cliffs, New Jersey, pp. 38–55.

Donaldson, T. (1989), *The Ethics of International Business*, Oxford University Press, New York.

Edmonds, P. Charles III and Hand H. John (1976), 'What are the Real Long Run Objectives of Business?' *Business Horizon*, 19 December, pp. 75–81.

Etzioni, A. (1988), *The Moral Dimension—Toward a New Economics*, Free Press, New York.

Fitch, H.G. (1976), 'Achieving corporate social responsibility', *Academy of Management Review*, vol. 1, issue no. 1, pp. 38–46.

Frederick, W.C. (1960), 'The Growing Concern over Business Responsibility,' *California Management Review*, Summer, vol. 2, issue no. 4, p. 60.

——— (1978), 'From CSR to CSR—The Maturing of Business and Society Thought,' working paper, Katz Graduate School of Business, University of Pittsburgh.

——— (1986), 'Towards CSR3—Why ethical analysis is indispensable and unavoidable in corporate affairs', *California Management Review*, vol. 28, issue no. 2, pp. 126–141.

Freeman, R.E. and D.R. Gilbert (1988), *Corporate Strategy and Search for Ethics*, Prentice Hall, Englewood Cliffs, NJ.

Friedman, Milton (1970), 'The Social Responsibility of Business is to Increase Its Profits,' *New York Times Magazine*, September 13, pp. 32–33, 122–126.

Ganguly, K.M. (tr) (1991), *Mahabharat*, 12 vols, Munshiram Manoharlal, New Delhi.

Hahlo, H.R. and M.J. Trebilcock (eds), *Hahlo's Casebook on Company Law 2/e*, Sweet and Maxwell, London (1977).

Hausman, D.M. (1992), *The Inexact and Separate Science of Economics*, Cambridge University Press, Cambridge.

Haynes, Douglas (1987), 'From Tribute to Philanthropy—The Politics of Gift Giving in a Western Indian City', *Journal of Asian Studies*, vol. 46, issue no. 2, May, p. 339–60.

Hirshman, A.O. (1981), *Essays in Trespassing—Economics to Politics and Beyond*, Cambridge Press, New York.

Hopkins, Michael (1998), *A Planetary Bargain—CSR Comes of Age*, Macmillan, London.

Interview with Björn Stigson, President of the World Business Council for Sustainable Development (WBCSD) http://www.wbcsd.org/plugins/DocSearch/result.asp?txtDocText=Definition%20of%20CSR&txtDocTitle=Definition%20of%20CSR, accessed on 22.6.2010.

Jones, T.M. (1983), 'An Integrating Framework for Research in Business and Society—A Step towards the Elusive Paradigm?' *Academy of Management Review*, vol. 8, issue no. 4, pp. 559–564.

Leitner, G.W., quoted in Majumdar, RC, *Social Work in Ancient and Medieval India*, in Wadia, A.R. (edited) (1961) *History and Philosophy of Social Work in India*, Allied Publisher Pvt. Ltd, Bombay, p. 5.

Lindblom, C.E. (1977), *Politics and Markets*, Basic Books, New York.

Majumdar, R.C., H.C. Raychaudhuri, and Kalikinkar Datta (1995), *An Advanced History of India*, Macmillan India Ltd, Madras, p. 809.

March, J. (1992), 'The war is over and the victors have lost', *The Journal of Socio-Economics*, vol. 21, issue no. 3, pp. 261–267.

Post, J.E. (1978), *Corporate Behavior and Change*, Reston Publishing Company, Virginia.

Preston, L. and J. Post (1975), *Private Management and Public Policy*, Prentice Hall, New Jersey, p. 9.

Rangarajan, L.N. (ed.) (1992), *Kautilya—The Arthasastra*, Penguin Books India, New Delhi.

Rudner, David West (1995), *Caste and Capitalism in Colonial India—The Nattukottai Chettiars*, Munshilal Manoharlal Publishers, Delhi.

Sharma, Subhash (2005), 'A Brief History of History—Some Models of History and Lessons for Leadership and Management', *Journal of Human Values* 11:2 (2005), Sage Publication, New Delhi, p. 131.

Singhi, N.K. (1991), 'A Study of Jains in Rajasthan Town' in Carrithers, Michael and Caroline Humphrey (eds), *Assembly of Listeners, Jains in Society*, Cambridge University Press, Cambridge, New York, pp. 149.

Steidlmeier, P. (1987), 'Corporate social responsibility and business ethics', in Sethi, SP and C. Falbe (eds), *Business and Society—Dimensions of Conflict and Cooperation*, Lexington Books, New York, pp. 101–121.

Steiner, A. George (1972), 'Social Policies for Business,' *California Business Review*, vol. 15, issue no. 2, pp. 17–24, 1972.

Sunder, Pushpa (2000), *Beyond Business, from Merchant Charity to Corporate Citizenship*, Tata McGraw Hill, New Delhi.

Swami Nikhilananda (tr.), Chandogya Upanishad (V.11.5), 2008, 'The Upanishads—A New Translation,' Advaita Ashram Calcutta.

Theodore, Levitt (1983), 'The Dangers of Social Responsibility,' in Tom L. Beauchamp and Norman E. Bowie, *Ethical Theory and Business*, 2/e, Prentice Hall, Englewood Cliffs, New Jersey pp. 83–86.

Upadhyaya, R.B. (1976), *Social Responsibility of Business and the Trusteeship Theory of Mahatma Gandhi*, Sterling Publishers, New Delhi, p. vi.

Velasquez, M.G. (2005), *Business Ethics—Concepts and Cases*, Pearson Education, Delhi.

Venkatsubbiah, H. (1977), *Enterprise and Economic Change, Fifth Year of FICCI*, Vikas Publishing House, New Delhi, pp. 169–172.

Vogel, D. (1991), 'The ethical roots of business ethics', *Business Ethics Quarterly*, vol. I, issue no. 1, pp. 101–120.

Votaw, D. (1973), 'Genius Becomes Rare', in D. Votaw and S. Sethi (eds), *The Corporate Dilemma—Traditional Values vs Contemporary Problems*, Prentice Hall, Englewood Cliffs, New Jersey, pp. 11–45.

Zadek, Simon (2001), 'Third Generation Corporate Citizenship', The Foreign Policy Centre, London.

――― (2001), *The Civil Corporation—The New Economy of Corporate Citizenship*, Earthscan, London, p. 29.

www.wbcsd.org.

CASE STUDIES

CASE 1 CSR IN HINDUSTAN UNILEVER LIMITED

Hindustan Unilever Limited (HUL) is a subsidiary of Unilever, one of the world's leading suppliers of fast-moving consumer goods (FMCGs) with strong local roots in more than 100 countries across the globe, and with an annual sales turnover of €40.5 billion in 2008. Unilever has about 52 per cent shareholding in HUL. It was recently rated among the top four companies globally in the list of Global Top Companies for Leaders by a study sponsored by Hewitt Associates, in partnership with *Fortune* magazine and the RBL Group. The company was ranked number one in the Asia-Pacific region and in India.

HUL believes that an organization's worth is also in the service it renders to the community. It focuses on hygiene, nutrition, enhancement of livelihoods, reduction of greenhouse gases, and water footprint. It is also involved in education and rehabilitation of special or underprivileged children, care for the destitute and HIV-positive, and rural development. HUL has also responded in cases of national calamities/adversities and contributes through various welfare measures. HUL's Project Shakti is a rural initiative that targets small villages populated by less than 5000 individuals. Through Shakti, it is creating micro-enterprise opportunities for rural women, thereby improving their livelihood and the standard of living in rural communities. Shakti also provides health and hygiene education through the Shakti Vani programme. The programme now covers 15 states in India and has over 45,000 women entrepreneurs in its fold, reaching out to 100,000 villages and directly reaching out to over three million rural consumers.

HUL also runs a rural health programme, Lifebuoy Swasthya Chetana. The programme endeavours to induce adoption of hygienic practices among rural Indians and aims to bring down the incidence of diarrhoea. As of 2010, it has already touched 120 million people in approximately 50, 676 villages across India.

HUL has been engaged in community projects in water management adjacent to their manufacturing sites.

The Vidarbha area in Maharashtra, a western state in India, is a dry and arid region. According to the district collector, V. Poreddiwar, 'of the total rainfall here, about 55 per cent of rainfall is lost in evaporation and 35 per cent is wasted as water runs away downhill. Merely 10 per cent is ultimately used for irrigation or drinking purposes.' In this scenario, farmers were constantly under financial crisis and felt helpless as they were dragged further into the vicious cycle of poverty. An NGO, Maharashtra Institute of Technology Transfer for Rural Areas (MITTRA), knew that water harvesting was the solution but did not have the required capital to implement it.

HUL had the capital and inclination to help farmers near its soap factory in Khamgaon village to be financially independent. Around 12 years ago, the factory started a pilot project on watershed management on a five-hectare plot to prevent soil degradation and conserve water. The efforts have resulted in the creation of a green belt, which is now a veritable forest of about 6300 trees.

Encouraged by the results, HUL extended the model to a neighbouring village, Parkhed, with an initial investment of Rs 80 lakhs in association with TERI and Bharatiya Agro Industries Foundation. The company believed that it would more than double the area under cultivation in Mandka, a nearby village. HUL aimed to get nearly 125 hectares of land owned by the farmers of Mandka under regular cultivation. The strategy was to first work on a demonstration land of 569 acres with a set of farmers to convince them of this model's utility.

The model had to be built on the hilly terrain in Mandka region, which has wide variations in elevation, slope lengths, and a fragile geological formation. When the water flowed down the hill, it triggered multiple problems like loss of vegetation, lack of fodder for cattle, and soil erosion. The water harvesting model encompassed building trenches and gullies, constructing check dams and wells, as well as planting a selection of tree species that would arrest water before it flowed away. Narrow excavations of about 0.3 metres wide and 0.6 metres long were made along the contours after furrowing the land. The available rubble was used for bunding. Agave/vetiver grass was planted to reduce run-off and to conserve soil. Where there was no debris, trench-cum-mounds were constructed to arrest surface water run-off. Three check bunds and six gully plugs were also constructed on the small 'nullahs' (narrow drains) running through the plot.

According to MITTRA officials, the project has benefited about 2000 people and about 120 landless farmers. Their income has soared three times. The cost of treating the plot was about Rs 6000 to Rs 8000 per hectare of land. The company also assisted women in forming 32 self-help groups, which collected a total savings of Rs 3.52 lakhs and helped local schools to give computer training. These developments reduced migration from the village, as 99 per cent of the people wanted to stay back after the success of the project.

HUL's Head — Corporate Social Responsibility Meeta Singh lays out the structure of each CSR project, which is later implemented by the company CSR team and local factory officials. Singh says, 'We developed this programme (Greening Barrens) according to the needs of the people here. Although we have other CSR projects running like Shakti, we realized that implementing a pan-India programme would not make sense, as every region has different needs.'

In Parkhed under the company's initiative, the farmers have been mobilized to build a community where they pool a part of their income. This fund is at the disposal of the farmers to use for repair work of existing dams. The community at Parkhed has already constructed 47 percolation bunds, 1600 trenches, 6000 running metres of continuous contour trenching over 100 hectares, and five permanent check dams. Around 350 families have reaped a second crop this year, which is only possible due to construction of check dams. The availability of water helped in the cultivation of vegetables and fruits. Total land under cultivation during the second crop season is 470 acres. With the increase in the number of crops, one acre of land is yielding production equivalent to five acres of land.

The annual income of the farmers in the vicinity of five check dams increased from around an average of Rs 36,000 to approx. Rs 85,000 per annum per farmer. This has been attributed to the availability of water in the wells during the *rabi* season and also increase in the level of water in the wells during the *kharif* season. Hence, along with reaping a *rabi* crop, the farmers have also been able to almost double the yield of the *kharif* crop. The initiative received appreciation at the Johannesburg World Summit on Sustainable Development.

Obviously, initiatives of this kind help to solve various social issues such as poverty, farmer suicides, migration to cities, and under-utilization of land. With the increase in the purchasing power of the farmers, they naturally become the future loyal customers of HUL products and intangible long-term benefit of brand building happens for the organization. HUL is a name that is the most trusted brand in FMCG products in India. The bottom line of an organization actually accentuates with such initiatives.

Source: Adapted from a report in *Business Standard*, 5 February 2008, Bangalore, http://www.hul.co.in/aboutus/introductiontohul/ and http://www.hul.co.in/sustainability/casestudies/water/WaterConservation/default.aspx, accessed on 4 June 2010.

Discussion Questions
1. Do you agree that HUL's CSR efforts add to its brand image in the public mind?
2. How does HUL ensure that business and CSR are not mutually opposed to each other?

CASE 2   CSR IN ITC

ITC (once called Imperial Tobacco Company) is rated among the World's Best Big Companies, Asia's 'Fab 50' and the World's Most Reputable Companies by *Forbes* magazine, among India's Most Respected Companies by *BusinessWorld* and among India's Most Valuable Companies by *Business Today*. ITC ranks among India's `10 Most Valuable (Company) Brands', in a study conducted by Brand Finance and published by the *Economic Times*. ITC also ranks among Asia's 50 best performing companies compiled by *Business Week*.

ITC has a diversified presence in cigarettes, hotels, paperboards and specialty papers, packaging, agri-business, packaged foods and confectionery, information technology, branded apparel, personal care, stationery, safety matches and other FMCG products. ITC is a market leader in its traditional businesses of cigarettes, hotels, paperboards, packaging, and agri-exports.

ITC's Agri Business Division, one of India's largest exporters of agricultural commodities, has designed e-Choupal, a community-based programme that has reached millions of farmers, and is expanding into 30 new villages a day. It is conceived as a more efficient supply chain aimed at delivering value to its customers around the world on a sustainable basis. The e-Choupal model has been specifically

> **ITC's vision:** Sustain ITC's position as one of India's most valuable corporations through world class performance, creating growing value for the Indian economy and the company's stakeholders.
>
> **ITC's mission:** To enhance the wealth generating capability of the enterprise in a globalising environment, delivering superior and sustainable stakeholder value.

designed to tackle the challenges posed by the unique features of Indian agriculture, characterized by fragmented farms, weak infrastructure, and the involvement of numerous intermediaries, among others.

Launched in June 2000, e-Choupal is one of the largest initiatives among all internet-based interventions in rural India. e-Choupal services today reach out to over four million farmers growing a range of crops—soyabean, coffee, wheat, rice, pulses, shrimp—in over 40,000 villages through 6500 kiosks across ten states (Madhya Pradesh, Haryana, Uttarakhand, Karnataka, Andhra Pradesh, Uttar Pradesh, Rajasthan, Maharashtra, Kerala, and Tamil Nadu).

The idea is a redefinition of *choupal*, which in Hindi means the village square where village elders used to meet to discuss important matters. The e-Choupal is a computer with an Internet connection for farmers to gather around and interact with people around the globe.

The problems encountered while setting up and managing these e-Choupals are primarily of infrastructural inadequacies, including power supply, telecom connectivity, and bandwidth, apart from the challenge of imparting skills to the first-time Internet users in remote and inaccessible areas of rural India.

ITC installs a computer with solar-charged batteries for power and VSAT Internet connection in select villages. A local farmer is made the *sanchalak*, i.e., conductor, and operates the computer exclusively for farmers on behalf of ITC. It offers five distinct services.

1. Information: Daily weather forecast, prices of various crops, e-mails to farmers and ITC officials, news, etc., in local language and free of cost.
2. Knowledge: Sourced from agricultural universities about farming methods specific to crops and region, soil testing, expert advice—all this is made available free of cost.
3. Purchase: Farmers can buy seeds, fertilizers, pesticides, and products like tractors and bicycles as well as services like insurance policies. About 35 companies are already using this portal to access the farmers to sell their products.
4. Sales: Crops can be sold at ITC centres or in local markets after verifying prices through the net.
5. Development work: NGOs working on various community development programmes like women self-help groups, cattle breed improvement, water harvesting, adult education etc., can now reach villages through e-choupal. Land records are also being made available online.

The sanchalaks are required to take a public oath of serving their community without discrimination and sign a social contract to spend a part of their income earned from e-Choupals on community welfare. The sanchalaks are selected from among the farmers, thus giving the message that the e-Choupals are for farmers and by farmers, though run by ITC. They become the agents of change as they are trusted and become the point man for all information. In return for their service, ITC gives Rs 5 for every quintal of the produce sold to ITC. In 2003–04, ITC distributed Rs 3 crore as commission. The sanchalak also gets commission on every product or service farmers buy through e-Choupals. This has made him an entrepreneur. Therefore, it is a win-win situation for all—the villagers, ITC, and the sanchalaks.

A coordinator or *sanyojak* is appointed to manage about 50 e-Choupals. He is either a former wholesale trader or a local dealer of ITC products. He is the link between the sanchalaks and ITC and also earns a commission on e-Choupal deals.

This human organization is a unique example where every stakeholder—farmers, traders, companies, government agencies, and NGOs—competes and collaborates with others.

The success of the system lies in the fact that

1. It is locally run. Since the sanchalak is a local villager, his prosperity is interlinked with local farmers and companies like ITC.
2. It encourages competition from within as more than one company supplies products to the villagers and they are not limited by selling at the 'mandis', i.e., the local wholesale markets. This ensures quality and fair prices. The farmers are no more dodged by arbitrary pricing, under-weighing, and delayed payments. The monopolies of the local markets controlled by unscrupulous trade cartels have been broken. Farmers have the advantages of 'bargain' and 'choice'. It surpasses the public distribution system, which lacks accountability and integrity, and therefore much leaks out through the porous distribution system. e-Choupals have broken the myth that farmers are unwilling to pay. In fact, they prefer paid and efficient products or services to free but inefficient products or services.
3. The power of scale can be leveraged. The bigger the scale, the more the transactions, the less the cost and the more the beneficiaries.
4. Availability of specialized knowledge as government institutions, NGOs, private companies, and local middlemen offer their expertise and also actively participate in the system.
5. A continuous process of improvement happens, based on experience and feedback from users of the network.

As India's *kisan* (farmer) company, ITC has taken care to involve farmers in the designing and management of the entire e-Choupal initiative. The active participation of farmers in this rural initiative has created a sense of ownership in the project among the farmers. They see e-Choupal as the new-age cooperative for all practical purposes.

This enthusiastic response from farmers has encouraged ITC to plan for the extension of the e-Choupal initiative to altogether 15 states across India over the next few years. On the anvil are plans to channelize other services related to micro-credit, health, and education through the same e-Choupal infrastructure.

No wonder the farmer's response is overwhelming—in 2001–02, ITC purchased 60,000 metric tonnes of crop through e-Choupal. In 2003–04, it increased to 2,10,000 tonnes, and in the four months of 2004–05, it picked up 1,80,000 tonnes of farm products. There is endless scope of making money from e-Choupals for every stakeholder. This has naturally led to a positive social spin-off as the purchasing power and self-respect of the under-privileged has increased. If the self-interest of each agent is strictly monitored and well aligned, it would translate into common good. This experiment at the 'outer circle' arena has proved the efficacy of CSR. This confirms that when corporate and community interests are aligned in a proactive way it serves both profitably. This answers the increasing pressure from society—expressed through legislation and in the courts—to hold business accountable to the same standards of conduct imposed on individuals.

In contrast to the view that national governments are powerless in front of the globalization challenge, domestic policies can integrate social progress. One positive approach is by ensuring cooperation between the academic institutions, voluntary organizations, and the corporates, which offers the right direction. There has to be a conscious effort to check exploitative patterns in the work environment. Family disintegration, rising consumerism, and discrimination need to be tackled by every stakeholder of society. There is a need to take account of the views of the social partners in economic and social policy formulation and implementation, as well as in enterprise and sectoral activities. Social dialogue at all levels is the necessity of the day. It is true that the process of implementation may take some time and effort before it bears fruit, but in the end it is worth it. We cannot remain complacent about corporate social responsibility. We have to orient ourselves to the sustainability ideal. 'We need visionary leadership, heartfelt commitment, and enduring hard work. And each of us, in our own way, in our own place, has a contribution to make.'

Discussion Questions
1. Tobacco is considered a 'sin industry'. After reading the case on e-Choupal of ITC, do you think marketing of tobacco products should be condoned?
2. How does ITC see to it that business and CSR are not mutually opposed to each other?

Sources: Adapted from the cover story 'Rural Markets', *India Today*, 13 December 2004, http://www.itcportal.com/sets/itc_frameset.htm and http://www.itcportal.com/sets/echoupal_frameset.htm, last accessed on 4 June 2010; Visser, Wayne, Analysis: Five Corporate Sustainability Challenges that Remain Unmet, ethicalcorp.com, 23 July 2004.

Evolution of Company and CSR

INTRODUCTION

Corporation is a concept that has evolved over time to become the single most significant overriding force in our modern lives. There is hardly a human activity that does not fall under the purview and 'shadow' of corporations. By definition, a corporation is a group or 'body' of individuals seeking some advantages for its members. A corporation achieves this end with the assistance of an extremely forceful state. It has no advantage by definition over other corporations, but it seeks to 'equal' itself, i.e., put itself on a level playing field with other corporations.

The concept of an economic system deals with human competition for scarce resources. In this race, to acquire the limited available resources for gaining profit, human beings create processes that help them to achieve the resources before others can do so. Once these resources are 'captured', they are either used to make other goods and services or sold in their natural form. This brings in the systems of production and exchange. Usually, it is not easy for a single individual to achieve this entire cycle. Therefore a group with different financial abilities and skills is created and thus the birth of a corporation—in economic terms what we know today in common language as a company or an organization—takes place. Because risks are involved in the entire process, the risk-takers, or those who have contributed, usually financially, to the formation of a corporation, become the owners and look for returns in financial terms and that, in simple terms, is called profit. Therefore, the economic corporation works on the basic principle of earning profits. 'Mediating the process of production and exchange that are governed by the laws of supply and demand, these institutions and organizations (developed as a consequence of "humanly devised constraints that shape human interaction") inhibit as well as stimulate economic growth and development' (North 1990; Hayami 1997).

LEARNING OBJECTIVES

After studying this chapter, you will be able to
- Understand the concept of corporation
- Trace a brief history of corporations
- Understand how modern corporations come into existence
- Provide a brief outline of corporate governance
- Analyse the importance of CSR in governance

SEEDS OF EARLY CORPORATIONS

The early corporations were either religious in nature or were conglomerates of people practising a particular skill. The English term 'confraternity' embraces a range of religious associations that have existed in the early Middle Ages and continue to exist even to this day and age. Members of the associations are committed to certain rules and guidelines, to promote their religious life. Western Catholicism pioneered and promoted confraternities. However, some Jewish and Muslim communities had their confraternities in early modern northern Italy, notably in Ferrara, in the Balkans, Levant, and the Maghreb, respectively. Most confraternities were for the laity and promoted by them, though confraternities did exist of clergy alone (Black and Gravestock 2006).

These confraternities played a significant role in religious-social life, in cities, towns, and sometimes in smaller rural communities from the central Middle Ages in western Europe. They catered to all levels of society; some solely for a specific group like women, nobles, a particular craft, students, etc. It is clear that large numbers of the laity were directly involved or indirectly affected by confraternity philanthropy. There were large numbers of confraternities and membership could be 'a mere handful, as in a rural Rosary society in Lombardy, or many hundreds (as in the top Venetian group of Scuole Grandi), or even thousands (as in Naples' actively philanthropic Santo Spirito company in the 1560s)' (Black and Gravestock 2006).

Banquets and feasts, which were an important part of confraternal life, were often used to raise money for various guilds. The leading money-raisers were Robin Hood guilds and guilds of Maidens. By the 16th century reformers like Bishop Giovan Matteo Giberti of Verona wanted a Corpus Christi fraternity in each parish. Like-minded bishops saw the 'value of lay confraternities, provided they were firmly linked to the parish. This control and supervision was taken up in the Tridentine legislation (formulated in 1562).' (French, 'Parochial Fund-raising, esp. pp. 125–27; Poska, 'From Parties to Pieties', esp. pp. 221–27 for some Spanish reactions; Black, *Italian Confraternities*, pp. 91–92; Diefendorf, *Beneath the Cross*, pp. 34–37, including 1551 French crown's attack on confraternal feasting). Some confraternities rebelled against the religious control and regained their independence.

These socio-religious entities were involved in philanthropic activities like providing food and medical aid. Though much of the activity was unorganized by the 'eleventh century in the Val d'Elsa, the statutes of a fraternity could enjoin its male and female members systematically to assist paupers' (Meersseman, *Ordo Fraternitas*, pp. 55–65, esp. p. 61; see also Henderson, *Piety and Charity*, pp. 14–15).

During the medieval and modern periods, there was much controversy about who should control philanthropy—state, municipality, confraternities, or other institutions. The vacillation of policies between central control and local initiatives, through the 16th to 18th centuries, reflects the conflicting policies and attitudes through Europe (Black and Gravestock 2006, p. 19).

Following the establishment of merchant guilds, the corporation of manual labourers was already very noticeable when towns began to flourish in the 12th century. Some examples can be traced to the 12th century Normandy, where guilds were attested for (Black and Gravestock 2006, p. 54). These associations provided aid to fellow workers and encouraged the celebration of communal religious festivities. Evidence in the form of statutes of confraternities of craftsmen earlier than 1300 have been discovered in sovereign regions of Flanders and Brabant. Many industries followed this trend of forming religious corporations during the 13th century. Confraternities of smiths, porters, carpenters, leather curries, stocking makers, and miners have also been found belonging to the period between 1280 and 1300. These early craft corporations were mainly involved in religious, social, and charitable activities. Economic activities fell outside the competence of these early corporations.

In India, the early corporations can be traced to the system of guilds, which can be traced as early as 800 BC. Their commercial character became more pronounced by the 3rd century BC. The guilds as corporations performed diplomatic, legislative, and administrative activities. They employed people and enjoyed immunity under specific charters. In fact, they evolved as one of the most important pressure groups in society.

However, a more organized concept of corporations emerged, with the entry of charter companies from Europe to India. Though the Portuguese were the first European traders to visit India, their commercial activities were controlled directly by the crown. The Dutch East India Company was formed in 1602. The most memorable and historical company was the English East India Company, which was formed by a charter. Queen Elizabeth incorporated it in 1600 under the title of 'The Governor and Company of Merchant of London Trading to the East Indies.' The French East India Company was formed in 1604 and underwent expansions leading to the establishment of the 'The Company of the Indies.' The Danish and the Ostend (incorporated by the King of Austria) East India companies are the other examples of early corporations in India (Report on the Miscellaneous Old Records of the India Office, 1 November 1878, London, 1879, p. 77, footnote).

DEVELOPMENT OF MODERN CORPORATIONS

Early corporations depended on age-old principles of property and contracts. As a result of this, firms either had single owners or a small number of owners, as the owners were totally liable for every activity of the firm, which included its profits and its debts. Therefore, every owner had to be vigilant because in case the company had to be wound up, the owner(s) would lose their entire personal wealth. This naturally meant that the early corporations usually began as small firms, since the capital available as well as the borrowing capacity was limited, as they depended upon the personal wealth of the proprietor(s). To counter this risk, legislation was devised to give the corporate entity a life of its own and separate the ownership from the management. That is how the concept of bonds and shares came into existence.

The agreed return on a share and a bond may be comparable but need not be equal. The return on the share is usually high because it is in the interest of the company (the proprietor of early corporations), as it does not lead to control and as finance by share issue reduces risks. Interest paid in the form of dividends would have to be paid in both profitable times and during times of loss, but the dividend can be reduced during bad times to reduce the burden of finance by shares. It is expected that it would go up during good times. However, it is during these good times that the increased payouts are borne more easily. Thus, in a way, the risk is diminished under this method.

We must remember that the proprietor always has more information than the outside shareholder; therefore company laws have been formed to reduce this inequality of information and ensure full and fair information sharing. In spite of this, the apprehension of loss built into the restricted transferability will dissuade investors from investing and that would limit equity for the firm. Restricted transferability means a long wait before gains may arrive (if at all) and the gains may not be worth the wait. Whereas, when shares can be easily transferred, gains can accrue even in a short term.

Transferable shares with limited liability are a liquid asset because they can be turned into money whenever the shareholders feel it is the right time to make profits. Since shares can be pledged to get loans as they are considered a liquid asset, a speculative drive is set in motion. One can either borrow to invest in more shares or make capital investment. Another advantage of limited liability and transferability is that investors can diversify their portfolios. As the adage goes 'all the eggs should not be in the same basket'; so the risk of loss is reduced and also, investors are more worried about the overall loss or gain in the portfolio. This leads us to the question of ownership of the companies and that brings us to the concept of corporate governance, which defines the laws, codes, structure, and processes put in place to run a company.

It begins with the proprietors being the first directors, but as the number of shareholders grows, they also become owners of the company and then profit needs to be shared between the proprietors and the shareholders. Besides, the succession planning of directors also needs to be done. This requires the formulation of rules and regulations that would create a win-win situation for the owners, the management, and the community at large in the activity of profit-making. This process of restraint and control imposed internally by the company and externally by the government relates to the concept of corporate governance (formal definition and legal details given later in the section on Governance and Management).

The limited liability concept is interesting because in a way it relates to CSR, because it asks what the liabilities are and this is where many of the stakeholders come into the picture. For example, the company has to pay for the resources, goods or services it receives, pay its employees' salaries and wages, pay its customers for any damages or losses, follow norms regarding environment and community protection, which also involves a cost and hence is a liability. We must keep in mind here that the criminal liabilities are not limited; it is only the civil liabilities which deal with paying money that is limited (refer to the idea of tradeoff between stakeholders given in Chapter 3).

The concept of unlimited liability also exists. This means that an individual or a small group of individuals have to bear the entire liability and pay the price. This may lead to loss of entire liquid assets as well as fixed assets like land, house, machinery, furniture, vehicles, etc. Normally, all shareholders are not 'hounded' and for this purpose the richest investor is targeted. However, certain professions are not allowed to practice limited liability, e.g., solicitors.

In any partnership business, the partners are fully liable to the extent of their personal property for the debts of the partnership. Of course, the aggrieved party cannot receive the full amount more than once from the partnership. The danger here is that as a partner one does not have full control on the other partner(s), vis-à-vis—the external business environment. The formal process of founding a modern public limited company is given below, which is the most common form of a business organization in modern times.

The Incorporation of a Company

Modern corporations have come into existence under the law in all countries and are recognized as a legal (artificial) person, quite separate and distinct from its owners. The corporation is recognized as artificial because it does not have a mind of its own and cannot take decisions. Its existence is ratified by law so that it represents the decisions taken by its members and in that sense is legally accountable and therefore answerable. This makes it easy for stakeholders to question the activities of a corporation because otherwise the wrongdoer in a corporation can hide behind the large number of members inside a corporation. An example of granting such legality is England, where the State can act to grant corporate personality. At common law, the crown can grant a Royal Charter or the parliament can confer by an Act of Parliament. However, the Joint Stock

Companies Act of 1844 brought in the concept of registering the corporation with the Registrar of Companies.

Even in India, the company is an artificial person with perpetual succession; or in other words, is a legal person 'who' can sue others and can be sued by others. Therefore, the shareholder of the company can enter into a contract with the company and if the contract is not honoured by any party, they can sue each other.

The shareholders are not agents of the company; they are legal members of the company. The shareholder is protected from any legal action by any other party (individual or organization) with whom the company may have entered into a contract. The shareholders enjoy limited liability, i.e., they are liable to the extent of the face value of the share. The shares of a company can be freely traded in the market.

These shareholders came to be considered as the owners of the company and ownership was the basis of power. There is an increase in the separation between the directors, whom the shareholders elected to manage themselves, as a result of the increase in numbers and geographical spread of shareholders. Berle and Means' (1932) argument that 'the rise of the modern corporation has brought a concentration of economic power, which can compete on equal terms with the modern state—economic power versus political power, each strong in its own field. The state seeks in some aspects to regulate the corporation, while the corporation, steadily becoming more powerful, makes every effort to avoid such regulation ... The future may see the economic organism, now typified by the corporation, not only on an equal plane with the state, but possibly even superseding it as the dominant form of social organization' appears like a prophetic truth today.

To rein in this super-economic giant, various efforts have been enumerated under the aegis of the term 'corporate governance'. It starts with incorporation, wherein the proprietors need to file the following documents with the registrar of companies in the place where the registered office would be situated:

(a) The memorandum of association
(b) The articles of association
(c) Notice of the situation of the registered office of the company
(d) List of persons who have agreed to act as directors
(e) Consent of the directors in writing to act as such
(f) A declaration confirming the due compliance to all legal liabilities to be endorsed by an advocate, a chartered accountant, or a director or secretary of the company

All the above documents are required when a public limited company is incorporated. In the case of a private limited company, the first three documents are the requirement. The registrar, after satisfying the needs, issues a certificate of incorporation that gives legal existence to the company and awards perpetual succession and a common seal.

Now, the company has to acquire the certificate to commence business (COB) by providing:

(a) The prospectus or statement in lieu of prospectus.
(b) Shares have to be allocated within 120 days from the date of the prospectus and/return of allotment of shares should be filed with the registrar.
(c) A declaration of all legal compliance also has to be submitted.

Therefore, to commence business, the company must have the memorandum of association, the articles of association, and the certificate to commence business.

GOVERNANCE AND MANAGEMENT OF COMPANY

'Corporate governance is not an abstract goal, but exists to serve corporate purposes by providing a structure within which stockholders, directors, and management can pursue most effectively the objectives of the corporation' (US Business Round Table White Paper on Corporate Governance, September 1997).

Governance is the prerogative of the board of directors, who are appointed by the shareholders. The board does not have a hierarchy and every director has equal responsibility and similar duties and powers. The management structure is a pyramid, headed by the chief executive officer (CEO) with a number of managers below. Authority and responsibility is delegated downwards and in return accountability is expected upwards. The CEO is the bridge between the directors (governing activities), and the managers (management activities).

The board consists of executive directors and non-executive directors. Non-executive directors include outside non-executive directors who have links with the company or are connected non-executive directors (CNED), and outside non-executive directors are those who have no links and hence are referred to as independent directors (INED). The main activities of the board can be summed up as formulating strategy, promulgating policies, supervising executive management, and being answerable and accountable to shareholders.

This brings us to the first principle of fiduciary duties. The fiduciary principle states that one having been entrusted with powers for another's benefit is under a general equitable obligation when dealing with those powers to act honestly in what they consider to be in the other's interests.

In reality, we find that though the board is seen as the major driver of good governance, it very often comes under external influences like large institutional investors who play a more important role than the individual shareholders.

The threat of hostile take-overs in liquid markets like the US and the UK also keeps the boards constantly vigilant about governance and share prices. In debt-driven markets, banks and financial institutions play a significant part as governance drivers. Even family members who sometimes can act as 'shadow directors', joint venture partners, and holding companies influence governance in companies. There is a fundamental difference between countries prescribing regulations through law and countries favouring a self-regulatory approach in governance styles, leading to vital differences in drivers of good governance.

THEORIES OF CORPORATE GOVERNANCE

'The directors of companies, being managers of other people's money than their own, it cannot well be expected that they should watch over it with the same anxious vigilance with which the partners in a private copartnery frequently watch over their own' (Smith 1776). This statement clearly describes the apprehensions of the shareholders when they select the directors and entrust upon them the responsibility to ensure regular higher returns on their investment. Therefore, let us look at a few theories that try to resolve the problem of separation of ownership and control:

- Agency theory
- Stewardship theory
- Shareholder versus stakeholder theory
- Transaction cost theory
- Sociological theory

Agency Theory

The agency theory describes the economic relationship that arises between two individuals, one being the principal and the other being the agent. In a corporate scenario, the principal stockholders/shareholders are the principal and the directors/managers are the agents. This relationship mainly requires three conditions to operate:

1. The agent has the freedom to choose between several courses of action, e.g., in an organization, the managers can choose various ways of utilizing the assets as they have effective control over the assets.
2. The actions of agents influence their own growth (through more stability and better remuneration) and also the growth of principals (through rise in share prices, dividends, etc.).
3. As a result of the geographical spread or complexity of activities, it becomes extremely difficult for the principals to observe the actions of the agents as information is not enough or equal. The crux of the agency theory is the agency problem or the relationship between the principal

and the agent. We can express the 'flow' of relationship in an organization in a very simple and basic manner as shown in Fig. 2.1.

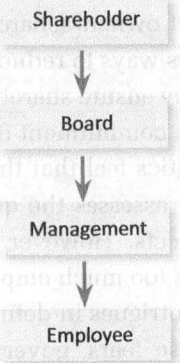

Figure 2.1 Basic organizational relationships

The suppliers of finance (principals signify shareholders in joint stock companies) to corporations need to assure themselves of getting a return on their investment. Therefore, they need to ensure that the directors (agent), appointed by the principal, return some of the profits to them, and do not steal the capital they supply or invest it in bad projects. Therefore, the suppliers of finance need to control the directors. The major issue with the numerically growing and geographically dispersed shareholders is the lack of transparency, and therefore the control is also dispersed and less effective. This has led to over-dependence on the directors to act honestly, keeping the shareholders' interest in mind.

With the growing complexity of business, tracing the agency chain becomes difficult, especially when investment is routed through various financial instruments/funds like bonds, equities, commodities, hedge funds, etc. Agency loss can occur in any form of a corporation like not-for-profit organizations, trade unions, and other professional bodies, private companies, cooperatives, etc. This loss was discovered by Jensen and Meckling (1976) when they wrote 'agency theory involves a contract under which one or more persons (the shareholders) engage another person (director) to perform some service on their behalf, which includes delegating some decision making authority to the agent. If both parties to the relationship are utility maximizers, there is a good reason to believe the agent will not always act in the best interest of the principal.'

The agency loss is compounded by factors such as unequal information between the two parties. The directors would always have more insider information of the organization and the shareholder has to trust and rely on the information that they receive from the directors. Prospective future investors can only judge the capabilities of the directors from the prospectus, the past performance reports. Therefore, the element of risk would always lurk in this relationship.

Strengths and Weaknesses of the Agency Theory

The main concern of this theory is to ensure that the agency loss is reduced. In modern corporations, because of the geographically dispersed and numerically large number of owners (shareholders), agency loss is a reality and therefore, the theory offers ways to reduce this loss. It provides for incentive schemes for managers, if they ensure shareholder profits. Senior members are offered shares to get long-term commitment from them.

However, critics feel that the theory is extremely narrow in its perspective because it only assesses the quantitative aspect and leaves behind important qualitative aspects. However, criticism is also labelled against the theory because there is too much emphasis on intangibles like altruism, interpersonal relations, and intrigues in defining the principal–agent relationship.

To allay these fears, governance procedures should include transparent and fair accounting practices and disclosures. The board of directors should include non-executive independent directors who would provide unbiased objective decisions that would lead to better productivity and thus increase shareholder value.

Stewardship Theory

This theory is built on the premise that the directors will fulfil their fiduciary duties to the shareholders. It assumes that human beings by nature are good and therefore directors are basically trustworthy. Personal reputation holds a very significant place in the directors/managers behaviour, hence they would not indulge in any activity that could damage their self-respect. This theory centres on the situations in which directors are stewards whose motives are aligned with the objectives of their principals.

Directors need to take into account the well-being of all the stakeholders of the organization, since they are serving as stewards, but under the law their first responsibility is to the shareholders. This is where governance has to incorporate corporate social responsibility. It is believed that the control of the stewards through rules can be detrimental because it undermines the pro-organizational behaviour of the steward by lowering his/her motivation. In fact, the trust reposed on the directors underpins company laws and governance codes. Donaldson and Davis (1991) highlighted the benefits when they explained that 'stewardship theory stresses the beneficial consequences on shareholder returns of facilitative authority structures, which unify command by having roles of CEO and chair held by the same person ... The safeguarding of returns to shareholders may be along the track, not of placing management under greater control by owners, but of empowering managers to take autonomous executive action.'

Strengths and Weaknesses of the Stewardship Theory

The trust entailed in this relationship is of a higher level. The faith that the stewards of the company would not at any point put themselves before the organization creates a highly motivated team. There is always an opportunity available to be innovative and offer new ideas of growth.

The theory has been criticized as a normative theory that cannot be used to predict future performance. The theory's weakness lies in the fact that the causal relationship between governance and performance cannot be assessed using this theory.

As is obvious from the above description of the theories, the agency theory is more control-oriented to keep the managers and administrators in check, whereas the stewardship theory is more liberal and believes in empowerment of managers and administrators. The differences have been well-summarized by Alfonso Vargas Sanchez (2003) and are given Table 2.1.

TABLE 2.1 Differences between agency theory and stewardship theory

Agency theory	Stewardship theory
1. Managers are agents.	1. Managers are stewards.
2. Governance approach is materialistic.	2. Governance approach is sociological and psychological.
3. Behaviour pattern is individualistic, opportunistic, and self-serving.	3. Behaviour pattern is collectivistic, pro-organizational, and trustworthy.
4. Managers are motivated by their own objectives.	4. Managers are motivated by the principal's objectives.
5. Interests of managers and principals differ.	5. Interest of managers and principals converge.
6. Role of the management is to monitor and control.	6. Role of the management is to facilitate and empower.
7. Owner's attitude is to avoid risks.	7. Owner's attitude is to take risks.
8. Principal–manager relationship is based on control.	8. It is relationship based.
9. Motivation revolves around lower order needs and extrinsic needs.	9. Motivation depends upon higher order needs and intrinsic needs.
10. Social comparison is between companies.	10. Social comparison is between principals.
11. There is little attachment to company.	11. There is great attachment to company.
12. Power rests with the institution.	12. Power rests with the personnel.
13. Management philosophy is control oriented.	13. Management philosophy is involvement oriented.
14. To deal with increasing uncertainty and risk, the theory advocates greater control and more supervision.	14. The theory advocates training and empowering people, making jobs more challenging and motivating.

Contd

Table 2.1 contd

Agency theory	Stewardship theory
15. Risk-orientation done through a system of control.	15. Risk-orientation is done through a system of trust.
16. Timeframe is short term.	16. Timeframe is long term.
17. The objective is cost control.	17. The objective is improving performance.
18. Cultural differences revolve around individualism and large power distance.	18. Cultural differences revolve around collectivism and small power distance.

Shareholder versus Stakeholder Theory

Shareholder approaches argue that corporations have limited duties/responsibilities, i.e., obeying the law and maximizing shareholder wealth.

The stakeholder theory is grounded in many normative, theoretical perspectives including the ethics of care, the ethics of fiduciary relationships, the social contract theory, the theory of property rights, and so on. All these theories deal with practical moral concerns and define what should be the way of achieving ethical relationship among stakeholders of business. Companies need to honour the trust that society places on them. With the growth of mammoth organizations, the impact on all aspects of human interaction is unquestionable. The inclusion of all constituents like shareholders, employees, customers, suppliers, bankers, partners in supply chains, community, environment, government, and non-governmental organizations is demanded under this theory.

With the collapse of a large number of corporations, the magic of the market has been challenged and there is a strong movement towards social responsibility and sustainability in the business world. Millstein and Katsch (1981) have opined that 'this strident and partisan concept of substantially unrestrained corporate power and discretion is, in a more moderate form, among the most important fundamental public concerns within large corporations ... as issue is whether the nation ... will accept larger private corporate size, accelerate the decline of pluralism by regulating or by giving greater responsibility to government, or by requiring fundamental changes in the internal governance structure of our major corporations.'

Strengths and Weaknesses of Shareholder and Stakeholder Theories

It is believed that by focussing on maximization of shareholder interest, societal benefit would automatically be addressed. The theory offers a clear focus. The results are easily quantifiable and adhere to the basic purpose of business, i.e., maximizing profits.

The criticism of this theory is based on the fact that shareholder interest maximizes social benefit and is dependent on the practice of perfect competition. It has been observed that in the real world of business, deviations from perfect competition are more common due to various reasons like imperfect information, government intervention, imperfect markets, development of unique competitive advantages, to name a few.

The stakeholder theory is more broad-based and takes into account the needs of all the parties that are affected by business, either directly or indirectly. It is more fair and just in terms of sharing the benefits that accrue to business.

The challenge for this theory lies in its implementation because very often the tradeoff between different stakeholders is not well-defined and therefore, accountability of managers cannot be judged. Authors and practitioners have tried to find an answer to this concern through unique methods like risk identification, prioritization of needs, value maximization, etc.

Transaction Cost Theory

Stiles and Taylor (2001) explained that 'both transaction cost economics and agency theories are concerned with managerial discretion and both assume that managers are given to opportunism (self-interest seeking) and moral hazard, and that managers operate under bounded rationality.' This theory is similar to the agency theory as it also discusses how managers may be selfishly driven to undertake transactions that benefit them personally, more than the company. They may also take transaction decisions without much study, as the money invested is not their personal money, and therefore, those deals may not yield the expected profits for the shareholders.

Therefore, to avoid such losses, transaction cost economics is entirely dependent on the mechanisms of internal and external controls like audit control, separation of board chairmanship from CEO, information disclosure, and non-executive independent directors.

Strengths and Weaknesses of the Transaction Cost Theory

This theory is based on financial economics, therefore quantification is easy. However, because of the complexities within an organization, it is difficult to draw conclusions about organizational performance. Since the shareholders are residual (left-over profit after paying off all liabilities) receivers of the profit, there is always a concern among shareholders regarding the safety of their investment. It is concerned about the losses that may occur to shareholder profit due to business transactions planned by the management.

The Sociological Theory

The theory has focussed mostly on broad compositions and wealth distribution. Under this theory, the composition of the board, transparency of financial reporting, disclosure, and auditing are considered central to realizing the socio-economic objectives of corporations.

Strengths and Weaknesses of the Sociological Theory

The theory is based on the fair distribution of wealth in society.

The challenge lies in ensuring that absolute power is not concentrated in the hands of the board that is selected by shareholders to ensure profit maximization.

Due to the above-mentioned fear, government control and interference may increase, leading to constraints and red tape. Creativity and innovation would suffer and motivation levels would be extremely low.

IMPORTANCE OF CSR IN CORPORATE GOVERNANCE

The requirement from corporates has moved beyond just getting shareholder value. The stakeholder theory is now an integral part of corporate governance. Socially responsible companies are lauded for their involvement in the welfare of all the stakeholders, the community, and the environment. There is a general acceptance that the government alone cannot manage the multifarious needs of the modern globalized society. Public-private partnerships have to be the order of the day to balance the interest of stakeholders with the profit requirements of the shareholders.

Carroll (1979) has succinctly summarized the concept of responsibility as given below:

Economic responsibility—The company has to be profit-oriented and market-driven

Legal responsibility—Since society gives the sanction to the business to operate, it is the duty of business to obey the laws and regulations laid down by society

Ethical responsibility—The company has to go beyond the law and honour the trust and expectations of society. The company should also be extremely culture-sensitive to provide the right services

Discretionary (or philanthropic) responsibility—Undertake voluntary activities and expenses, keeping the greater good of society in mind

Many countries have created company laws, which incorporate CSR as a formal duty of the company. For example, The Companies Act of 2006 of the UK formally includes CSR as a responsibility to be undertaken by companies. In India, the Narayana Murthy Committee also recommends CSR as an integral part of corporate governance (see Annexure for details on various important corporate governance committees).

Corporate governance is a powerful tool, which can ensure that CSR permeates throughout the company. It should operate at the internal, intermediate, and outer circles, as explained in Chapter 1. However, we must remember that every company would have to find and frame its own framework for implementation of CSR because every company is unique, and similarly, every culture in which it is operating is distinct. Today, environmental pollution has become a major concern and many companies are including their efforts to improve the situation in sustainable reports that they are issuing along with CSR reports.

A brief list of obligations catering to important areas related to some important stakeholder is given in Table 2.2.

TABLE 2.2 List of obligations to society, investors, and employees

Obligations to Society
1. National interest should take priority
2. Political non-alignment
3. Legal compliances
4. Rule of law
5. Honest and ethical conduct
6. Corporate citizenship
7. Ethical behaviour
8. Social concerns
9. Corporate social responsibility
10. Environment-friendly
11. Healthy and safe working conditions
12. Trusteeship
13. Accountability
14. Effectiveness and efficiency
15. Timely responsiveness
16. Uphold brand of the country

Obligation to Investors
1. Towards shareholders
2. Measures promoting informed shareholder participation
3. Transparency
4. Financial reporting and records

Obligation to Employees
1. Fair employment practices
2. Equal opportunities employer
3. Encouraging whistle-blowing
4. Humane-treatment

Contd

Table 2.2 contd

5.	Participation
6.	Empowerment
7.	Equity and inclusiveness
8.	Participative and collaborative environment

Source: Adapted from *Corporate Governance, Principles, Policies, and Practices* by A.C. Fernando (2006).

LEADERSHIP CRISIS

The obligations listed in Table 2.2 can be discharged only when leaders of the corporate world believe in them and are committed to them. It is the human aspect of the company that would ensure the success or failure in every field because they are the process creators, process owners, and process deliverers. The need for moral leadership and social responsibility were rightly stressed and highlighted by business leader Kasturbhai Lalbhai (1963) when he stated, 'industry and trade have to discharge many responsibilities to the community. They should provide support—moral, personal, and financial—to institutions and causes which make their towns and villages better for living and which are intimately connected with our spiritual heritage. We should advertise what we produce and sell, but in doing so also convince the public that free enterprise exists to serve the community by improving social and economic standards. We should also provide leadership to the community. We should also impress upon the people that no business can continue for long without profits. Profits are a measure of effective, efficient operation and should be worn as a badge of accomplishment and honour.' (Taken from a speech at the Indian Merchants Chamber, Bombay, on 27 February 1963, and reprinted in Tribute to Ethics, Gujarat Chamber of Commerce, Ahmedabad, pp. 108, 109.)

Therefore, organizations need a team that can identify with their mission statement. 'If the organization is defined by management solely in economic terms of its objective function ... the management fails to realize the deeper values that the organization offers to employees in terms of security, personal growth, purpose in life, and self-realization (or whichever the deeper values might be)' (Gustavsson 1995). Unless people within the organization feel responsible for the company's activities, they will not perform to their optimum capacity. It is in the determination and subsequent implementation of how to do things right that the success of business lies. Business has to face the bitter truth that making money is the result and is, of course, essential but is certainly not its purpose. The point is that we cannot have two sets of moral standards, one for business and another for the rest of the world. We see increasing pressure from society—expressed through legislation and in the courts—to hold business accountable to the same standards of conduct imposed on individuals. Business does not operate outside society, therefore, it has a responsibility towards society. This call can be fulfilled only by the value-orientation of the people within business.

Relation between Values and Skills

This brings us to the obvious question, are the leaders in the professional sphere value-oriented? Society offers them a high pedestal as they are considered experts in their fields and have dedicated their time and energy in mastering their art. This respect demands that these professional leaders fulfill their obligations to society. With increasing specialization, the degree of interdependence has also increased and we cannot have rules for every relationship because rules are good as guidelines, but are not the end-all of every activity. Usually, organizations use mutually understood vision and values to guide decision-making and rely on collaboration and trust to get things done. This can operate only when leaders are truly committed to their work, to the extent that work becomes their motivation and not pay and perks. Often, rules and regulations lead to complacency because we believe that we have done 'our job' if we have followed the code. The code always denotes the minimum necessary. Hence, one has to move above the code in a positive direction. When we are limited by goals of good salary, status, recognition, etc., how can we be visionaries? The concept of compassion and common good should be a significant guiding factor for a professional leader while reviewing work and its results. Leaders are required to be balanced, rational, and objective with a steadfastness (not attachment because attachment leads to achieving the goal by any means, right or wrong) towards the goals, which will ensure that the means to achieve the goals are also value-oriented. The statistics given below about the controversy on CEO compensation highlights the need to curb the selfish interests of leaders and encourage shared community growth if we want holistic development.

According to *Business Week*'s Annual Executive Compensation Survey, the gap in pay between average workers and large company chief executives surpassed 300-to-1 in 2003, up from 282-to-1 in 2002 and just 42-to-1 in 1982. Between 1990 and 2003, the chief executives pay rose 313 per cent, compared with profits rising 128 per cent and average worker's pay increasing only 49 per cent (just ahead of inflation at 41 per cent). During 2003 alone, average chief executive pay was $8.1 million, up 9.1 per cent from the previous year, a year in which US employees' average pay inched up only 1.5 per cent and the economy shed 410,000 jobs (Visser 2004). This gap increased further with the increase in greed for more profit to satisfy selfish personal goals of the leaders in recent years. The recession that struck the world from 2008 highlighted this discrepancy in CEO compensation, and many cases were lodged questioning the justification of such high remuneration for the leaders in spite of corporate governance in every country recommending regulation in the remuneration of the top management. Many such statistics can be found highlighting the intra-company inequalities as well. Professionals have to unite to create a leadership cadre that can fight the catastrophe of such unethical conduct that is sustained in the name of professionalism and expertise. This can happen only when one man's gain is not another man's loss.

Leaders, therefore, have to take a proactive stand and exert authority to shape policies conducive to human good. A responsible leader is the only guarantor of the ultimate conduct of the entire socio-economic environment. Commitment from leaders should be active, obvious, and informed. Now the macho aggressive image of management is no longer relevant. Only such a leader would be able to create an organization, which will help develop unique qualities in every stakeholder, as every person knows something nobody else knows, and such an organization will certainly have a higher chance at success.

THE SOCIAL IMPACT

We all know that long-term success is an outcome of interdependence and the people we are dealing with have their unique emotions and feelings. The business fraternity needs to realize that the law and order situation is also dependent on the economics of the country, its roots are often embedded in a terrible sense of deprivation felt by the local community. Anger is usually directed towards big businesses which, it is felt, have cornered all the benefits of development without giving anything back to society. The unprecedented labour unrest in West Bengal during 1969–70, especially the Naxalite movement of 1970, as well as the recent Maoist movements in Nepal and India, are examples of such emotions. If business needs customers with buying power, then it has to ensure that the common man's condition must improve. Unless the business community contributes to the basic development needs, its very survival would be threatened and it is in its own interest to participate in the 'nation-building' effort. Another famous business tycoon of India, Shri Ramakrishna Bajaj (1970), grandson of Jamnalal Bajaj, also expressed the same view when he said, 'The business community is an essential ingredient of our democratic society and it has a duty not only to create wealth but also to promote the ethical and social goals of the community. Unless it fulfills both these functions and thereby plays its due role as a responsible section, it will not be able to ensure its own survival'. Yet, we as managers behave as if we are alone and only our needs matter. The commonly heard cliché is that we have no choice. It is this seeming lack of choice that is the real killer of humanity in organizations that are undergoing massive and speedy change. People suffer from the insecurity that they are not in control of anything and try to control whatever they can, in any way they can. Problems are assuming huge proportions and gigantic shapes. They can only be solved when looked at in the broader light of global interaction. This certainly needs an inter-cultural awareness and an attitudinal change in accepting everyone (more details on this are provided in the chapter on Models of CSR). The original intent of management scientists who developed models was to consider only objective judgements of the costs to the company, but it has become obvious in recent years that the models also have to include subjective estimates of the costs to the employees, the customer, and the general public. Estimates of the costs external to the firm and of the economic damages caused by the firm are also required to be taken into account.

Sir Julian Huxley (1957) has rightly pointed out that 'human evolution is not biological but psychological'. Therefore, the concept of survival of the fittest does not fit human civilization in literal terms because, in that case, how do we define and measure fitness, and who among us should be given the right to judge fitness. The spirit of cut-throat competition only for wealth has led us to accumulation of more and more wealth at the cost of ethics. This has wrought social havoc at every level leading to fear, purposelessness, drug addiction, anxiety, neurosis, unethical life, and untimely death. As early as 1939, Arnold J. Toynbee questioned the efficiency of scientific management when he wrote 'what was the extent of sacrifices of personal freedom that workers would be prepared to make for the sake of increasing size of the cake of which they were each demanding a larger slice? How far would the urban industrial workers go in submitting to scientific management? ... Western man had brought himself into concentration on a sensationally successful endeavour to increase his material well being. If he wants to find salvation, he would find it only in sharing the result of his material achievement with the less materially successful majority of the human race.' Toynbee called him the western man, but is it not true for all our self-seeking materially motivated professionals? 'Consensus management' with vertical, horizontal, and diagonal consensus among workers and management, is becoming common. To achieve this, an individual has to move beyond himself and create a family within the corporation. The idea of family carries with it the concept of basic human values of love, integrity, honesty, selflessness, etc. Therefore, we are again back to the principle of being ethical, which leads to good business.

Corporate social performance encompasses an organization's commitment to behave in an economically and environmentally sustainable manner, while honouring the interest of the direct stakeholders and benefitting the greater community at large. The success of this performance depends totally on what people really think about business and that entirely is based upon how people behave within a corporate. Figure 2.2, borrowed from Dr Bengst Gustavsson's (1997, p. 82) *Research Monograph*, lucidly explains the value of CSR, which is actually a transcendent (inspirational) value. When such inspirational ideology is combined with formalized structures, it can create that transcendent (awe-inspiring) organization. Such an organization can withstand any challenge, internal or external, as it would be strongly rooted in its endogenous (own, developed from within the organization) collective value system. This value system becomes the foundation of an organization and continues to guide the organization while taking strategic decisions. The value foundation helps an organization to judge between various options available, to choose the right ethical action to be taken.

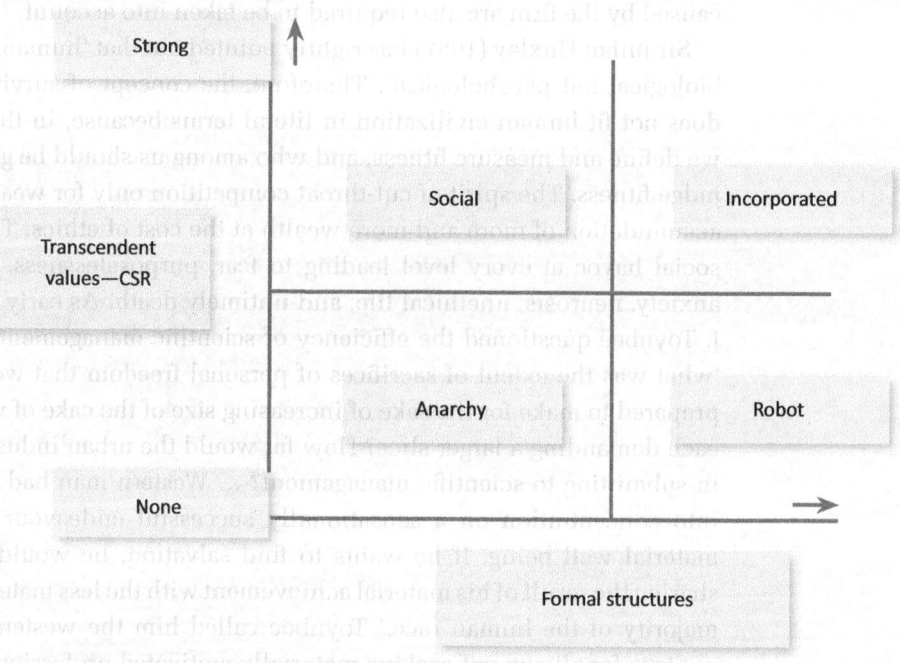

Source: Bengt Gustavsson, 1997, p. 82.

Figure 2.2 Matrix of transcendent and formal organization

A brief analysis of the various combinations in the matrix given in Fig. 2.2 will help us understand that a transcendent organization is an incorporated organization.

Anarchy This is mainly a hypothetical state because it is quite unthinkable that an organization would be devoid of any structure, subjective or objective. However, we may think of this state as a state of flux between an old value structure and a new one. This state is highly dangerous because it can lead to extinction of the organization with chaos, internal turmoil, conflicts, and lack of hope and direction for the future.

Robot This represents the mechanistic view. This view explains how an organization works like an objective machine and the subjective human factor within the organization acts in a predefined pattern. It is a highly rational way of comprehending the organization. It can also represent a state of regeneration of the organization, i.e., the man-made organizational structures are recognized as real.

Social In this state, the subjective (human entity) is the only structure that exists. It is found in highly cohesive (unified) groups and organizations, where there is a strong sense of interconnection between common values and direction. It is characterized by spontaneous, endogenous (growing from within) group action, unquestioned and harmonious. In practice, it is probably difficult to find this state other than in certain small organizations.

Incorporated This is the ideal state where endogenous values and structures are forceful and strong within the framework of dependent organizational structures. The basis for creating a truly integrated organizational structure is the value foundation of the collective consciousness of all the members of the organization.

CONCLUSION

The management heads should remember that CSR is a process, not an event. There should be a continuous effort to keep the process moving in a positive direction and generate collective support within the organization in support of CSR. For this purpose, a few simple steps are needed:

1. The organization should reflect the confidence of its management in the role play. This means the management of an organization should do what it preaches and promises or 'walk the talk'.
2. It should be consistent in upholding values over the long run.
3. The organization should show respect and courtesy to all stakeholders of the organization.
4. There should not be any contradiction between verbal and non-verbal activities of the organization.
5. There should be a positive and sincere attitude and the motivational activities should be fresh and interesting.
6. There should be a constant endeavour to find a common ground between the different stakeholders and society at large, based upon emotional understanding of the close connection between them.
7. Organizations should stay focussed in proving that good ethics means good business in the long run.

The quickest path to success is to decide on the process and put down the goals, objectives, and action plan, so that the focus is visible and transparent to all. There is then an unseen pressure to live up to the plans. It becomes a living document. There should be a study of the return on investment (ROI) on CSR, so that it proves the value of the activities and also gives a system to improve the CSR process. ROI is a performance measure used to evaluate the benefits of an investment or compare the benefits between a number of investments incurred by an organization.

$$ROI = \frac{\text{Gain from investment} - \text{Cost of investment}}{\text{Cost of investment}}$$

The best method of studying ROI would be to analyse programme measures and tactic measures. The stakeholders should be updated about ROI plans in the planning stage, in order to get their total committment on CSR.

It is true that the process of implementation may take some time and effort before it bears fruit, but in the end, it is worth it. We cannot remain complacent about CSR. We have to orient ourselves to the sustainability ideal. 'We need visionary leadership, heart-felt commitment, and enduring hard work. And each of us, in our own way, in our own place, has a contribution to make' (Visser 2004).

The Satyam Computers case, given as a case study at the end of this chapter, aptly highlights how greed and failure of leadership can lead to the downfall of renowned well-established organizations. The lack of true CSR inspiration can put so many stakeholders in jeopardy. This can be understood from this case.

SUMMARY

The corporation has evolved as an important entity touching every aspect of human existence. The early corporations developed as confraternities or guilds. Legal existence was attributed when chartered corporations came into existence. Legislation was devised to give the corporate entity a life of its own and to separate ownership from management and that is how the concept of bonds and shares came into existence. Modern companies are based on the concept of limited liabilities. Management and governance are two distinct activities of the company. The board of directors has to follow the fiduciary principle, which states that those who have been entrusted with powers for the benefit of others are under a general equitable obligation when dealing with those powers to act honestly in what they consider to be in the interests of others.

CSR is an integral part of governance and modern corporations cannot ignore it. Corporations have to balance the growth of values and skills to achieve success. CSR, which is actually an inspirational value, when combined with formalized structures can create that awe-inspiring magnificent organization that can withstand any challenge as it would be strongly rooted in its endogenous collective value system.

KEY TERMS

Charter companies Grant of authority and right by a sovereign, legislature, or other authority to conduct business.

Confraternity An association of persons united in a common goal and interest, especially Christian laymen organized for religious or charitable service often referred to as brotherhood.

Corporate personality Providing an identity, usually by making it legal.

Fiduciary duty Is a relationship based on total trust, good faith, and honesty. It can be an individual, corporation, or an association. They hold assets for another party under moral and legal obligation to act primarily for the other's benefit.

Laity Commoners not related to clergy.

License-permit Raj Refers to the controlled economy of India where licences and permits were required for any business deals. This led to unprecedented red tape and bureaucratic corruption in India.

Perpetual succession The company would continue to exist in spite of the death, bankruptcy, insanity, change in membership or an exit from the business of any owner or member, or any transfer of stock.

Proprietor Owner of a business.

Return on investment (ROI) The performance measure used to evaluate the efficiency of an investment; the benefit of an investment divided by the cost of the investment.

Solicitors Related to the legal profession.

Transaction cost Cost incurred during an economic exchange while participating in the market. It can be related to finding information, negotiating deals, etc.

Transcendent value Inspirational.

Utility maximizers Trying to gain benefits for themselves.

EXERCISES

Concept Review Questions

1. Define a corporation and its unique qualities.
2. Give a brief description of early corporations and give the steps followed to incorporate a modern corporation.
3. What do you understand by the term 'corporate governance'? Briefly describe the theories of corporate governance.
4. What is the relationship between good leadership and CSR?

Critical Thinking Questions

1. According to you, which theory of corporate governance best suits the modern corporations and why?
2. What is the role of CSR in corporate governance? Explain with examples.
3. How can a leader help to improve the social impact of an organization?

Research Question

Select a company of your choice and read their annual reports and analyse the relationship between corporate governance and corporate social responsibility.

REFERENCES

Bajaj, Ramakrishna (1970), *Social Role of Business*, Maharashtra Chamber of Commerce, Bombay, p. 52.

Berle, Adolf A. and Gardiner C. Means (1932), *The Modern Corporation and Private Property*, Macmillan, New York.

Black, Christopher and Pamela Gravestock (2006), *Confraternities in Europe and the Americas, International and Interdisciplinary Perspectives*, Ashgate Publishing Ltd, Surrey, U.K.

Carroll, Archie B. (1979), 'Three–Dimensional Conceptual Model of Corporate Performance', *Academy of Management Review*, vol. 4, issue no. 4, pp. 497–505.

Donaldson, L. and J.H. Davis (1991), 'Stewardship Theory or Agency Theory—CEO Governance and Shareholder Returns', *Australian Journal of Management*, vol. 16, issue no. 1, 1991.

Gustavsson, Bengt (1995), 'Consciousness and Experience—Implications for Organizations and Management', in S.K. Chakraborty (ed.), *Human Values for Managers*, Wheeler Publishing Company, New Delhi, p. 217.

────── (1997), *Transition or Transcendence? A Study of Indian Managerial Values*, Research Monograph, Sir Ratan Tata Visiting Fellow, Management Centre For Human Values, Indian Institute of Management Calcutta, March.

Hayami, Y. (1997), *Development Economics—From the Wealth to Poverty of Nations*, Clarendon Press, Oxford.

Huxley, Julian (1957), *Transhumanism in New Bottles for New Wine*, pp. 13–17, Chatto and Windus, London.

Ira M. Millstein and Salem M. Katsch, in Tricker Bob (2009), *Corporate Governance, Principles Policies and Practices*, Oxford University Press, New Delhi, p. 230.

Jenson, M. (2001), 'Value Maximization, Stakeholder Theory, and the Corporate Objective Function', *Journal of Applied Corporate Finance*, vol. 14, issue no. 3, p. 8–21.

North, D.C. (1990), *Institutions, Institutional Change and Economic Performance*, Cambridge University Press, Cambridge, pp. 3–4.

Smith, Adam (1776), *An Inquiry into the Nature and Causes of The Wealth of Nations*, in George J. Stigler (ed.), Strand, MDCCLXXVI (1776), University of Chicago Press, Chicago, 1977.

Stiles, P. and B. Taylor (2001), *Boards at Work—How Directors View their Roles and Responsibilities*, Oxford University Press, Oxford.

Toynbee, Arnold (1939) in *The Study of History* p. 233, (Abridgement Of Volumes I–VI Paperback), Oxford University Press, US (1987).

Vargas Sanchez, A. (2001), La Teoría de la Agencia versus la Teoría del Servidor—una aplicación a las sociedades cooperativas agrarias de la provincia de Huelva. In—*Best*

Papers Proceedings. X International Conference of AEDEM, Reggio Calabria, Italy, pp. 1067–1076.

——— (2003), La Teoría de la Agencia versus la Teoría del Servidor—una aplicación a las sociedades cooperativas agrarias del País de Gales (Reino Unido), *Proceedings of XIII Jornadas Hispano–Lusas de Gestión Científica,* Lugo, Spain, vol. I, pp. 1–10.

Visser, Wayne (2004), *Analysis—Five corporate sustainability challenges that remain unmet, EC Newsdesk,* 23 July.

Web Resource

http://www.uhu.es/alfonso_vargas/archivos/EURAM%202004.pdf, accessed on 10 July 2010.

CASE STUDY

THE SATYAM ODYSSEY

Introduction

Byrraju Ramalinga Raju—founder of the former Indian IT giant Satyam Computer Services now known as Mahindra Satyam—was one of the new millionaires of India. He hailed from a farming background and belonged to a middle-class family. He pursued his MBA degree in the US and received the recognition of 1999 Ernst & Young Entrepreneur. Raju founded Satyam in 1987 after venturing earlier into other businesses such as construction and textiles. He started the IT company with 20 employees that obtained contracts for IT projects, mostly from US companies. Satyam rapidly developed and became a multinational company, with thousands of employees spread over many countries. Raju, along with the then Chief Minister of Andhra Pradesh, Chandrababu Naidu, was able to obtain high-scale government contracts worth of USD $1.2 billion in information technology for Andhra Pradesh and Indian government.[1]

The astounding confession of Raju that for the quarter ending September 2008, though the company reported a revenue of Rs 2,700 crore and an operating margin of Rs 649 crore (24 per cent of revenue), the actual revenue was Rs 2,112 crore and actual operating profit was Rs 61 crore (3 per cent of revenues) hit investors and employees badly and tarnished the Indian corporate sector, especially the IT sector. Raju wrote in his letter to the board (7 January 2009) 'gap in the balance sheet has arisen purely on account of inflated profits over several years. What started as a marginal gap between actual operating profit and the one reflected in the books of accounts continued to grow over the years. It has attained unmanageable proportions as the size of the company operations grew significantly.'

The news caused Satyam's stock to crash by 66.5 per cent to Rs 58 from a high of Rs 188.70. The BSE Sensex crashed 470.23 points or 4.55 per cent to 9,865.70, after rising to a high of 10,469.72. Investors aggressively cut their positions. The BSE IT Index plunged 7.70 per cent and BSE Realty tumbled 11.20 per cent. IT and other stocks in related sectors took a beating as the Satyam fraud raised questions over corporate governance of other companies also, especially in the IT sector.

There was the possibility of other Satyams being out there, waiting to be discovered. The general feeling among people was that serious investigation needs to be carried out into the country's business ethics and corporate governance.

Why was Satyam tempted to break the Law?
In the case of a software exporting company like Satyam, inflating sales is far easier for three reasons[2]:
1. Fictitious revenue for selling software solutions originated either from group companies incorporated in foreign countries or from a friendly customer.
2. Since software solutions are sold or supplied online, as opposed to physical movement of goods out of a factory gate after paying excise duty, there is no record keeping by any outside agency.
3. As revenue from software exports are tax-free, there is no government authority to monitor it. Generating orders from a company abroad is easy as IT companies have clients all over the world (Satyam has clients in 66 countries).

The liberalization period was heralded post 1990, with the opening of the Indian economy. This, along with the increasing competition, forced some corporations to seek unethical ways of conducting their business to stay ahead in the game of profit-making. What probably started off as an attempt to cover-up the bad performance in one quarter, as Raju admitted in his letter written to the board (and also sent to the Securities Exchange Board of India), became unmanageable as the company expanded. Raju may have believed that the minor adjustment was in the general interest of everybody concerned, as it would retain investors' confidence in the company.

Overconfidence in his ability to turn things around before they got out of hand could have been another compelling reason. Experts refuse to believe that the operating profit of Satyam could be as low as 3 per cent. This leads to speculation that some of the money could have been siphoned off and Raju believed that he would be able to eliminate the gap. However, as he said, 'What started as a marginal gap between actual operating profit and the one reflected in the books of accounts continued to grow over the years. It has attained unmanageable proportions as the size of company operations grew significantly. As the promoters held a small percentage of equity, the concern was that poor performance would result in a takeover, thereby exposing the gap. The aborted Maytas acquisition deal was the last attempt to fill the fictitious assets with real ones. It was like riding a tiger, not knowing how to get off without being eaten'. As per the deal, Maytas Properties (unlisted) is being valued at Rs 91.47 lakh per acre (Rs 6,220 crore; land bank of 6,800 acres), despite the fact that the bulk of the land is in tier II and III cities such as Vizag, Vijaywada, Kakinada, and Nagpur. Analysts say that, on a realistic basis, the per acre price should average at Rs 40–45 lakh per acre or even less, given the current scenario.

On the other hand, Maytas Infra has been valued at nearly 1.6 times FY08 revenues even as mid-cap construction stocks on an average are trading at less than half their FY08 revenues.[3]

Looking beyond Numbers

Rs in crore	Satyam Com		Maytas Infra	
	FY09E	FY10E	FY09E	FY10E
Net sales	11,403	12,633	2,154	3,238
EBITDA	2,600	2,705	268	450
EBITDA (%)	22.8	21.4	12.4	13.9
Net profit	2,267	2,363	112.6	149.5
EPS (Rs)	33.4	34.6	19.1	25.4
P/E (x)	4.9	4.7	13.0	9.8

Source: Bloomberg.

This is an example of what is known as 'controlled fraud'. The fraud is meticulously executed by the management of an organization. They manage to dupe all stakeholders and regulators to earn huge profits, which they pocket. 'William K. Black, who as regulator, fought off savings and loan scandal, which too was built on the real estate bubble, was one of the first to explain control frauds. Explaining the mechanism on which these frauds are built, Black says control frauds routinely enlist top lawyers and academics to aid their frauds. Shopping for appraisers is even easier than shopping for auditors and attorneys. The grossly-inflated valuations made by appraisers allow outside auditors to rely on them, which in turn provide the cover of apparent neutrality to the control fraud to carry out his loot. So, in essence, regulators instead of defending the interests of investors end up advocating interest of the client. One should remember that no frauds, in India or abroad, perpetrated by company managements have ever been uncovered by external auditors. When the fraud unfolds auditors often seek reduced liability.'[4]

Inaction of the Board

In his now famous (or rather infamous) letter, Raju absolved all the members of the board and senior executives of the fraud. However, the pertinent question is how the board could not be aware of the activities of the company. What happened to the fiduciary duties of the board? The board consisted of luminaries like Vinod K. Dham of Pentium fame; T.R. Prasad, former cabinet secretary; Prof. M. Rammohan Rao, Dean of ISB Hyderabad; Dr Mangalam Srinivasan, and V.S. Raju, who were all independent directors, while Prof. Krishna G. Palepu, Professor of Harvard Business School was the non-executive director.

It is obvious that while the promoters of Satyam were manipulating the account books, the board was happy pocketing its money. According to many newspaper editorials, the board members should return Rs 14 crore, which also include payments made to auditors, in the last two years. This shows the scale of mismanagement that was on at the cost of all other stakeholders. In fact the Dean of ISB, M. Rammohan Rao, chaired the board meeting that approved the controversial buying of Maytas (Satyam spelled in reverse), Infra and Satyam Properties, both belonging to Raju's family. T.V. Mohandas Pai, director and head, education and research and human resource development at Infosys commented, 'You need to get incredible independent directors who have the mindset to ask questions and get into details. Independent directors need to do more work and auditors need to be more vigilant.'[5]

Another opinion as expressed by Vimal Bhandari, country head, Aegon NV, a Dutch financial firm, is if management wants to do something, they can do it and so that everything is in order (because) 'The role of directors is not to look at minute details when the accounts are placed. They would rely more on the auditor's report and go by the confidence in the management.' Otherwise, the directors are unlikely to continue on board.

A quick analysis of the above two opinions raises the question: Is corporate India still unclear about the role of independent directors? All codes of corporate governance emphasize that independent directors would ensure objectivity and take care of the interest of shareholders and other stakeholders. Yet, the reality seems to be far from the truth. Does this lead to the more provocative question of personal subjective ethicality of members of the board? At least, if the board could not be a detective, they could have been the judge by asking probing questions to keep the management on its toes. For example, as Sanjay Sinha, CEO, DBS Cholamandalam Mutual Fund says, '... in this particular case, they could have asked why such a big sum (Satyam had close to Rs 1000 crore in current accounts of banks as on 30 March 2008) was placed in non-interest yielding current accounts in banks year after year.'

Accountability, integrity, transparency, and disclosures—the pillars of corporate governance—were dismantled (broken) and hence, the edifice (building or superstructure) came crumbling down.

The Role of the Auditors

Considering the role of the audit firm, PriceWaterhouse Coopers (PWC), in the fraud, there are a number of discrepancies. PWC response has been the usual 'client confidentiality': 'Over the last two days, there have been media reports with regard to alleged irregularities in the accounts of Satyam ... PWC are the statutory auditors of Satyam. The audits were conducted by PWC in accordance with applicable auditing standards and were supported by appropriate audit evidence. Given our obligations for client confidentiality, it is not possible for us to comment upon the alleged irregularities. PWC will fully meet its obligations to cooperate with the regulators and others.'[6]

In fact, the issue cannot be condoned either as a case of gross negligence or on terms of first-hand involvement. The basic question remains as Sastry, economist, financial analyst, and country head of Firstcall points out, '... At the time of preparation of the balance sheet, auditors cross-verify the bank statements and tally the same with cash and bank balance numbers. Even if we presume that inflating cash and bank balance is possible, it cannot be to this volume.' What is baffling is why the enormous cash reserves were not earning interest. In fact, Kotak Securities pointed out in a report, 'We had previously raised issues about use and deployment of cash, especially the increasing amount of cash balance in current accounts and believe that the market may no longer be charitable to the company on such issues.' Therefore, the great conspiracy and nexus between auditors, management, and bankers cannot be ignored.

The auditors come under the purview of the Institute of Chartered Accountants of India (ICAI) and punishment that an auditor is liable to in such cases of fraud is a nominal penal fine, i.e., striking off the names from the membership list and cancelling the certificate of practice. If the firm's certificate is cancelled, then the auditors can re-group and form another firm as in the case of Arthur Anderson, the auditors in the Enron debacle. Therefore, the ethical question again remains, 'Is it subjective individual ethics that needs to be developed?'

The audit firm can be sued only under tort, if enough evidence can be given that the creditors or shareholders relied upon the auditors and suffered losses. It also has to be proven that the auditors owe a duty of care to shareholders and stakeholders. If this kind of case actually gets filed then '... this would be the first ever case in India that would challenge the extent to which an auditor is liable due to incorrect documentation revealed in the books of a troubled company,' says Sujjain Talwar, a partner with a law firm, Economic Law Practice.

Ved Jain, President of ICAI, made a public statement that if found guilty, the chartered accountants involved in the Satyam case would be banned for life and that PWC would be issued a showcause notice as per the Chartered Accountants Act of 1949. PWC is already under the scanner because the Reserve Bank of India had barred it from auditing any Indian bank after the great fiasco of the Global Trust Bank (GTB). The RBI's inspection report for GTB for the year 2002–03 showed a scam of around Rs 742 crore (Rs 7.42 billion), which was not disclosed by GTB. Oriental Bank of Commerce, which merged with GTB, inherited gross non-performing assets of about Rs 1200 crore (Rs 12 billion) and impaired assets of Rs 300 crore (Rs 3 billion). This implied that GTB's share capital and reserves were wiped out by a good margin and the listed shares of the bank were worthless.[7]

Since Satyam had raised money from American investors by American depository receipts listed on the NYSE, two class action suits have been filed against Satyam. These are claims made against fraudulent mis-statement and common law fiduciary duty claim. This claim has been given more teeth by the Sarbanse Oxley Act (see Annexure), which was passed after the Enron scam in the US. Therefore, PWC may have some major answering to do in the US in the near future.

Awards
Satyam Computers and Raju were showered with awards and anointed as best employer by various national and international institutions. Some of them have been revoked since the discovery of the fraud.

- Ernst & Young Entrepreneur of the Year Services Award 1999
- Dataquest IT Man of the Year Award 2000
- Asia Business Leader Award 2002
- Ernst & Young Entrepreneur of the Year 2007 (revoked)
- Golden Peacock Award for Corporate Governance 2008 (revoked)
- CNBC TV 18 rated it as No. 7 in the Best Employers list.
- *Business Today* ranked it the third best company to work for
- *Business World* gave it the top award for corporate social responsibility: 'Corporate Citizen No. 1'
- An international award for best financial disclosure procedures. At that time, Satyam CFO Vadlamani had commented 'These awards recognize (our) commitment to keeping the market and our investors informed, and having our financial information clearly and easily understood by the stakeholders.'

Now, rating agencies are under suspicion and the public is wondering whether the awards signify the real worth of an organization.

The Aftermath

All the independent and non-executive directors resigned and left the sinking ship to sail to its disastrous destiny, displaying their level of committment to the organization. Raju quit as chairman on 7 January 2009 after confessing he cooked up the company's account books and inflated profits over the past several years.

On 10 January 2009, the Company Law Board decided to bar the current board of Satyam from functioning and appointed ten nominal directors. 'The current board has failed to do what they are supposed to do. The credibility of the IT industry should not be allowed to suffer,' said Corporate Affairs Minister, Prem Chand Gupta, in a public declaration. C.P. Gurnani is the new chairman of Satyam, replacing the earlier chairman, A.S. Murty.

It was also reported that PWC will be scrutinized for complicity in this scandal. SEBI, the stock market regulator, also said that, if found guilty, its license to work in India may be revoked.[8]

The New York Stock Exchange halted trading in Satyam stock as of 7 January 2009 (http://sify.com/finance/nyse-halts-trading-in-satyam-stock-news-national-jegu0achifi.html). India's National Stock Exchange announced that it will remove Satyam from its S&P CNX Nifty 50-share index on 12 January. The founder of Satyam was arrested two days after he admitted to falsifying the firm's accounts. Raju is charged with several offences, including criminal conspiracy, breach of trust, and forgery.[9]

The Government of India has stated that it may provide temporary direct or indirect liquidity support to the company. It was reported in IANS, New Delhi, 29 May that the Satyam fraud case is top priority of the government, and the investigating agency, the Serious Fraud Investigation Office (SFIO), has been asked to put the prosecution on fast track. Minister of State for Corporate Affairs (independent charge) Salman Khurshid said after taking charge, 'The case is required to be put on the fast track so that the guilty can be punished quickly. SFIO has completed the investigation in the case and the ministry has asked it to chalk out a strategy for prosecution in coordination with the CBI (Central Bureau of Investigation),' he added. SFIO has already submitted a 14,000-page report on the Satyam case to the Ministry of Corporate Affairs.

According to Khurshid, the next priority of the ministry would be to re-introduce the Companies Bill, 2008, which was introduced in the last Lok Sabha and has since lapsed. 'The government's focus will be on the protection of interest of average investors, particularly small investors, and ensure that nothing goes wrong, in addition to bringing in more transparency for boosting public confidence.' A number of issues related to the corporate governance framework, including the role of directors and the role of auditors, also need to be examined carefully, Khurshid added.[10]

On 22 January 2009, the CID said in court that the actual number of employees is only 40,000 and not 53,000 as reported earlier and that Raju had allegedly been withdrawing Rs 20 crore every month for paying these 13,000 non-existent employees. (Sourced from *The Times of India*, (TNN, 22 January 2009.) Satyam Fudged FDs, Has 40,000 Employees: Public Prosecutor.

Should Satyam be saved at all costs?[11] Yes, because

- Satyam is a flagship company of the Indian IT sector. Its downfall will leave an indelible impact on the reputation of the entire industry.
- With the outsourcing industry constantly increasing in size, it is becoming strategic in nature; therefore, clients would look for long-term sustenance of firms who are their vendors. Keeping the larger good in mind, the government needs to rally around and pull the company out of its present state. Only this will re-establish the confidence of clients and investors in the IT industry.
- Should the shareholders and employees be punished for no fault of theirs? Jobs of nearly 40,000 employees are at stake. If you add to this the number of people who have bought Satyam shares, you end up with a significantly huge number of people whose lives could be badly affected by the fall of this giant.

No, because

- There should be zero tolerance for such controlled fraud. Satyam must pay for its actions. The government must not set a precedent by bailing it out. They will have to do the same in all cases where a company finds itself in a similar situation.
- This is a clear case of market justice meting itself out. If rules have been tampered with, then the consequences cannot be condoned. Satyam should be an example to all other players in the arena not to indulge in nefarious tactics.
- Satyam does not represent the entire Indian IT industry. Nandan Nilekani, former co-chairman (at the time of the Satyam debacle he was acting co chairman) of Infosys Technologies concurs with this view when he says, 'Every industry and country has its rogues and bad apples. When you have a $50 billion Bernie Madoff scandal on Wall Street, you don't say that all asset managers are tainted. I don't think that this (Satyam) will have any impact

on the IT industry.' Satyam's fall will not be the death knell of the sector. This needs to be made clear to clients and investors.
- If a tainted organization like Satyam is allowed to continue, the IT sector stands to lose a lot more than it hopes to gain.
- Any possibility of a loss of projects on account of the fall of Satyam is unfounded. Any large customer normally deals with multiple vendors. Therefore, the option to shift to other players in the market is a strong possibility. According to some estimates, around $300 million worth of contracts were due for renewal at Satyam since January 2009. Therefore, there is always an opportunity for redistribution of these projects among companies with a good track record.
- The same applies to the employees of Satyam. Trained professionals like them are bound to be lapped up by other companies to handle the redistributed projects.

The above question with its pros and cons has been a discussion point in the international business community. The question that readers of this case need to analyse is, 'Did Satyam fulfil its corporate social responsibility?' More important than that, we must realize that CSR is not philanthropy or charity, it is about incorporating ethics in the entire operation of a company. Historically, many companies and industries have faced major challenges of this kind. Companies that aspire to be the best should learn from these events and put processes based on ethics in place, which allow them to survive and make them stronger. Trust is at the crux of any free market economy because it is built on relationships that are based on trust, and incidents like this erode the very basis of such an economy.

Conclusion

Today, Satyam has been taken over by Tech Mahindra, a surprise for many market watchers. The takeover bid came only a month after Satyam announced it was up for sale. Tech Mahindra bid Rs 58 per share, above what Larsen & Toubro and billionaire tycoon Wilbur Ross offered. It now owns 31 per cent of the IT mammoth at a cost of Rs 1757 crore, or slightly more than US$350 million.[12]

'It looks like Mahindra got a bargain, considering the firm is worth a reported $2.1 billion. Who knows what the real value is, but it's surely more than Rs 1757 crore for almost a third of the firm,' commented Francesco Gopalakrishnan, *EconomyWatch* correspondent. Tech Mahindra plans to extend its ownership up to 51 per cent by purchasing an additional 20 per cent at the same value. This brings Satyam's valuation in Mahindra's eyes to $1.1 billion. Tech Mahindra bid 20 per cent more than the next highest bidder and more than double the lowest bidder.

Satyam has offices in a dozen countries and employs 40,000 people. It has more than 650 clients around the world, and 185 of them are Fortune 500 corporations. Tech Mahindra is an Indian conglomerate famous for its SUVs, tractors, and financial services. This foray into IT and outsourcing demonstrates the firm's eagerness to diversify and expand. Tech Mahindra Chairman, Anand Mahindra, explained the synergy as 'both companies can benefit from each other'.[13]

Extra Information
Financial Times—Buck Stops at Raju,
Subhomoy Bhattacharjee,
posted online: 7 January 2010. Given below are extracts.
- A total loss is estimated at Rs 14,162 crore and the CBI has charged the Raju brothers in this fraud.
- However, this 80-page chargesheet does not implicate any other entity other than those run and owned by the Raju family in India's biggest corporate fraud. The CBI report emphasises that the fraud began more than a decade ago in 1999.
- The main culprit of the chargesheet is Raju and his team members who created seven fake customers to create an inflated sale of Rs 430 crore in April 2006. To cover the fictitious sale, they spent another Rs 68 crore of company money on salary of the employees who were made to work on the non-existent project. They inflated the accounts and flouted audit rules and coerced internal audit employees to stay silent on the deals. The report gives a detailed breakdown of the way in which the then finance heads established the possible complicity of the two external auditors from PriceWaterhouse in the episode.
- In an unrelated transaction, Ramalinga Raju and the other accused borrowed Rs 160 crore from front companies in 2007 to buy the shares of Nipuna, a BPO company floated by the Raju family. The transaction cost Satyam Rs 229 crore.
- It is further alleged that from the proceeds of the insider trading in the shares of the company, the Raju family built up real estate of Rs 350 crore between 1999 and 2006.
- However, there are certain pertinent exclusions in the report. While the chargesheet gives details of the massive Rs 1,951 crore loans the accused raised from several financial companies, the final summary does not mention the sum or the need to follow the money trail. The money was offered against Satyam shares pledged through a shell company. The chargesheet makes it clear that the seven non-banking financial companies sanctioned loans worth more than Rs 100 crore each to front companies like Samudra Greenfields, Vamadeva Greenlands and Vyaya Agro on the surety of the pledged shares of Satyam when the IT company was building up huge cash balances.
- The chargesheet has also used Raju's statement to trace another set of loans of Rs 1221 crore raised from HDFC Bank, HSBC, Citibank, Citicorp Finance, BNP Paribas, and ICICI Bank between 2000 and 2008. The document notes the banks were paid a consolidated interest of only Rs 43 crore in the eight years. All these loans were raised on fictitious authorisations created by the accused on behalf of the Satyam board. Surprisingly, the report does not investigate if any or all of these banks had inquired why a supposedly cash-rich company needed to raise such large loans. In fact, this huge borrowing is not given due importance by the report and is mentioned only in the 'sidelines'.

Time Line[14]
- December 16—1. Satyam Computer Services Ltd. announces that it will buy two construction and property firms—the listed Maytas Infra and the unlisted Satyam Properties for $1.6 billion. These firms were promoted by the Rajus, the founder of Satyam.
- 2. Satyam ADRs (American Depopsitory Receipts) plunges 55% as investors react negatively to the news.
- December 17—1. In the early hours of the morning (India time) Satyam says it will not go through with the deal, which would have involved borrowing $400 million to add to Satyam's cash balance of $1.2 billion
- 2. Share prices fall, nevertheless, on the Indian bourses. Satyam Chairman B. Ramalinga Raju says the negative investor reaction had prompted the change in thinking. But Satyam shares are down 30% plus on doubts over corporate governance issues.
- December 18—Satyam calls a board meeting on December 29 to consider a share buyback to try and restore confidence.
- December 23—World Bank reveals that it has barred Satyam from doing business with it for eight years for providing improper benefits to its staff. Shares fall further.
- December 25—Satyam demands that the World Bank withdraw its 'inappropriate' statement. The Bank refuses. Satyam shares mark time as the company is seen as an attractive takeover target.
- December 26—Mangalam Srinivasan, an independent director on the board of the company since 1991, resigns. Srinivasan, an US based academic, says she resigned owning 'moral responsibility for not opposing in writing the management's decision to buy out the two Maytas firms.'
- December 28—Satyam defers December 29 board meeting.
- December 29—Three more directors—Krishna G. Palepu, a professor at Harvard Business School, Vinod Dham, the father of the Pentium chip, and Medhu Rammohan Rao, the dean of the Hyderabad-based Indian School of Business—resign. Strength of the board reduced from nine to five.
- December 30—Satyam shares on a rollercoaster as hope battles dismay and there is speculation of a takeover or a shotgun marriage.
- January 2—Satyam says the Raju stake is down by a third to 5.13%. The company is obviously more vulnerable.
- January 5—Satyam shares down 9%; corporate governance issue to the fore.
- January 6—Shares rise more than 7% as predators are reported to be circling. The company announces that Raju's holding has fallen further to 3.6% as institutional holders sell shares pledged with them.
- January 7—Raju admits falsifying accounts and that there is a hole of Rs 5000 crore in the company's accounts. Resigns. Satyam shares plummet some 80%; Sensex drops 750 points.

- January 9—The government dissolves the Satyam board and cancels the meeting scheduled for Jan 10. The government says it will appoint a new board.
- January 24—PriceWaterhouse auditors arrested for their involvement in the scandal.
- January 27—Board of Satyam announces it will sell the company. They hire Avendus and Goldman Sachs.
- April 5—Three Satyam finance employees arrested.
- April 7—Police file charges against Raju.
- April 9—Board of Satyam announces bidding for the firm is open.
- April 13—Bid by Tech Mahindra wins, at Rs 58 per share. This values Satyam Computers at $1.1 billion.

Discussion Questions
1. What were the failures of the corporate governance structure in Satyam?
2. Explain the importance of CSR in corporate governance with reference to the Satyam case.
3. What role can informed stakeholders play in a company? According to you, which stakeholder(s) played a major role in the Satyam case?
4. Give suggestions on the role that the management of Tech Mahindra needs to adopt to overcome the crisis.

End Notes
1. http://www.moneycontrol.com/company-facts/mahindrasatyam/history/SCS.
2. Adapted from *Deccan Herald*.
3. http://www.rediff.com/money/2008/dec/22maytas-deal-impact-on-the-companies. htm, accessed on 10 July 2010.
4. *Financial Times*, Subhomoy Bhattacharjee, accessed on Monday 19 January 2009.
5. This and other facts and quotes in this case study are from *Business India*, 25 January 2009.
6. 9 January 2009 in *India Knowledge@Wharton*. http://knowledge.wharton.upenn. edu/india/article.cfm?articleid=4344.
7. http://www.rediff.com/money/2004/aug/30gtb.htm, accessed on 6 July 2010.
8. http://www.livemint.com/2009/01/07165018/ICAI.
9. http://en.wikipedia.org/wiki/Satyam_scandal#cite_note-15, Annexure.
10. http://www.thaindian.com/newsportal/business/government-to-put-satyam-case-on-fast-track_100198455.html#ixzz0cWFRIFRU.
11. Adapted from http://www.indiabroad band.net/news-views-business-world/14171-satyam-case-why-now-what.html.
12. Satyam's website on 14 April 2009 announcing Tech *Mahindra*'s highest bid.
13. http://www.economywatch.com/economy-business-and-finance-news/India_News_ Tech_Mahindra_Wins_Bid_to_Take_Over_Satyam_Computers.html.
14. Adapted from *Business India*, 25 January 2009 and http://www.economywatch.com/ economy-business-and-finance-news/India_News_Tech_Mahindra_Wins_Bid_to_ Take_Over_Satyam_Computers.html.

ANNEXURE

AN OVERVIEW OF IMPORTANT CORPORATE GOVERNANCE COMMITTEES*

Cadbury Committee, 1992

The Cadbury Committee investigated the accountability of the Board of Directors to the shareholder and to society. It has 19 recommendations in the nature of guidelines for the board of directors, executive directors, non-executive directors, and such other officials.

Important recommendations include enhanced information to the shareholder and the setting up of the audit committee with independent members. Its model is one of self-regulation. The most controversial and revolutionary requirement was the 'Code of Best Practice' proposed by the committee. It required that:

The directors should report on the effectiveness of a company's system of internal control. The services of the directors should not extend beyond three years without the approval of the shareholders.

Every listed company should create an audit committee with a minimum of three non-executive directors.

It was the extension of control beyond the financial matters that caused the controversy.

The Paul Ruthman Committee

The committee mitigated the controversial element of reporting beyond the financial matters by limiting the reporting to internal financial control. However, it continued the thread of the progressive element by extending the directors' responsibilities to 'all relevant control objectives including business risk assessment and minimizing the risk of fraud ...'

The Greenbury Committee, 1995

The committee was set up to provide an answer to the general concern about accountability and the directors' remuneration.

The committee believed in strengthening accountability by proper allocation of responsibilities for determining directors' remuneration, accurate reporting to shareholders, and greater transparency in the process. The committee did not endorse statutory control for achieving the best practice.

The Code of Best Practice devised by the committee was divided into four sections: Remuneration Committee; Disclosures; Remuneration Policy; Service contracts; Compensation.

---

* Adapted from Singh S., Corporate Governance, Global Cocepts and Practices, 2005: Fernando A.C. Corporate Governance Principles, Policies and Practices, 2006, and http://www.accaglobal.com/students/student_accountant/archive/2002/30/665132, accessed on 24 May 2010; http://en.wikipedia.org/wiki/Sarbanes%E2%80%93Oxley_Act), accessed on 24 May 2010.

All public limited companies were expected to produce annual compliance statements and encourage maximum implementation of the Code of Best Practice.

The Hampel Committee, 1995

The committee further developed the Cadbury Committee Report.

It recommended that:

The auditors should report on internal control privately to the directors.
The directors should maintain and review all reports, not just financial controls.
Companies that do not already have an internal audit function should, from time to time, review their need for one.
The committee introduced a combined code that consolidated earlier reports, specifically Cadbury and Greenbury reports.

The Combined Code, 1998

The Combined code was basically derived from the Hampel Report, the Cadbury report, and the Greenbury report. The recommendations aimed at:

Maintaining a sound system of internal control to safeguard shareholders' investment and company's assets.
To review at least annually the internal controls covering financial, operational, and compliance and risk management and report to shareholders that they have done so.
Importance of risk management was highlighted as an important ingredient in the success of the corporate.
It was mandatory for all listed companies to adhere to the combined code.

Turnbull Committee, 1999

The committee was set up by Institute of Chartered Accountants in England and Wales to assist in implementing the requirements of the Combined Code relating to internal controls.

It recommended that internal audit should be carried out annually, specially in companies that did not have an internal audit function.

To manage risks the board of directors were advised to confirm the existence of procedures of evaluating and managing key risks.

Sarbanes Oxley Act, 2002

The Sarbanes Oxley Act or SOX Act, 2002 is one of the most comprehensive Acts to control fraud and achieve quality governance. For the first time an Act tried to monitor minute details of organizational governance. It was aimed at protecting the investors and other stakeholders from corporate failures. Therefore, it provided detailed recommendations on various aspects:

1. Establishment of Public Company Accounting Board (PCAOB)
2. Audit Committee
3. Conflict of Interest

4. Audit Partner Rotation
5. Improper influence on conduct of audits
6. Prohibition of non-audit services
7. CEOs and CFOs required to affirm financials
8. Loans to Directors
9. Attorneys
10. Securities Analysts
11. Penalties: Studies should be conducted by the Securities and Exchange Commission (SEC) or the Government Accounting Office in:
    (a) Auditor's rotation
    (b) Off-balance sheet transactions
    (c) Consolidation of accounting firms and its impact on the accounting industry
    (d) Role of credit-rating agencies
    (e) Study of violators and violation during the years 1998–2001
    (f) SEC enforcement actions over the past five years
    (g) Role of investment banks and financial advisers
    (h) 'Principle-based' accounting

Indian Committees

The Companies Act of 1956 was rooted in an environment of License and Permit Raj. The deficiencies were:
1. Though non-executive directors can play a significant role in providing independent and objective opinion, the Act does not assign any formal role between executive and non-executive directors. The effective control was in the hands of the executives, whole time directors, and the MD.
2. Non-executive directors have only ornamental value as no commitment from them is expected, since the Act allows them to be members of as many as 20 companies at the same time. Financial reporting was not transparent.
3. No formal qualification for a director of a company was laid down.
4. Formal provision of auditors to be appointed by shareholders was available, but auditors worked in collusion with the management.
5. Hardly any service was provided to investors.

CII'S Recommendation, 1998

This body recommended
1. A single board can maximize long-term shareholder value. It should meet at least six times a year, preferably at an interval of two months.
2. A listed company with a turnover of Rs 100 crores and above should have professionally competent and recognized independent non-executive directors who should constitute: at least 30 per cent of the board if the chairman of the company is a non-executive director, or at least 50 per cent of the board if the chairman and MD is the same person.
3. A person should not hold directorship in more than ten listed companies, which excluded directorship in subsidiary companies where over 50 per cent

stake was held by the group company, and directorship in associate companies where more than 25 per cent but less than 50 per cent equity stake was held by the group company.

4. Non-executive directors should:
   (a) Become active participants in boards, not just passive advisors.
   (b) Have clearly defined responsibilities within the board, such as the audit committee.
   (c) Know how to read a balance sheet, profit and loss account, cash flow statements, and financial ratios and have some knowledge of various company laws. This excludes those invited as experts in other fields such as science and technology.

5. To secure better efforts from non-executive directors companies should:
   (a) Pay a commission over and above the sitting fees for the user of the professional inputs. Commissions are rewards on current profits.
   (b) Consider offering stock options, so as to relate rewards to performance. Stock options are rewards contingent upon future appreciation of the corporate value.

6. While reappointing members of the board companies should give the attendance record of the concerned directors. If the director has not been present, i.e., absent with or without leave, for 50 per cent or more meetings, then this should be explicitly stated in the resolution that is put to vote. One should not reappoint such directors.

7. Key information that need to be placed before the board must contain:
   (a) Annual operating plans and budgets as well as updated long-term plans, capital budgets, manpower, and overhead budgets.
   (b) Internal audit reports including cases of thefts and dishonesty of material nature show-cause, demand, and prosecution notices from revenue officers.
   (c) Fatal and serious accidents, dangerous occurrences, any effluent and pollution problems.
   (d) Default in payment of interest or non-payment of the principal on any public deposit and/or any secured creditor or financial institution.
   (e) Default such as non-payment of intercorporate deposits by or to the company or materially substantial non-payments for goods sold by the company.
   (f) Any issue that relates to public or product liability claim of a substantial nature.
   (g) Details of any joint venture or collaboration agreement.
   (h) Transactions that involve substantial payment towards goodwill, brand equity, or intellectual property.
   (i) Recruitment and remuneration of senior officers just below the board level, including appointment or removal of the CFO and the Company Secretary.
   (j) Labour problems and their proposed solutions.
   (k) Quarterly details of foreign exchange exposure and the steps taken by management to limit the risks of adverse exchange rate movement.

8. For all companies with paid-up capital of Rs 20 crores or more, the quality and quantity of disclosure that accompanies a GDR issue should be the norm of any domestic issue.

    Listed companies with either a turnover of Rs 100 crore or a paid up capital of Rs 20 crore, whichever is less, should appoint an Audit Committee within two years.
9. Under 'Additional Shareholder's Information', listed companies give data on the following:
    (a) High and low monthly averages of share prices in a major stock exchange where the company is listed for the reporting year
    (b) Greater detail on business segments up to 10 per cent of turnover, giving a share in sales revenue, review of operations, analysis of markets, and future prospects
10. Companies that default on fixed deposits should not be permitted to accept further deposits and make inter-corporate loans or investments or declare dividends until the default is paid.
11. Major Indian Stock Exchanges should insist upon a compliance certificate signed by the CEO and the CFO, which should clearly state:
    (a) The company will continue in business in the course of the following year
    (b) The accounting policies and principles conform to the standard practice
    (c) The management is responsible for the preparation, integrity, and fair presentation of financial statements, and other information contained in the annual report
    (d) The board has overseen the company's system of internal accounting and administrative controls either directly or through its audit committee.

SEBI's Initiatives

SEBI appointed a committee on 7 May 1999 under the chairmanship of Kumara Mangalam Birla with a view to promoting and raising the standard of Corporate Governance.

Mandatory recommendations:
1. Applicability—all listed companies with paid-up share capital of Rs 3 crore and above had to comply.

    Board of directors—Optimum combination of executive and non-executive directors was suggested. The number of independent directors should be at least one-third in case the company has a non-executive chairman and at least half of the board in case the company has an executive chairman.
2. Independent directors were those who, apart from receiving director's remuneration, do not have any material pecuniary relationship or transaction with the company, its promoters, its management, or its subsidiaries, which in the judgement of the board, may affect the independent judgement of the directors.
3. Audit committee—Qualified and independent audit committee to enhance credibility and encourage transparency had to be created.

The audit committee should have a minimum of three members, all being non-executive directors with a majority being independent and at least one director having financial and accounting knowledge.

The audit committee should invite such executives as it considers appropriate, besides which the required head of internal audit and external audit representative should be present as invitees for meetings of the committee.

The audit committee should meet at least thrice a year with a gap of not more than six months.

The quorum should be two members or one-third, whichever is higher, with a minimum of two independent directors.

As in the earlier recommendation, this committee also required confirmation that:
(a) The company will continue business in the course of the following year.
(b) The accounting policies and principles conform to standard practices.
(c) The management is responsible for the preparation, integrity, and fair presentation of financial statements and other information contained in the annual report.
(d) The chairman should be an independent director and must be present at the AGM to answer shareholder questions.

4. Remuneration committee of the board should decide the remuneration of the non-executive directors.
Full disclosure of the remuneration package of all the directors including salary benefits, bonuses, stock options, pension-fixed component, performance-linked incentives, along with the performance criteria, service contracts, notice period, severance fees, etc., should be made available in the section on Corporate Governance of the annual report.

5. Board procedures: The board meetings should be held at least four times a year with a maximum time-gap of four months. Minimum information on annual operating plans and capital budgets, quarterly results, minutes of meeting of audit committee, and other committees, information on recruitment and remuneration of senior officers, significant labour problems, material default in financial obligations, statutory compliance, etc., should be placed before the board for its deliberation.
A director should not be member in more than ten committees and act as chairman of more than five committees across all companies in which he is a director.

6. Management: Management discussions and analysts report about industry structure, opportunities and threats, segment-wise or product-wise performance, risks, internal control systems, etc., are to form part of the director's report or an addition to it.
The management must make disclosure to the board relating to all material, financial, and commercial transactions where they have personal interest that may have potential conflict with the interest of the company.

7. Shareholders: In case of a new director or re-appointment of existing director, information on resume, qualification, companies where he holds directorship

and committee membership for shareholders' perusal should be available.

Sharing information of quarterly results on website for the benefit of shareholders.

A board committee under the chairmanship of a non-executive director should be created to look into redressing shareholder grievances.

For share transfer authority should be delegated to officer, committee, registrar, and share transfer agents to attend to issues at least once in a fortnight.

Manner of Implementation: A separate section on Corporate Governance in annual reports is to be introduced.

Non-mandatory recommendations:
1. Chairman of the board: The chairman's role, in principle, should be different from that of the chief executive. A non-executive chairman should be entitled to maintain an office at the company's expense.
2. Remuneration committee: Credible and transparent policy should be put in place. Remuneration should be good enough to attract, retain, and motivate. The committee should comprise of at least three directors, all of whom should be non-executive directors, the chairman being an independent director. The chairman should attend the AGM to answer shareholder queries.
3. Shareholder's right: Half-yearly declaration of financial performance including summary of the significant events of the six months should be sent to the shareholders.
4. Postal ballot: The following important activities should be decided by postal ballot to ensure shareholder participation:
   (a) Matters relating to alteration in the memorandum of association, e.g., change in name, address of registered office, etc.
   (b) Sale of whole, or substantially the whole, of the undertaking.
   (c) Sale of investments in the companies where the shareholding or the voting rights of the company exceeds 25 per cent.
   (d) Making a further issue of shares through preferential allotment or private placement basis.
   (e) Corporate restructuring.
   (f) Entering a new business not germane to existing business.
   (g) Variation of rights attached to class of securities.
   (h) Matters relating to change in management.

In 2000 SEBI adopted the recommendation that the stock exchanges should modify the listing requirements by incorporating in them a new clause—Clause 49—so that disclosure is made in the following areas: board of directors; audit committee; remuneration of directors; board procedure; management; shareholders; report on corporate governance; compliance certificate from auditors.

SEBI's Code of Corporate Governance requires that the following information by a company should be made available to the board of directors periodically:
(a) Annual operating plans and budgets and any updates
(b) Capital budgets and any updates

(c) Quarterly results for the company and its operating division or business segment
(d) Minutes of audit committee meetings
(e) Information on recruitment and remuneration of senior officers just below the board level
(f) Material communications from government bodies
(g) Fatal or serious accidents, dangerous occurrences, or any material effluent pollution problems
(h) Details of any joint venture or collaboration agreement
(i) Labour relations
(j) Material transactions that are not in the ordinary course of business
(k) Disclosures by the management on material transactions, if any, with potential for conflict of interest
(l) Quarterly details of foreign exchange exposures and risk management strategies
(m) Compliance with all regulatory and statutory requirements.

Naresh Chandra Committee Report, 2002

Department of Company Affairs appointed the Naresh Chandra (NC) Committee.

Recommendations mainly concerned: (a) The auditor–company relationship; (b) disqualifications for audit assignments; (c) list of prohibited non-audit services; (d) independence standards for consulting; (e) compulsory audit partner rotation; (f) auditor's disclosure of contingent liabilities; (g) auditor's disclosure of qualifications and consequent action; (h) managements' certification in the event of auditor's replacement; (i) auditor's annual certification of independence; (j) appointment of auditors; (k) certification of annual audited accounts by the CEO and CFO; (l) auditing the auditors; (m) setting up of the independent quality review board; (n) proposed disciplinary mechanism for auditors; (o) independent directors; (p) audit committee charter; (q) exempting non-executive directors from certain liabilities; (r) training of independent directors; (s) establishment of corporate serious fraud office and; (t) SEBI and subordinate legislation, etc.

The difference between the two committees: The NC Committee made no distinction between a board with an executive chairman or with the non-executive chairman. It has recommended that all boards should have at least half of its members as independent directors.

About audit committee, the KM Birla Committee suggested it should have non-executive directors as its members with at least two independent directors. The NC committee recommended all should be independent directors.

The NC Committee was strict about the relationship between auditors and their clients.

The committee has recommended that along with its subsidiary, associates or affiliated entities, an audit firm should not derive more than 25 per cent of its business from a single corporate client. This move could affect small audit firms, because new firms which are usually small, may not be able to get business from a number of companies as they would have to establish their credentials in the market. Therefore, if it is regulated that not more than 25 per cent of business can be earned from one business, these small firms would never be able to establish themselves and would be taken over by bigger firms in the market who would continue to hold monopoly sway. This monopoly may become the breeding ground for corruption and ultimately impact the socio-economic structure of a country.

To ensure transparency, the proposal for compulsory rotation of audit firms was suggested. It stressed the partners and at least 50 per cent of the audit team working on the accounts of a company, need to be rotated by the audit firm once every five years.

The NC Committee drew up a list of prohibited non-audit services.

It said nominees of institutions (FIs) cannot be counted as independent directors.

The committee aimed at tightening the noose around the auditors by asking them to make an array of disclosures.

By calling upon the CEO and the CFO of listed companies to certify their company's annual accounts it brought in accountability.

It suggested setting up of quality review boards by the Institute of Chartered Accountants of India, Institute of Company Secretaries of India and the Institute of Cost and Works Accountants of India, instead of a public oversight board, as in the US.

To attract quality independent directors, the committee recommended that these directors should be exempt from criminal and civil liabilities under the Companies Act, the Negotiable Instruments Act, the Provident Fund Act and the Employee State Insurance Act, the Factories Act, The Industrial Disputes Act, and the Electricity Supply Act.

The Narayana Murthy Committee Report, 2003

The terms of review were:
1. To review the performance of Corporate Governance.
2. To determine the role of companies in responding to rumour and other price-sensitive information circulating in the market in order to enhance the transparency and integrity of the market.

The committee agreed with the NC Committee on:
- Disclosure of contingent liabilities
- Certification by CEOs and CFOs
- Definition of independent directors
- Independence of audit committees

Mandatory recommendation:
1. Audit committee: Should review:
   (a) Financial statements and draft audit reports including quarterly and half-yearly information.
   (b) Management discussion and analysis of financial condition and the result of operations.
   (c) Report relating to compliance with laws and risk management.
   (d) Management letters of internal control weaknesses issued by statutory internal auditors.
   (e) Records of related party transactions.

2. Related party transactions: A statement of all transactions with related parties including their bases should be placed before the audit committee.
3. Proceeds from initial public offerings: Companies raising money through IPO should disclose to the audit committee the uses and application under major heads on a quarterly basis. Each year the company shall prepare a statement of funds utilized for purposes other than those stated in offer document/prospectus.
4. Risk management: Procedures to inform the board members of the risk assessment and minimization procedures.
   Management should place a report before the entire board every quarter documenting the business risks faced by the company, measures to address and minimise such risks, and any limitation to the risk-taking capacity of the company. The board should formally approve this document.
5. Code of conduct: The code should be posted on the company's website and all board members and senior management personnel shall affirm compliance with the code on an annual basis. The annual report of the company shall contain a declaration to this effect signed by the CEO and COO.
6. Nominee directors: Recommended removing the concept of nominee directors. Shareholders should appoint any director. An institutional director, if appointed, would have the same responsibilities and liabilities as other directors.
7. Compensation to non-executive directors should be approved by the shareholders in the general meeting, restrictions were placed on grant of stock option, and it was required to make proper disclosures of compensation.
8. A whistle-blower policy was to be created in a company.

Non-mandatory recommendations:
Providing unqualified financial statements, training of board members, evaluation of non-executive directors' performance by a peer group comprising the entire board of directors excluding the one being evaluated.

Stakeholder Theory

INTRODUCTION

At ground level, resources include land, labour, and capital and their productive utilization needs the consideration of economic, social, and environmental costs. At the higher end, the resources include information, knowledge, and wisdom, which again require judicious application. Effective and efficient utilization of these resources is the focus of every business. Management theory and practice are continuously trying to evolve the best methods of value-added utilization of resources. Therefore, the process of business requires interaction with a number of entities who become the stakeholders. The relationships with these stakeholders have been analysed from simple economics to moral and value levels. To give credence to the economic aspect and skill-driven entrepreneurship, authors like Drucker (1999) and McGrath and MacMillan (2000) have highlighted capabilities like innovativeness, managing change, risk-taking capacity, and surviving competition as the driving force behind successful leaders. Similarly, there can be found propagation of strengthening of the values by drawing on an inner sense of spirituality, along with operational expertise as the vital force behind success, by management writers like Boleman and Deal (2001), Covey (1999), and Jager and Ortiz (1997).

Obstacles to ethical, responsible growth may range from the levels of the individual, to groups, to society, and to the outer world. The genuineness of the professional in ensuring holistic growth would help them make the right choice and impact. Concept and implementation would need to be synchronized in a symbiotic (co-existence of two parties that is mutually beneficial) manner, as there would always be a gap between theory and practice. The movement has to be towards quality along with quantity. Therefore, the question of CSR would require defining acceptability in the 'right' sense. A concise understanding of the tussle between the two forces of individualistic self-growth and collective shared growth would help us to gauge the issues better.

LEARNING OBJECTIVES

After studying this chapter, you will be able to
- Understand the definition of stakeholder
- Understand why the stakeholder theory is important
- Learn the taxonomy of stakeholder
- Analyse stakeholder relationship
- Understand holistic growth through tangible and intangible manifestations in a corporate business

If we trace the history of ancient civilizations, we find that economics was rooted in local community exchanges, based on barter, which required a high sense of morality and character. The frontier culture of America—the home of modern management science—also glorified harmonious existence (Oaks 1997; Handy 1998). Industrial Revolution was driven by processes that needed rules and control for success, and social scientists like Max Weber (2001), Fayol (2001), and Taylor (2001) endorsed rule-driven hierarchies, scaler chains, and quantification of results. These naturally led to creation of high standards and efficiency but slowly and silently led to the demise of the human spirit (Maney 2003; Morgan 1998). The free human spirit driven by equal opportunities was now in search for security. Therefore, either willingly or forcefully, people submitted to the domination of business entrepreneurs. This created a need to find justice in measuring efficiency and productivity (Hassard 1994; Morgan 1998). Superficial justice and equality was offered by creating the stockholder relationship. The relationship between the organization and employees became an exchange of unconditional loyalty and regimentation through employee appraisals in return for 'lifetime employment,' good salary, and excellent perks. The lack of human sensitivity and individual freedom led to the formulation of theories like the self-actualization by Maslow (2001), two-factor theory by Hertzberg (1966), and many such documentation on empowerment, motivation, teamwork improving morale, etc. (Singer and Singer 1990).

The emergence of the market forces as a result of post-war developments and political movements gave importance to the individual. This individualism was the central idea of the concept of free market, proposed by economists like Milton Freidman. The market system tried to create the amoral economic man who believed that economic activities should not be judged on moral values. This was explained by Friedman (1970) with the help of the principle of unanimity. According to this principle, in an ideal free market, cooperation is voluntary and all parties to cooperation benefit or they need not participate. This principle does not include any social responsibility, or values and morals. It only concerns itself with the shared values and responsibilities of individuals. Therefore, the only responsibility of business, which was an economic activity, was to earn economic gains. In this race to earn more to satisfy the needs (greed), the consumerist culture (or consumerism) was born. This culture led to human burnout and resource exploitation (Hage and Powers 1992). Thus, the market lost its stability as it had to face the challenges of socio-economic concerns. This volatility in the market has brought questions of stakeholder relations in business to the forefront.

TAXONOMY OF STAKEHOLDERS

In simple terms, stakeholders can be defined as individuals or groups who either get advantage or are disadvantaged by corporate decision or action. Very often, the terms society and community are used interchangeably. This raises certain discrepancies, which can be settled if the stakeholder approach is accepted. The social responsibility of organizations does not lie outside the organization. It is a part of the entire process, from planning to production and marketing (refer to Chapter 1).

The stakeholder theory highlights this dimension of corporate involvement. Freeman (1984) describes the stakeholder as 'any group or individual who can affect or is affected by the organization's purpose, because that group may prevent our accomplishment'. Evan and Freeman (1988) extend the concept of stakeholder to those who 'benefit from or are harmed by, and whose rights are violated or respected by, corporate actions.' A similar idea is expressed by Eden and Ackermann (1998) when they say stakeholder is 'people or a small group with the power to respond to, negotiate with, and change the strategic future of the organization.' Clarkson (1995) described stakeholders as those who 'have or claim, ownership, rights, or interests in a corporation and its activities.' This group has been defined as 'constituents who have legitimate claim on the firm… established through the existence of an exchange relationship' and those who supply 'the firm with critical resources (contributions) and in exchange each expects its interests to be satisfied'. Post et al. (2002) define 'the stakeholders in a corporation as the individuals and constituencies that contribute, either voluntarily or involuntarily, to its wealth-creating capacity and activities, and they are, therefore, its potential beneficiaries and/or risk-bearers'.

Perhaps a more cogent definition of stakeholder is provided in Wheeler and Sillanpaa's (1997) work. They have offered a very convenient classification by dividing the stakeholders into categories, as shown in Table 3.1.

TABLE 3.1 Classification of stakeholders

Primary social stakeholders	Secondary social stakeholders	Primary non-social stakeholders	Secondary non-social stakeholders
Investors	Government and regulators	Natural environment	Environmental pressure groups
Employees including managers	Civic institutions	Future generations	Animal welfare organizations
Local communities	Social pressure groups	Non-human species	
Suppliers	Media and academic commentators		
Other business partners	Trade bodies		
	Competitors		

A similar detailed description of stakeholders is provided by Carroll and Buchholtz (2000): Primary stakeholders are shareholders (owners), employees, customers, business partners, communities, future generations, the national environment. Secondary stakeholders are local, state, and federal governments, regulatory bodies, civic institutions and groups, special interest groups, trade and industry groups, media, competitors.

STAKEHOLDER RELATIONSHIP

To understand the relationship of the above-mentioned stakeholders, let us take a closer look at their actual functioning, as shown in Fig. 3.1.

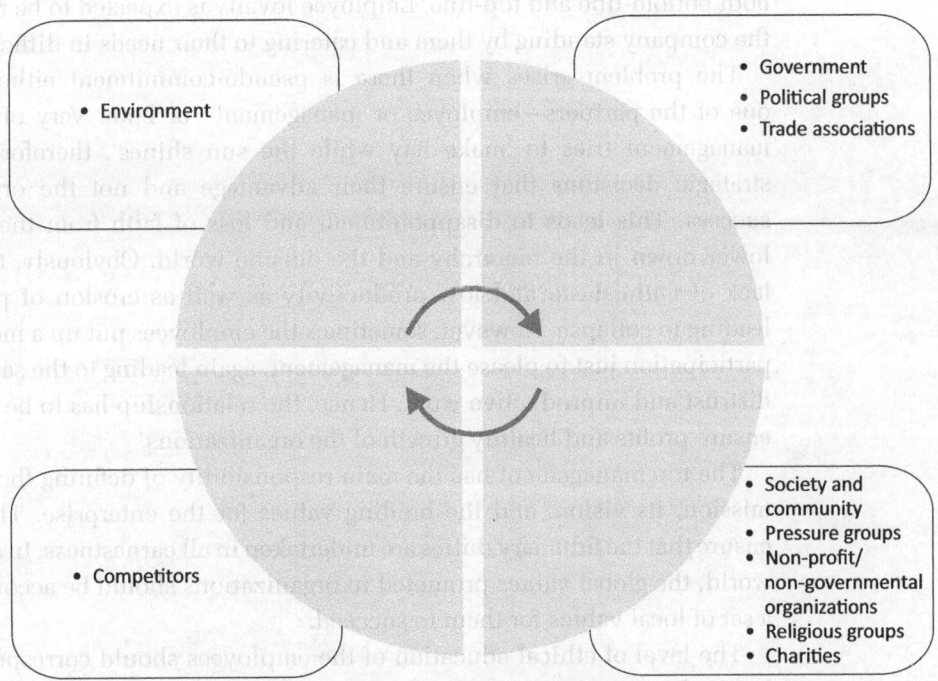

Figure 3.1 Stakeholder relationship

Stockholders

Shareholders and investors have a financial stake in the organization, in the form of investment in stocks, bonds, etc. Having invested directly or indirectly through certain exchanges, these investors would certainly demand returns and the corporation would have to honour this demand to ensure future investments for carrying on business. Of course, the stakes of the stockholder will differ, based on the type of owner and their preferences, as well as on the type of company or firm, i.e., whether the stocks are widely distributed or held closely by a small group (e.g., a family).

Employees

Employees, including the management, are hired based on their skills and expertise. Therefore, in return for their contribution, they demand wages, benefits, meaningful work, and security. Their jobs and their livelihood are at stake in this relationship. They are supposed to be disciplined and work as per the instructions at the lower level of the hierarchy. The senior members are supposed to contribute by considering a systems perspective that helps to define goals and long-term strategies and decisions for the companies. In those decisions, the social aspects are absolutely vital to ensure the steady growth of both bottom-line and top-line. Employee loyalty is expected to be rewarded by the company standing by them and catering to their needs in difficult times.

The problem arises when there is pseudo-commitment either from any one of the partners—employee or management—or both. Very often, the top management tries to 'make hay while the sun shines', therefore they take strategic decisions that ensure their advantage and not the organization's success. This leads to disappointment and loss of faith from the employees lower down in the hierarchy and the outside world. Obviously, the result is lack of enthusiasm and low productivity as well as erosion of public trust, leading to collapse. However, sometimes the employees put up a mock show of participation just to please the management, again leading to the same result of distrust and unproductive work. Hence, the relationship has to be nurtured to ensure profits and healthy growth of the organizations.

The top management has the main responsibility of defining the company's mission, its vision, and the binding values for the enterprise. They have to ensure that the fiduciary duties are undertaken in all earnestness. In a globalized world, the global values promoted in organizations should be accompanied by a set of local values for them to succeed.

The level of ethical education of the employees should correspond to their level of action, so that identifying conflicts becomes much easier. All the members of a company should be committed to the common value as that is the foundation of the company.

Suppliers

As a stakeholder, there is an interdependent relationship between the suppliers and the organization. They provide products and services to the organization to facilitate their operations and the organization in return rewards them by giving the suppliers business. Therefore, the suppliers gain if the organization is successful because they get more orders, and vice versa.

For the relationship to be a win-win situation for both, the partners' firms have to look beyond the traditional relationship based on a number of short-term suppliers. Modern business is moving more towards partnership-based approaches emphasizing a long-term relationship based on mutual trust and collaboration with core supply firms (Duran and Sanchez 1999). The problem in the relationship stems when any of the parties underplays social responsibility and only focuses on profits. Organizations in their competition to reduce cost may unwittingly agree to low quality inputs believing that the impact of products and services on customers would be over a long period and therefore it would not be noticed. Suppliers may misuse the trust of the organization by supplying poor quality supplies by taking recourse to questionable tactics. The outsourcing industry often comes under such attack.

Customers/Consumers

Customers have been variously described as 'God', 'guests', 'king', etc. of business. Older tradition promoted the concept that customers are solely responsible for making the right decision in the market to get the best gains, but modern business principles consider that the success of companies depend upon how closely the customer relationship is monitored. The more satisfied the customer is with the products and services provided by the business, the more profits business can reap.

The relationship often does not get honoured because traditionally the producers have the following rights (Boatright 2003):
1. The right to make decisions regarding products offered for sale, such as their design and sale
2. The right to set the price for products and all other terms of sale, including warranties
3. The right to determine how products will be made available to consumers (that is, right to make decisions about distribution)
4. The right to promote products in any way that they choose, including the use of any truthful advertising method.

The consumer only has the 'veto' option against the products and services offered for sale. Consumers have to protect themselves from any unethical activities of the producers. The main right that consumers can exercise is that they can switch from one product to another, but that depends on the availability of similar products. Therefore, the market exchange relationship between the consumer and the business was largely defined in terms of 'caveat emptor' or 'buyer beware' (Smith 1995).

Keeping this precarious condition of the consumers in mind, they have been offered legal protection through consumer rights. Today, businesses have realized that they cannot continue to cheat the consumer as various institutions are active in creating consumer awareness. Government and the media play an important role in this and help to protect the consumer. With markets opening up and an increase in globalization and liberalization, consumers have got the benefit of choice. Therefore, consumers can now dictate their terms in the market to a large extent but not completely, because cartels and monopolies limit choices even today.

Competitors

Though competitors are not always given a very important position as stakeholder, it is important to remember that they play an important role because the concept of free market encompasses certain rights that must be adhered to. Free market is based on free entry and free exit, which allows enterprises to fix their prices and share information with consumers. Here, the question of moral obligations comes into force, i.e., 'Is it ethical for competitors to enter the market space by cheating, lying, poaching, or using similar unfair means?' Thus, competitors affect and get affected by mutual behaviour and can either benefit or be harmed by the organization's response to such activities. Thus, competitors play an extremely important role as stakeholders by creating a network of relationships where they can impact market share by impacting consumers, suppliers, employees, and other actual and potential stakeholders.

Government

It is widely believed that government and business have a strong nexus and often work to benefit each other at the cost of other stakeholders. We need to understand that the term 'government' encompasses a large number of actors and institutions that have the right to issue laws. These actors and institutions vary from the local level to international level. Since society gives sanction to business, laws normally codify what society regards as right and wrong.

The relationship of government as a stakeholder in business relates to two distinct activities of government. First, government as a representative of community and society trying to regulate business, usually through rules, laws, and taxes and facilitate business through providing infrastructure, subsidies, tax holidays, licensing, and protecting from competition. Second, government is dependent on the economic prosperity of the nation and the economy is run by business, therefore, there is a covert dependence of government on business for it to retain its own power. Overtly, the government is also a competitor to business because very many products and services are provided by public organizations. In fulfilling these roles, the concept of corporate social responsibility comes to the forefront (see Chapter 4 for more details).

Society and Community

Society and community include all the players in the community and society, such as non-profit organizations, non-governmental organizations, charities, religious groups, pressure groups related to human rights, environment, welfare, etc. This sector was given prominence by writers like Bendell (2000), Reece (2001), Baker and Chandler (2005), and others. The idea of a global civil society has also been created (Baker and Chandler 2005). The civil society, through its social organizations, actually represents the voice and needs of the individual stakeholder.

Corporate social responsibility requires that an analysis be made about the lack of employment opportunities and low income as both these aspects have tremendous macro-level impacts that ultimately would demand answers from the business community. Technological change and global competition are accelerating changes in market demand. This is manifested in violation of human rights and destruction of natural resources. These challenges, though not immediate, would have to be proactively handled by businesses if they want long-term sustenance and viability (Chapter 4 for more details on NGOs).

Today, business can no longer ignore this stakeholder or behave in a confrontational or high-handed manner. Business has realized that a multi-faceted relationship is advantageous to them in the long run, as both the bottom-line and top-line of business needs the assistance of society. However, we must remember that sometimes unscrupulous social groups may misuse their power to seek out personal gains by harassing business, e.g., by targeting specific companies, indulging in yellow journalism, spreading false information, etc. Therefore, the relationship has to tread the line of a mutual win-win situation.

IMPACTS AND DILEMMAS OF BUSINESS

Till recently, the process of development pursued capital formation and raising of gross national product (GNP) in the erroneous belief that the mysterious 'hidden hand' and 'trickle down' effects would ensure the fair distribution of the gains of development. The hidden hand and trickle down is a traditional economic theory that advocates providing incentives to businesses to restart the economy from the top and letting businesses flourish, in the belief that their profits will ultimately trickle down to lower-income individuals and the rest of the economy.

However, in the course of time, it has become amply evident that affluence alone cannot be the goal for society, as by itself it is not an indicator of the quality of life. Corporates have to recognize this philosophy of 'empty plenty', which means the availability of abundant material goods that only fulfil the physical needs but do not actually ensure emotional happiness and satisfaction. The business community has to work towards a process of change management that ensures holistic growth of both the physical and emotional needs of human beings, because money and material goods cannot guarantee necessary human feelings like love, friendship, sharing, loyalty, etc., in a society. The transition to knowledge economy gave a semblance of equality in the power hierarchy by creating a concept of the virtual world but equality has also probably remained virtual.

Though cooperation is the best option, when rationally analysed, yet the lack of trust and values in interpersonal relationships leads to rationality itself being challenged. Therefore, to get out of this strange human dilemma, do we need to devise systems that would focus beyond the material gains to spiritual value systems? To answer this dilemma, various researches on systems have revealed that open self-directed systems are better than closed entropic structures (Katz and Kahn 2001). The word entropy has been borrowed from thermodynamics to explain systems that do not allow innovation and therefore begin to degrade and degenerate.

To be meaningful, organizations have to make life reverent and just. This requires an honest assessment of the internal and external environment, so that the realities are matched. 'The categorization of the issue as an opportunity or a threat can affect the decision maker's subsequent cognitions, motivations, levels of risk taking, involvement, and commitment' (Thomas, Clark, and Gioia 1993). This is where the structure and process of an organization may be compatible or incompatible. An organization needs to understand that it must allow the expression of diverse ideas, even if they may be opposite to each other, because that is what would encourage change. Change in a positive direction requires that both the extremes, one of total conformity with set patterns and the other of absolute disregard for traditional processes, have to be avoided. For example, the need to hold together cannot be seen as a blind following of laid-down systems; encouragement should be provided to think out-of-the-box, to seek opportunities by thinking creatively if the organization wants to emerge with a unique brand of its own. Diversity of thought and practices need to be respected and enjoyed for CSR to be effective both internally and externally in the organization. The vital balance between two opposing forces that are actually complementary needs to be understood as shown in Fig. 3.2 (Padaki and Vaz 2005).

The above-mentioned structure and process needs to be driven by professionals. Thus, professionals have an influence on business. They are the 'right' people who need to step in to provide the right direction to the organization system, strategy, process, and function. The word professionalism is associated with certain values and ideals. It is intricately intertwined with a concept of social well-being as that is the prerequisite for any kind of survival—individual or group.

Stakeholder Theory | 91

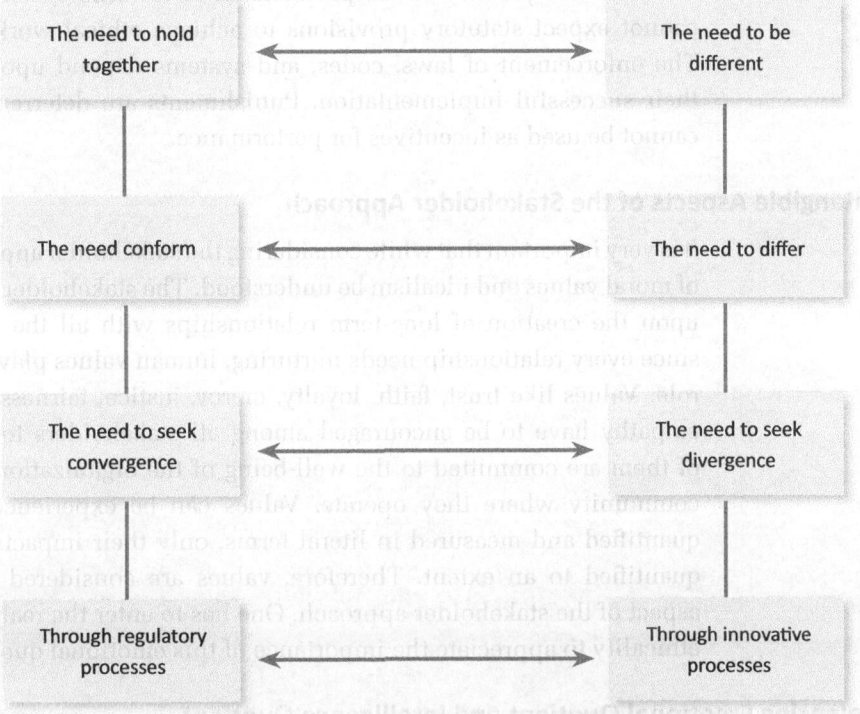

Figure 3.2 Complementary needs in an organization

As professionals, we have to understand that we can no longer have stereotyped images of different identities because professionals are not supposed to follow an algorithmic meaning, simple step-by-step processes or heuristic referring to working on the basis of thumb-rule, which gives fixed solutions. The responsibility of the professional is to use his knowledge to diagnose, infer, analyse, and then offer solutions on a 'case-to-case basis'. It is only in this process of creativity and innovativeness that we can hope for a genuine appreciation of human rights.

The danger that the world faces from these so-called 'right people' or professionals is the misuse of the specialized knowledge that gives extraordinary power and status to them. Society respects and gives social sanction to this knowledge and offers the highest pedestal to the professional. The common man has no other alternative but to trust the professional and hope for the honouring of that trust. It is the individual values that determine the organizational values. No codes, systems, or structures can ensure success, as the dangerous manipulative managers can always bend them or twist them to suit their personal gains. Here, we need to take the argument a little further by distinguishing between the concept of success, which is usually measured in material terms, and perfection, which goes beyond the material ratings.

Unless the journey of the professional is towards excellence in spirit, we cannot expect statutory provisions to achieve ethical working environment. The enforcement of laws, codes, and systems depend upon punishment for their successful implementation. Punishments are deterrents and, therefore, cannot be used as incentives for performance.

Intangible Aspects of the Stakeholder Approach

It is very important that while considering the stakeholder approach, the concept of moral values and idealism be understood. The stakeholder approach is based upon the creation of long-term relationships with all the stakeholders, and since every relationship needs nurturing, human values play a very significant role. Values like trust, faith, loyalty, mercy, justice, fairness, forgiveness, and empathy have to be encouraged among all stakeholders to ensure that each of them are committed to the well-being of the organization, society, and the community where they operate. Values can be experienced but cannot be quantified and measured in literal terms, only their impacts can be seen and quantified to an extent. Therefore, values are considered as the intangible aspect of the stakeholder approach. One has to enter the realm of morality and ethicality to appreciate the importance of this emotional quotient.

Balancing Emotional Quotient and Intelligence Quotient

If we sift through the literature on human resources management, organizational behaviour, organizational development, or anything related to quality in an organization, we would come across statements like 'human resource management is a distinctive approach to employment management which seeks to achieve competitive advantage through the strategic deployment of a highly committed and capable workforce, using an array of cultural, structural and personnel techniques' (Storey 2000).

The famous Hawthorne study leading to the concept of the Hawthorne Effect was done by Elton Mayo and his colleagues of the Hawthorne plant of the Western Electric Company in Chicago, during 1929–35. They found that workers' feelings, attitudes, and beliefs played a huge part in their productivity. They also concluded that performance at work depended not only on pay, but also on their emotional feelings, about how they were treated, and their perceptions of the supervisor's style of dealing with them. All these relate to the concept of motivation and emotional rewards, beyond codes and laws.

Therefore, the search has to be of the right professional who is 'emotionally purified' to make the incentive-oriented journey towards perfection. However, instead of purifying emotions, attempts are made to annihilate emotions. We have tried to do this by creating the neutral amoral human by giving him the credentials of the 'economic man'. Can the economic man be really devoid of emotions and are not emotions the secret choice-makers for us?

The extreme fallacy of asking our professionals to keep their emotions at home, while they are involved in activities that have profound influence globally, is a matter of concern. It is the emotional intelligence that decides whether the subjective individual is going to deliver the correct objective. The intelligent brain can justify any activity, and therefore, an individual whose emotions are not managed can commit the most heinous crimes. Unfortunately, modern management focuses more on skill development than value development. Intellect and reasons are tools for skill development and action. However, these skills and action need to be guided by the intangible, subtle, and enduring values of human existence. This is the choice our 'right' people would have to make because there is no area of life that does not contain values/ethics elements.

Importance of Ethics

Any focus on healthy and wholesome growth in the corporate world cannot ignore ethics. The main concern of business is to make profit and ethics has to be a proactive part of business if profits need to be sustained. Any process of business to be perfect pre-supposes accountability and integrity. Both qualitative and quantitative assessment require professionals to be committed and passionate about the activity and these qualities stem from the emotions of human beings, not from their skill sets.

Knowledge has no value if it is not creative. Creativity always relates to positive sustainable growth. One can understand this very well when we analyse the recent liquid bomb threat that has put the entire process of air travel in turmoil. Certainly, the man who designed it is extremely knowledgeable but is he really creative? This is the difference between the 'right' professional and the 'wrong'. The right people are supposed to make life more comfortable by reducing drudgery and inhumanity.

The purpose of business is to create material wealth for society to make living more enjoyable. As a reward for this creation, society offers economic sanction and allows business to make profits. The material wealth is of value only when it leads to preservation of human life. Therefore, professionals have to understand the distinction between need, want, and greed. Selfish individual preservation is always fuelled by want and greed. This naturally makes earning wealth primary for an individual. Thus, collective and holistic preservation of life becomes secondary. Such economic activity can have a Mephisthophelean impact on human existence. The recent global recession has raised the question of greed in no uncertain terms.

Professionals have to understand the need for 'destruction' and 're-creation' in the perspective of change and innovation. The old order has to give way to the new exactly as the ripe fruit cannot hold on to the branch of the tree and must fall off in order for the new fruit to come. A mindset to unlearn and relearn needs to be created to accept change.

The learning to 'give up' power is as significant as 'acquiring' it in the sustenance of an organization. Unfortunately, there is no training given to professionals on this aspect of management. Therefore, it becomes exceedingly painful and depressing for a professional to give up authority and power. These emotional upheavals often get expressed in various acrimonious and destructive ways, which the world can only live to regret.

The Tussle between Means and Ends

Means are as important as the end. One becomes free from the stress and fear of non-achievement when one is committed to both the means and the end. This dedication leads neither to extreme elation at achievement nor total despondency in non-achievement. One is balanced, or as Lord Buddha had termed it, one is walking on the Middle Path. There is total satisfaction that one has done ones best. Therefore, in this paradigm, failure becomes the 'stepping stone to success' as it is not perceived as a personal failure but a result of factors that were probably beyond control or unknown at that particular time, as per Murphy's Law. Hence, there is always a hope and an inspiration to try again! Professionals should always be sure that the goal or the success will not disappear; it is bound to come as a reward of the hard work. There is no alternative to performance of work; it is the subjective motivation and inclination that decides whether the result is positive or negative. Dissatisfaction or unhappiness occurs when somebody else achieves success quicker than us by using unfair means. But how long can such success last, e.g., if he has used force, somebody stronger may come along and snatch it from him. Does he really gain the satisfaction that professionalism stands for? Above all, is not using unfair and corrupt methods unprofessional?

Combining Tangible Gains with Intangible Satisfaction

Can a business really ignore any of its stakeholders? Business is nothing but building and sustaining the relationships with these stakeholders. Relationships depend totally on trust and certainly trust is not a skill. It is a value. If the subject (the individual) is not value-oriented, how can the object (action and result) be? If the input is not regulated, the output in the production process cannot be right.

Business depends on a vision and the vision is achieved through smaller missions. For achieving this, professionals need to have sight, insight, and foresight, as shown in Fig. 3.3. Sight involves the day-to-day activity; insight

Stakeholder Theory | 95

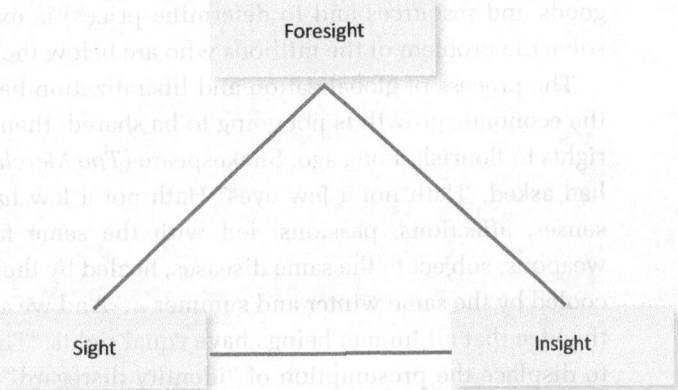

Figure 3.3 Organizational decision-making process

is like a debriefing session where an appraisal is made of the activities and their results; and foresight is setting the goal towards which the company has to proceed.

To complete this triangular journey, the professional has to learn to move away and review the work. This is well expressed in the Chinese saying 'you can view the forest only from a distance; standing under a tree in the forest you cannot see it.' This requires the talent of learning to delegate and let go, to do intelligent work in a detached manner. Develop the spirit of introspection so that learning is complete and no gaps are there. The true leader needs to be alert and relaxed to give the right decision and this attitude can be developed only when we learn to curb our desires, which lead to attachment, wrath, and fear. The basic value system of the organization has to be strong, then the peripheral systems can always be grafted by adhering to it. The 'right' people need to enhance the strength of standing by the values and others would follow. These basic values are universal to all countries and cultures, for they spring from the depth of human existence and survival.

Holistic Growth

This brings us to the understanding of holistic growth encompassing the economy, polity, and society. Professionals cannot work in silos within their respective areas and believe that development would happen. The greatest examples of this skewed vision are the processes of outsourcing, mergers and acquisitions, free market zones, SEZs, patents, etc., which are all driven only by economic criteria and the rest are left to fall in place. This is where the common people are dependent on the professionals to ensure that these are achieved with the least disturbance.

The mantra of the 'magic of the market place' (an economy where all business deals are decided in the market, as it relies chiefly on market forces to allocate goods and resources and to determine prices) is excellent, but does it really solve the problem of the millions who are below the poverty line?

The process of globalization and liberalization has to have a human face. If the economic growth is not going to be shared, then we cannot expect human rights to flourish. Long ago, Shakespeare (*The Merchant of Venice*, III. i.49–61) had asked, 'Hath not a Jew eyes? Hath not a Jew hands, organs, dimensions, senses, affections, passions; fed with the same food, hurt with the same weapons, subject to the same diseases, healed by the same means, warmed and cooled by the same winter and summer ...' And we are still trying to cope with the idea that all human beings have equal rights. 'The time has certainly come to displace the presumption of "identity disregard" from the exalted position it has tended to occupy in a substantial part of economic theory woven round the concept of the "economic man" ...' (Sen 2006), and knowing that the beauty and justification of human existence lies in accepting each culture and country with its human wealth in its totality, and not trying to give the same economic colour to every activity.

STAKEHOLDER TRADE-OFFS

While implementing the stakeholder theory, we have to keep in mind that very often the real business world with its dynamism would demand trade-off between stakeholders because it is not possible to meet the demands of all equally. To understand this, let us first look at a few analyses of stakeholder importance.

Donaldson and Preston (1995) proposed three uses of the stakeholder model: descriptive, instrumental, and normative. The descriptive model helps one to understand how corporations are organized and managed. Basically, it provides a description of the organization and what people in corporations believe their roles are in it. The authenticity of the description should be verified empirically, while using the stakeholder model in this perspective.

The stakeholder model can be used instrumentally to explain to managers how to handle stakeholders as a practical method of earning profits. It is often observed that those corporations who care about their different stakeholders reap in higher profits.

When the stakeholder model is used normatively, it relates to the interest of the stakeholders, which should be promoted for their own sake as 'the interests of all stakeholders are of intrinsic value' (Donaldson and Preston 1995).

Similar thoughts can be discerned when Mitchell et al. (1997) suggest that the importance or salience of the stakeholder can be judged from the parameters of power, legitimacy, and urgency:

Power is the ability of the stakeholder to influence organizational decision-making and action.

Legitimacy relates to how far the organization perceives the activities of stakeholders as appropriate and desirable.

Urgency as the word suggests, judges the importance of stakeholder claim to immediate action.

Based on which stakeholder demonstrates how many attributes, they are segregated as (1) latent, possessing only one, (2) expectant, showing two, and (3) definitive, having all the three attributes. Now the organization can decide how it would engage with its various stakeholders by prioritizing them.

According to Hill and Jones (2001), 'stakeholder impact analysis enables a company to identify the stakeholders most critical to its survival and to make sure that the satisfaction of their needs is paramount. Most that go through this process quickly reach the conclusion that there are three stakeholder groups the company must satisfy if it is to survive and prosper: customers, employees, and shareholders.' The idea is to understand the importance of the influence of the stakeholder to take strategic decisions in a milieu of stakeholders.

However, there are critics of the stakeholder theory as well as those who believe that the theory has practical shortcomings. Ansoff (1965) feels that the theory actually restricts a firm from performing to reach its objectives. He contends that 'responsibilities' and objectives are not the same. The former are obligations to various stakeholders that actually create confusion in achieving the main objective of the corporation, which is 'profit'.

It has been pointed out that the stakeholder model is unable to provide a clear-cut guide for action as it leaves many questions unanswered, specially about trade-offs. Structuring an organization on the basis of priority of various stakeholders is not easy.

A framework for making the trade-off is offered by Jenson (2006). He calls it the enlightened value maximization and enlightened stakeholder theory. According to him, stakeholder theory directs corporate managers to serve 'many masters' and companies 'embracing stakeholder theory will experience managerial confusion, conflict, inefficiency, and perhaps even complete failure.' Therefore, value–maximization, which includes not just the value of equity but all financial claims on the firm—debts, warrants, and preferred stock of a firm—should be the value-objective around which the stakeholder theory should fit into.

Therefore, the enlightened value maximization principle is: we cannot maximize the long-term market value of an organization, if we ignore or mistreat any important constituency. The value criteria would help the organization to decide the trade-off more effectively and efficiently. Jenson cautions that the stakeholder theory can play into the hands of special interest groups who would legitimize using resources for their needs under the guise of stakeholder welfare. The danger would be that instead of increasing social welfare, the stakeholder theory would actually reduce it. The theory can be used to cater to those stakeholders whom the leaders of the management like. Therefore, the theory can become person-dependent instead of process-dependent and fail to realize its actual aim. Hence, the value maximization should be the guiding force. He opines that 'we must not confuse optimization with value creation or value seeking. To create value we need not know exactly what maximum value is and precisely how it can be achieved. What we must do, however, is to set up our organization so that managers and employees are clearly motivated to seek value—to institute those changes and strategies that are most likely to cause value to rise.'

CONCLUSION

If we analyse the development of the concept of the stakeholder theory, we find that it is an extension of the rights enjoyed by the stockholders of a firm to other constituents of the firm. This is so because the stockholder is also a stakeholder in the ultimate analysis. Since the stockholders originally provided the capital to start business, they staked the first claim on the firm. This special right of the stockholder to demand certain privileges from the management was questioned when it became evident that business is not just the product of capital or money. The realization that business requires the involvement of the entire ecosystem that develops around it gave significance to the stakeholder concept. Now it was proclaimed that every entity that in any way impacts business or is impacted by business have some special claim on the firm. Thus, the traditional view that the only responsibility of business was to earn profit and in that process it was doing social responsibility because it provided employment and goods and services was challenged.

The main question that the stakeholder theory brought into focus was 'for whose benefit and at whose expense should the firm be managed' (Evan and Freeman 1988). This gave birth to a number of ways to resolve this issue and gave importance to values, along with skills. The stakeholder theory does not give importance to one stakeholder over another. Therefore, in real life, corporations have to design a just trade-off between the stakeholders based on the prevailing circumstances, both in the internal and external environment. However, management must keep relationships amongst stakeholders in balance (Freeman 2001).

Thus, the stakeholder theory has brought in the concept of holistic growth. The business world cannot expect to earn profits if it does not take care of the rights of every stakeholder. Business also has to be extremely alert about the effect it has on the stakeholders. Today, the numbers of stakeholders have increased and include the environment and community. This has happened because the influence of business has grown in leaps and bounds and has become an integral part of life. This growth has naturally shifted the focus to the purpose of business and new theories are emerging to define the legitimacy of business. Central to all this thought is the responsibility that the business world has to discharge and this has been expressed through the concept of fiduciary relationship (see Chapter 2 for details of fiduciary duties).

SUMMARY

The question of CSR would require defining acceptability in the 'right' sense of the economic and social aspects of business. The emergence of the market forces as a result of post-war developments and political movements envisaging individualism as the core of existence encouraged the concept of free market. The market volatility has brought to the forefront questions of stakeholder relations in business. The social responsibility of organizations does not lie outside the organization. It is a part of the entire process, from planning to production and marketing. The stakeholder theory highlights this dimension of corporate involvement.

Stakeholder is any group or individual who can affect or is affected by the organization's purpose, because that group may prevent our accomplishment. Stakeholders are those who benefit from or are harmed by, and whose rights are violated or respected by, corporate actions. The process of development, till recently, pursued capital formation and raising of GNP in the erroneous belief that the mysterious 'hidden hand' and 'trickle down' effects would ensure the fair distribution of the gains of development. However, while implementing the stakeholder theory, we have to keep in mind that very often the real business world, with its dynamism, would demand trade-off between stakeholders because it is not possible to meet the demands of all equally. Finding the balance between stakeholders needs great acumen and commitment from the business leaders. The stakeholder theory has been criticized on the basis of the confusion it can create because it appears to cater to many masters. However, if a well-structured process is put in place, this dilemma can be met.

KEY TERMS

Cartel When independent business organizations form an association to regulate production, pricing, and marketing of goods by the members.
Emotional quotient Capacity and ability to identify, manage, and control emotions.
Fiduciary Power held on trust by the management under equal obligation to deliver benefit by using it for the sole purpose specified.
Holistic Concerned with the whole and the interdependence of the separate parts.

Mephistophelean Evil or fiendish.
Professional An individual who specializes and gains expertise in a particular field of interest.
Stakeholder Independent entities influenced by business activities.
Sustainable Endure over a long period.
Trade-off Exchange, specially as a compromise.
Yellow journalism Journalism that exploits, distorts, or exaggerates the news to create sensations and attract readers.

EXERCISES

Concept Review Questions

1. Define stakeholder theory and its importance in the modern business environment.
2. Give a detailed description of the various stakeholders and analyse their relationship to business.
3. Briefly explain the tangible and intangible impacts of the stakeholder theory.
4. Why do we need to understand stakeholder trade-off?
5. Evaluate the advantages and disadvantages of the stakeholder theory.

Critical Thinking Questions

1. According to you, what led to the development of the stakeholder theory?
2. Do you think that the stakeholder theory is best suited to achieve CSR?
3. How should an organization design its stakeholder trade-off?
4. How important are the intangible impacts of the stakeholder theory on CSR practices of an organization?

Research Question

How can a company manage trade-offs between stakeholders?

Project Question

Choose a company and analyse who is the most important stakeholder for that company.

REFERENCES

Anderson, D. and L.A. Anderson (2001), *Beyond Change Management—Advanced Strategies for Today's Transformational Leaders*, Jossey–Bass/Pfeiffer, San Francisco.

Ansoff, H. Igor (1965), *Corporate Strategy—An Analytical Approach to Business Policy for Growth and Expansion*, McGraw–Hill, New York.

Baker, G. and D. Chandler (eds.) 2005, *Global Civil Society*, Routledge, London and New York.

Baulch, Bob and John Hoddinott (2000), 'Economic Mobility and Poverty Dynamics in Developing Countries', *Journal of Development Studies*, vol. 38, issue no. 6, p. 1–24.

Beck, L.C. and C.C. Cowan (1996), *Spiral Dynamics—Mastering Values, Leadership and Change,* Blackwell Publishing, Massachusetts.

Bendell, J. (2000), 'Introduction—Working with Stakeholder Pressure for Sustainable Development', in J. Bendell (ed.) *Terms for Endearment—Business, NGOs and Sustainable Development,* Greenleaf, Sheffield.

Boatright, R. John (2003), *Ethics and the Conduct of Business,* Pearson Education, India, p. 276.

Boleman, L.G. and T.E. Deal (2001), *Leading with Soul—An Uncommon Journey of Spirit,* Jossey–Bass, San Francisco.

Carroll, Archie B. (1979), 'A Three Dimensional Conceptual Model of Corporate Performance', *Academy of Management Review,* vol. 4, issue no. 4, pp. 497–505.

Carroll, Archie B. and Ann K. Buchholtz (2000), *Business and Society—Ethics and Stakeholder Management,* South Western College Publishing, Cincinnati.

Covey, S.R. (1999), 'Success on the Far Side of Failure', *Executive Excellence,* vol. 16, issue no. 1, pp. 3–5.

Donaldson, T. and L.E. Preston (1995), 'The Stakeholder Theory of the Corporation—Concepts, Evidence and Implications', *Academy of Management Review,* vol. 20, issue no. 1, pp. 65–91.

Drucker, P.F. (1999), *Management Challenges for the 21st. Century,* HarperBusiness, New York.

Duran, J.L. and F. Sanchez (1999), 'The Relationship between the companies and their Suppliers', *Journal of Business Ethics,* vol. 22, issue no. 3, pp. 273–80.

Eden, C. and F. Ackermann (1998), *Making Strategy—The Journey of Strategic Management,* SAGE Publication, London.

Evan, W.M. and R.E. Freeman (1988), 'A Stakeholder Theory of the Modern Corporation—Kantian capitalism', (eds) T. Beauchamp and N. Bowie. *Ethical theory and business.* 75–93. Englewood Cliffs, NJ, Prentice Hall, Also see, Hoffman M.W. and R.E. Frederick (eds) (1995), *Business Ethics—Readings and cases in corporate morality* 3/e, McGraw–Hill Inc, US, pp. 145–154.

Fayol, H. (2001), 'General Principles of Management' in J.M. Shafritz and J.S. Ott (eds), *Classics of Organization Theory,* pp. 48–60, Harcourt Publishers, Orlando, Florida, US.

Freeman, E.R. (1970), Business Ethics—Readings and cases in corporate morality, Hoffman M W., Frederick R.E., Schwartz M.S. (eds) (2001), 4th edn, McGraw–Hill Inc, US, pp. 160–168.

——— (1984), *Strategic Management—A Stakeholder Approach,* Pitman Publishing, Boston.

Friedman, Milton (1970), 'The Social Responsibility of Business is to Increase its Profits', in Hoffman, W.M., R.E. Frederick, and M.S. Schwartz (eds) (2001), *Business Ethics—Readings and Cases in Corporate Morality* 4/e, McGraw Hill Inc, US, pp. 156–160.

——— (1970), 'The Social Responsibility of Management is to Increase Profits', *The New York Times Magazine,* September 13.

Hage, J. and C.H. Powers (1992), *Post Industrial Lives—Roles and Relationships in the 21st. Century,* Sage Publications, California.

Handy, C. (1998), *Beyond Certainty—The Changing World of Organizations*, Harvard Business School Press, Boston.

Hassard, J. (1994), 'Postmodern Organizational Analysis—Towards a Conceptual Framework', *Journal of Management Studies*, vol. 31, issue no. 3, pp. 303–24.

Hertzberg, F. (1966), *Work and the Nature of Man*, World Publishing Company, Cleveland.

Hill, C.W.L. and G.R. Jones (2001), *Strategic Management—An integrated approach*, Houghton/Mifflin Publishing Co., Boston.

Jager, R.D. and R. Oritz (1997), *In the Company of Giants—Candid Conversations with the Visionaries of the Digital World*, McGraw Hill, San Francisco.

Jensen, C. Michael and William Meckling (1976), 'Theory of the Firm—Managerial Behaviour, Agency Costs and Ownership Structure' *Journal of Financial Economics* October, vol. 3(4) pp. 305–360.

Jenson, C. Michael (2006), 'Value Maximization, Stakeholder Theory, and the Corporate Objective Function', in Donald H. Chew Jr. and Stuart L. Gillan (eds), *Corporate Governance at the Crossroads, a book of readings*, Tata McGraw–Hill, New Delhi, pp. 7–20.

Katz, D. and R.L. Khan (2001), 'Organization and the System Concept', in J.M. Shafritz and J.S. Ott (eds), *Classics of Organization Theory*, Harcourt, Orlando, Florida, US, pp. 257–67.

Maney, K. (2003), *The Maverick and His Machine—Thomas Watson, Sr. and the Making of IBM*, John Wiley and Sons, New York.

Maslow, A.H. (2001), 'A Theory of Human Motivation', in J.M. Shafritz and J.S. Ott (eds.), *Classics of Organization Theory*, Harcourt Orlando, Florida, US, pp. 167–78.

Mayo Elton, (1933), *The Human Problems of an Industrial Civilization*, MacMillan, New York, Chapter 3.

McGrath, R.G. and I. MacMillan (2000), *The Entrepreneurial Mindset—Strategies for Continuously Creating Opportunities in an Age of Uncertainty*, Harvard Business Press, Boston.

Mitchell, R.K., B.R. Agle, and D.J. Wood (1997), 'Toward a Theory of Stakeholder Identification and Salience—Defining the Principle of Who and What really Counts', *Academy of Management Review*, vol. 22, issue no. 4, pp. 853–888.

Morgan, G. (1998), *Images of Organization*, Berett–Koehler Publishers, San Francisco.

Oaks, D.H. (1997), 'Following the Pioneers', *Ensign*, vol. 27, issue no. 11, pp. 72–74.

Padaki, Vijay and Manjulika Vaz (2005), *Management Development in Non–Profit Organizations, A programme for Governing Boards*, Sage Publications, New Delhi, p. 61.

Post, E. James, Preston E. Lee, and Sachs Sybilee (2002), 'Managing the Extended Enterprise—The New Stakeholder View', *California Management Review*, vol. 45, issue no. 1, p. 8.

Reece, J.W. (2001), 'Business and the Civil Society—The missing dialectic', *Thunderbird International Business Review*, vol. 43, issue no. 5, pp. 651–67.

Roethlisberger J. Fritz and W.J. Dickson (1939) (Mayo supervised the study), *Management and the Worker*, Harvard University Press, Cambridge.

Runge, C. Ford (1984), 'Institutions and the Free Rider; The Assurance Problem in Collective Action', *Journal of Politics*, 46, 154–81. Cited in Ian Maitland, 'The Limits of Business Self Regulation', *California Management Review*, vol. 27, issue no. 134, Spring, 1985.

Russell, Hardin (1971), 'Collective Action as an Agreeable n– Prisoners' Dilemma', *Behavioral Science*, 16, pp. 472–79.

Sen, Amartya (2006), *Identity and Violence The illusion of Destiny*, Penguin Books, New Delhi.

Singer, M. and A.E. Singer (1990), 'Situational Constraints on Transformational Versus Transactional Leadership Behaviour, Subordinates' Leadership Preference, and Satisfaction', *Journal of Social Psychology*, vol. 130, issue no. 3, pp. 385–97.

Smith, N.C. (1995), 'Marketing Strategies for the Ethics Era', *Sloan Management Review*, vol. 36, issue no. 4, pp. 85–97.

Storey, J. (2000), *Human Resource Management—A critical text*, Routledge, London.

Taylor, F.W. (2001), 'The Principles of Scientific Management', in J.M. Shafritz and J.S. Ott (eds.), *Classics of Organization Theory*, Harcourt College Publishers, New York, pp. 61–72.

Thomas, J., S. Clark and D. Gioia (1993), 'Strategic sense-making and organizational performance—Linkages among scanning, interpretation, action, and outcomes' *Academy of Management Journal*, 36: 239–270.

Weber, Max (2001), 'Bureaucracy', in J.M. Shafritz and J.S. Ott (eds), *Classics of Organization Theory*, Harcourt College Publishers, New York, pp. 73–78.

Wheeler, David and Maria Sillanpaa (1997), *The Stakeholder Corporation—The Body Shop Blueprint for Maximising Stakeholder Value*, Pitman Publishing, London.

CASE STUDY

The case study presented here is based on the Tata initiative in their leather unit in Dewas, Indore, in Madhya Pradesh. It highlights a company's effort to add to the sustainability concept of CSR by balancing the stakeholder needs. The authors have written the case based on published material and interviews with the process-owners at Tata International Dewas, India, and is meant solely for class discussion. The case is not intended as an endorsement, source of primary data, or a comment on effective or ineffective management.

CSR IN THE TATA GROUP

Dr Madhumita Chatterji and Prof. Ashoke Rao

Abstract
The business world, with its multifarious activities and myriad influences, has tried various ways to cope with the demand of sustaining profit and still be socially responsible. This is exemplified by the variety of ingenious initiatives that the Tata group has taken. The authors decided to showcase the gainful utilization of hazardous solid leather waste, an initiative of the Tata International Limited, a

Tata group company. It is considered a breakthrough in the area of treating and managing toxic waste, which for a long time was considered untreatable and not eco-friendly. The case aims at showcasing one of India's most loved organization's methods of doing business. It highlights that doing business in India has to go beyond the 'bottom line'.

Key terms   corporate social responsibility (CSR), stakeholder, trusteeship, hazardous waste, bottom-line

Introduction

The business world, with its multifarious activities and myriad environmental influences, has tried in various ways to cope with the demand for sustaining profit and still be socially responsible. Some have proactively got involved and some have tried to find ways to rationalize non-performance in the social area, by hiding behind the jargon of the 'magic of the market place'. There is a growing awareness that government alone cannot bear the responsibility for development. Freedom is accompanied by responsibility, and therefore, the more 'free market' is advocated, there is more responsibility and need to stay 'within the rules'. This is exemplified by companies who have strong value-based foundations like the legendary Tata Group.

Stakeholder Approach

Very often, the terms 'society' and 'community stakeholders' are used interchangeably. This raises certain discrepancies, which can be settled if the stakeholder approach is accepted. CSR is a proactive process of business and not just a one-time philanthropic activity. Philanthropy is certainly an important aspect of corporate planning, but it cannot substitute CSR. At every stage of corporate life and in its processes, there is human involvement, either directly or indirectly, and this cannot be ignored by the corporates if they want to succeed. The stakeholder theory highlights this dimension of corporate involvement.

However, it is true that at the implementation level trade-off between the stakeholders responsibilities are bound to occur. How much this trade-off should be stretched to is where the corporates have to be extremely cautious. For example, cutting cost by reducing quality and yet maintaining high prices to earn profits for the shareholders, is satisfying one stakeholder (shareholders) at the cost of another (customers). This type of strategy cannot ensure sustainability and survival. CSR is a process that would help us to understand this balance, since it is involved at all levels—inner, intermediate, and outer levels of the organization. The inner level is where the core strength of the organization lies and the efficient execution of the economic function—products, jobs, and economic growth is the main thrust area. The intermediate circle encompasses responsibility to exercise this economic function with sensitive awareness of changing social values and priorities. The outer circle outlines newly emerging and still amorphous responsibilities that business should assume to become more broadly involved in actively improving the social environment (as explained in Chapter 1 of this book).

Identification with Organization

The gist of all CSR research is that for economic survival, social responsibility is a prerequisite, but the process of finding an accurate measure or crisp definition still continues. This concept is certainly not new. Every age in history has tried to find a symbiotic relationship between the economic man and the social man.

Arriving at a consensus for CSR checklists may not be easy. There will be the perennial and inevitable disagreements on 'cause and effect' in the development process, as every organization has its own perspectives and perceptions regarding service to society. However, it does seem worth the effort to work towards defining the minimum acceptable criteria, and the authors felt that the best way to demonstrate this is to portray a process already in practice. 'Seeing is believing' and therefore it was felt that if we can give a live example of an effort being undertaken by a successful business organization, the process of practicing CSR may become more acceptable and worthy of emulation. Thus, feasible directions may evolve out of this endeavour, because Indian business can actually check and authenticate the findings. To understand and appreciate this phenomenon, the authors have showcased a company and one of its initiatives and demonstrated how the company has successfully integrated social responsibility and responsiveness with profit-making.

The organization in question is the Tata Group, which has discovered what WBCSD describes as its 'magnetic north' (refer to Chapter 1). This organization is an exceptional entity that has stood tall in the business scenario because its core values have shaped its philosophy and direction towards social responsibility. The group is determined to tread this path and translate values into implementable working systems and that has made them the legend they are today.

A Brief History of the Tata Group

The Founder and His Vision

Jamsetji Nusserwanji Tata, the founder of the group, had a unique vision of development. He knew that political means alone cannot suffice to retain the independence of a nation in its true sense, and that economic development and strength was equally essential. Therefore, he emphasized the need for application of science and technology and modern methods in industrial management. To quote Jamsetji Tata (1839–1904)[1] 'I am far from decrying the noble spirit, which seeks to help a poor or suffering fellow being... (But) What advances a nation or community is not so much to prop up its weakest and the most helpless members as to lift up the best and the most gifted, so as to make them of the greatest service to the country. I prefer this constructive philanthropy, which seeks to educate and develop the faculties of the best of our young men' and with this proactive vision Jamsetji set out on his pioneering journey. His commitment to give back to society was based on the trusteeship concept, propagated by Mahatma Gandhi (see Chapter 1). He embraced the concept of trusteeship and propagated that to survive and prosper, free enterprise must serve the needs of society. These practices were to later become the driving force of the Tata Group.

Jamsetji Tata was a staunch believer in indigenization. He knew that a country can achieve actual freedom only when economic freedom becomes a reality. Therefore, he put his entire energy in creating indigenous organizations to help in India's growth in the economic sphere. Jamsetji Tata founded a trading firm in 1868. He established the Swadeshi Textile Mills, Tata Hydro-Electric Supply Company, and the genesis of the Tata Iron and Steel Company were a part of his vision and struggle.

The Successors' Commitment
His successors founded the Tata Sons Ltd. in 1917, and through its subsidiary Tata Industries Limited, it acted as the managing agent of all the Tata companies. When the Managing Agency System was abolished, respective boards were formulated in each company to manage them professionally. The title legend fits the Tata group because of the extraordinary contribution it has made in every field of human endeavour. It has created an aspiration for achievement in others and is still in the mode of continuous progress. There are many 'firsts' the Tatas have: they gave India its first integrated steel plant, The Tata Iron and Steel Company; India's first power-generating company, Tata Power; one of the first science and technical institutes, the Indian Institute of Science. Airlines were also a dream venture of the Tatas. In fact, J.R.D. Tata was known as the 'father of Indian aviation'.

J.R.D. Tata's comment is an eye-opener to many of today's business leaders who lack the vision that Tata Group leaders had: 'The private sector should realize that they have to play their part in the spirit of trusteeship advocated by Mahatma Gandhi. There is no room in India today for selfish men indulging in understanding acquisitiveness, tax evasion, black marketing, illegal foreign exchange transactions, and conspicuous spending. All these have brought distrust and disrepute to the Indian business community and jeopardized its very survival.'[2]

Walking the Talk
Under J.R.D. Tata's guidance, various agencies were created to discharge social welfare activities. In fact, in 1970, a special resolution was passed that incorporated Clause 3A in its Articles of Association: '...the promotion and growth of the national economy through increased productivity... The company shall be mindful of its social and moral responsibilities to consumers, employees, shareholders, society and the local community'.[3] Further, the ethos is clearly entrenched and reflected in J.R.D. Tata's inaugural speech at the Tata Management Conference in 1955, 'to create good working conditions, to pay the best wages to its employees, and provide decent housing to its workers are not enough for the industry, the aim of industry should be to discharge its overall social responsibilities to the community and society at large where the industry is located.' Historically, the Clause 3A is very relevant because it was in the same year (13 September 1970) that the *New York Times* published an article by eminent economist Milton Friedman in which he pronounced, 'the only social responsibility of business is to make profits'. The event therefore is extremely momentous, as it clearly brought to the forefront, the value-orientation of two extremes.

This ethos can also be seen in Jamsetji's letter, written in 1902, to his son Dorab, describing his vision of the steel town: 'Be sure to lay out wide streets planted with shady trees, every other of a quick growing variety. Be sure that there is plenty of space for lawns and gardens. Reserve large areas for football, hockey, and parks. Earmark areas for Hindu temples, Mohammedan mosques, and Christian churches.'

Core Values

Thus, we find that the core foundation of this much-loved and respected group has been value-based and passed on from generation to generation. This has been the strength of the Tatas, as they were able to create an organization culture that was self-sustaining and did not beg the presence of an individual to manifest its ideas. The fall-back system during a crisis was available in the form of the founding values that guided them to take the 'right' decisions, however stressful they may have proved to be. This is succinctly expressed in the Second Social Audit Report[4] of Tata Iron and Steel. There was a pattern of service to the community, which transcends communal, caste, or state barriers. One may call it 'a pattern of tradition and standards introduced by Jamsetji, in regard to fair and honest management, product quality, human relations in industry, industrial philanthropy, all of which I (J.R.D. Tata) am glad to say have become widely recognized as the Tata industrial ethos.'

The Tatas believe in:
- Ploughing back the wealth generated from efficient business to the community where it was earned
- Treating employees as the producer of the wealth, like members of a joint family
- Treating all stakeholders with due respect and fairness
- Improving the quality of life in the eco-system where it operates

Contemporary Ethos

Given the high degree of internationalization of production, the extensive liberalization of markets that has happened after 1991 in India and the rapid growth in applying technologies and acquiring knowledge in techniques of business management demands an inter-disciplinary macro-approach to issues related to business and economics. The Tata group has always tried to keep pace with this need. Today, the Tata group has footprints in almost every sector, viz., engineering, energy, materials, consumer products, chemicals, communication and information systems, automobiles, and services. The combined group companies enjoy a market capitalization of Rs 2,51,487 crore ($5661 crore) as on January 10, 2008.[5]

Looking at the variety of modern ingenious initiatives that the Tata group has taken, the authors had to choose one of the initiatives due to constraint of space and time to give an understanding of the group's commitment to holistic development. We decided to showcase the gainful utilization of hazardous solid leather waste, as this initiative has been a breakthrough in the area of treating and managing this toxic waste, which for a long time was considered untreatable as well as not eco-friendly, of the Tata International company at Dewas.

Tata International Limited[6]

Background

Established in 1962, Tata International has evolved from an export house into an international business company, with a global turnover of US$850 million in 2006–07. In international trading, it encompasses the entire value-chain from sourcing products to delivery. The company has taken on various value-added roles and has stakes in a cross-section of businesses.

Its business lines include leather, engineering, and pharmaceutical products. With the worldwide reach provided by a well-integrated network that spans the globe, the company has strengthened its capability to source globally, deliver world-class quality, work with global brands, and has developed some key international alliances for sustaining future growth. Its major markets are Europe, Africa, SAARC, ASEAN, West Asia, the Far East, and Oceania.

Tata International has an estimated turnover of US$28.8 billion (equivalent to 3.2 per cent of India's GDP). Besides its trading-house profile, the company has stakes in mines, a five-star hotel, distributorships, trailer and railway wagon manufacturers, and IT ventures. It has customer support facilities for Tata vehicles, design studios for leather, and warehouses dotted across the world.

In tune with the Tata ethos, Tata International is a signatory to the United Nations' Global Compact. The R&D division of Tata International's Leather GBU, the company's only manufacturing operation, fosters environmental projects that look at the future needs of the leather industry, including patented technologies for energy generation from waste and for leather processing. In this respect, in 2003 the company won the Rajiv Gandhi Award for Environmental Protection and in 2005 it won the TERI Corporate Environmental Award.[7]

Some of the Developmental Activities[8]

Tata International has undertaken various developmental activities in and around its production facilities. It has tried to keep the needs of the indirect stakeholders in mind while designing these activities, as can be seen from the list of community-related activities encouraged by the group:

- Co-operatives to generate leather industry-related employment for women at Indore and Mhow in Madhya Pradesh
- Maintenance of a public children's park in Dewas town
- A public library in Dewas, supervised by workers as a volunteer activity
- Marketing consultancy and computer classes for NGOs as a volunteer activity
- Commencement of Tata Public School in Dewas
- Provides training to women in the manufacture of leather articles at a vocational training centre, the Leather and Jute Training Centre at Indore, in collaboration with the Madhya Pradesh Handicraft Development Board (Hasta Shilp Vikas Nigam)
- Donation of finished leather to a leprosy hospital every year for making shoes for patients

- Tata International is also a member of the Tata Council for Community Initiatives and participates in regional programmes.

Environment protection activities include
- Planting of 200,000 trees at the leather factory at Dewas
- Building a deer park at the leather factory at Dewas
- Reforestation of the Tekri hillock in Dewas town
- Construction of a sophisticated effluent treatment plant at the leather factory
- Building a reverse-osmosis plant for liquid waste
- The inception of the pioneering biomethanation pilot plant
- Undertaking research and development projects, like processes for chrome-free leather and process changes study for eco-labelling of leather products.

Efforts at energy conservation can be seen in the commencement of one of India's largest solar thermal water-heating systems at the leather factory.

To provide support to the community, Tata International provides financial assistance to NGOs in the fields of education, environmental consciousness, healthcare, medical research, and social welfare.

Core Values of Tata International

As in all Tata Group companies, the core values revolve around the company's Articles of Association and the Tata Code of Conduct (as mentioned earlier in this case study). This document is signed by every Tata International employee. It seeks commitment to community development and social responsibilities from all members of Tata International. The core value states: 'We must always conduct our business with fairness, honesty, and transparency, so that we can at all times stand public scrutiny. We will never undermine the heritage of trust that comes with the *Tata brand*'. The company's vision statement endorses the role of a socially responsible manager by encouraging them to 'become a proactive, integral, and responsible member of our environment and communities'.

The Modern CSR Initiative

High-rate Biomethanation Plant Based on Hazardous Solid Waste from the Leather Industry[9]

Place of installation:	Dewas, Madhya Pradesh
Date of commissioning:	September 2002
Status functioning on 1 January 2008:	Running continuously
Implementing agencies:	Tata International Limited and MNES (Govt. of India)
Technology:	Tata International Limited
Patents:	IN 188788 and IN 188789
Technology institution for monitoring:	Central Leather Research Institute, Chennai

Background

The biomethanation demonstration plant, based on Tata International Ltd., R&D, patented technology at TIL, Dewas, sets an example for the entire global leather industry. Before this technology, it was considered that chromed leather solid wastes is non-biodegradable (due to the presence of bonding between collagen and chromium) and hence, these wastes had to be disposed in a secured landfill, leather board manufacturing, or as a low-grade fuel in brick kilns. This mode of disposal is not an environment-friendly method, but this technology takes care of utilization of these wastes gainfully, vis-à-vis, reducing greenhouse gas (GHG) emission. As the technology developed with non-degradable solid waste (all bio-digesters technologies are based on self-bio-degradable solid waste, e.g., cow dung, municipal wastes, etc.), no in-house/outside expertise was available. Thus, it would have been a challenging task for a commercial scale-up of this technology.

Leather processing solid wastes like shaving dust, wet blue trimming, and others have now been classified as hazardous wastes because of chromium, as per Schedule–2 by Ministry of Environment and Forests, Government of India. The work presented here forms the later part of a comprehensive process developed and awarded to two patents for gainful utilization of these hazardous solid wastes to solve their disposal problem through:

1. Energy recovery from these renewable non-conventional sources by biomethanation
2. Resource recovery of chrome as basic chromium sulphate (BCS) for process need

The process involves treatment of shaving dust/trimming with alkali at an elevated temperature and isolating the inorganics. These inorganics are treated with H_2SO_4 and the chrome is ultimately recovered as BCS. The BCS is obtained in solution form, ready for use as a tanning agent.

Other than the high-value environment care of solving the hazardous solid waste disposal problem, the other advantages of the comprehensive process are:

1. Recovery of energy through biomethanation
2. Recovery of chrome from waste as a resource recovery for recycling and economic viability
3. The remaining 5 to 10 per cent of original material left as residue would no longer be hazardous waste, as the chrome has been removed and recovered
4. Solving of hazardous waste disposal problem saves soil/ground-water pollution
5. Reducing GHG emission

These advantages drew application from the Ministry of Non-conventional Energy Sources (MNES) G.O.I., New Delhi, for this work. As a result, a full-scale demonstration plant as a J/V between MNES and Tata International Ltd. DEWAS (TIL, Dewas) using this TIL-Research and Development (R&D) technology is implemented for the benefit of the leather industry as a whole.

Technology involved
No process is presently available commercially for the treatment of hazardous chromed leather solid wastes. Hence, after exploring several possibilities, a novel method of gainful utilization of these hazardous solid wastes through energy and resource recovery was conceived and work was started in this laboratory quite some time ago.

TIL, R&D Concept
TIL, R&D worked proactively to look for a process, which can use this waste gainfully. An innovative concept of utilizing these wastes towards a self-sustaining environmental care project was worked out as a composite process.

The concept was to treat the solid wastes to separate the chrome and the organics. The organics would go for biomethanation and chrome would be recycled for leather-making. The steps needed for this to be successful are:
- Pre-treatment of waste to make it amenable to biomethanation
- Establish the biomethanation parameters to generate substantial fuel gas to be used in-house
- Recover chrome as BCS for captive consumption

Wet blue being almost 85 per cent collagen and 15 per cent inorganic, the collagen is extracted by hydrolysis and used for anaerobic digestion (UASB mode). Simultaneously, chrome is recovered and recycled as BCS for wet-blue making/rechroming with equal efficiency as commercial BCS. The process leaves behind less than 5 per cent residue containing mainly $CaSO_4$ for disposal, which has become non-hazardous. Biomethanation parameters for this collagen hydrolysate called gelatin have been established, giving bio-gas (65–70 per cent CH^4). Pilot trials had shown efficiencies of gelatin extraction and chrome recovery to be around 95 per cent and above. This comprehensiveness of energy and resource recovery, together with low cost makes this environmental care process unique and self-sustaining.

For the first time in the world, this kind of new technology commercially demonstrated a totally sustainable solution of treating chromed leather solid wastes gainfully, generating bio-gas using the organic part of chromed solid wastes and recovery of chromium, which is recycled for the process needs of the leather industry. Due to the uniqueness of this technology, MNES came forward sharing 50 per cent of the total project cost with TIL, Dewas. CLRI, Chennai, monitored the project execution. The plant is running well since 2002, and at present generating almost 6000M^3 biogas/month and 10000 kg BCS (10 per cent solution)/month with a processing capacity of 700 tons of hazardous waste per annum. A core team led by the Chief, R&D, addresses environmental issues associated with production, products, use, and recycling of materials from which they are made, on a continuous basis.

Since the leather industry is divided into small clusters and most of the companies are not as big as TIL, the initial investment may be a constraint. To overcome this problem, the technology can be implemented in the form of CSTPs (common solid waste treatment plant) like CETP (Common Effluent Treatment

Plant). The Government of India, along with TIL, CLRI, and CII can work together to implement this technology in different leather clusters to generate electric power from leather waste.

A brief view of the environment-friendly technology and the chronological and technical details of the process in the leather plant of Tata International is given below:

A Way Forward to Sustainable Development

Hazardous Waste Recycling
- Recycling capacity of 700 tons per annum of chromium containing leather waste
- Bio-gas from chromium containing leather waste project 50 per cent sponsored by MNES (Project cost ~ 1 crore)
- Methane gas production 200m^3 per day
- Chromium recovery and recycling 12 tons per annum as chromium sulphate
- Two patents on 'hazardous waste recycling'

Water Recycling
- Reverse osmosis plant on treated effluent recycling
- RO plant capacity 100 m^3 per day
- Ground-and roof-water harvesting

Energy Saving
- Large solar array (~700 nos.) for heating boiler feed-water
- Capacity 50 m^3 per day to 80°C
- Specific power consumption reduction in leather processing (~ 2 per cent each year)
- Bio-gas from leather waste

Air Pollution Prevention
- Cyclone dust separator
- Membrane panel in boiler

Maintaining Bio-diversity
- 2 lac trees planted all around the complex
- Plantation at Dewas Tekri
- Distribution of saplings for plantation, to employees

Chronology of Events for Bulk Implementation
1994–96: Bench-scale data established
Late 1996: Ministry of Non-conventional Energy Sources brainstorming session on leather industry's waste treatment process
1997: MOU signed by Tata, CLRI, Chennai, and MNES, GOI
1998: DPR preparation
March 2002: Plant installed
August 2002–December 2004: Commissioning testing, and completion of the project

Technical Information

Solid waste treatment:	Chromed leather waste
Plant capacity	700 ton/year
Chromed leather dust:	1.2–1.5 tons/day
Digester effective volume:	240 m³ approx.
Feed rate:	10–15 m³/day
Biogas produced:	~ 200 m³/day
Digester retention time:	16–24 days
Efficiency of digesters:	~ 60%
Chromium recovery:	~ 99%
BCS recovery	1.0–1.5 ton/month
Power consumption	60 kwh/day

Manpower Requirement

Engineer	1
Chemist	1
Operators	2
Workers	6

Cost Economics

Total cost of the project is approximately 1.0 crore; 50 per cent has been borne by MNES and the remaining 50 per cent by TIL, Dewas. The land and other supportive facilities were borne by TIL, Dewas.

Benefits Achieved

The construction of this unique solid waste management plant has helped various stakeholders by providing: cost reduction, so more profits to shareholders; employment to local people, ensuring better environment management; and thus, improving the quality of life of the community. The benefits can be summed up as: the creation of an environmental care plant, which is self-sustaining and helps in solving the hazardous solid waste disposal problem. This has improved the efficiency of production processes and reduced wastage and cost of disposal by recycling waste gainfully. Clean technology has been achieved through scientific and technical processes such as the following:

- Converting—hazardous non-degradable waste to non-hazardous waste gainfully
- Recycling of chromium, which saves the soil/underground water pollution
- Environmental-friendly disposal of hazardous waste
- Energy generation from non-degradable waste
- Reduction in GHG emission

Awards

Naturally, this innovation brought much recognition and accolades to the Tata organization. It helped the Tata brand become stronger and it continues to be respected as a socially conscious organization. Some of the awards received by Tata International are:

- TERI Corporate Award for Environmental Excellence in 2005
- 'Environment Award for Best Practices' Madhya Pradesh Fovernment in 2004
- National Award for Prevention of Pollution in 2002–03 by Ministry of Environment and Forests
- Rajiv Gandhi National Quality Award 2000 in best of all categories
- ISO 14001 and ISO 9001–2000 certification

Argument: Making Sense of CSR

The question may be asked, specially keeping in mind Friedman's description of social responsibility, 'Has the Tata International actually wasted the shareholders money by foraying into activities that should actually be the responsibility of the government of a country?' The answer can be found in the answer to counter questions like, 'Is it just and right on the part of an organization to destroy the socio-cultural fabric and devastate the environment for their personal profits? Can the government be held responsible to find answers for all ills that plague a nation? Do the citizens have a responsibility to ensure that the future generations are better provided for? As individuals, should we not honour the trust that society places on us to make life more comfortable and enjoyable?'

Beyond the Bottom line

The Tata House understood right from its inception that the narrow adherence to the bottom-line does not automatically improve common good as proposed by Friedman, and therefore, the focus has always been to balance the satisfaction of all stakeholders (as mentioned in the beginning of the case). This 'enlightened self-interest' (as business ethics theories define it), which goes beyond measuring activities on the basis of whether they are legal or honourable to a higher level of holistic human existence, has become the core foundation values on which all Tata group businesses are founded.

Social Perceptiveness

The interesting aspect is that the technological innovation that the R&D department of Tata International conceived of was about low-cost detoxification of the waste that was the residue in leather production. Leather industries are functioning in several developed countries but the initiative came from the Tatas in India, where actually the pollution laws are not as stringent as elsewhere. Tata International did not wait for a law to innovate. It was proactive in trying to solve a problem that, as experts, they knew could have a devastating impact in social and environmental terms. The cost was kept low because small plants supplying leather products cannot meet the cost of putting up the treatment plant. Today, with this innovation, small clusters of leather SMEs can also ensure environment protection and control pollution.

The best practice followed by the Tata group has helped many other similar industries to ensure that the environment is protected and there is saving of a scarce resource like water. This aim of greater good for the long-term health of the economy has lived up to the Tata culture. It highlights the role of early conditioning among Indian business houses and demystifies the myth that CSR is a very novel concept, and more so to India.

The need, an obligation, and an opportunity for the field of CSR practice to reclaim a prominent position of influence in leadership and ethics, particularly in the global domain, has been well-exemplified by the Tata Group. The above-mentioned innovation of the Tata Group gives a glimpse into the fundamental value-system of the organization. The use of science and technology for the comfort and convenience of mankind is the hallmark of a true professional vision. The plant is situated in one of the most water-scarce areas of Madhya Pradesh—Dewas. When the Government of India requested the Tata Group to help in the development of the region, they could not refuse.

Conclusion

Today, the Tata Group has emerged as the world's sixth most reputed company and has been ranked fifth in governance and third in leadership.[10] The Tatas have epitomized that 'beyond the bottom-line' value accelerates and accentuates profit, rather than slowing it or diminishing it. This is amply demonstrated by the fact that three of the group companies form a part of the sensex (the most to represent a corporate) and the combined weightage of the market-cap of the three companies in the sensex is 6.4 per cent. The Tatas also have 13 other listed companies, excluding the three that are part of the sensex.[11]

The latest community-related project that they are involved in is a wasteland management project. Tata Steel will initiate 6,500 acres of wasteland development programme in Jharkhand and extend it to Orissa and Chhattisgarh (it should be noted that all these states are ranked low in both economic and social development parameters). The initiative is to boost agricultural income and motivate people. The company targets to boost agricultural income from Rs 8,000–Rs 12,000 crore per year to Rs 20,000 crore per year.[12] These efforts highlight the fact that:

- Tatas have tried to balance the stakeholders' demands in the best possible way. The Tata share has always traded at levels that has brought returns to the shareholder and instilled confidence in the investors
- The organization has always tried to look beyond the immediate contracts to innovative services for both its employees and customers
- The community has always played a very important role in the Tata agenda of growth and they have ensured that contributions to public events, programmes, and services have been undertaken ungrudgingly
- The vision of the founding fathers of ensuring the socio-economic growth of India has been undertaken in a proactive manner by the Tata group
- The Tatas have carried the Indian brand to the global platform by providing an authentic image of being responsible and following high standards in its activities. The 'Made in India' image owes much to this pioneer. In doing all this, it has earned for itself the brand of being the legend, in every aspect of quality.

The Tata group has truly justified 'business is part of the solution and its potential is driven by its engagement', as stated by Björn Stigson, President of the World Business Council for Sustainable Development (WBCSD).[13] 'Doing business' for this group can be simply defined as 'looking beyond the bottom line' and proving that the strategy actually leads to achieving higher returns in the bottom-line.

Discussion Questions

1. Taking into account the history of the Tata Group, how do you think the group built an ethical business foundation?
2. What was the role played by the leaders in creating the value-foundation of the organization?
3. In your opinion, how has the Tata group used the 'stakeholder theory'?
4. How do you think the initiative of Tata International has helped in catering to the stakeholder theory?
5. In today's competitive world, is it a wise decision of the Tata group to spend company resources on CSR? Justify your answer.

End Notes

1. Quoted in Manshardt, Clifford, 'Pioneering on Social Frontiers in India', *TISS*, Bombay, 1967, p. 76.
2. *Economic Times*, 1980.
3. Pandey S.N., *Social Side of Tata Iron Steel*, Tata McGraw-Hill, New Delhi, pp. 20–21, 1991.
4. Tata Iron & Steel, The Second Social Audit Report, 1991, Steel City Press, Jamshedpur, January, 1992.
5. http://www.tata.com.
6. http://www.tatainternational.com/
7. http://www.tatainternational.com/
   http://www.tatainternational.com/abt-intro.html.
8. http://www.tatainternational.com/abt-social.html.
9. Tata International in-house report reproduced with the permission of Tata International.
10. Press Trust of India, New York, 5 June 2008, as reported in the *Global Pulse Report* compiled by Reputation Institute, US.
11. http://www.tata.com.
12. *Business Standard*, 24 June 2008.
13. Geneva, 6 August 2008, Business in Deep at World Water Week, http://www.wbcsd.org/Plugins/DocSearch/details.asp?DocTypeId=251&ObjectId=MzEwMDE.

Role of Various Institutions in CSR

INTRODUCTION

The concept of CSR brings to the forefront the human aspect of development. It reminds every professional that they are people first, and therefore, human relationships have to be managed efficiently. Development cannot be uni-dimensional; it has to cater to all the players in the economy, polity, and society. A matrix of relationships based on trust between the partners of growth needs to be established. CSR signifies the concept that it is better to have a shared interest in a successful development process than to dominate a failed, dissatisfied, socio-economic structure. Therefore, the role of major institutions in the CSR process needs to be analysed and understood. Each institute can act as a check and balance on the other to ensure distributive justice in the sharing of the development synergies. For example, the government can check the destructive growth by private industries for profit. The media and NGOs can reveal corruption and weaknesses in the government system. The system has to move beyond the laws and rules to the value arena to create a symbiotic existence among all the stakeholders. This chapter deals with the four major institutions, namely the government, non-governmental and non-profit organizations, educational institutions, and the media, since they all make extremely important contributions to CSR, either directly or indirectly. There are other smaller institutions that also contribute but can be put under the aegis of the major institutions portrayed here.

LEARNING OBJECTIVES

After studying this chapter, you will be able to
- Understand that CSR is integral to the development process
- Understand the role of the major institutions of the civil society in CSR
- Create an awareness of certain institutional initiatives in progress and the need for further contribution in the field

ROLE OF GOVERNMENT

In spite of exponential economic growth, globalization, and liberalization, there has not been any real progress in addressing human issues. Instead of ensuring a holistic growth, economics has been used to amass wealth and increase the division between the haves and the have-nots. Therefore, there seems to be a growing consensus that government should intervene to ensure justice and fairness. However, this requires extremely fine balancing between autocracy and democracy, which is the actual challenge, and so let us look at how CSR can be used to balance the two.

It is believed that governments should accept moral responsibility for the well-being of their citizens. History is witness to kings and empires (and the governance structures built by them) recorded as great because of their contribution to the growth of the nation. Whatever the form of a political institution, it cannot ignore the common folk. Governments throughout history have either used force to keep manpower and money power coming together, or used manipulative methods to seduce the common man into believing that his welfare is at the top of the list. Some have actually contributed to the greater good of the masses. Therefore, we need to carefully analyse what is the role that the government is playing through its values, vision, and strategies in promoting CSR. The modern concept of public-private partnership (PPP) has to be debated impersonally, creating a win-win situation in all the three dimensions—society, economics, and politics. It cannot work as a nexus between government and business under the pseudo-umbrella of providing space to each other. The complex set of relationships that have to be taken care of as a social responsibility of the government needs a very clear focus on the understanding of development and its tangible and intangible benefits.

The magical concept of the virtue of the market seems to have faded when we are faced with the underbelly of progress throwing up issues of human degradation, pollution, climate change, ecological imbalances, 'gendercide' (specifically female infanticide), to name a few. The questions are: Why has the market failed to deliver? All human beings are supposed to be basically good and believe in collectivist living and therefore, great civilizations and social institutions like family, marriage, and festivals have been created to celebrate the feeling of sharing and giving. Then why is the divide between the rich and the poor increasing? Have our own mechanisms failed us by creating unethical negative emotions like greed, hatred, and jealousy in our search for happiness?

Different Markets

The answer may be found when we analyse the different markets in which business operates. The three major markets are the capital market, the labour market, and the consumer market.

Capital Market
The capital market provides the basic necessities for production in terms of resources like land, finances, machinery and technology, raw materials, etc.

While participating in this market, does the firm operate with CSR as a high priority? Probably not. The search is for cheaper, quicker, sources rather than ethical sources because the name of the game is competition. Very often, the quality of inputs is compromised because it is a cost to the company and profits may suffer. The long-term perspective may not be attractive to business when performance is measured quarterly. Investors measure opportunities based on the financial well-being of the company and CSR may not be playing a very prominent role in such performances. One can argue that CSR will bring better financial returns in the long run, but it seems so elusive and qualitative that capital markets are not actually driven by CSR. Firms may be using CSR only as a seductive notion to keep any kind of external control, like government regulations, away from their activities.

Labour Market

The labour market is another interesting arena. It is believed that education creates responsible, trustworthy, dependable people. This is also the need of the highly specialized world of today. As we specialize, the depth of knowledge increases but the width of knowledge decreases (one learns more and more about less and less!). This means today we are more interdependent than we were in the past and to honour this interdependence we need trust. In a professional course class if students are asked to identify their favourite company, it would always relate back to the pay package and turnover of the company. It is never about how responsible the company is. Therefore, the company that offers the highest package gets the best brain. Since our system of education worldwide is based more on sharpening the intellect than the human emotional aspect, the labour market also participates in exploitative behaviour in collusion with the organization (see Chapters 2 and 3). The big question is, 'Who will honour the common man's trust on professionals and business to create a more comfortable life?' This truth is borne out by the fact that today Harvard Business School has a student initiative where students sign up to take an oath that they would not consent to any organizational activity that is unethical. There is talk in academic circles whether business professionals, like doctors or lawyers, should also have external sanctions from business bodies or government that disqualify them from practicing their skill when they indulge in unethical practices. (See the Aspen CBE initiative in the section—Role of Educational Institutions.)

Consumer Market

It is interesting to note that the consumer market is also not really driven by responsible behaviour, although they can play a big role in promoting CSR. First, consumers are not willing to bear the extra cost of CSR in the form of higher prices. It is only a few niche brands that can command an extra price on the basis of a responsible product or service. Usually, consumers are driven by advertisements to buy a product and not on whether the company has been operating ethically. Therefore, companies say that since CSR does not sell, we do not highlight it in the market. Though business touts that consumer is the king, what actual power does the king have besides the veto power (the power to reject a product by not buying it)? Veto power can operate only when there is transparency and equal information available for a consumer to make a choice. Monopolies (single product or a company ruling the market) and oligopolies (small groups coming together to rule the market) limit this free choice, thus limiting the virtue of the market from providing the best to the consumer. The consumer is at the mercy of the producer. As a result of expertise and resources, the producer has the right to design, price, and distribute the product. Consumers have to come together to create the collective bargaining power to ensure responsible behaviour in the market, otherwise the 'king would be toppled everyday' and kingship of consumers would remain a myth. This effort is, to an extent, supported by the government through its consumer forums and consumer courts. However, there is still room for further growth. The Wal-Mart supply chain issue (Exhibit 4.1) highlights how consumer-centric behaviour can lead to unethical behaviour with other stakeholders and also how only consumer activism can stop this kind of rapacious (greedy and grasping) behaviour.

EXHIBIT 4.1

The Wal-Mart Controversy

Terry Collingsworth, attorney of the International Labour Rights Fund, took up the cause of workers from China, India, Indonesia, Nicaragua, Swaziland, and California. He filed a lawsuit on behalf of workers against Wal-Mart for denial of basic wages, forced extra hours of work, as well as not allowing the right to organize on 13 September 2005. Sam Walton, the founder of Wal-Mart, did not dream of becoming the world's largest retail chain. Throughout his career, he wanted to bring development and relief to the rural American South by bringing in a large variety of products at low prices to his consumers. He believed in respect for the individual, service to customers, and striving for excellence.

The success of such a benevolent vision can be seen from the statistics: sales recorded in 2006 were over $4312 billion worldwide and net income exceeded $11 billion. It had 1.8 million associates and 6100 stores worldwide. However, this dream, pursued by qualified professionals, lost its focus somewhere in the process of its growth. In its search to be on top by continuing to offer consumers the best deals, Wal-Mart turned a blind eye to many unethical practices. For example, Wal-Mart shifted its purchasing to China, where labour was cheaper, environment and pollution control less stringent, and laws and regulations manipulative. In trying to continuously please the retailer, Wal-Mart contained the profit margins of the suppliers to beyond survival limits as illustrated by the Vlasic pickle company's bankruptcy. The 'gallon jars' of Vlasic pickle were priced by Wal-Mart at $2.97. Though it sold well, the profits reduced by 25 per cent because the smaller jars were no longer popular and since Wal-Mart was selling at this forced controlled price, the consumers did not purchase from other stores. In forcing Vlasic to comply with its pricing policies, the Wal-Mart business model had changed Vlasic from a brand-led business into a commodity discounter, with disastrous results. These and similar events have led to the Wal-Mart brand suffering, specially under consumer scrutiny, and today Wal-Mart is struggling to regain its consumer trust.

It is interesting to note that such unethical business practices have occurred in spite of Wal-Mart having incorporated high standards of belief and values for suppliers and a stringent inspection checklist. Therefore, the contention is that CSR needs to be woven into the strategy of an organization to ensure benefits to all stakeholders.

Sources: www.walmart.com; Sevin, Molly, 'Wal-Mart Faces Suit by Labor Group', *Los Angeles Times*, 14 September 2005, http://laborrights.org, http://walmartstores.com; Lichtenstein, Nelson, ed. *Wal-Mart: The Face of Twentieth-Century Capitalism*. Misha Petrovic and Gary G. Hamilton—'Making Global Markets—Walmart and Its Suppliers', The New York Press, New York, 2006, p. 133; Lichtenstein, Nelson, opcit. James Hoopes, 'Growth through Knowledge', p. 92; http://www.laborrights.org/creating-a-sweatfree-world/wal-mart-campaign/news/11611, accessed on 17 July 2010.

Looking at the above concerns, the only viable alternative is that the government plays a very proactive role to ensure that CSR is promoted. Even companies that practice CSR very aggressively, such as the Tatas, Johnson & Johnson, Unilever, Infosys, Mattel Toys, etc., need the necessary support from a publicly accepted body because there is a limit to a corporation's efforts. It is the responsibility of the government to create the necessary safe environment for business investment, provide basic infrastructure, reasonable regulatory processes, and public policies. Governments have to create a level playing field for all players, but it is easier said than done. Some of the reasons are given below.

(a) Every country with its unique culture, history, and political institutions needs to address the socio-economic issues exclusively.
(b) Multi-national corporations (MNCs) may bring about an increase in the standard of living in a country, but the fall-out in areas of resource exploitation, environmental disasters, employment policies, and financial and marketing concerns may nullify CSR.
(c) The vested interests of corporates may lead to the formulation of policies that may keep out fair competition or may be aimed at promoting their

products and services behind the facade of social responsibility, e.g., the controversy over genetically modified food, which is about a choice of having higher yields to feed more hungry people, against health issues over a long period. More importantly, genetically modified crops cannot be recycled as seeds, like traditionally grown crops, for the next sowing season. Therefore, large corporations involved in agricultural products would have the monopoly over seeds, which actually translates into endangering the food sufficiency of a country.

(d) Governments themselves may have a vested interest in engineering policies that may cater to their party funds by favouring certain industrial lobbies and cartels, especially in multi-party democracies like India, or even in developed countries like the US, or in the European Union.

Therefore, the role of the government needs to be understood as a collaborative process that seeks a balance between authority and responsibility. An equitable distribution of cost and benefits between the two entities, government and business, has to be the ground reality and not a patchwork of certain CSR policies that remain on paper. Governments everywhere have to wake up to the reality that their purpose is to ensure that social responsibility is incorporated in their role, relationship, and influence, otherwise the whole concept of the term 'governance' is defeated. Governance relates to enforcing of laws and regulations with the objective of ensuring justice, fairness, and peace, to encourage economic development. Governance is about the proactive actions that need to be implemented to reduce the gap between the haves and the have-nots of society. Governments were created to ensure the welfare of people, so they must represent people in the true spirit and not be dominated by elitist or interest groups seeking selfish personal gains.

Most governments tend to justify their activities on the utilitarian principle of greatest good for the greatest number. The danger here is that moderate benefits may be provided to large numbers at the cost of severe discomfort to smaller groups. The discomfort may fester into activities like terrorism or fundamentalist movements in the name of offering justice to the ignored smaller groups. This naturally would eat into the process of development by creating fear psychosis, extra security expenditure, and destruction of national wealth. It creates a vicious cycle of deprivation and violence, questioning the very basis of the freedom of the human spirit. Every regulatory body, as part of the government of a country, has to ensure distributive justice. To ensure justice and fairness in the process of distributive justice, it has to be based on the absence of specific information, which is called the veil of ignorance (Rawls 1958). The absence of specific information means it prevents anyone from knowing whether he/she is advantaged or disadvantaged, based on social class and fortune. Thus, the problem of better bargaining power from the position of better knowledge, physical prowess, or economic strength does not impact the principle of fair distribution. Under this principle, governments have to rise above petty self-centred consumerism. This would ensure that markets remain competitive, there is equality of opportunity in every sphere, resources are utilized efficiently, and the outcome of business in the form of wealth is distributed to ensure appropriate minimum socio-economic existence. The political machinery has to work towards providing civil liberties and freedom of thought and choice. The social capital has to be enhanced through developing human capital by providing overheads like free education, family allowances, graded taxation, mandatory disclosures, and the right to information. Corruption has to be rooted out to ensure true competitiveness in the markets by preventing socio-economic barriers to achieving desirable profits. Thus, the government has to oversee the spread and distribution of the above-mentioned activities through strict rules and vigilance. The growth of a well-balanced and viable socio-economic system depends on a strong political will.

The case on the Internet privacy issue in China (Exhibit 4.2) shows the misuse of authority by government to forge a nexus with business for self-interest.

EXHIBIT 4.2

The Internet Privacy Issue In China

The nexus between government and business to mutually benefit each other is not a new phenomenon. Even during the era of Hitler, business and technology was used to further government ideology. This was revealed when E. Black, the author of *IBM and the Holocaust*, revealed that between 1933 and 1945, IBM's Hollerith punch card technology was used by Nazi Germany to automate the prosecution of Jews. A similar kind of repression of human rights by American Internet companies in China has continuously been reported. Since China provides a large market of Internet users, these companies are willing to bend rules of individual privacy and cater to government authority, as they earn huge profits from this market. The events that forced the issue of questioning unethical partnership between government and business to further each other's agenda were: the arrest and conviction of a journalist because Yahoo! handed over the personal details that were stored in the search service of the company's server. 'Yahoo! was roundly condemned for hurriedly turning over user-information on reporter Shi Tao to the Chinese security forces in 2005. Their actions resulted in a long prison term for Shi for sharing Chinese media coverage policy with foreign sources. The late US Congressman, Tom Lantos, called CEO Jerry Yang a 'moral pygmy' for his collusion and subsequent slippery 'excuse-making'.[1]

Similar incidents like the removal of a politically sensitive blog hosted on a Microsoft server, the self-censorship of search results generated by Google on its Chinese site, the reconfiguration of routers and hubs provided by Cisco Systems in filtering out sensitive key words and phrases, have brought to the forefront the tussle between right to privacy and right to information. Finally, public pressure has led to a bill on the Global Online Freedom Act being introduced in the US in February 2006. Recently, Google threatened to walk out of China on ethical and moral grounds. The conflict between the Chinese government and Google arose in January 2010 because Google decided to end its four-year practice of omitting search results that the Chinese government considers subversive or pornographic. Google blamed the Chinese computer hackers for an attack that it said was aimed at stealing the company's technology and e-mail information from human rights activists. Based on this accusation, Google decided to end its practice of filtering. The showdown was resolved in July 2010, when an official announcement was made by the Ministry of Industry and Information Technology, which regulates internet operations in China, that the government had approved the license for Beijing Guxiang Information Technology Co. Ltd., the operator of Google's China website, according to the official Xinhua News Agency.[2] Again, it becomes obvious that the people who hold power and status and take decisions that have universal repercussions need to view the issues more holistically, rather than in economic profit-making terms.

Sources: 1. http://www.readwriteweb.com/archives/china_yahoo_accounts_hacked.php, accessed on 20 July 2010; 2. http://www.google.com/hostednews/ap/article/ALeqM5gKrY51v O2V86xiICf35Q05J0FIEAD9GSQSR00, accessed on 20 July 2010; Black, E., *IBM and the Holocaust: The Strategic Alliance between Nazi Germany and America's Most Powerful Corporation*, New York, 2001; Morais, R., 'People's Liberation', *Forbes Asia*, 27 February 2006; Briggs, S., 'US Draft Bill Targets China Censorship', *South China Morning Post*, 20 February 2006.

The role of the government lies in providing clear guidance to the business world about CSR policies. Today, companies are struggling to find the right way of pursuing CSR as they have to adhere to an excessive number of complicated rules and norms. Unethicality thrives best in chaos because no one is accountable. Expectations regarding public welfare have to be clearly stated with a proper chain of accountability laid out for monitoring the activities related to the public domain. The limitation of the corporate world and government mechanisms has to be understood mutually by both the actors. Governments can insist on internalizing (bearing the cost) the social and environment costs created by business and business, can pressurize governments for better mechanisms of distribution of wealth, leading to the creation of more purchasing power among more aware consumers.

In a globalized world, the business world represents the nation and its governance structure. Therefore, it is in the interest of the government that they ensure that domestic firms adhere to the norms of responsible social behaviour in the international business world. Very often, a large multinational company's misadventure can compromise a country's reputation. For example, companies like Coca Cola, Nike, De Beers, Shell, and Wal-Mart have given the image of profit-mongering to the developed world, or in common parlance, the western world. On the other hand, countries like India and China have earned the reputation of being corrupt and not quality-conscious because of the shortcuts to profit practised through cost-cutting on quality and integrity. Governments can play an important role here by being the independent regulatory body monitoring such business behaviour through CSR legislation. A two-pronged approach has to be adopted by the government—on the one hand, it should ask for mandatory disclosure of the activities impacting society, and on the other hand, it must educate its people to be able to understand such information. This would promote an environment of informed choices, resulting in more just and fair decisions. It is only the government, as a publicly sanctioned body, that can enforce legislation for companies to internalize their externalities, which means, bear the cost for rectifying the damages that may occur in the environment or socio-economic sphere, as a result of their activities. Since this demand that companies engage in socially relevant activities that are not profitable, and thus, do not meet the market test (success cannot be measured in terms of earning profit from the market), monitoring may become a big challenge. Corporations can falsify information if the checking by government machinery is not strict or if the government officials join hands with the company to get personal gains. Besides macro-level issues like divergences based on cultural and political framework, the organizational structures and the business and economic background in each country can create specific problems needing unique solutions. While monitoring the activities, government has to be careful that its involvement does not become an interference and legal coercion.

Besides the usual companies that we see in the market every day, there are many other businesses, which also require to be regulated. An interesting example is sports and its commercialization in modern day. The incidence of some unethical practices in sports exemplifies lack of morality among professional sportsmen using the taxpayer's money. Should the government intervene in this? Exhibit 4.3 highlights a few such incidents.

EXHIBIT 4.3

Unsportsman-like Behaviour

Sports professionals have also started participating in the commercialization of their profession. The spirit of sportsmanship is lacking and values have reached a new low of degeneration. The unsportsman like behaviour can be gauged from initiatives and activities such as the number of 'umpires' that are there to judge a game because of sportsmen no longer owning up to mistakes and foul play, the unholy nexus between the underworld and players based on betting, sledging in the field, use of drugs, etc. Fixing matches at a price, tampering with the ball to win at any cost, these are everyday stories in the cricket world. Use of drugs by athletes and weight-lifters are examples of extreme commercialization of every activity and the insensitivity and apathy to human excellence.

The IPL scandal in India, which brought to the forefront the deep-rooted corruption involving the sports authority, government servants, players, and individual owners of teams, is a blatant example of profiteering at the cost of the country. When the world was undergoing an economic recession, with people losing livelihoods and not being able to earn even one square meal for the family, there seemed to be enough money available among select individuals to buy players (who actually do not need that kind of money). Honesty seems to be in short supply. When money or material comfort becomes the measure of success, then we are bound to go on a downward journey of inhuman behaviour.

Sources: Times of India, Bangalore, 8 February 2007; *The Hindu*, News Update Service, 28 March 2007.

Therefore, the conclusion that one arrives at is that a broad-based social and moral consensus in the global arena is the need for effective CSR practices. International principles have been designed, like the 'Sullivan Principle' by Reverend Leon Sullivan, a member of the Board of General Motors, US. It was issued originally in 1977 to persuade US companies with investment in South Africa to not participate in the apartheid practiced by the then South African government. This principle gained popularity and was relaunched in 1999 as Global Sullivan Principles to foster human dignity. The Global Sullivan Principles refer to the support for universal human rights, equal opportunities, respect for freedom of association, levels of employee compensation, training, health and safety, sustainable development, fair competition, and working in partnership to improve quality of life. This and other United Nations institution principles can become ready reckoners for phased-out surveys by home governments to evaluate their CSR activities.

Finally, one cannot ignore the fact that at the final assessment, every regulation is dependent on the human subjective as it is the human being who designs them, works with them, and therefore, can also break them if they want to.

Governments, especially democratic governments, have to be careful about the balance between freedom and responsibility. If the government allows direct democracy, which allows citizens to vote on any initiative that they believe should be allowed or disallowed, it can often lead to the 'tyranny of the majority'. This is actually where the utilitarian concept of ethics that speaks of the greatest good for the greatest number faces a road-block. This happens because the concept of majority is rather flexible, e.g., in a group of ten, six is a majority and so is nine. Therefore, if an initiative is supported by six, actually almost half are not represented. In the case of nine, those who get left out may suffer such extreme disadvantage compared to the moderate comfort of the majority that destabilization is ensured. The danger is that direct democracy, like in the state of California (where citizens are allowed to vote on any initiative they want or do not want), may actually undermine and overrule representative government (democracy). As direct democracy is about citizen participation in every decision, it is a threat to individual freedom as the minorities may lose out in the race of representation. Therefore, while the government has to be vigilant about misuse of power by the corporates, it also has to ensure that citizens do not abuse their rights and freedom to exploit others.

The hazards of extreme involvement of the business world in the governance and administrative duties of the state can be understood from Exhibit 4.4.

EXHIBIT 4.4

What Role Should Corporates Play in Politics?

A recent Supreme Court ruling in the US granted corporations the same rights as people with regard to full first amendment political rights, which means that corporations have the right to 'stand' as candidates in the race to be elected as representative of people. It is a landmark decision in the world's biggest democracy. The idea behind it is to 'create the best democracy money can buy'. The first firm to take advantage of this unique ruling and file for candidacy in the election was Murray Hill, a start-up company that is only five years old. The question is, 'Does this company fit the bill of being an adult, i.e., 18 years old before standing for election or are the rules going to be different for companies standing for election?' The candidate running for Congress is not a person but a company. It is indeed a political campaign unlike any other. This candidate is obviously going to put business before people in its agenda. How attractive that would be for the voting community is for the future to decide.

This candidacy promises 24/7 availability to its supporters, unlike persons who are hard to reach once they become political leaders. Since this is a firm doing business, it cannot withdraw from the scene of action. According to the *Washington Post*, the candidate unavailable for interview said in a statement, 'Until now, corporate interests had to rely on campaign contributions and influence-peddling to achieve their goals in Washington. But thanks to an enlightened Supreme Court, now we can eliminate the middle-man and run for office ourselves. Murray Hill will bring enlightened self-interest and corporate accounting to Congress.'

The future of democracy and the role of business within it is the controversial topic that needs to be debated, along with the unique judgement. This influence of business is widely perceived negatively. In fact, Barack Obama, President of the United States, has expressed concern that it will 'open the floodgates to special interests, including foreign corporations, to spend without limit in our elections.'

The big question is, 'Should this influence be encouraged or should there be control mechanisms put in place to restrain companies, and encourage them to exercise self-restraint?' 'Corporate citizenship' is preferred by a growing number of companies to describe their social efforts aimed at making a difference in society. Some companies take these efforts far more seriously than others. 'The Supreme Court ruling takes the corporate-citizenship metaphor a step further by equating what is an artificial creation of the law with flesh-and-blood citizens, at least when it comes to the right to free speech. Yet, just because companies have new rights, that does not mean they must exercise them—or must exercise them through the grubbiest, most unenlightened forms of lobbying.'

It was debated that companies should be transparent about their involvement in government and political processes, just as they are about their activities related to sustainable development. In fact, Robert Monks (a veteran agitator of CSR) highlighted that corporate members have to act responsibly in the way they conduct their business, and also about their relations and engagement (working with or for) with government. Ideally, a firm's involvement in politics should be subject to approval by shareholders and to an annual audit.

This would require a big cultural shift for businesses. There is a pervasive fear that such a law of Supreme Court will give business even more influence over the political process than it has already. But if firms take Mr Monks' advice, it could instead make them more open and accountable with respect to their political activities. This may be a lot to hope for, but surely it is more likely than a company winning a seat in Congress.

Source: 'Campaign stunt launches a corporate "candidate" for Congress' by John Wagner, *Washington Post*, 13 March 2010; 'Conference on Corporate Governance', *The Economist*, 15 March 2010, New York.

ROLE OF NGOs AND NOT-FOR-PROFIT ORGANIZATIONS

The full form of NGO is 'non-governmental organization'. As the name suggests, it is a legally constituted body without any government involvement. Even those NGOs that receive government funding keep their non-governmental status intact and do not allow any government representative to be their members. Though this is a common term, it is not a legal definition and therefore, such organizations are referred to by different names in many countries, like civil society, independent sector, volunteer sector, grassroots organizations, transnational social movement organizations, private voluntary organizations, self-help organizations, and non-state actors' organization. It is estimated that in India there are about one to two million functional NGOs. Though the history of NGOs in different countries can be traced to antiquity, as a generally accepted concept, it became popular with the establishment of the

United Nations Organization in 1945, as per the provisions in Article 71 of Chapter 10 of the United Nations Charter for a consultative role for organizations that are neither governments nor member states. The international NGO got its definition from the 288(X) resolution of the ECOSOC in 1950, stating 'any international organization that is not founded by an international treaty'.

An incorporated organization that exists for educational or charitable reasons, and from which its shareholders or trustees do not benefit financially, is referred to as non- (not) for-profit organization (NPO). Any money earned must be retained by the organization, and used for its own expenses, operations, and programmes. Many non-profit organizations also seek tax-exempt status and may also be exempt from local taxes, including sales taxes or property taxes. Well-known non-profit organizations include Habitat for Humanity, the Red Cross, and United Way, and are also called not-for-profit organizations.

In India, they can be registered in four ways: (1) Trust; (2) Society; (3) Section-25 company; and (4) Special licensing. Registration can be done with the Registrar of Companies (RoC). The following laws or Constitutional Articles of the Republic of India are relevant to the NGOs:

- Articles 19(1)(c) and 30 of the Constitution of India
- Income Tax Act, 1961
- Public Trusts Acts of various states
- Societies Registration Act, 1860
- Section 25 of the Indian Companies Act, 1956
- Foreign Contribution (Regulation) Act, 1976

NPOs need to be managed just as any other corporate. The inherent structure of a NPO is the high level of dedication and commitment to work with and for the disadvantaged groups in society. This naturally needs specialized skills and expertise. Considering the socio-economic condition of the country or region where these NPOs and NGOs operate, the work can be extremely demanding. The funds are usually public donations that get routed either through donor agencies, government bodies, or are given directly to the organization. Unlike the corporate world where investors get a share of the profit, in a NPO or NGO, there is separation between the cause supported and the donor. Actually, the NPO works as the bridge between the beneficiary and the donor, and hence is accountable to both (Padaki and Vaz 2005).

From the above description of a NPO or NGO, we can assess the important role that these institutions can play in CSR. In fact, they can play a very proactive role if they work to facilitate social responsibility by joining hands with the corporate and government. They can work as the conscience of the business world. However, they can also become agents of money laundering by unscrupulous business organizations or government bodies, by posing as the social wing and camouflaging the actual activities. Businesses often tend to use them as facades to keep away legal collective bargaining processes, like trade unions, from questioning the social responsibilities of business. Since the NGOs and NPOs receive funds from donors and venture capitalists, the donors often decide what social cause needs to be addressed. If the donor is residing in a foreign country, they would like to address social issues that is the priority in their country or considered fashionable among the rich. Therefore, very often the priority social causes in the country where the NGO or NPO is operating get ignored. It often happens that donors may insist on changing the focus of work, even if the earlier project is not completed, because a particular social cause is being promoted in the media or social circles. All these often lead to just superficial social work without any concrete results of social upliftment. Therefore, one needs to assess the true worth of such voluntary organizations in their role as CSR promoters.

With the unbridled growth of commercial activities, countries are faced with both positive and negative fallouts. Often, tradition suffers at the hands of commercial growth. This makes people rootless and the fear of such displacement can be addressed by NPOs and NGOs in a more professional manner than either government or corporates. An excellent example is the practice of child labour in India. Children are caught in a vicious cycle of lack of opportunities and poverty, leading to promotion of child labour. Till India does not create enough infrastructure, like better connectivity between rural and urban areas, accessibility to schools, and provision of meals to ensure children do not run away from school, employment, and social security schemes, child labour would remain as a source of livelihood for children and the families they belong to. If by law, child labour is totally eradicated, then social issues like street crimes, drug abuse, human trafficking, and other related concerns would plague society, as has happened in Bangladesh where child labour was banned due to international pressure but there was no contingency plan to absorb these children more productively.

Another major concern is that traditional forms of art are dying because once children are educated, they do not want to go back to their hereditary forms of earning a livelihood. For one, it is hard work and the economics are also not very encouraging for young people to follow traditional professions. This is an area where NPOs can play a major role in conjunction with the government and corporate world, by designing education in a manner that keeps the traditions alive and also by ensuring that right esteem and price is offered to such products. These kinds of initiatives are actually beneficial to all parties concerned because it reduces the burden on the already overstretched facilities of the urban centres and also creates employment and purchasing power, leading to a more viable economic development.

Exhibit 4.5 explains the rice culture of a developed country like Japan, which exemplifies such issues.

EXHIBIT 4.5

Japan and Its Rice Culture

Japan is renowned for its veneration of traditional cultures like the celebration of the rice harvest. The obsession with rice is rooted in the history of Japan. In spite of its affluence, technological advances, and development, Japanese still hold rice as a symbol of pride and the government endorses it with trade restrictions on rice. However, when one journeys through modern Japan, a different story comes to the forefront, like the village of Tochikobu, which nestles in the cold mountainous region of Japan. The variety of rice called 'minami uonuma', from the farms of this village, is one of the best in Japan. It is believed that the snow gives it special purity.

At first glance, the village appears to be prosperous with new cars on the road and a modern school building. The alarming part is that today the school has only 11 students of such varying ages that the school has seven teachers! A decade ago the same school boasted of 120 students. This is the consequence of the trend among young couples to abandon such villages in search of a better life in the cities. The population consists of 40 per cent people above 65 years of age. This phenomenon is described in Japanese as genkai shuraku or the ageing precipice. According to the OECD, 18,775 such communities will lose their traditional character.

The story is the same anywhere else in the world: 'It's a tough life. Even those who have grown up in the village don't want their children to work in the rice fields.' Not only is the physical effort discouraging, even the financial remunerations are not attractive. Each of the 60 households in Tochikobu village own about a hectare of land, but the government pays them to leave a part (one-third) of the land fallow for fear of overproduction. The income from the cultivated land is about 8,00,000 yen (Japanese currency), which is not sufficient to even buy farm machinery.

After the Second World War, when the US ended Japanese isolation, the socio-economic turmoil underwent a change. By the 1960s Japan became a thriving nation with extraordinary growth in agriculture and industry. The farms became flatter encouraging mechanized farming. The use of fertilizers and pesticides improved yields and Japan became self-sufficient in the mystical grain—rice. The industrial renaissance led to a growing demand for labour and attracted the young to these hi-tech goods industries. They were becoming the 'salary-men'.

All this has come at a cost to Japan. As more and more people moved to the cities and became the heralds of modernization, their tastes also changed. Rice no more remained the favourite dish. It was replaced with more westernized food habits of bread and meat. Therefore, the self-sufficiency in rice became surplus rice. The fall in rice consumption is as drastic as half. Today each Japanese consumes about 60 kg of rice annually, which is almost half of the consumption pattern in the 1960s. Since the 1970s, the government is paying farmers to produce less. The elderly Japanese lament this loss of tradition, for farmers suddenly feel redundant in the social scheme.

> The common Japanese grumble about how their money is used to support farmers. Farmers naturally oppose free trade and a substantial number of Japanese support this stand. The catch-22 situation is that if the government allows free trade, then prices would fall and that may lead to more rice consumption. Thus, there appears to be confusion at one end and paralysis at the other, in searching for a remedy to this malady of a disappearing tradition, which results in various socio-economic issues. A glimmer of hope and change is visible in activities undertaken jointly by students, environmentalists, and businessmen, who are promoting organic farming and restoring traditional farming practices. This is where NGOs and NPOs can play the role of saviour and encourage entrepreneurship. The ageing population needs support to continue in their entrepreneurial venture of reviving Japanese traditions. Farmers are hoping that such initiatives would bring back enthusiasm and the danger of succumbing to obsolete Soviet-style collective farming may be averted. The farmers who were the backbone of Japan may recover their pride through these efforts and thus Japan may regain its ancient self-esteem as well.
>
> *Source:* Adapted from 'You Are What You Eat', an article in *The Economist*, 19 December–1 January issue, 2010, pp. 37–39.

Poverty is described as 'pronounced deprivation in well-being' and being poor as 'to be hungry, to lack shelter and clothing, to be sick and not cared for, to be illiterate and not schooled ... Poor people are particularly vulnerable to adverse events outside their control. They are often treated badly by institutions of the state and society and excluded from voice and power in those institutions' (*IBRD*, 2000–2001, 15). Thus, poverty is the sum total of multiplicity of factors. Often, the mistake of taking only income as the indicator of poverty results in flawed solutions to eradicate it. Poverty has to be understood from a wider perspective that includes health, which relates to calorie intake, nutrition, safe drinking water, sanitation, and longevity. Access to land and credit, education, and other infrastructural facilities define the various causes of poverty. The related issues of poverty, like female infanticide, gender discrepancy, illiteracy, and subservience are factors that impact the development of the country. In the long run, poverty causes multifarious damage to healthy human capital, which in turn can lead to an unproductive, unhealthy workforce. This would raise the cost of production in companies, as labour would not be competitive in the world market, because the cost to the company and country on health concerns may be enormous. These are some of the areas where the experience and expertise of NPOs become irrevocable. CSR needs to address these forces unleashed, either because of market forces, government apathy, and corruption, if a true economic environment conducive to investors needs to be created.

CSR would have to confront the issue of women empowerment, along with decrease in the number of tomorrow's workforce and the underlying female foeticide that still plagues the world. The matrix of these factors is related and not amenable to easy solutions. On the one hand, we are celebrating women's economic empowerment that has released women from the shackles of low-paid repetitive menial jobs to aspire for the board room. But the question of balancing motherhood with the challenges of catering to the demands of a well-paid job and a promising career needs serious intervention from government, corporates, and NPOs. How does a society ensure that the next generation is well taken care of, both physically and emotionally? A large number of women opt to remain childless, against the guilt of not providing adequate attention to the child. In the context of fundamental rights, it is the right of an individual to decide whether one wants a child or not. But the bigger issue is the social cost—countries are becoming old like Japan, Canada, and affluent European countries. Tax users are becoming larger in number than the tax payers. How would it be possible for the states to continue to provide the benefits that were symbols of growth and progress, when the revenue is going to become a trickle? Deciding to have children at a later age or using technology to create 'banks' that can store the future generations, in the form of 'eggs', has its own biological hazards concerning the health of the child.

Corporates have to reinvent their human resource policies to support women to balance family life with professional life. Already efforts like flexi-work hours, paid maternity leave, etc. are being put in place but these may also lead to women not being hired, as the cost of hiring women becomes higher when such benefits have to be provided. Therefore, the celebrated women empowerment may not actually fructify and the percentage may remain far below the desirable rate.

It was believed that education would reduce female infanticide in societies that favour boys over girls. Unfortunately, exactly the opposite seems to have happened. In educated couples belonging to the middle class, where incomes are on the rise, the desire for a small family is very strong. Traditional customs of more respect to the mother of a son against that of a daughter, dowry to get the daughter married, and the fact that once the daughter is married, her earnings would contribute to her husband's family income, still have strong roots in societies like India. Therefore, the need for a son to take care of the couple when they are old may bear a strong influence on the desire to have a son. Since one is educated, the knowledge of using technology to detect the sex is prevalent and abortion is legalized to control population—and both technologies are being used to ensure that the baby girl never sees the light of day. In rural societies, where hard physical labour is required, boys are preferred to girls, and therefore, female infanticide is common. A government policy, like the one-child policy in China, has led to more female deaths. Because China is an authoritarian communist state, policies are enforced strictly, unlike in democratic countries like India. Therefore, couples do not want to reveal the birth of a child, if it is a daughter, as they can continue to show that they have one child till they get a son.

All these aspects have resulted in a much-skewed gender ratio. Northern India and China show alarming ratios of almost as high as 124 boys to 100 girls. This means more men are finding it hard to get wives. This again is a social stigma in many Asian societies and such men are considered as 'outlaws', and in China they are called 'bare branches' (*The Economist*, 6–12 March 2010). This naturally is a challenge to natural human instincts, and therefore, there is bound to be a rise in the flesh trade, women trafficking, women suicides, sexual violence, and crime rates.

Thus, it is clear that what may not seem like a problem for the business world on the surface, is actually going to impact it in a major manner in the form of either lack of a qualified healthy workforce, or a social imbalance that can spell disaster to the future development of a country.

These are areas where NGOs and NPOs can contribute with proactive initiatives, in collaboration with the government and the corporate world to ensure that the future developments are sustainable.

ROLE OF EDUCATIONAL INSTITUTIONS

Adomssent and Michelsen (2006, p. 86) state that a university 'does not only need to become more open-minded, it also needs to transform itself into a learning academia, constantly adapting itself to new challenges and comprehending itself as one player interacting with others'. The same argument is also applicable to smaller educational institutions.

Educational institutions should promote an ecosystem suited to CSR throughout their organizations and in the outside world. The advantage of educational institutions is that they are far better positioned to influence and mould the young minds to value-sharing and giving. This is an important aspect of CSR that businesses are unable to handle, for lack of resources that can mould mature minds.

Communication to the stakeholders is an activity that education institutions have to undertake vigorously because they are the training grounds of the future corporate leaders. The immediate stakeholders of a university include present students, future students, corporates and other financial supporters. These students would carry the baggage of their conscious and unconscious learning to the corporate world. This subjective dimension is the cause of the nature of corporate culture. Satisfaction and dissatisfaction and happiness and discontent influence the smooth functioning of the organizations and thus its performance and policies. Academic institutions have to provide the platform for interaction between the corporates and academics for encouraging innovative processes of CSR practices. Students are the largest stakeholders who should be given the opportunity to learn hands-on about CSR.

The ultimate objective is the enhancement of the quality of life of the population. In this, educational institutions can play many roles, essentially to achieve social dynamics. For example, education is a great tool that can persuade people to stop polluting, to adopt healthier lifestyles and diets, to engage in family planning, ensure gender equality, etc.

Academic institutions have a social responsibility to create a better future through processes such as those mentioned below:
(a) Educating the human capital
(b) Promoting the development of knowledge in society by encouraging lifelong learning
(c) Creating an environment for scientific and technological innovations that make human existence more comfortable
(d) Collaborating with the corporate world to help in the processes of advancement through research and development
(e) Disseminating knowledge that creates synergy for socio-economic development

Educational institutions have to play a major role in removing the myth that inequality is natural because only then can solutions be obtained to fight it. Inequality is a major hurdle in the distribution of the fruits of progress. CSR encompasses this issue and academic institutions have to partner with government and civil society to eradicate inequality.

Academic institutions have to play a very proactive and influential role in redressing the fundamental power imbalances between the political realm, the economic realm, and the civil society. The imbalance of power between the major actors, that is the state and the economic realm represented by the business world, cannot be accepted because in the long run, whether the state has more power or the business world has more power, it is the common man in the social sector who really feels the brunt of exploitation. In an ideal scenario, power would be equally divided among the three actors—politics, economics, and society.

The ongoing global crises like the economic recession, climate change, economic imperialism in the name of progress, and patents and sanctions have unleashed concerns about how academic institutions are going to revamp their curriculum and teaching processes to ensure that future leaders and professionals do not plunge the world into similar catastrophes. Similar concerns were raised by the public during 1960s and the 1970s as well, showing that people have constantly questioned unethical behaviour. The media actively supported these issues during the 1970s and most US schools offered a course in business ethics by 1980. The next five years saw consolidation of the idea of business ethics as a field of academic interest with its inclusion in journals, research centres, and conferences. The offering of courses in business ethics paved the way for it to be recognized as an academic discipline (Shaw 1996). The debate whether CSR is a part of business ethics as a discipline or vice versa still rages in academic circles. However, there is certainly a consensus that both are normative sciences that relate to values and morality and need significant attention in academic institutions training future managers.

Realizing the influential role academic institutions play, the United Nations has created a charter, which when signed, binds the academic institutions voluntarily to commit to ten principles of action, encompassing institutional commitment, environmental ethics, university employees' education, environmental education, inter-disciplinary approaches, knowledge dissemination, networking, strategic partnerships and alliances, continuing education programmes, and technology transfer. They have the freedom to decide whether or not to teach themes such as social responsibility and sustainable development. They should not ignore the norms and guidelines of organizations such as UNESCO, UNDP, and EU, since they are in fact key players in promoting CSR.

The Aspen CBE initiative, shown in Exhibit 4.6, is an illustration of the impact of CSR awareness and commitment to social well-being in the academic circle.

EXHIBIT 4.6

Aspen CBE Announces the Launch of TheOathProject.org

To support and promote the idea of a business professional oath, Aspen CBE has joined with three other organizations in undertaking The Oath Project. Aspen CBE and its partners—Association for Professional Business Managers, MBA Oath, and the World Economic Forum for Young Global Leaders—launched TheOathProject.org in 2009 to support this endeavour.

The idea is not new and has been in circulation for quite some time. Strong impetus was given to this idea when more and more professional dishonesty and governance malfunctioning surfaced. In fact, one of the aims of the MBA programmes in the US was a desire to 'professionalize' the practice of management by creating an accountability code. Several MBA programmes have experimented with oaths at various points. For example, in 2005, the Thunderbird School of Global Management adopted a 'professional oath of honor', which has since been taken by students upon their graduation. Recently, the concept has gathered momentum with a number of institutions and academic circles supporting it. In a widely read November 2008 article in the *Harvard Business Review*, Professors Rakesh Khurana and Nitin Nohria suggested a draft oath. World Economic Forum Executive Chairman, Klaus Schwab, has also spoken extensively about the need for an oath. In January 2009, the World Economic Forum at Davos hosted a special session on an oath for business leaders that inspired a group of young global leaders from around the world to begin the process of creating a 'global business oath'. In May 2009, an enterprising grass-roots movement led by Harvard Business School students created the MBA Oath, which was signed by more than half the HBS graduating class of 2009 and also by 1000 other business school students from MBA programmes across the globe. More and more people and organizations are showing interest in this 'self regulatory' method of promoting ethicality.

The leaders of The Oath Project agree that for a universally acceptable oath to be created, continuous upgradation and sharing of information is required. The Oath (as adopted in February 2010) is available on the Aspen CBE website and students can register and sign the oath. According to the founders, the published oath should be used as a common standard by all participating institutions and individuals.

The Management Oath (as adopted in February 2010)
As a business leader, I recognize my role in society.
- My purpose is to lead people and manage resources to create values that no single individual can create alone
- My decisions affect the well-being of individuals inside and outside my enterprise, today and tomorrow

Therefore, I promise that:
1. I will manage my enterprise with loyalty and care, and will not advance my personal interests at the expense of my enterprise or society.
2. I will understand and uphold, in letter and spirit, the laws and contracts governing my conduct and that of my enterprise.
3. I will refrain from corruption, unfair competition, or business practices harmful to society.
4. I will protect the human rights and dignity of all people affected by my enterprise, and I will oppose discrimination and exploitation.
5. I will protect the right of future generations to advance their standard of living and enjoy a healthy planet.
6. I will report the performance and risks of my enterprise accurately and honestly.
7. I will invest in developing myself and others, helping the management profession continue to advance and create sustainable and inclusive prosperity.

In exercising my professional duties according to these principles, I recognize that my behaviour must set an example of integrity, eliciting trust, and esteem from those I serve. I will remain accountable to my peers and to society for my actions and for upholding these standards.

This oath I make freely, and upon my honour.

To learn more about the idea of a business oath and The Oath Project itself, please visit http://www.theoathproject.org.

Source: Adapted from http://www.aspencbe.org/E-newsletter/jan2010.html#1, accessed 12 July 2010.

ROLE OF THE MEDIA

The media is one of the most powerful engines of social change. Unfortunately, due to reasons internal and external to the media world, it has not been tapped to bring about responsible social change. History is witness to the fact that autocratic oppressive governments have always tried to control the media because of its influence and reach. This industry has remained unregulated because democratic political systems shy away from being seen as regulators of free expression of speech and thought. Also, the media with its powerful 'pens' often have 'shot' the hapless regulators.

The benefits of the free press cannot be overlooked. Whenever the media world has wished to achieve some good, it has had a tremendous positive influence on society. We have examples in India like the Jessica Lal case, where the murder case of Jessica was reopened because of the campaign carried out by the media in partnership with the civil society. But the danger is when media companies become the tools of their proprietor for self-promotion or camouflaging unethical activities through biased reporting.

The competition for survival is strong and media companies often trade value and integrity to remain in business. The media world justifies this by saying that they show or write what the public wants. Sensational scoops are considered the highest-selling products of the media companies and with 24-hour channels, very often news needs to 'created'. So where is the business case for social responsibility?

The media has to play the role of a true detective who weighs all the evidence carefully and offers a balanced opinion. It must expose the truth but also keep in mind that the dignity and privacy of the citizens should be maintained. The ethical issue is that media has to balance between two rights in the literal as well as the legal sense—right to information and right to privacy. It has to play the role of not just the entertainer, but also of the informer. Taking sides is not its privilege because society trusts it and it must honour that trust. Media cannot encourage conflict of interest in the name of open journalism. The media world has to create a self-regulatory process keeping the well-being of the civil society in mind.

This is where the concept of CSR fits into the media world. As we have seen in the earlier chapters that rules, codes, systems, and processes can only produce minimum standards. They cannot lead to excellence, which CSR can provide as a best practice. Considering the power and pressure that media can create, it has to create a strong value foundation by embedding virtue into the system. The argument that the inherent virtue of the profession would take care of the media world is flawed. The media is described as the conscience-keeper of the nation and it has to live up to this reputation. It is not the moral police, but certainly, it can highlight and promote morality by reporting cases that enhance human dignity. It has to act as the channel for dialogue between different stakeholders in a society and be the instrument for disseminating development and goodwill. It can infuse solidarity and appeal for joint action across borders to enhance the positive contributions of globalization.

Both the government and the corporates can be monitored by the honest media, and in fact, the media can often play the role of a mediator in sensitive issues by creating a platform for debate. This naturally means that the media itself must be transparent and accountable to be the credible judge of other institutional players, like the government and business stakeholders in CSR. Media companies have often faced the criticism that they do not want to track stories related to social responsibility because it does not ensure readership or viewership and, therefore, demand payment from institutions to print such issues. The fall-out of this attitude is that unscrupulous business organizations can use CSR as a publicity gimmick by joining hands with deceitful media companies. Therefore, the role of media has to be that of a role model of CSR. It has to enhance its understanding of CSR and build public awareness. Media can motivate corporations who are involved in value-added service to society by publicizing their work, and thus creating awareness in society of the need for socially relevant activities and sustainable development. This kind of strategic communication is an important mechanism of social awareness resulting in change. Such communications would create a cycle of sustainability as society would demand responsibility and corporates involved in such responsible behaviour would come into the limelight, thus improving their brand image. This would encourage other corporates to follow suit, as the advantages would be obvious.

When the media strongly supports CSR, it would gain public support and almost blind faith. However, if the underlying motive behind media activism is only brand building, then it would remain an attention-seeking effort without yielding any real change for the better. The media needs to create its ethical code of conduct and a transparent governance procedure to ensure its credibility among the citizens of the world. Perhaps the best advice was given by the erstwhile media baron Joseph Pulitzer, 'Always fight for progress and reform. Never tolerate injustice or corruption; always fight demagogues of all parties—never lack sympathy for the poor; always remain devoted to public welfare; never be satisfied with merely printing the news; always be drastically independent; never be afraid to attack wrong.' Joseph Pulitzer (1847–1911), was a media mughal (Denis 2001).

CONCLUSION

The role of the different institutions can be summed up as providing a path 'between the exploration of new possibilities and the exploitation of old certainties' (March 1991). This means that the different institutions can play specific roles in providing support to the concept of CSR by bringing to the forefront the traditional practices that need to be strengthened and by creating new practices in a changing environment. The most important role of the various institutions is to showcase for business the need to adapt and change in a globalized world. As communication is reducing distances, it is bringing diverse forces closer. To address this challenge, businesses now have to redefine their processes, products, employee relations, and other factors in the value chain. This is where each institution can help to provide the necessary support to ensure long-term success.

As explained above, these institutions help to create the check and balance in each others' spheres of activities and therefore help a nation to decide between controlling, i.e., keeping under government command and restriction, and autonomy which means allowing freedom to everybody interested in the various decisions, initiatives, and programmes. Together, the institutions help to create an environment that goes beyond just compliance to rules to moral responsibility. Therefore, they help to create 'ambidextrous' organizations (idea adapted from O'Reilly and Tushman 2004) that balance between earning profits from society and giving back to society by honouring the trust of society on business. Organizations can no longer take cover under the argument that their responsibility is limited to their authority over resources employed by them. The institutions can create an ambidextrous environment of control and enforcement to ensure that CSR receives the necessary attention it deserves.

An example of this is the Bhopal gas tragedy, which caused the death of more than 20,000 people, with still more suffering till date. Even today, many children are born with congenital defects because of the toxins that were released at that time. This disaster was caused due to negligence on the part of the multinational company Union Carbide (which has been taken over by Dow Chemicals now). The case has dragged on for 25 years and in a recent judgement on 8 June 2010, only two years of imprisonment is the punishment given to the members of the management. 'Too little too late' is the cry of the people who are still suffering. These instances of inhuman treatment can be put in check if the different institutions play their roles in CSR.

Thus, the various institutions have to answer the call of public pressure for radical social change. The public interest in CSR, expressed by questioning the relations of the firm with its customers, the community, and the general public, can no longer be ignored. A well-informed consumer can exert moral pressure on a company's social and environmental performance. The power of the public seeking better corporate policies can be enhanced by the support of the various institutions like government, NGOs, academic institutions, and the media, to name a few of the non-corporate actors. The institutions can bring about better sustainability by promoting authenticity, accountability, and achievability. These three As would make business realize that CSR is not a liability but an asset. A quick check-list for implementing accountability, transparency, governance, and trust in various institutions is provided in the Annexure at the end of this chapter.

SUMMARY

In spite of exponential economic growth, globalization, and liberalization, there has not been any real progress in addressing human issues. Instead of ensuring a holistic growth, trade and commerce has been used to amass wealth and increase the division between the haves and the have-nots. The role of the government lies in providing clear guidance to the business world about CSR policies. Today, companies are struggling to find the right way of pursuing CSR, as they have to comply with a number of complicated rules and norms. Governments, especially democratic governments, have to be careful about the balance between freedom and responsibility. Another important institution is the non-governmental organization (NGO) and the not-for-profit organization (NPO). Unlike the corporate world, where investors get a share of the profit, in a NPO or NGO, there is separation between the cause supported and the donor. Actually, the NPO works as the bridge between the beneficiary and the donor, and hence, is accountable to both. In fact, they can play a very proactive role if they work to facilitate social responsibility by joining hands with corporates and the government. Academic institutions are the other extremely important contributors to the process of CSR. They have to play a very proactive and influential role in redressing the fundamental power imbalances between the political realm, the economic realm, and the civil society. The media is described as the conscience-keeper of the nation and it has to live up to this reputation. It is not the moral police but it can certainly highlight and promote morality by reporting cases that enhance human dignity. The ultimate objective is the enhancement of the quality of life of the population.

KEY TERMS

Ambidextrous A person who can use both hands equally well and competently. Therefore an organization that can balance both profit-earning and social responsibility competently is an ambidextrous organization.
Autocracy Absolute government by one person.
Collectivist A number of individuals coming together and cooperating.
Democracy A system of government by the whole population, usually through their elective representatives who help to run the country.
Enforcement Impose or persist on following an action.
Globalization Related to worldwide acceptance.

Liberalization Opening up of the economy and prevalence of market forces.

Lobbying An organized attempt by a group to influence important decisions.

Monopolies Exclusive control on the trade of a commodity or service by a single company or individual.

Non-governmental organization and non-profit organization Organizations that are not run by the government and organizations that are created to help in the development of a nation without any profit-making motive.

Oligopolies Exclusive control on the trade of a commodity or service by a small group of companies or individuals.

Public-private partnership Sharing of responsibilities by the government and private organizations for initiatives related to the development of a nation.

Specialization Devoting oneself to earn training in a particular branch of interest, skill, or profession.

Strategic communication Extremely important information related to a plan of action.

EXERCISES

Concept Review Questions

1. Analyse the role government or political structure in promoting CSR.
2. Describe how NGOs and NPOs can help in creating purchasing power in a society.
3. Should academic institutions include CSR and business ethics as a part of their curriculum? Justify your answer.
4. What recommendations would you offer for media to play the role of the conscience-keeper of a nation?

Critical Thinking Questions

1. Which form of political structure can best support CSR activities and why?
2. Do you think NGOs and NPOs are being used as a facade to shield irresponsible behaviour by corporations? Debate and justify.
3. How can educational institutions promote the concept of CSR?
4. Today media is a big business. Do you think that in such a scenario media can justify its role as a promoter of CSR? Justify your answer.

Research Question

Analyse how CSR can be impacted by different forms of political ideology.

Project Question

Visit a NPO or NGO and find out whether CSR is being carried out in its true spirit there.

REFERENCES

Adomssent, M. and G. Michelsen (2006), 'German Academia heading for sustainability? Reflections on policy and practice in teaching, research and institutional innovations', *Environmental Education Research,* vol. 12, issue no. 1, pp. 85–99.

Denis, Brian (2001), *Pulitzer—A Life,* John Wiley, New York.

Lichtenstein, Nelson (ed.), 'Wal-Mart—The Face of Twentieth Century Capitalism', Misha Petrovic and Gary G. Hamilton, *Making Global Markets—Wal-Mart and Its Suppliers,* The New Press, New York, 2006, p. 133.

March, J.G. (1991), 'Exploration and Exploitation in Organizational Learning', *Organization Science,* vol. 2, issue no. 1, pp. 71–87.

O'Reilly, C.A. and M.L. Tushman (2004), 'The Ambidextrous Organization', *Harvard Business Review,* vol. 82, issue no. 4, pp. 74–81.

Padaki, Vijay and Manjulika Vaz (2005), *Management Development in Non–Profit Organizations, A programme for Governing Boards,* Sage Publications, New Delhi.

Rawls, John (1958), *Justice and Fairness in Philosophical Review,* vol. LXVII (2): 164–194, reprinted in John Rawls, Collected Papers, Samuel Freeman (ed.) Cambridge: Harvard University Press, 1999.

Shaw, W. (1996), 'Business Ethics Today—A survey', *Journal of Business Ethics,* vol. 15, pp. 489–500.

Web Resources

For more information on the role of media in CSR, see http://www.grainesdechangement.com/docs/medias/Good–News–and–Bad.pdf, accessed 31 March 2010.

http://www.theoathproject.org.

CASE STUDY

JANAAGRAHA CENTRE FOR CITIZENSHIP AND DEMOCRACY

Not-for-profit (NPO) organizations highlight the check-and-balance effect that institutions can play on others. More often than not, it is believed that CSR relates more to rural concerns than urban issues. But this is a myth that needs to be rectified. With increasing liberalization, privatization, and globalization (LPG), urban areas are under tremendous strain, especially in terms of basic infrastructural facilities. Since the demand is higher than the supply of facilities, it gives rise to rampant corruption and exploitation, which naturally in the long run is detrimental to any sustainable growth. Janaagraha Centre of Citizenship and Democracy is one such NPO that is trying to address urban issues through citizen participation and demand for transparency.

Janaagraha is a Bengaluru-based NPO that works with citizens and the government to improve the quality of life in Indian cities and towns. Founded in 2001 by Ramesh Ramanathan and Swati Ramanathan, it started as a movement to enable citizen participation in public governance and has now evolved into a robust institution for citizenship and democracy.

The term 'quality of life' as defined by Janaagraha has two distinct and inter-related aspects. The first is 'quality of urban infrastructure and services', i.e., the quality of urban amenities such as roads, drains, traffic, transport, and water supply. The second aspect is the 'quality of citizenship', i.e., the role that urban residents play by participating in civic issues.

Janaagraha's guiding principle to define quality of life and bring about changes in public governance is a comprehensive framework called REED. It is an acronym for the four defining aspects of urban governance, which are

- *Regional* perspective to urban issues
- *Empowered* citizens and local governments
- *Enabled* citizens and local governments with
- *Direct* accountability of the government to the people

Some of its initiatives like Jaagte Raho! and I Paid a Bribe are very innovative and have received overwhelming support, thus creating awareness among common citizens to know their rights and demand them.

Jaagte Raho!
About Jaagte Raho!
Jaagte Raho! inspires values of active citizenship in urban India by bringing out the citizens to vote in local, state, and union elections and by promoting participation in neighbourhood areas. It is a non-partisan campaign by Janaagraha Centre for Citizenship and Democracy.

Best Initiative
In continuation of the mission to improve the quality of urban voter rolls, Janaagraha and the Election Commission of India (ECI) signed a memorandum of understanding on 23 July 2010 to pilot a vigorous electoral roll cleanup in Shanthi Nagar Assembly Constituency of Bangalore over a period of six months. Christened Bengaluru Electoral System Transformation (BEST), the pilot aims at near 100 per cent error-free electoral rolls in the chosen constituency. The BEST project will work with two key stakeholders of the electoral process—the ECI and the citizens. Technological and infrastructure-related interventions will be undertaken by the ECI to handle voter registration in a time-bound, transparent, and citizen-friendly manner.

Objectives of the BEST project:
1. To achieve 100 per cent accuracy in the voter list
2. To maintain a clean voter list on an ongoing basis

The BEST project seeks to involve citizen volunteers called area voter mitras (AVMs) in the constituency. An AVM is a booth-level volunteer as recognised by the ECI, who will
1. Be the guide on voter registration in their residential area
2. Identify and correct inaccuracies in the voter list pertaining to their area

The institutions of democracy offer a space for citizen participation. Janaagraha has delved into these spaces and formalized a structure to allow citizens to participate effectively in urban governance. Thousands of citizen volunteers have dedicated their time and talents to causes close to their hearts. They are driven by their commitment to Janaagraha's motto 'Be the change you want to see'.

I Paid a Bribe

About I Paid a Bribe

IpaidaBribe.com is Janaagraha's unique initiative to tackle corruption by harnessing the collective energy of citizens. Citizens can report on the nature, number, pattern, types, location, frequency, and values of actual corrupt acts on this website. The reports will, perhaps for the first time, provide a snapshot of bribes occurring across the cities in India. They will be used to argue for improving governance systems and procedures, tightening law enforcement and regulation, and thereby in reducing the scope for corruption in obtaining services from the government.

I Paid a Bribe launched

The website was informally launched on 15 August 2010. Within the first month, the website had received over 35,000 hits from across the world. Some were victims, some were surprised that they did not have to pay a bribe, while others took a stand against bribing. Under these different heads, people from all walks of life have told their stories on actual corrupt acts. There have been stories pouring on this website. The intention is to use these actual incidents to press for improved governance systems, procedures, better law enforcement, and stricter regulation in the government.

Within a month of its launch, the website has
- Received 35,000 hits from 109 countries
- Got 535 reports of bribes being paid
- Been intimated of 100 incidents of bribes not being paid
- Already inspired people to stop paying bribes

The website has a section for 'Ask Raghu' questions, which within a month had received over 350 queries. From how to deal with policemen asking for bribe for passport renewal to how to deal with people who refuse to provide service where it is legally required, the section answers many commonly seen situations. The website also provides space for people who paid bribes against their will to tell their stories. The initiative seeks to uncover the market price of corruption.

Find more details at www.IPaidABribe.com.

Source: Swati Ramanathan, Ramesh Ramanathan, and the Janaagraha team.

Discussion Questions

1. What does the term 'Janaagraha' mean? What role can institutions like Janaagraha play in the modern economic scenario?
2. What is unique about the initiatives of Janaagraha?
3. How can citizens contribute in promoting CSR concepts?
4. Discuss the socio-economic issues of urbanization.

ANNEXURE

Recommendations on Accountability, Transparency, Governance, and Trust

No organization or institution can design and practice CSR without believing in accountability and implementing transparent governance that can induce trust among the stakeholders. A quick checklist of initiatives and activities that can be reviewed to ensure that basic CSR is being followed in the organization is given below:

1. Establish specifically at the board level, i.e., the strategic level of a company, NGO, NPO or government, whether the balance between public interest and commercial imperatives is being strategically reviewed, properly managed, and publicly disclosed.
2. There should be a proper review of goals, targets, and performance against leading governance codes (including the UN Global Compact, the Global Sullivan Principles, and SA 8000) and socially responsible investment (SRI) criteria.
3. It should be remembered that compliance with laws, regulations, industry, and codes is the absolute minimum for good governance and therefore, they should commit to 'beyond compliance' standards wherever possible.
4. Walking the talk should be implemented by adopting and publicizing ethical codes of conduct and clear statements of corporate values and principles.
5. Efforts to involve and engage regularly the key stakeholders should be honestly practiced. This would ensure that inclusive policies and processes are adopted right across the business.
6. The government, business community, NGOs, NPOs, as well as the media, should provide leadership in terms of triple bottom-line accounting, auditing, and reporting.
7. A policy of disclosing all proprietorial cross-ownerships and influence should be rigorously followed.
8. Open declaration of editorial policy (in case of media)—both general and issue-specific—and political allegiances should be made.
9. There should be transparency in relation to all sources of funds that could influence production operation and marketing in business corporations, editorial, and programming content—including their biggest advertisers, sponsors, and production subsidies for media and deployment as well as usage of funds by government, NGOs, and NPOs.
10. Regularly report direct and indirect lobbying activities that impact socio-economic development, either positively or negatively.

Source: Adapted from http://www.grainesdechangement.com/docs/medias/Good-News-and-Bad.pdf, accessed on 31 March 2010.

Creating CSR Framework

INTRODUCTION

Development is a universal phenomenon, but its issues differ from country to country. The essence of development lies in proper 'contextualization' of the problems and concerns in terms of both the ethos and culture of the country. The process of CSR helps to create this contextual understanding. Therefore, CSR needs to be integrated into the strategic framework of the organization. The indisputable purpose of business is to earn profit. To achieve this end, we have to understand the basic management process in an organization. Profit is a culmination of risk, return, and growth of an organization. All the three have a deep relationship with the internal and external environment of business, and CSR caters to both these environments. If CSR is not woven into the organization's day-to-day activities, then the danger of overthrowing CSR activities will always lurk as and when the organization goes through a downturn. Firms grappling with an economic crisis use resources hitherto devoted to social issues for immediate financial remedies, like cost saving, by discontinuing socially relevant activities.

Let us begin by appreciating the role that history and culture play in the economic development of any country and then understand how a strategy to incorporate and implement CSR can be created.

RELEVANCE OF HISTORY AND CULTURE

Today, a business aiming for total development cannot remain insulated from the historical and cultural aspects of a country. A durable and resilient socio-economic environment has to create a harmonious relationship with new changes without losing its originality and ethos. Our view of history shapes the way we view the present, and therefore, it dictates what answers we offer for existing problems. We have to learn from history carefully, because 'the historian's distortion (subjective bias) is more than technical, it is ideological; it is released into a world of contending (opposing) interests, where any chosen emphasis supports (whether the

LEARNING OBJECTIVES

After studying this chapter, you will be able to
- Understand the importance of historical evidence in exploring the concept of CSR
- Examine the processes of integrating CSR into the strategic framework of organizations
- Provide simple suggestions on implementation processes of CSR for organizations
- Understand that CSR perception and delivery have to take into account both global and local practices

historian means to or not) some kind of interest, whether economic or political or racial or national or sexual' (Zinn 1980). Therefore, when we use history to evaluate the relevance of a concept, empirical data, and implementation methodologies, we should be aware that 'true history' and 'pseudo-history' can exist together. This tricky situation should be demystified for any social activity to be acceptable. Early historicism emphasized the ways in which the institutions of capitalism and industrialism evolved (Hodgson 2001). Historical sociologists, Webber and Simmel (Weber 1904, English translation 1930; Simmel 1908, English translation 1950; Sombart 1911) explored the role of religion and social relations in the development of modern capitalist attitudes towards economic gain and economic opportunity. According to McCraw (1986), an eclectic approach that history provides helps in understanding temporal changes in the industries, markets, societies, economies, and political systems in which they operated.

Management and the industry have to respond to cultural elements that include psychographics and the physiological needs of its various stakeholders. Taylor (1871) offered one of the earliest definitions of culture as 'that complex whole which includes knowledge, belief, art, morals, law, custom, and any other capabilities and habits acquired by man as a member of society.' Culture, outlined by Geertz (1973), is 'a system of inherited conceptions expressed in symbolic forms by means of which people communicate, perpetuate, and develop their knowledge about and attitudes toward life.' A more recent definition proposed by Ferraro (2002), culture is 'everything that people have, think, and do as members of society.'

Generally, culture is regarded as society's way of life and therefore comprises of politics, economics, law, religion, language, literature, art, philosophy, and other related systems and substances. Some also believe that culture refers to people's world outlook, values, and outlook on life. Values, in particular, reflect the main body of cultural practices.

Therefore, while designing strategies for growth and corresponding profits, the business world would have to take into account the history, culture, and the various business processes to create a sustainable socio-economic environment.

CREATION OF STRATEGY

Strategy refers to an elaborate and systematic plan of action pursued consciously to achieve a particular goal or objective. Strategy is concerned with analysing, projecting, and directing the different engagements. It is about understanding how each engagement is linked with the other. It operates in an uncontrolled environment. Therefore, it is not about how an engagement is conducted or done. Strategy is an in-depth visualization of terms and conditions that need to be assessed to evaluate the future of any undertaking. Strategy is not a guessing game based on intuition, rather it is a rational and conscious reaction to situations. Some of the important assessments that an organization needs to make on pursuing CSR are given below.

Risk Analysis

Building on the information gathered from history and culture, the organization would have to create its strategy to succeed in the market. The foremost policy that the corporate needs to articulate is, what it is planning to do in the market place, i.e., its goals and objectives, both long term and short term? While defining its objectives and goals, the firm has to analyse its impact, both long term and short term on the community and society. This is required because the resources and markets required to fulfil the aims and objectives have to be drawn from society.

This is where the stakeholder theory finds its legitimacy. However, to implement this, organizations have to be committed towards governance and transparency in their activities. Accountability and integrity are strong 'brand ambassadors' (help to build brand) of a corporate and often cannot be quantified. These intangible assets have a significant impact on the quantifiable financial profit, which is the central aim of the business entity. Since the real world would demand a trade-off between the stakeholders, the firm would have to find a sync (matching, harmony) between its value foundation (its vision) and the designed trade-off, otherwise it would look farcical.

Therefore, risk management would have to be undertaken with immense sincerity, not only within the corporate as a whole, but also in its departments. This would help the organization to evaluate the trade-off and the consequences on a long-term basis, and that would certainly be a more fair and just decision than a short-term profit-oriented trade-off. The firm has to periodically take stock of its assets, relationships, processes, technology, and capabilities to achieve its mission. The mission has to be crafted ingeniously, so that it is neither too broad nor too narrow. An unfocused broad concept, like increasing profit or creating customer satisfaction or catering to the investor, etc., can lead to the firm venturing into every kind of activity, as there is no clarity about the journey that the firm wants to pursue. Extremely focused statements like producing only one product or part of it, for example offering only electronic entertainment or offering one service such as hotels catering only to tourists, can constrict the innovativeness and flexibility of the firm. The mission should aim at creating competitive advantage that would lead to long-term viability. The World Economic Forum 2007 has listed the following risks that need to be assessed by a company if it wants to mitigate the fears of the investors:

business environment, competitive issues, compliance matters, employee problems, operational factors, reputational loss, security and fraud, strategic failure, technological change and trade credit, and customer insolvency.

Building Trust

An investor-friendly environment can be created only when the company increases the quotient of trust in the minds of the customers. Since trust is not a unilateral process, the firm has to build a reciprocal relationship with all its stakeholders. CSR is the prime intervention required here to create that congenial (friendly and pleasant) co-existence of all stakeholders. This would help the company to go beyond financial reporting and report on the 'soft' or intangible aspects, sometimes termed as extra-financial issues. Today, every governance code is demanding a reporting of the non-financial factors impacting profits. The corporate has to streamline its value chain to bring about transparency in the process. This would allow stakeholders to judge the corporate strategy and action related to quality and sustainability, and thus create trust. The product lifecycle, i.e., the stages that a new product is believed to go through from beginning to end (introduction, growth, maturity, and decline) can also be used by corporations to identify sustainability issues.

Subliminal Impact of History

History and heritage provides individuals with a number of basic tools and methods with which to pilot everyday lives. In order to understand the thoughts, feelings, and actions of a community, it is crucial for the corporate world to comprehend history. The history of a country underpins (supports) its culture, which actually reflects the way of life. According to Jones (2008), 'the (this) loss of history has resulted in the spread of influential theories based on ill-informed understandings of the past.' For example, the current accepted advice is that wealth and growth will come to countries that open their borders to foreign direct investment. 'The historical evidence shows clearly that this is an article of faith rather than proven by the historical evidence of the past' (Jones 2008). This reflects that very often policy formulations are based on mono-causality (single cause) and a uni-dimensional (one aspect or characteristic) view of the world, thus emphasizing lack of historical understanding.

Social cohesion is one of those values that need an in-depth appreciation of the history of a nation. The form of government and political system plays a large role in deciding the terms of social reforms, as can be seen in the following modern examples. Though Greece has a socialist government, it is unable to balance its economic needs in this era of global recession. This is because being a socialist country it cannot immediately cut public sector pay, though that is required to ease the economic pressure on the country. Similarly, Spain's socialist government continues to retain the labour market laws, which make retrenching permanent employees extremely expensive. Italy's right-wing government is reluctant to remove the burdensome regulations on small business because it fears large-scale strikes. Similarly, Sweden's centre-right leadership does not want to revisit the generous social model, which needs trimming of benefits, pay, and pensions. Even a developed nation like France fears trouble if it pushes for reform in the labour market, pension, and welfare schemes. Now the question is: Is CSR being trampled in the name of social cohesion? (Information regarding the countries mentioned here have been adapted from *Economist*, 30 January 2010, p. 16.)

The above examples show the strategy to trade-off between permanent and temporary workers behind the façade of social cohesion. But this strategy can have long-term negative impacts because the temporary or the unemployed are bearing the cost of protecting those who are in permanent jobs and/or are members of trade unions, and thus have the benefit of collective bargaining or hold privileged jobs. These temporary workers are usually the young workforce of the country, and also the immigrants. Thus, on the one hand, the young are being denied training and the immigrants are not being assimilated into the mainstream. This is increasing the divide in the society and production in industry is lagging behind as trained employees are in short supply. In the name of cohesion, public sector employees continue to retain their perks and privileges, while the private sector employees feel the brunt of their pay and privileges being reduced or frozen. This again highlights the disparity in CSR within the same country as a fall-out of their past historical traditions.

Mosseau, who carried out two different studies, tried to find a suitable explanation between democracy and economy. In 2005, he noted that democracy is only a factor when the country has a high level of democracy, well above the global median. He also noted that 21 per cent of the poorest democracies in the study were more likely to go to war. Both world wars were fought between economically developed nations. Both these findings show that conflict cannot be directly related to economic prosperity or depravity. Mosseau, Hegre, and Oneal in 2003 argued that USSR (during the Cold War) and Saudi Arabia and China (today) have state-managed economies that are not thrown open to market norms. They show that democracy and civil peace are correlated only when the country has a high literacy rate and development. Conversely, the risk of civil war decreases with development only for democratic countries. Thus, it becomes evident that formulating business strategies without understanding these contradictory factors may not lead to expected gains by the business world.

Corporate Ideology and History

The history and culture of countries play a crucial role with respect to accountability, integrity, and transparency. Fritzsche and Becker (1984) presented a correlation between the level of economic growth and economic behaviour. According to their study, the level of development/advancement in the legal system and/or social expectations and the need of the involved parties attributed to this difference. This is corroborated when the corruption index of the country is viewed. The international watchdog, Transparency International, has released a list of 180 countries in terms of public-sector corruption (*Times of India*, 18 November 2009). A glaring example is India, which, though it is considered one of the fastest-growing economies and a world player in the economic arena, is ranked 84th in the index. Thus, though good governance usually relates to better law and order and less corruption, corruption and growth have moved hand-in-hand in India. This has happened because corruption in India is broad-based and corrupt money is spread over a larger number of people, who return it to the economy through their spending. This is when CSR gives the warning that such practices would corrode the economy over time and sustainable growth would be a mere mirage or illusion.

Corporations need to realize that corruption is a cost that they are passing on to the unit price of their products. This obviously means that such businesses can never be competitive in the world market. The nexus between the governments and the corporate world in this game of corruption is actually harming national competitiveness. This activity is further fuelled by availability of 'tax havens' in countries practising secrecy in banking laws. Transparency International for the first time recommends that tax havens like Switzerland and Liechtenstein should do away with the secrecy in banking laws (*Times of India*, 18 November 2009). 'Corrupt money must not find safe havens. It is time to put an end to secrecy in banking laws' (Huguette 2009). The advantages of a free market economy can never be reaped in such an environment. Therefore, the root of the CSR concept is being challenged here due to the unique practices of different countries.

Appreciating Culture

Society comprises of the people who carry the baggage of their culture because culture includes 'behaviour, artefacts, values and beliefs, systems of meaning, and as ways of knowing, going from the most accessible to that which can only be inferred' (Schein 1992). Therefore, decisions can highlight bounded (limited) perceptions and conflicting goals ... (Allison 1971; Cyert and March, 1963). As a result of historic events leading to the development of unique cultural processes, we may also find 'group think' (Janis 1981) or it may induce 'satisficing', (meeting the requirements or gratification) 'solution selling', or failure avoidance behaviour, and decision process may lack order or rational structure (Anderson 1983; Mintzberg et al., 1976; Nutt 1984). Different strategic decisions in the corporate world may result from different value systems, which differ from country to country. However, forces of globalization and liberalization may push the same countries towards convergence of ideas about business. Therefore, while formulating strategies, corporates have to take into account this tension between the local and global perspectives.

An excellent example is Japan, where hurried efforts, without really understanding the deep roots of its culture, were made to redefine its ways and processes to find a solution to the above tension. Therefore, today the belief that Japan has adapted to new challenges by brilliantly reinventing itself is being questioned as it is suffering from nearly 20 years of economic stagnation and an ageing and shrinking population. The historical insular nature and rigid systems of Japan have to be understood and modified for corporate social responsibility to deliver the expected results to all its stakeholders. The case of Toyota Motors, shown in Exhibit 5.1, shows the importance of understanding cultural practices while creating strategies for success in business.

EXHIBIT 5.1

Fiasco at Toyota Motors

Toyota Motor's failure and recall of its hybrid and other celebrated brands has exposed how a cultural practice can lead to overwhelming challenges in the arena of branding, quality, market capitalization, and dissatisfaction among shareholder, employees, consumers, suppliers, and other stakeholders. The problem began with complaints regarding the accelerator and brake of the car. The technological issue got magnified due to the inflexible system of seniority and hierarchy. This tradition prevents juniors from passing bad news up the chain in a misguided effort to protect the seniors from loss of face. The family ties (common to most Asian countries) make it almost impossible for anyone to challenge the boss. Not following the hierarchical chain is considered as disloyalty and violation of consensus culture. Groupthink as a practice gets embedded in such systems as mobility is restricted between companies. Any employee wanting to move is stigmatized as 'disloyal job-hoppers' and hiring outsiders is considered a threat to internal harmony. With extraordinary emphasis on harmony, diversity and alternative viewpoints are stifled. This led to failure in assessing the issues and concerns in the right perspective, especially in a global market that is diverse, and created enormous embarrassment for the world famous company.

Source: Adapted from *The Economist*, 13 February 2010.

Governance and Culture

The recent problems of Japan mentioned in Exhibit 5.1 and the western model of governance, which showed chinks in its armour during the Enron, Worldcom, Tyco, and other mishaps, have shown the importance of drawing lessons from history and culture in governance strategies. There is a need to continuously re-evaluate production processes, emphasising efficiency and effectiveness, along with understanding the value of human capital, because CSR is a measure of how a company journeys through the three tiers of internal, intermediate, and external levels of development (as explained in the definition of CSR).

CSR demands that corporates understand that balancing internal culture with the external opportunities and realities would need certain sacrifices, and that can happen only when one is aware of one's history and culture as a country and as an organization. The history and culture of the country also determine the impact of governance on growth. For example, 'poor countries suffer from a multitude of growth constraints and effective reforms address the most binding among them. Poor governance may, in general, be the binding constraint in Zimbabwe and a few other countries, but it was not in China, Vietnam, or Cambodia—countries that are growing rapidly despite poor governance ...' (Dani 2008). While designing strategies related to institutional arrangements (encouraging any form of institution that relates to development and prosperity), economists have to minimize behavioural distortions by assimilating local knowledge and being creative. 'Unfortunately, the type of institutional reform promoted by, among others, the World Bank, IMF, and the World Trade Organization is biased towards a best-practice model, which presumes that a set of universally appropriate institutional arrangement can be determined and views convergence towards them as being inherently desirable. But best practice institutions are by definition, non-contextual and cannot take local complications into account' (Dani). Thus, we see that understanding local culture is very important. It is a prerequisite even if we want to implement some practice that may be successful in some other culture because it would fail in spite of good intentions.

Apprehensions of Societies

Businesses have to rethink their strategies, as sweeping changes in global economy have created an environment of uncertainty. The 1990s was hailed as the age of abundance and there was a movement towards a 'do good' value by the developed countries debating issues of human rights, abortion, mercy killings, suicides, etc. With the recession, there is the fear of scarcity looming large. Common people are facing scarcity of food and water, rise in prices of all necessities, changes in the demographics due to multifarious reasons, ranging from higher education, liberating women, better medical facilities increasing longevity, government policies limiting number of children, to lack of hygiene and sanitation decreasing lifespan. Today the debates have shifted to each country trying to save themselves and grab power. This effort cannot insulate (save) a country or state from a network of threats that would emanate (come) from multiple sources, which would include non-state actors, social and economic factors, and environmental issues.

History and culture shape the sub-conscious behaviour of managers who design the strategies, and of other stakeholders who are either directly or indirectly impacted by the strategies. Culture provides the cushion in times of uncertainty by offering guidelines to social integration. Since the concept of CSR relates to social concerns like unemployment, poverty, illiteracy, child labour, social exclusion arising out of caste, class or gender discrimination, degradation of environment, preservation of scarce resources, etc., it has to enter the domain of history and culture to understand their origin. The efforts to improve basic amenities like health, nutrition, employment, leisure, education, shelter, and other infrastructural facilities are again embedded and integrally connected to the history and culture of the country.

For example, the mobility of labour and capital in an industrial economy is far more advanced than in an agriculture predominated economy, as the individual is not tied to land or other fixed assets and has to only carry his or her skills. To create a symbiotic relationship between global economic interests and local socio-economic interests, local communities should be encouraged in their effort to preserve and follow local practices. These practices are reflected in the historically shared values, spirituality, rituals, and beliefs. Local residents and civic leaders are questioning the flawed assumption that traditional societies are static and homogenous. They are pointing out that every culture has an inner dynamism and diversity that lends it its unique identity. This identity should not be destroyed if we want growth that is acceptable to all. Communities' economic future cannot ignore distributive justice and autonomous self-expression in every activity. The anxiety of being uprooted from the historical moorings can often lead to discontent and aggressive denials by the different stakeholders of all change processes, both internal and external, to the organization.

True Nationalism

Similarly, local communities and political will must ensure that companies do not shy away as a result of protectionism and isolationism. In the global economy, disparities cannot increase, leading to unequal distribution of benefits because that is going to increase discontent. These discontented masses are an easy target for propagators of 'nativist' (fundamentalist) culture, ethnicity, or terrorism. Therefore, understanding of CSR has to take these into account. A firm and its practices should be seen as the product of a specific historical era and a particular place. Small and mid-size companies are joining the league of corporate giants in exploiting opportunities in international growth markets to become world-class to meet the demands of the alert and conscious local customers. This needs to be monitored because the danger of misuse of resources in their rush for reaching the top will manifest itself in stringent protectionism, human rights violation in outsourced markets, or health and environmental hazards in undeveloped communities.

A good measurement of nationalism is how honestly the corporations and citizens of a country remit their taxes. Transfer price is another fraudulent practice that is practised under the cover of legality. Again, CSR implementation would differ as it demands that company ideology reflect honesty and integrity. According to a recent Harvard University study, US companies avoided paying tax on nearly $300 billion in income in 1998. ... In 1940, companies and individuals each paid about half the federal income tax collected; now the companies pay 13.7 per cent and individuals 86.3 per cent (Byrnes and Louis 2003). Tax evasion itself causes loss of revenue to the government and distorts the economy, leading to failure of policies. The flow of products, services, trademarks, funding, and technology is having a significant impact on the issues of transfer pricing. The rise of tax haven states is a corollary to this practice. Curbing international tax evasion is a challenging and difficult task. Therefore, a determined and adequate action needs to be formulated with the consent of the government agencies and business firms. An official US report shows that tax havens harbour deposits of around $5 trillion and the US government itself loses about $70 billion by way of tax on account of such deposits (Verma 2002). We can imagine how many times it must have increased by now.

CREATING A FRAMEWORK FOR CSR

From the above discussion it is clear that CSR requires an in-depth understanding of the history and culture of the country and also a committed integration into the strategy of an organization for it to succeed. Therefore, keeping these in view, certain suggestions are given below to help in designing the framework that would help to implement CSR in each organization.

Creation of a Corporate Culture

The relationship between an organization and its environment has been extensively discussed by sociologists in the form of institutional theory (Scott and Meyer 1995). For example, Scott's (1992) book, now seminal, stresses the importance of organizations as open systems in which the boundary between an organization and its environment is permeable (porous). The institutional environment of an organization refers to the written and unwritten rules to which organizations must conform in order to maintain legitimacy, to survive, and to prosper. In essence, they reflect the beliefs, values, and norms of the members of the institution. Thus, industry culture can be thought of as the organizational manifestation of institutional beliefs and values. While implementing CSR in an organization, one has to keep in mind the concept of 'invented traditions' as explained by Hobsbawm: '"Invented tradition" is taken to mean a set of practices, normally governed by overtly or tacitly accepted rules. These rules have ritualistic or symbolic nature; therefore, they seek to inculcate certain values and norms of behaviour by repetition, which automatically implies continuity with the past. In fact, where possible, they normally attempt to establish continuity with a suitable historic past ... insofar as there is such reference to a historic past. The peculiarity of "invented" traditions is that the continuity with it is largely factitious' (Hobsbawm 1983, pp. 1–2). Factors such as the founder's beliefs (Schein 1985; Pettigrew 1979), national cultures (Hofstede 1984), and industry pressures are likely origins of widespread and consistent practices. An example of an 'invented tradition' in most Indian organizations is the practice of doing 'puja' (asking for the blessings of the Almighty) before launching any new venture.

Since specific cultural practices have a crucial impact on corporate performances, CSR practices in an organization have to be woven into the fabric of operations of the organization. CSR cannot remain as a separate voluntary entity anymore. Corporate scams and disasters like the Bhopal gas tragedy, Exxon Mobil oil spill, Enron, and Satyam, to name a few, have clearly exposed that parking a part of profits in trusts and foundations, run by the mother organization doing social work, however brilliant they may be, does not protect society against fraud and disillusionment. The big questions are how is the profit being earned and distributed among the stakeholders? If the means of earning is dishonest and selfish, and the distribution is not just, the repercussions would be Mephistophelean, i.e., extreme devastation as a result of wickedness. Therefore, CSR is the basic source of success for all stakeholders.

Three-Level Implementation Framework

The framework for implementation has to be integrated through three stages: the inner corporate level, the intermediate national level, and the outer universal level. This is shown in Fig. 5.1.

Inner Corporate Ideology

The core value foundation based on integrity, accountability, and transparency of the organization needs to be built. This would provide the direction to strategic decision-makers to choose between alternatives that may be either

158 | Corporate Social Responsibility

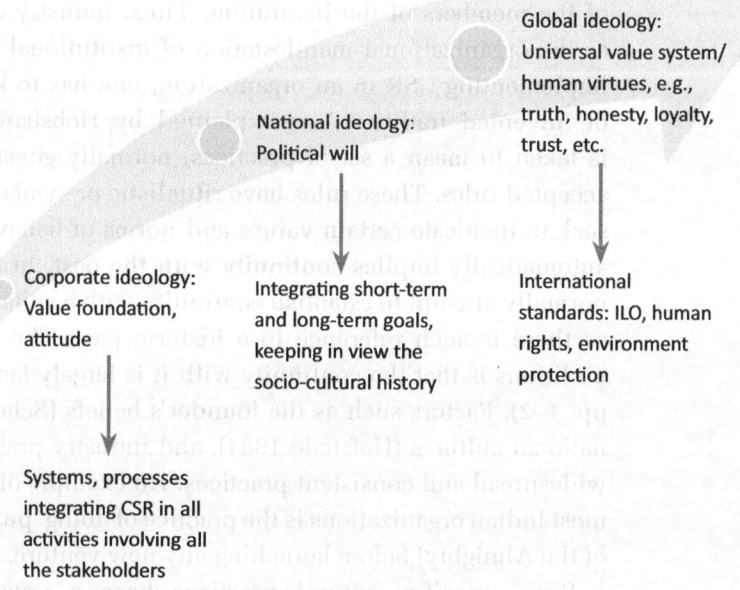

Figure 5.1 Three levels of implementation

right or wrong or between two rights. Choosing between right and wrong is easy but when it comes to a choice between different decisions that seem both valid and just, e.g., the right to information and the right to privacy, both of which are fundamental rights, the choice becomes rather difficult. Therefore, the decision-makers have to be extremely cautious in such situations. This is where the concept of CSR can become very handy because if CSR is already woven into the business plan and mission, it would be easier to see which 'right' needs priority at that particular time and location.

The business fraternity needs to realize that the law and order situation is also dependent on the economics of the country. Its roots are often embedded in an unfair distribution of benefits to the local community of both government schemes and organizational benefits. The anger is usually directed towards the big businesses, which become symbols of disrupting local subsistence in collusion with the government. The promises of larger growth are not trusted because very often development does not put anything back into the local society. The unprecedented demands for community-based settlements like the Gorkhaland movement in West Bengal, the ULFA movement in Assam and the North East, as well as the recent Maoist movements in India are examples of such emotions. Unless the business community contributes to the crucial development needs, its very survival would be threatened and it is in its own interest to participate in 'nation-building' effort.

A few suggestions of the approach to the implementation of CSR are given below.

A practical approach for judgeing value-based management would be to understand the micro-level integration by the firm and macro-level integration by the government (Chatterji 2005).

Micro-level Integration by the Firm

This relates to individual activities that firms undertake, both as suppliers of products and as consumers of labour and capital. The concept of integration helps the firms to examine how values can become an integral part of the various activities that they undertake to allocate the resources drawn from society to earn profit. The individual activities that need to be viewed in their pursuit of CSR can be summarized as given below:

1. Position in the stock market
2. Value creation to be judged through
   (a) Portfolio management
   (b) Choice between strategic options
   (c) Assessment of impact of business plans
   (d) Target-setting and bench-marking
3. Analysing resource sourcing. Prioritizing and allocating resources conscientiously
4. Appraisal of business performance and analysing organizational image
5. Focus on business and operational strategies and opportunities that maximize value in everyday management
6. Learn the skill to enhance delegation as well as to increase responsibility and accountability
7. Move from subsidiary level to the corporate level by breaking down plans into key objectives and prioritizing them. This would ensure value throughout the organization
8. Provide undiluted support for difficult but essential long-term initiatives to tackle stakeholder issues
9. Invest in research and development to increase invention and innovation
10. Be transparent about the risks and benefits of technology and be open to disruptive innovation, even if it means short term disturbances to existing business but ensures long-run universal benefit

Macro-Level Integration by the Government

As the name suggests, this level refers to national and international level of policies that impact business. When policymakers in government adhere to

accountable and responsible behaviour while formulating economic policies, then CSR becomes easy to achieve. The immediate areas of implementation are:
1. Draw up long-term unambiguous policy framework of targets and regulations.
2. Establish mandatory minimum standards for public participation, supported by improved incentives and performance appraisals.
3. Systematically incorporate public welfare in decision-making at each stage of the firm's project/policy cycles.
4. Improve the transparency of its governance and operations, particularly for project-affected people.
5. Expand and protect political space for democratic and participatory decision-making at the national level.
6. Find new and attractive ways to co-finance social initiatives related to sustainable growth of all stakeholders.
7. Accountability of global international organizations like the World Bank, ILO, UNICEF, and other agencies.

Integration of CSR at the Operation and Process Level

A quick check for this can be done by studying the organization production and operation flowchart and analysing whether the responsibilities are being handled ethically. This strategy would ensure that a poor substitute for collective agreements are not made. This would remove the danger of many stakeholders becoming docile and flexible, at the cost of overall profit mongering. The long-term viability would be addressed because at every stage quality would be scrutinized. The potential danger—of companies choosing partners like pseudo-NGOs who suit them by setting aside real partners of growth behind the facade of CSR—would be addressed. Figures 5.2 and 5.3 are adapted from Schroeder's (1993) work. Similar production and operation flowcharts can be used to ensure CSR is practiced at every stage.

The flowcharts give quick overviews of the activities that a firm undertakes to ensure that they are able to achieve effective and efficient (at the lowest cost) usage of resources. If a firm, while pursuing its activities of sourcing raw materials to supplying products to consumers, builds in CSR at every level, it would emerge as a responsible company in the business world. The firm can start by ensuring the following.

Resources These include energy, material, labour, capital, and information. How these are sourced and allocated for the most profitable as well as for the most socially sustainable economic activity should be studied by the business enterprise, so that from the beginning of their production process the social concern is built into the working of the company.

Creating CSR Framework | 161

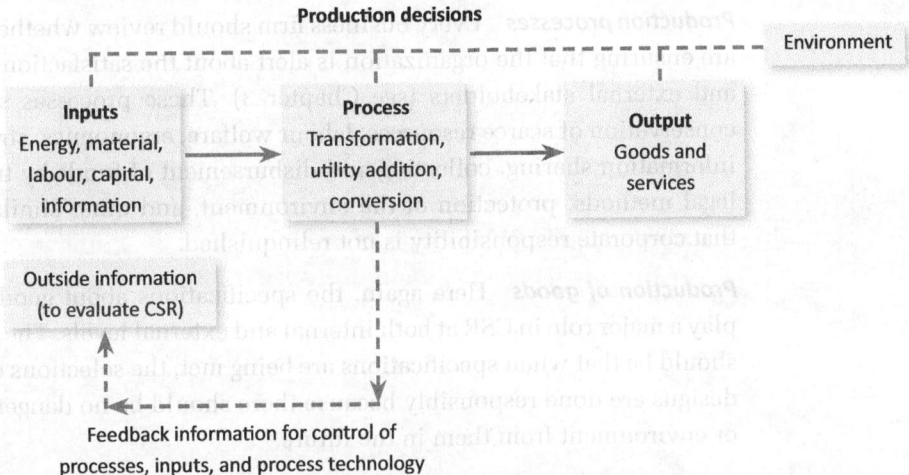

Figure 5.2   Production flow chart

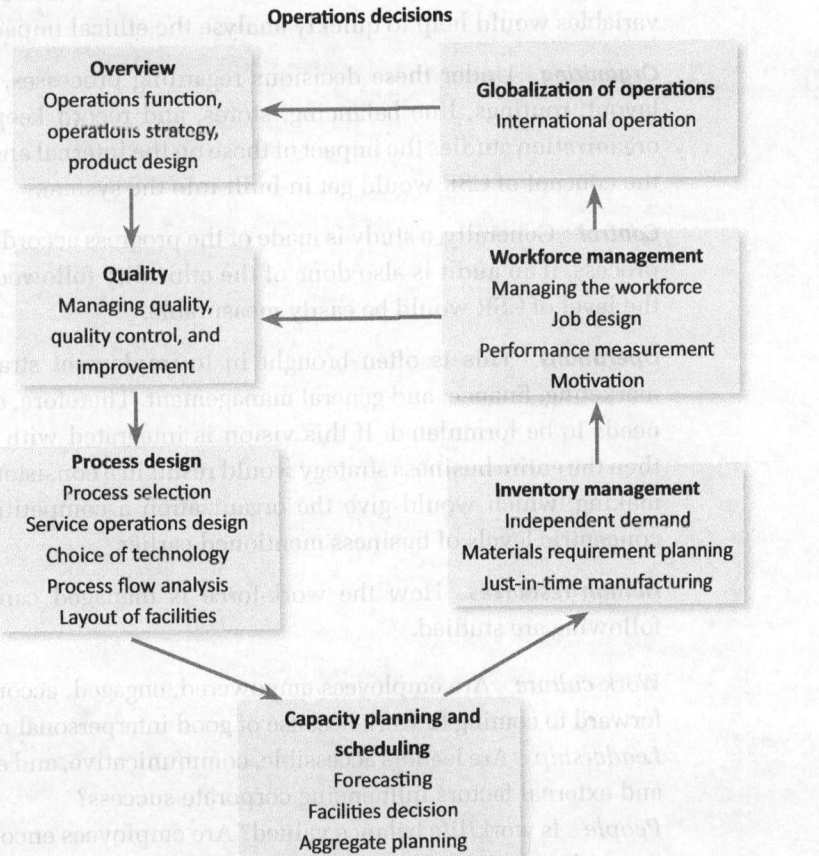

Figure 5.3   Operation flow chart

Production processes Every business firm should review whether the processes are ensuring that the organization is alert about the satisfaction of the internal and external stakeholders (see Chapter 3). These processes should include conservation of scarce resources, labour welfare, ergonomics, strict vigilance of information sharing, collecting and disbursement of funds by transparent and legal methods, protection of the environment, and other similar activities so that corporate responsibility is not relinquished.

Production of goods Here again, the specifications about goods and services play a major role in CSR at both internal and external levels. The understanding should be that when specifications are being met, the selections of material and designs are done responsibly because there should be no danger to human life or environment from them in the future.

Planning While planning the selection of machinery and men in 'need-based marketing', which analyses the product, basic need, existing solution, and current problem is taken into account, then the focus on this handful of variables would help to quickly analyse the ethical impacts.

Organizing Under these decisions regarding processes, plant location, plant layout, routings, line balancing, stores, and record keeping are made. If the organization studies the impact of these on the internal and external conditions, the concept of CSR would get in-built into the system.

Control Generally, a study is made of the progress according to the plan. In this process, if an audit is also done of the ethicality followed during the progress, the level of CSR would be easily measurable.

Operations This is often brought in to implement strategic plans made by marketing, finance, and general management. Therefore, an operations strategy needs to be formulated. If this vision is integrated with social responsibility, then the entire business strategy would result in a consistent pattern of decision-making, which would give the organization a competitive edge in the three concentric levels of business mentioned earlier.

Human resources How the work-force is managed can be measured if the following are studied.

Work culture Are employees empowered, engaged, accountable? Do they look forward to coming to work because of good interpersonal relationships?
Leadership Are leaders accessible, communicative, and empathetic to internal and external factors influencing corporate success?
People Is work/life balance valued? Are employees encouraged to take care of themselves and their families? Are flexible policies regarding where, when, and how people work available?

Work Do all employees feel that their work is significant? Are there appraisal/recognition for the difference/contribution they make in the lives of others?

Growth and opportunity Are training and education valued? Do all employees receive similar opportunities to learn and grow? Do the employees have career growth options?

Compensation and benefits Are people paid fairly for the work they do? How well-aligned to the needs and interests of the employees are benefits programmes?

Social awareness Does the employer facilitate opportunities for employees to volunteer their time and expertise to improve life for others—in the local community, around the country, around the world?

Intermediate National Ideology

CSR often becomes a difficult issue when companies build and maintain production facilities in countries without an appreciation of the national culture and history. The basis for the relation of culture and CSR depends on the size of the company as well as on the products and services it offers and markets in which it operates. Companies are confronted with pressing problems that may vary from consumerism to poverty, state-run mandatory health facilities to inadequate health care, HIV infected workforce, corruption, child labour, educated unemployed, restrictions on trade, organized and unorganized labour, organized and unorganized business sectors, poor education systems, as well as the absence or non-implementation of rules on working conditions and environmental protection.

Therefore, companies have to be actively committed to a sustainable improvement in the macro-economic situation and introduce measures that go beyond statutory requirements of the countries in which they operate. With globalization and outsourcing as a business model, to enjoy economies of scale and efficient and effective supply chain models, corporations have to be extremely alert about the practices followed by/in their subsidiaries, contractual partners, suppliers, and licence-holders.

Statutory Regulations

The statutory provisions of any country have to take account of the socio-economic situation in the countries in question. Hence, very often rigorous implementation of high social responsibility standards may not be immediately possible in developing countries. This is because:
   (a) the infrastructure to support such implementation may not be available;
   (b) the implementation may actually reduce the competitive advantage of low cost of production;

(c) removal of social evils without proper contingency plans may increase rate of crime and substance abuse in the society; and
(d) it has been found that formal modern education has led to decline in vocation-based skills training or pursuance of traditional crafts followed by their forefathers. Hence, there is a decline and in some cases, disappearance, of vocational skills and indigenous heritage.

The national-level policy should incorporate the welfare state concept in its policies. Instead of a general boycott or piecemeal ameliorating (betterment) activities, the nation should have a structured policy aimed at reducing red tape, corruption, and increasing fair distribution.

Achieving the brand of being a quality conscious nation is as important as that of the corporate entities. The nation has to be seen by people as a nation that is safe, peaceful, and friendly. Corruption levels have to be checked and bureaucratic red tape has to be lessened. If a nation is unable to create an investor-friendly environment and brand equity through its transparent business policies and systems, as well as honest and just government and legal institutions, economic growth will remain a mirage.

Danger of Stereotyping

To create an environment at the national level that promotes sustainability, very often the mistake of copying systems is committed. Stereotyping relates bracketing problems and solutions under a common frame because theoretically they look similar. The reality is, when we analyse a problem at the practical level and try to implement solutions, the stark differences and challenges are revealed among similar-looking problems and solutions. An excellent example of this dilemma can be seen in the way poverty is viewed.

Poverty is usually defined in a limited way in terms of an income-based poverty line.

Several forms of human deprivation (which cause poverty) including poor survival chances, unjust employment of children, child prostitution, bonded labour, environmental pollution, domestic violence, and social exclusion arising out of caste and gender discrimination, are not related to income in a predictable manner (UNDP 1997). As explained earlier, poverty includes factors like hygiene, education, nutrition, credit, etc., which cannot be measured through the income parameter alone. Technological changes and global competition are accelerating changes in market demand. This, in turn, is rendering traditional skills redundant, enhancing development-related displacement, harming ecological factors, etc. Businesses would have to proactively handle these concerns related to poverty, if they want long-term sustenance and viability. 'Governments themselves are often a source of shocks to households. This comes about through the way governments influence the economic, legal, and political settings within which the household is embedded' (Baulch and Hoddinott 2000). The shocks mentioned above result from government policies that impact everyday life of citizens. For example, in May 2010, the Government of India decided to increase the price of petroleum products. This would naturally increase the price of almost all consumer goods as the cost of transportation would go up. Since the inflation rate is already high, such a policy becomes an added shock for households. These changes in policies creating different issues of poverty not directly related to the income of an individual or community may be due to the demands of liberalization and globalization (Chatterji 2006).

Another interesting example of misinterpretations that can occur due to the stereotypical belief is that poverty leads to child labour. For example, it is fascinating to observe that though poverty is rampant both in India (which got independence in 1947) and Georgia (which became independent when the USSR broke up in 1991), Georgia does not have child labour, whereas it is widespread in India. In Georgia, there is no child labour as every child goes to school, because the communistic past has created the culture of sending children to school by providing state-aided free education. The children there suffer from other factors like war (see section on 'Challenges' in the Poti case study). Since industrial development is almost negligible, there is an enormous number of educated unemployed in Georgia. When people are not employed for a long time, skill redundancy occurs and a vicious cycle of poverty continues. Therefore, here the challenge of eradicating poverty is different from the challenge in India. In Georgia, industries need to partner with government to provide skill training and employment to ensure a productive workforce of the future.

It is propagated that because of poverty children in India have to seek employment to survive. The Indian government cannot immediately and strictly implement its policy of removal of child labour because contingencies like number of schools and availability of food for all is not yet totally implemented. If under international pressure from businesses or international organizations a ban is strictly imposed on child labour, it may lead to increased street crimes, drug addiction among children, spread of sexually transmitted diseases, and other kinds of child abuse. Therefore, the Indian corporate world has to partner in a proactive manner with the government to tackle and eradicate poverty from a totally different perspective. Initiatives like free and compulsory education, better schools, availability of meals in schools to retain students, availability of free books and uniforms have to be undertaken by the business world, along with the government, to ensure a healthy workforce of tomorrow.

Therefore, stereotyping should be avoided and answers should be found as per the unique history of each country.

Outer Global Ideology

The general standards laid down by the United Nations and the International Labour Organisation need to be practised. However, certain areas of conflict that may arise in this are collective bargaining of workers, gender equality, human rights, environment protection, free trade, financial transparency, and corporate governance, to name a few. To overcome such conflict, in addition to ensuring social responsibility and understanding cultural relativism, the issue of economic justice would have to be taken care of.

An example of how the above-mentioned responsibilities can be ignored is when companies in the international arena operate by propagating. As Friedman (1962) wrote 'there is one social responsibility of business ... to use its resources and engage in activities designed to increase profits so long as it stays within the rules ... engages in open and free competition without deception or fraud.' From Friedman's perspective, an individual leader has a primary obligation to increase profits and maximize the return for the shareholders within the law. Friedman maintained that it is the political authority that has the responsibility to foster social objectives.

Ethical conduct under this capitalistic model could include using low-cost labour in countries where it is not illegal, regardless of working conditions and employee treatment. Similarly, operating plants that cause environmental damage or reckless depletion of natural resources would be considered ethical if it is legal in that jurisdiction. Conversely, Marxists believe that capitalism destroys the intrinsic value of human labour, if treated as merely a means of production or other input commodity (Krasemann 2001). The danger in this ideology is behind the façade of social justice, personal freedom of thought, speech and initiatives may be curtailed. 'Equality of poverty' (everybody being provided the same material welfare by the state) may be encouraged instead of actual development by disallowing any individual from taking advantage of opportunities.

Therefore, the social cost needs to be assessed fairly in every form of political ideology. It would require a balance between total control and absolute laissez-faire at the macro-level. Hence, international bodies have to be proactively involved in bringing about social justice and economic welfare in an accountable and transparent manner.

CREATING AN IMPLEMENTATION FRAMEWORK

The organization strategy needs to build the CSR structure that actually helps analyse risks and builds trust, so that it can achieve its purpose of earning profits without controversy. This can be visualized as different levels of value implementation as shown in Fig. 5.4. The foundation (inner circle of the core values) is where the values of the organization is entrenched, the second layer is where the application of the values occur, and the third is the visible layer of rules, structures, systems, processes, and codes that are put in place. The journey of the professional leader of an organization can be towards excellence when he/she draws from and relies upon the strong foundation of the organization, and builds the basic value system for the in-group and out-group of the organization.

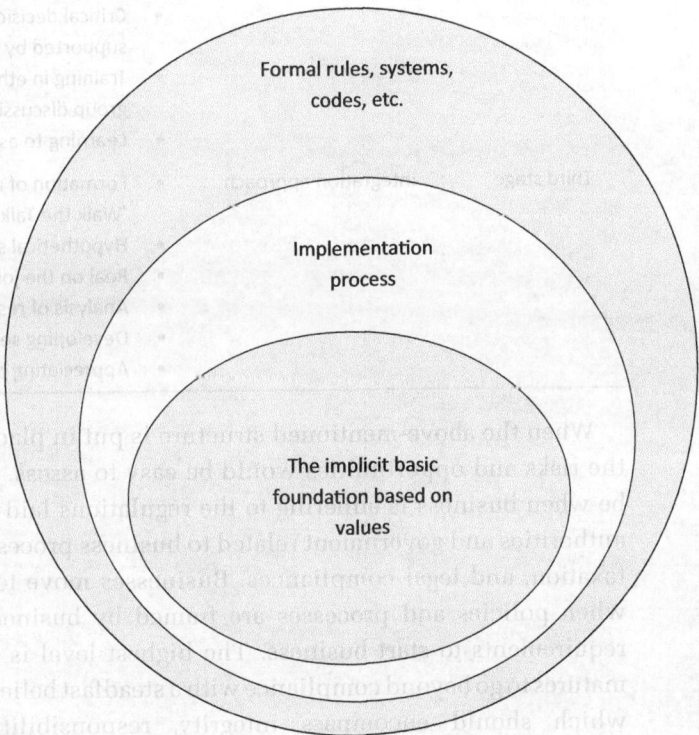

Figure 5.4 Levels of value implementation

The training approach for value implementation should follow three simple stages:
1. information sharing,
2. checking effectiveness, and
3. integration approach.

Table 5.1 shows the different continuums.

TABLE 5.1 Value implementation continuum

Levels	Function	Activities
First stage	Information sharing	• About organization values • About vision and mission • Cultural briefings • Tolerance/intolerance of unethical activities—'zero tolerance concept'
Second stage	Checking effectiveness	• Reminder of values, vision, and mission • Problems faced- solved or unsolved • Critical decisions and incidents should be supported by core values • Training in ethics—counselling, cases, group discussions • Learning to assimilate ethics at work
Third stage	Integration approach	• Formation of an assessment centre—'Walk the Talk' • Hypothetical simulation • Real on the job experiences • Analysis of responses • Developing sensitivity • Appreciating differences

When the above-mentioned structure is put in place, then an evaluation of the risks and opportunities would be easy to assess. The lowest level would be when business is adhering to the regulations laid down by the regulatory authorities and government related to business process, technical parameters, taxation, and legal compliances. Businesses move to the intermediate level when policies and processes are framed by business to cater to the basic requirements to start business. The highest level is reached when business matures to go beyond compliance with a steadfast belief in its value foundation, which should encompass integrity, responsibility, accountability, and compassion. Figure 5.5 provides the framework for understanding and rating the reciprocal relationship between the value foundations, the practical and implemented processes, and the creation of the excellent or immortal brand of an organization. This emphasizes how responsible behaviour (CSR) can create opportunities that are sustainable. The value foundation or core values of an organization should be geared towards mutual sharing of benefits with its immediate and peripheral stakeholders. Then building the organizational processes and policies based on transparency and humanity would not be difficult. Once this is achieved, brand becomes unquestionable and helps organizations to continue to build on the same cycle with renewed strength and confidence.

Creating CSR Framework | 169

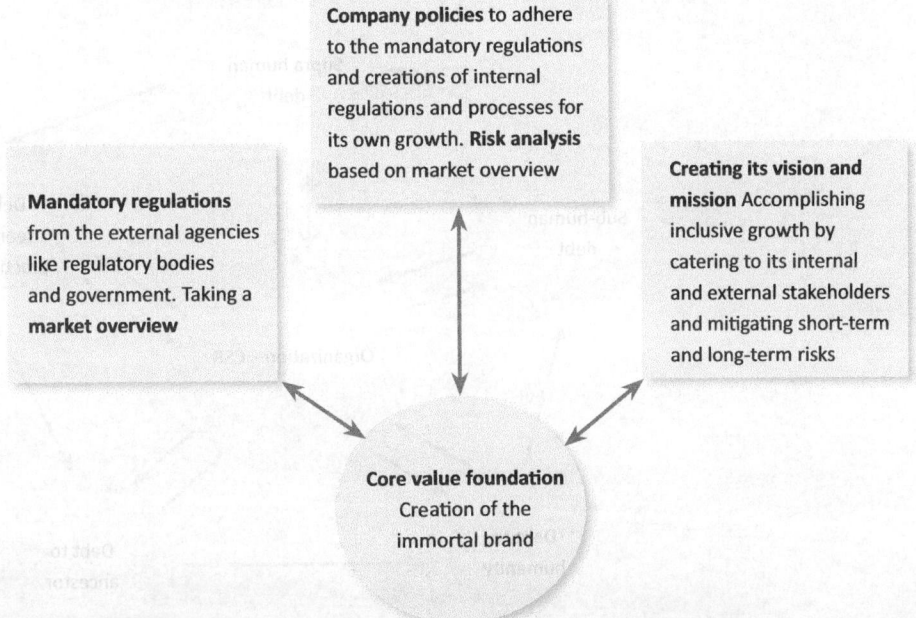

Figure 5.5 Reciprocal relationship between CSR and organization

The usual methods of taking CSR decisions are result dependant, duties dependent, and virtue or moral obligation dependant. As a result, a practicing manager is confused as he/she tries to analyse from his/her cultural understanding about what exactly to do for behaving ethically. The concepts that ensure maximization of profit with least social waste and disharmony are becoming popular. Long-term value creation should be the practical objective of any business entity in society. This can be understood if we analyse the ancient Indian tradition of 'debts' that human beings owe to implement CSR, as shown in Fig. 5.6 (Chatterji 2006).

The supra human forces These are those forces that have not been created by human effort but are inevitable necessities for survival of any life, like the sun, the earth, air, water, etc. The human race can repay the debt to these life-giving forces by protecting them. This relates to what we are today debating as environment protection and management.

The seers and practitioners These are those who have led lives of selflessness and achieved the highest truths and satisfaction in sharing and giving. Those who have shown that '... consciousness of personality begins with the feeling of separateness from all but has its culmination in the feeling of unity with all ...' (Sri Aurobindo 1985). This converting of 'me' to 'we' needs to be imbibed and practised. It actually is a debt to the knowledge that we inherit from such

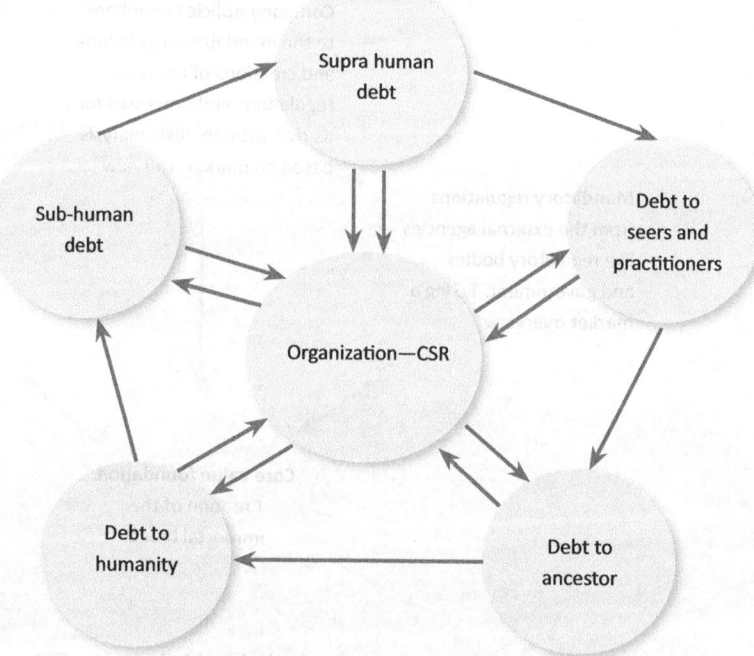

Figure 5.6 Organizational debt analysis for CSR

visionaries, which helps us to move ahead without repeating the mistakes. The repayment of the debt is by adding value and disseminating that ever-valuable knowledge.

Our ancestors If we do not preserve what our ancestors have given us, we would perish. The debt to our ancestors is repaid when we add to the wealth and development that we inherit and pass on a better world to the next generation. One cannot work in a vacuum and therefore, we have to be eternally grateful to the older generation for giving us life and learning and show respect by adding value to both.

Humanity, in general We are indebted to all people, as each one of us has a contribution to make in the working of the socio-economic system. We may never meet each other but the interdependence cannot be denied, especially in today's globalized and specialized world. People who are constantly doing or have done their work to ensure cumulative contribution to the present standing of the world need to be respected and appreciated to ensure repayment of the debt.

The sub-human life forms This relates to the understanding of the eco-diversity and the need for balance in it for everyone's survival. It is referred to as sub-human not because they are less important, but because they represent forms of life that are lower in the chain of evolution than human beings. The debt to such important forms of life in the ecological environment can be repaid by not disturbing the wonderful balance in nature. For example, if the butterflies and earthworms disappear, there would be no fruits for future seeds and no fertile land for future sowing. In the cost-benefit analysis, the long-term costs would be more and may be irreversible.

If an organization's attitude towards social existence is driven and inspired by the above orientation, then certainly the journey would be towards duties, responsibilities, and sacrifice, which are the core essence of CSR. This particular framework would help to rectify the weak linkages between various institutions like governmental, intergovernmental, as well as private organizations. The linkages need to be strengthened to access world markets, technology, credit, and managerial know-how.

Another simple way of implementation is the integrated model of development C^3 covering the 'three Cs'—understanding concepts, acquiring competencies, and building connectivity (see Fig. 5.7). This would translate excellent ideas into tangible products and services, leading to intangible value-addition through brand equity acquired as a result of connecting with all the stakeholders.

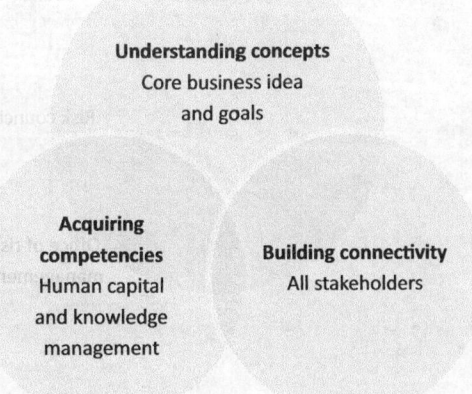

Figure 5.7 The C3 model

Exhibit 5.2 portrays Infosys Technologies, which is driven by ethics as its core-value foundation. Their process for sustainability includes every employee who is lovingly known as the Infoscion.

EXHIBIT 5.2

Infosys Technologies

One of the most eminent IT companies in India, Infosys offers a stellar example of ethics woven in their business processes. When we look at their sustainability strategy, we find it is based on the practical analysis of risks and opportunities of the organization. As per their website, their enterprise risk management programme is aimed at sustaining and enhancing long-term competitive advantage, thus adding value to their stakeholders. They are driven by their core values and ethics, which provide the platform for their risk management. Infosys analyses its risks by dividing the risks into various categories: strategy, industry, counter-party, resources, operations and regulations, and compliance. These are further divided into components under the heads of risk governance structure and key risk management processes.

Under the governance structure, it is very interesting to note that the responsibility of risks flows down to every Infoscion. The flowchart in Fig. 5.8 shows how it starts from the board of directors and moves downward, finally ending at the employee

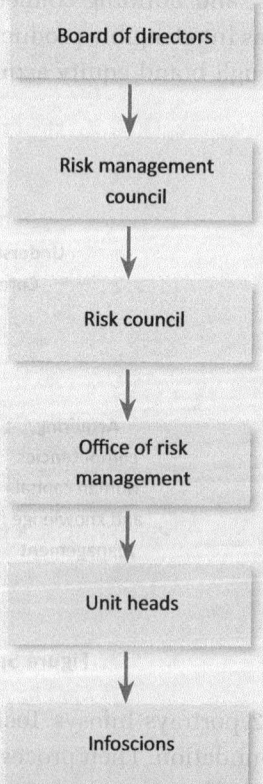

Figure 5.8 The Infosys risk management structure

known as Infoscion. Thus, the responsibility of risks is shared by every member of the organization and hence, there is a commitment from every member to ensure that risks are mitigated at every level.

The risk management process comprises of risk assessment, risk measurement and monitoring, risk reporting and disclosures, and finally integration with strategy and business plan. Thus, we see that an extremely simplified and streamlined process has been put in place for understanding risks and being accountable for the activities.

In keeping with the guidelines of the Global Reporting Initiative (GRI), Infosys published its sustainability report for the year 2008–09. As per the requirements, the report discloses information on the company's economic, social, and environmental activities and dimensions. Infosys published its first sustainability report in 2008. The report is aligned with the GRI sustainability reporting guidelines and meets the requirements of Application Level A+. The report also conforms to the principles of the UN Global Compact (UNGC).

According to Kris Gopalakrishnan, CEO and Managing Director, Infosys, 'in this sustainability report, we present the progress we have made in 2008–09 and also our charter for the future. The sea change in the world's economic scenario has highlighted the importance of and sharpened our focus on sustainability initiatives. These measures have been conceptualized and implemented, keeping in mind our responsibilities towards key stakeholders, our role in the economy and society, and our impact on the environment.'

Source: http://www.infosys.com/sustainability/Documents/infosys-sustainability-report-0809.pdf, accessed 18 May 2010.

CONCLUSION

CSR, as we know it today, can be traced historically to 1968, when the United Nations began debating it. Traditional deep-rooted practices hidden in the history of the countries where business operates influences the reputation and long-term success of enterprises. Foreign companies moving into new regions have to tread cautiously because they would be entering into new cultures and encountering social expectations drawn from the historical background of the countries they have moved into. Domestic companies would have to create trust among the stakeholders by demonstrating their adherence and understanding of the ethos and culture of the country.

These can be achieved only when CSR becomes an integral part of the business strategy of organizations. Profit is a culmination of long-term and short-term vision and is the mission of an organization and CSR is integral to both. CSR cannot remain as a peripheral philanthropic activity if long-term sustainability is the aim of the business world. The business world has to balance between the 'I' as the individual and the 'we' as the collective needs by going beyond compliance requirements and building strong value-based ideology. The best practices of today cannot remain the best practices of tomorrow unless they relate to the universal virtues, which are not relative in their existence. In science nothing can be defined as cold or dark, only the absence of heat and light. Similarly in socio-economic sphere honesty, truth, trust, loyalty, and similar virtues cannot be defined under a cultural or individual relativity. Absence of honesty is dishonesty. There cannot be levels of it from country to country for these values do not need human sanction for existence. Global recession and challenges of global warming are eye-openers for us to realize how important it is to understand that individual success can be sustainable and reaches its culmination only when it creates collective welfare.

SUMMARY

To understand CSR, building on the strong roots of history and hermeneutics (interpret ancient texts and find their relevance in the modern day) one has to visit the domain of values, beliefs, and idealism. CSR perception and delivery, therefore, differs from country to country depending upon whether the country has a business system that is able to learn and absorb new knowledge and an appropriate public policy framework. Very often, one set of definitions from one culture and ethos does not find place in another culture and ethos. Practising managers have to create an organization with a strong value-foundation, which helps to design CSR strategies that revolve around result, duties, and virtue or moral obligation. We need to have rational understanding, based on the history and socio-cultural environment of a country, for CSR practices. This will help managers develop business plans and strategies to evaluate the trade-offs and gauge variations in prioritization and acceptability that practical implementation would demand. Changing societal expectations have to be understood in the light of history. Only such a logic-based system will permit us to classify CSR understanding unambiguously, and thus enable a more sustainable course of action at the macro-level of human sustainability and the micro-level of finding a framework for measurement.

KEY TERMS

Debt theory This is borrowed from Indian spirituality. It highlights the concept of giving back to society and environment as each of us is obligated to society and nature for our own existence and growth.

Groupthink This refers to when members of a group try to minimize conflict and reach consensus without critically testing, analysing, and evaluating ideas.

Hermeneutics The science and art of interpretation of text and an attempt at seeking the contemporary relevance of ancient texts.

Creating CSR Framework | 175

Nationalism Identifying with and supporting one's country and culture.
Nativist and fundamentalist Extreme emphasis of indigenous and traditional culture and total resistance to any other culture.
Public policy Decisions or actions of government that addresses problems and issues
Stereotype Refers to conforming to a set image or type about specific social groups, or types of individuals.
Sustainability Meeting the needs of today without compromising the needs of the future generations. This relates to long-term endurance.
Transfer pricing The practice that multinational enterprises adopt in their accounting practices, so as to declare high incomes and profits in geographical areas with low taxation rates.

EXERCISES

Concept Review Questions

1. Do history and culture have any relevance in CSR? Justify your answer.
2. How can an organization build the concept of CSR into its strategy?
3. To design a corporate strategy that would include CSR as an integral concept, what aspects would you take into account?
4. Give suggestions on implementation framework of CSR.

Critical Thinking Questions

1. Why is it difficult to replicate the CSR framework from one country to another?
2. What do you understand by the term 'risk management'? Why is it relevant in CSR evaluation?

Research Question

Analyse the form of political structure that can best promote CSR. Justify your answer with historical examples.

Project Question

Select any CSR project of a corporate of your choice and find out how closely the project is aligned to local community needs.

REFERENCES

Allison G.T. (1971), Essence of Decision—Explaining the Cuban Missile Crisis, Boston, MA: Little Brown and Co.
Allison, Paul D. (1984), *Event history analysis—Regression for longitudinal event data*, Sage, Beverly Hills, CA, London, and New Delhi.
Anderson, J.R. (1983), *The Architecture of Cognition*, Harvard University Press, Cambridge.

Asmus, Peter (2003), '100 Best Corporate Citizens of 2003', *Business Ethics Magazine*, Spring 2003, pp. 6–10.

Baulch, Bob and Hoddinott John (2000), 'Economic Mobility and Poverty Dynamics in Developing Countries', *Journal of Development Studies*, vol. 38, issue no. 6, p. 1–24.

Byrnes, Nanette and Louis Lavelle (2003), 'Special Report—The Corporate Tax Game—How blue–chip companies are paying less and less of the nation's tax bill', *BusinessWeek*, March 31, pp. 79–87.

Chatterji, M. (2005), 'Building Strategic Advantage through Values and Culture', *International Conference organized by NICOM 2005*, Institute of Management Nirma University, Ahmedabad.

——— (2006), 'Corporate Social Responsibility in Practice—An Audit' www.crrconference.org, accessed on 25 May 2010.

——— (2009), 'Learning from the Legend–Case study of The Tata Group', *Focus*, vol. 5, issue nos 1 and 2, p. 127–143.

Committee for Economic Development (1971), *Social Responsibilities of Business Corporations*, CED, New York, 15.

Cyert, Richard M. and March James G. (1963), *A Behavioral Theory of the Firm*, Prentice Hall, Englewood Cliffs, NJ.

Denison, Daniel R. (1990), *Corporate culture; Organizational effectiveness*, Wiley, New York.

Ferroro, G.P. (2002), *The Cultural Dimensions of International Business* 4/e, Prentice Hall, NJ.

Friedman, M. (1962), *Capitalism and Freedom*, University of Chicago Press, Chicago.

Fritzsche D. and H. Becker (1984), Linking Managerial Behaviour to Ethical Philosophy—An Empirical Investigation, *Academy of Management Journal*, no. 17, pp. 166–175.

Geertz, Clifford (1973), *The Interpretation of Cultures*, Basic Books, New York.

Gordon, G. George and Nancy DiTomaso (1992), 'Predicting corporate performance from the strength of organizational culture', *Journal of Management Studies*, vol. 29, issue no. 6, November, pp. 783–798.

Hansen, Gary S. and Birger Wernerfelt (1989), 'Determinants of firm performance—The relative importance of economic and organizational factors', *Strategic Management Journal*, vol. 10, issue no. 5, pp. 399–411.

Hobsbawm, Eric (1983), 'Introduction—Inventing traditions' in E. Hobsbawm and T. Ranger (eds.), *The Invention of Tradition*, Cambridge University Press, Cambridge.

Hodgson, Geoffrey (2001), *How Economics Forgot History—The Problem of Historical Specificity in Social Science*, Routledge, London.

Hofstede, G. (1980), *Culture Consequences—International Differences in Work–Related Values*, Sage, Newbury Park, CA.

——— (2001), *Culture's Consequences—Comparing Values, Behaviours, Institutions and Organizations across Nations* 2/e, Sage, Thousand Oaks, CA.

Huguette, Labelle (2009), *Times of India*, November 18, 'India 84th in corruption list, Singapore top'.

Janis, I.L. (1972), *Victims of groupthink*, Houghton-Mifflin, Boston, MA.

Kotter, P. John and Heskett L. James (1992), *Corporate Culture and Performance*, Free Press, New York.

Krasemann, K.W. (2001), *Business ethics—Problems principles practical applications*, Copley Publishing Company, Acton, Massachusetts.

Maslow, A.H. (1943), 'A Theory of Human Motivation', *Psychological Review*, vol. 50, issue no. 4, pp. 370–396.

McCraw, Thomas K. (1986), 'Why history matters to managers', *Harvard Business Review* (January–February), pp. 81–88.

Mintzberg, H., D. Raisinghani, and A. Théorêt (1976), 'The structure of 'unstructured' decision processes', *Administrative Science Quarterly*, vol. 21, issue no. 2, pp. 246–275.

Mosseau, Michael (2003), 'The Nexus of Market Society Liberal preferences and Democratic Peace—Interdisciplinary Theory and Evidence', *International Studies Quarterly*, vol. 47, issue no. 4, pp. 483–510.

Mosseau, Michael, Harvard Hegre, and John R. Oneal (2003), 'How the Wealth of Nations Condition the Liberal Peace', *European Journal of International Relations*, vol. 9, issue no. 4, p. 277.

Nutt, P.C. (1984), 'Types of Organizational Decision Processes', *Administrative Science Quarterly*, vol. 29, issue no. 3, pp. 414–450.

Pettigrew, Andrew M. (1979), 'On studying organizational cultures', *Administrative Science Quarterly*, vol. 24, issue no. 4, pp. 570–581.

Press trust of India 2008—New York, June, 5, as reported in the Global Pulse Report compiled by Reputation Institute, US.

Roger, G. Schroeder (1993), *Operations Management Decision Making in the Operations Function*, McGraw Hill, New York, Fig. 1.2, p. 14 and Fig. 1.4, p. 17.

Salk, J.E. and O. Shenkar (2001), 'Social Identities in an International Joint Venture—An Exploratory Case Study', *Organization Science*, vol. 12, issue no. 2, pp. 161–178.

Schein, E.H. (1985), *Organizational culture and leadership*, Jossey–Bass, San Francisco.

——— (1992), *Organizational Culture and Leadership* 2/e, Jossy–Bass, San Francisco.

Schroeder G. Roger (1993), *Operations Management Decision Making in the Operations Function*, McGraw Hill New York, Fig. 1.2, p. 14 and Fig. 1.4, p. 17.

Scott, W.R. and J.W. Meyer (eds) (1995), *Institutional Environments and Organizations—Structural Complexity and Individualism*, Thousand Oaks, CA: Sage Publications.

Scott, W.R. (1992), *Organizations—Rational, natural and open systems*, Prentice Hall, Englewood Cliffs, NJ.

Silverthorne, Sean (2008), *The Lessons of Business History—A Handbook Q&A with Geoffrey G. Jones*, Harvard Business School Working Knowledge, Boston March 17, Harvard Business School Working Knowledge.

Simmel, Georg (1908, English translation 1950), 'The Stranger', in KH Wolff (ed.), *The Sociology of Georg Simmel*, The Free Press, New York.

Sombart, Werner (1911, English translation 1982), *The Jews and Modern Capitalism*, Transaction Books, New Brunswick.

Sri Aurobindo (1985), *The Human Cycle*, Pondicherry (India): Sri Aurobindo Ashram, p. 160.

—— (1985), *The Human Cycle*, Sri Aurobindo Ashram, Pondicherry, p. 160.

Swaminathan, M.S. (2009), 'Towards an Ever–Green Revolution', *Manorama Year Book 2009*, Malayala Manorama Press, Kottayam, Kerala, pp. 567.

Taylor, E. (1871), *Origins of Culture*, Harper and Row, New York, p. 1.

Toynbee, Arnold (1939) in *The Study of History* (Abridgement Of Volumes I–VI Paperback), Oxford University Press, US 1987, p. 233, 245.

Verma, M.N. (2002), 'Havens of Terrorism', *The Times of India*, January 10.

WBCSD, 2008—Geneva, 6th Business in Deep at World Water Week—http://www.wbscd.org/Plugings/DocSearch/detaiks.qsp?Doc; TypeID=251&ObjectID=MzEwMDE, accessed on 16 December 2008.

Weber, Max (1904, 1930 English edition), *The Protestant Ethic and the Spirit of Capitalism*, Scribner, New York.

Zadek, Simon (2001), *The Civil Corporation The New Economy of Corporate Citizenship*, Earthscan, London, p. 29.

—— (2001), *Third Generation Corporate Citizenship*, Earthscan, London, published by The Foreign Policy Centre.

Zinn, Howard (1980), *A People's History of the United States*, Harper and Row, New York, p. 8.

CASE STUDY

THE POTI PORT IN GEORGIA

History of Georgia

The long history of Georgia, the country in eastern Europe, is steeped in occupation and fighting—which is, unsurprising, due to the strategic location of the country. The rule under Russia was welcomed and introduced aspects of Georgian nationalism that still hold strong in the hearts of the natives. The Soviet Socialist Republic of Georgia was one of the most prosperous areas of the former Soviet Union. After the fall of Communism, Georgians voted unanimously for independence and soon elected their first president. Unfortunately, the 1990s brought a period of instability and fighting, which has left scars the country is still healing from—governments have been displaced and officials have died in 'mysterious circumstances', but the people let their government and the rest of the world know they were not going to stand for it with the 'Rose Revolution' of November 2003, which swept the old leaders out and threw in Europe's youngest leader, 35-year-old Makhail Saakashvili. While tensions in breakaway regions are still present and dangers still abound, Georgia has steadied itself and stability has returned.

The World Bank recognized Georgia as the world's fastest-reforming economy in its 2008 'Doing Business' report, ranking it as the world's 15th easiest place to do business, in the same league as countries such as Germany, Sweden, and Estonia.

The World Bank's 'Anti-Corruption in Transition' report places Georgia among the countries showing the most dramatic improvement in the struggle against corruption, due to implementation of key economic and institutional reforms, and reported reduction in the bribes paid by firms in the course of doing business.

The History of Poti Port
One of the engines of Georgia's growth is the historical port of Poti. Georgian ports were involved in trading with the Greeks. The story of Jason and the Argo in which he set out to find the Golden Fleece probably was a voyage into Georgia where it was a custom to hang sheep fleeces in rivers to catch gold dust from the river sediments. Such a system has been observed in use in recent times both in Georgia and Romania.

On 3 April 1858, the Russian Emperor Alexander II converted the executive visa into a perfect significant state document—the resolution # 451 of the Caucasian Committee 'On establishment of an international Commercial Port on the East Coast of the Black Sea in Poti' (official brochure of Poti Sea Port). Wedged between Ponto, Paliastomi Lake, and the river Rioni, mythical Pazisi—present Poti—has been renowned since time immemorial. With its advantageous geographical location, high throughput, terminals, well-developed transport communications and its rich ancient traditions, Poti has the potential to be on the list as one of the best ports of the world in the 21st century.

Poti, the first seaport of Georgia, played a crucial role in the economic advancement of the country. It is a legal entity of public law and has been an integral part of the politics and economy of Georgia. Fortune favoured Poti when Niko Nikoladze was elected the head of the town in 1894. He initiated the mechanization of the port and built the Rioni-Porti and Rioni-Kaparchi channels, which had strategic military importance. During World War II it was an important military base of the Soviet army.

Importance of the Port
The historical port is a transit centre and a junction point of the Caucasian Corridor. The port has an important role in the TRACECA Project, which envisages providing sea, rail, and land communications after its modernization has been completed, and its infrastructure has been enlarged. The TRACECA Project is the result of the formation of the Common European Market and the activation of relations with Asian Countries. The project aims at developing trade relations between East and West in order to connect Central Asia with Europe.

Poti's coveted location has drawn the EU and other western countries to be actively involved in its development. It has been unanimously agreed by the western institutions that Poti has great potential in international deliveries. The growth of the Euro Asian transport corridor includes the construction of a new port in Poti. The port is a member of the Black and Azov Sea Port association.

The port defines the industrial character of the town. The port has open and closed storage facilities, road and railway passages, a distribution station and other support functions. There are eight cargo-handling complexes and different types of bulk cargo such as coal, coke, ore, metal wares, non-ferrous metals, paper, food products, wheat, general cargo, and oil products are handled. The social and economic development of Georgia greatly depends on the normal functioning of the port.

The Social Aspect

Considering the economic importance of the port, it has played an important part in the local community's advancement. The policies of the port were framed keeping in mind the dependence of the local people on the port for their livelihood and growth. Therefore, the CSR has operated mainly at the inner circle level and the outer level has seen more philanthropic activity than a structured CSR policy.

The port boasts of employing on the basis of merit. According to their HR department one of the greatest attractions for seeking employment in the port is the timely disbursement of salary. The relevance of this can be best understood when it is compared to situations such as—Brussels, 28 June, 2002 (on-line): With output in the Georgian energy sector in rapid decline due to government corruption and incompetence, wage arrears of 10–15 months have accumulated and the situation for many workers is desperate.

Some examples of the employee-friendly attitude of this industry are: The labour code is strictly followed and women employees are given a few extra advantages. Women are given the facility to come one hour late if they have children below the age of eight. Every family is given 200–300 Lari (local currency) during child-birth or death in the family. Bonuses, holidays and sports facilities are the other incentives. It is the largest employer in the region, therefore a major source of livelihood.

At the outer circle level the port has played a crucial part in the lives of the local residents through philanthropic activities like building orphanages, providing children books, computers, and organizing visits to amusement parks and other gifts for children. The renovation of the city hall, schools and hospitals has been monitored by the port management. The Department of Public Relations oversees these activities.

Considering today's market conditions and competition in a globalized world the government of Georgia has a tie-up with RAK Investment Authority, which is a nodal agency of Ras Al Khaima Government, to improve productivity and modernize the operations so that it becomes the central hub of business in Eastern Europe.

The Challenges for CSR Implementation

As mentioned above CSR is not philanthropy but demands the integration of social responsibility in the entire business process. Therefore the history of the nation and the organization both become extremely important while designing policies. Georgia faces many challenges in attracting foreign investment and growing its economy. In 2007, more than 23 per cent of the population lived below the official poverty line. With only 4.7 million people, most of whom have little disposable income, it is a small market in itself. The major market to which Georgia has traditionally been linked is Russia. 'Of all CIS countries, Georgia has the sad honour to be in the first place regarding wage arrears. Most of the concerned workers make no more than the minimum wage, which does not even secure the most minimal level of subsistence. The situation has been exacerbated by the policies of MNEs whereby profit comes at the expense of all other factors,' explained Vadim Borisov, ICFTU representative for CIS countries.

Unemployment has to be addressed as the purchasing power of the country is dependent on the earning capabilities. Therefore the vicious cycle of unemployment and poverty has to be broken with proactive efforts of the corporate and the political will. The organizations would have to address accessibility to basic amenities, which would be the natural demand of a population that was historically provided with such amenities under the socialistic regime of Russia. After meeting those the organization has to develop the future competencies like teaching English, providing scientific and technological knowledge and skills, improving infrastructure, creating credible systems within the organization and actively participating with the government to reduce corruption and establish independent judiciary and legal framework and credible financial institutions. CSR demands that philanthropy, at the edges of the corporate existence, can no longer be propagated as socially responsible behaviour.

The government faces a major challenge in controlling the persistent problem of corruption. The survey by the World Bank and the EBRD, published as part of the EBRD's annual Transition Report, concludes that bribery and corruption remain widespread due in part to the continued reliance of companies on direct ties to government officials. Also, widespread lack of confidence in the Georgian courts and system of justice is a major obstacle to both foreign and domestic investment. The new government has promised to tackle this difficult task, which requires balancing the objective of judicial independence with honest, fair, and competent decision-making.

According to a United Nations report, children face worse deprivation and danger in post-communist eastern and central Europe than under the old authoritarian regimes, UNICEF, the UN Children's Fund, says the social, political, and economic upheavals since the collapse of communism have taken a heavy toll among children in the region's 'transition' countries. There are now about one million children living in public care, mostly in big institutions, in these 18 countries, the UN agency estimates. This figure is higher than in the 1980s. Children have been the victims of armed conflict in transition countries such as Georgia. 'One might have expected families to pull together in times of economic crisis', the report's authors commented. 'But the huge pressures of the transition appear to be splitting families apart and eroding parental responsibility'. The report describes as frightening the pace of the spread of drug abuse, child prostitution, and juvenile crime, in the post-communist period. The UN agency calls on governments in the region to give up their 'piecemeal, crisis-led approach' and to devise a long-term strategy to help families meet their child-raising responsibilities. 'Communism's fall means misery for children in need.' 'Eastern Europe reform leaves children behind. The long-term impact of this would be reflected in the lack of a healthy workforce in the future. Unhealthy workers not only cannot contribute to higher production but also become a drain on the finances of the organization and the country, as employee welfare schemes would require large allocations of money. The cost to the company for delivering goods and services would increase and thus it would neither be competitive in the world market nor serve national needs, as the prices would be high for the common people to afford. Thus, it becomes clear that CSR has to address community issues to increase the bottom line of organization and add to social welfare.

Advantages of Georgia
The United States and other international donors have targeted foreign assistance to promote democratic reform, resolve regional conflicts, foster energy independence, assist economic development, and reduce poverty. Georgia is one of the first countries to receive a compact, an amount of $295 million over five years, from the United States Millennium Challenge Corporation (MCC). MCC offers grant assistance to countries that meet certain requirements for good governance and commitment to reform. In 2004, Georgia's debt to the Paris Club was restructured. From 2004, the International Monetary Fund (IMF) monitored a Poverty Reduction and Growth Facility that was to terminate in 2007. The World Bank, European Bank for Reconstruction and Development, EU, OSCE (Organization for Security and Cooperation in Europe), and the UN are all active in Georgia. Their goals are complementary, and include assisting in conflict resolution with Russia in Abkhazia and South Ossetia, energy and transportation development, legal and administrative reform, health, and many other areas. In response to the damage suffered during the 2008 conflict with Russia, 38 countries and 15 international organizations pledged to provide US$4.55 billion to Georgia at the Brussels donors' conference on 22 October 2008. Of the US$4.55 billion, US$2 billion are grants and the rest are low-interest loan guarantees. The pledges amounted to some US$3.7 billion to meet the urgent post-conflict and priority infrastructure investment needs over three years—2008, 2009, and 2010—with the rest going to shore up the financial and banking sector.

Georgia's location situated between the Black Sea, Russia, Armenia, Azerbaijan, and Turkey gives it importance as a transport corridor far beyond its size. It is developing as the gateway from the Black Sea to the Caucasus and the Caspian basin. It signed a partnership and cooperation agreement with the European Union, and in 2006 signed an action plan under the European Union's European Neighborhood Policy for reforms aimed at building a closer relationship with the EU. Georgia participates in NATO's Partnership for Peace programme. In addition, Georgia has reached out to a number of countries that have expressed interest in investing in the country.

Since the collapse of the Soviet Union, Moscow and Washington have been jockeying to control the route that will eventually take these enormous resources more rapidly to market in the West. Georgia and neighbouring Azerbaijan, which borders the Caspian, quickly came to be seen not only as newly independent countries, but also as part of an 'energy corridor'. The old, Soviet-era pipeline runs from the Azerbaijani capital Baku north into Russian territory, then west to the Black Sea port of Novorossisk, in the process running through the troubled separatist region of Chechnya. Anxious to build a more secure route, Western investors built a second line in 1998, from Baku to the Georgian port city of Supsa. Plans were laid for an even larger pipeline that would run through Georgia to Turkey and the Mediterranean.

INTEGRATING CSR AS A CORPORATE PROCESS

Learnings from the case

Georgia has just emerged out of the Russian block therefore the need to convince the people and orient them towards a new vision of market led growth is going to be one of the big challenges. To reap the advantages of the free market economy and globalization, the management of the Poti Port would have to chalk out the growth trajectory by utilizing the inner dynamics of the ancient Georgian history and culture. This would allay the fears of the local people and minimize forces of destabilization.

Poti port, like the Tata group in India, can play a crucial role by pioneering and initiating socially relevant activities as both have an honourable historic past. It can become the role model for other organizations in the urgent need of nation building. Poti Port can take great advantage of Georgia being a natural transit corridor. Because of its strategic physical reason Poti can invite investment in any kind of warehousing, terminaling, product assembly—anything that takes advantage of and uses the country's position as a corridor between Europe and Central Asia. Georgia is a beautiful country where tourism remains a promising sector for future development, and the port can take benefit of this economic opportunity and thus help in increasing employment and add in other ways to the social scenario.

The Georgian government has done a lot to encourage incoming investment in Georgia as a transit corridor, such as the Free Industrial Zone legislation and infrastructure privatization initiatives. Once the international economy gets better, things in Georgia will also improve. The port like the Tata group can utilize the government initiatives to promote socially responsible economic activities and increase its own bottom-line as well.

International initiatives are also adding to Georgia's journey towards CSR, and by getting involved in their agenda and activities organizations can re-define their boundaries of responsibility vis-à-vis the society and environment and subsequently come up with a new 'social contract'. The ILO EMP/SEED conducted tripartite meetings on socially sensitive enterprise restructuring (SSER) in Georgia, during which a seminar was conducted jointly with ILO Turin at the request of the Georgian Employers' Federation, and was attended by the high-level representatives of government, employers, and workers. A project proposal has been developed, which is under consideration by potential donors.

To better understand the potential of responsible business practice for sustainable development of Western Balkans as well as how to move the agenda forward, UNDP undertakes a base-line study as a diagnosis exercise. This aims to map out the actors' engagement in CSR in the project countries through research and consultations. UNDP encourages national debates in these countries on the results of the mapping and broad-based discussion on the way forward.

Poti Port has to design value-based systems and processes to ensure that CSR is incorporated in the management practices of the organization. The entire operation of the organization needs to be guided by strong value-based policies. This would enhance the trust that the port already enjoys of all the stakeholders and that would increase the bottom-line and the top-line of business. The new management of Rash Al Khaima government is already taking positive steps towards this requirement.

(The case has been developed for class discussion and is based on published data and a few personal interviews. The POTI Port case has been provided to understand how historical events lead to the development of different systems of ethics for understanding business responsibilities.)

Discussion Questions
1. What are the historic and cultural issues that need to be addressed while designing CSR programme in Georgia?
2. What is the significance of the port at Poti and how can it play a major role in setting a standard for CSR?
3. What are the major challenges that need to be addressed by CSR initiatives of the Poti port?
4. Read the Tata cases given in chapters 3 and 6 and compare them with the Poti Port Case and design a CSR framework for the Poti port.

Sources: http://georgia.offplanproperty.info/about.html; http://www.traveldocs.com/ge/economy.htm; http://www.ewpnet.com/georgia/history.htm; *ICFTU online*, 128/280602/SV-J, 28 June 2002; Profit at all costs: Irish and Spanish multinationals flout international standards in Georgia *ICFTU online*, 128/280602/SV-J, 28 June 2002; Gordon Martin, *Daily Telegraph*, 24 April 1997, Unicef report; http://www.traveldocs.com/ge/economy.htm; International Labour Office Governing Body, Geneva), November 2007 Sub-committee on Multinational Enterprises (MNE, GB.300/MNE/3/1; http://europeandcis.undp.org/gender/georgia, The CSR Western Balkans Baseline Study.

Framework for Rating Corporate Social Responsibility

INTRODUCTION

Today, there is a widespread realization that the business world has to create its own code of 'decency' if it wants long-term sustainable existence. The reality is that business operates inside society and, therefore, it has to create a relationship with society, which is based on trust stemming from transparency in its dealings. To achieve this, businesses have to portray to all stakeholders their intentions and the best way to do that is to provide a measurement of its impact on stakeholders. This has created an awareness that CSR should be rated. In terms of business history, this idea of measuring socially responsible behaviour is a comparatively new concept. Obviously, the idea draws heavily on prevailing credit ratings and securities analysis. Since CSR includes the socio-cultural paradigms, it is difficult to create a universal rating mechanism. Therefore, in spite of similarities between different frameworks, we have to provide for diversity and heterogeneity for a true rating result. The rating mechanism at best works as a signalling factor for stakeholders to re-evaluate their financial and economic commitment to the business world and also helps the business world to rectify its processes, to remain in the good books of the stakeholders.

LEARNING OBJECTIVES

After studying this chapter, you will be able to
- Understand the importance of CSR reporting
- Create awareness about the various reporting criteria followed to report CSR
- Understand how conscientious organizations are committed to the concept of CSR
- Learn from CSR reporting frameworks of various agencies and organizations

UNDERSTANDING CSR RATINGS

If we trace the history of the rating process, then two important international conferences come to the forefront: the UN Biosphere Conference and the Conference on the Ecological Aspects of International Development by the Conservation Foundation and the Centre for the Biology of Natural Systems, 1968. In 1972, *The Limits to Growth* was published by the Club of Rome, representing initial steps in the direction of sustainability reporting. During the same year, the United Nations Conference on Human Environment was held in Stockholm. Following these initiatives, many more such sustainability related publications were launched, e.g., World Conservation Strategy (1980), UN Global Compact (2000), the Green Book of the EU-Commission on CSR (2001), and the OECD-Guidelines for Multinational Enterprises (2004).

Business is undertaken to cater to the prevailing or created needs of society. A business operator has to analyse the overt (immediately visible) and covert (not visible, hidden) impacts of its activities on society. This relates directly to the market forces that impact and are impacted by the following factors: (a) What is the need that is being catered to? (b) What are the alternatives available? (c) What is the competitor offering and at what price? (d) The demands of the regulations promulgated by the government and other regulatory bodies, like SEBI (Securities and Exchange Board of India), RBI (Reserve Bank of India), CII (Confederation of Indian Industry) in India, SEC (Securities and Exchange Commission), and FED (Federal Reserve) in the US, etc., which impact business processes; (e) Macro economic factors like change in the demographic factors, new economic policies, and the political ideology of the ruling party also need to be factored in by the corporates, for both their economic and social activities. Similar ideas are expressed in what Gladwin et al. (1995) define as intra-generational justice, in particular between the first and the third world, and inter-generational justice between the present and future generations.

CSR rating tools help in corporate governance processes by providing information and helping in monitoring socially responsible behaviour. They provide the incentive to screen activities, thus both agency loss and transaction cost can be reduced by capturing opportunistic, irregular behaviour and activities (refer to Chapter 2). This adds value to the corporate because it provides the quality parameters on which a corporate has been screened. Since this kind of an evaluation requires organizational structure analysis, which would highlight both the direct and indirect interventions, this may lead to the creation of a sustainability sensitive organization that caters to holistic growth. See Annexure for details on environmental reporting.

AVAILABLE ACCEPTED RATING FRAMEWORKS

Let us now look at some of the established quantitative rating frameworks that are available for organizations to report on sustainability.

Global Reporting Initiative

Global Reporting Initiative (GRI) is a forerunner among the standard frameworks for sustainability reporting. The birthplace of this reporting framework is the US. It was envisioned by non-profits CERES (formerly, the Coalition for

Environmentally Responsible Economies) and Tellus Institute, with the support of the United Nations Environment Programme (UNEP) in 1997. In 1999, the first version known as the 'exposure draft' of the Sustainability Reporting Guidelines was published. The full version was released at the World Summit for Sustainable Development in Johannesburg in the year 2000. It was a momentous occasion, as the organization and the guidelines were referred to in the Plan of Implementation and were signed by all the attending member states. During the latter half of the year, it became a permanent institution. It has its Secretariat in Amsterdam, in the Netherlands. GRI is an independent body but has close connection with the United Nations Global Compact and functions as a collaborating centre of UNEP.

It is a network-based organization that seeks consensus from business, civil society, labour, and professional institutions. It offers principles and indicators that organizations can use to measure and report their economic, environmental, and social performance. It prides itself for quality, credibility, and relevance.

To ensure continuous improvement and applicability worldwide, GRI keeps updating its Sustainability Reporting Guidelines. The third version is named G3, and was published in 2006. It is a free public good, i.e., the guidelines can be used by anybody free of cost. As of January 2009, more than 1500 organizations from 60 countries use the guidelines to produce their sustainability reports.

The G3 guidelines are relevant to all organizations, regardless of their geographical location, industry sector, or size. Therefore, it is recommended that it should be used as the basis for annual reporting by an organization on its sustainable and responsible behaviour. The framework is flexible and has an inbuilt incremental process. However, it is a voluntary initiative of firms and not a mandatory global practice.

Exhibit 6.1 gives the basic features of the reporting methodology and how it is quantifiable and therefore measurable.

EXHIBIT 6.1

Features of Reporting Methodology

Principles for Defining Report Content

Materiality What should be the major content of the report? The information in a report should cover topics and indicators that reflect the organization's significant economic, environmental, and social impacts, and all that would substantively influence the assessments and decisions of stakeholders.

Stakeholder inclusiveness The reporting organization should identify its stakeholders and explain in the report how it has responded to their reasonable expectations and interests.

Sustainability context The report should present the organization's performance in the wider context of sustainability.

Completeness Coverage of the material topics and indicators and definition of the report boundary should be sufficient to reflect significant economic, environmental, and social impacts and enable stakeholders to assess the reporting organization's performance in the reporting period.

Principles for Ensuring Report Quality

Balance The report should reflect positive and negative aspects of the organization's performance to enable a reasoned assessment of overall performance.

Comparability Issues and information should be selected, compiled, and reported consistently. Reported information should be presented in a manner that enables stakeholders to analyse changes in the organization's performance over time, and could support analysis relative to other organizations.

Accuracy The reported information should be sufficiently accurate and detailed for stakeholders to assess the reporting organization's performance.

Timeliness Reporting occurs on a regular schedule and information is available in time for stakeholders to make informed decisions.

Clarity Information should be made available in a manner that is understandable and accessible to stakeholders using the report.

Reliability Information and processes used in the preparation of a report should be gathered, recorded, compiled, analysed, and disclosed in a way that could be subject to examination and that establishes the quality and materiality of the information.

Source: http://www.globalreporting.org/NR/rdonlyres/DDB9A2EA-7715-4E1A-9047-FD2FA8032762/0/G3_QuickReferenceSheet.pdf, last accessed 11 April 2010.

Specialized Securities Indexes

Specialized Securities Indexes are also used for rating CSR-oriented activities of a firm. These basically replicate stock sector reporting in social and environmental sectors. The Dow Jones US Water Index is an interesting index as it reports about the water resources and looks at it from stock option perspective (see Fig. 6.1). As it brings to the fore the issues related to water in terms of scarcity, pollution, etc., it serves the social interest by alerting about scarce, non-renewable natural resources. It is estimated that about 70 per cent of the earth's surface is covered with water, but 97 per cent of it is saltwater. Since saltwater cannot be used for drinking, irrigation, and most industrial uses in its natural form, this huge body of water is unfit for human usage. Therefore, only the remaining 3 per cent of the world's water resources can be utilized. Unfortunately, due

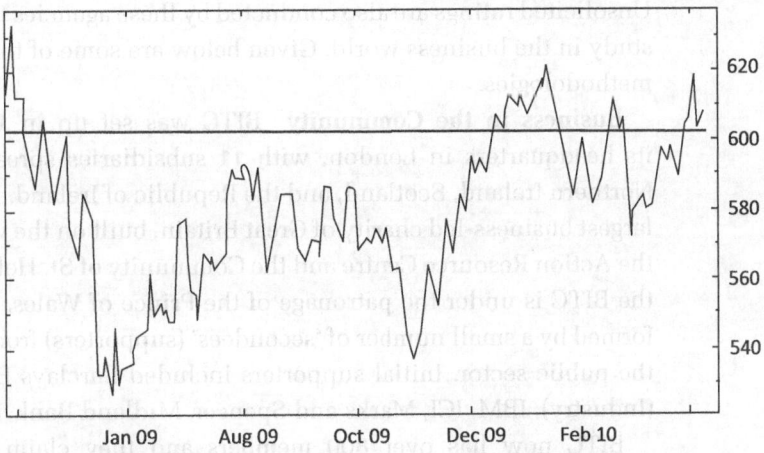

Source: www.advfn.com

Figure 6.1 Dow Jones US water index historical stock chart

to rapid industrialization, unplanned cultivation, and deforestation, much of this amount is polluted and unsafe for human consumption. Only about 1 per cent is readily available for human consumption. Naturally, as a commodity, now water becomes a good stock option and companies are looking at various options to fill this requirement gap and earn profit.

Another similar index is the European Renewable Energy Index (ERIX), issued by the French bank Société Générale in collaboration with Stoxx Ltd. and the SAM Group. The index tracks the stocks of companies providing renewable energy and related issues. This index also concerns sustainability issues as it provides pointers towards sustainable development in the environmental sector.

Regulatory Bodies and Stock Exchanges

Regulatory bodies and stock exchanges also provide tools for rating CSR. For example, SEBI in India, SEC in the US, and similar authorities in other countries provide guidelines on corporate governance, which helps to protect the stakeholders of organizations. The London Stock Exchange has created a tool named Corporate Reporting Exchange (CRE) to measure CSR in collaboration with the UK Social Investment Forum.

Besides the above mentioned rating propositions, companies do in-house CSR reporting and publish it for public consumption. Certain institutions like Allianz Global Investors, BHF-BANK AG, and UBS (Union Bank of Switzerland), are a few institutional CSR-rating agencies.

There are agencies that help in rating socially relevant activities and companies often solicit their intervention in rating their sustainable activities.

Unsolicited ratings are also conducted by these agencies to create a comparative study in the business world. Given below are some of these agencies and their methodologies.

Business in the Community BITC was set up in 1982 in the UK, with its headquarters in London, with 11 subsidiaries spread over Great Britain, Northern Ireland, Scotland, and the Republic of Ireland. It has evolved into the largest business-led charity of Great Britain, built on the work of groups such as the Action Resource Centre and the Community of St. Helens Trust. Since 1987, the BITC is under the patronage of the Prince of Wales. The organization was formed by a small number of 'secondees' (supporters) from both companies and the public sector. Initial supporters included Barclays Bank, BP, British Steel (Industry), IBM, ICI, Marks and Spencer, Midland Bank, and WHSmith.

BITC now has over 800 members and they claim 'we inspire, engage, support, and challenge companies to make a positive impact in the community, workplace, marketplace, and environment'. They have identified five principles that form the heart of their strategy and the commitment to action that represents membership of business in the community: integrity, inspiration, integration, innovation, and impact.

BITC has so far gone through three major phases. During Phase I in the 1980s, BITC was dedicated to regenerating local economies across the UK through charitable contributions. The main aim was to encourage small businesses and support re-skilling. In their own words, BITC acted as a broker for companies supporting local enterprise agencies with cash, secondees, premises, equipment, expertise, and employee volunteering.

The 1990s saw the second phase, which was marked by trying to create a community corporate involvement by helping organizations to better organize their involvement. This widened to CSR and the process of integrating sustainability into the core business strategies of organizations was the main agenda. The business driver was that competitive advantage could be gained by individual companies by following CSR. It looked at the concept of sustainability as a business challenge and worked at offering solutions. Therefore, BITC promoted companies to work in individual capacity as well as collectively, sharing concerns and resources. It has helped to institutionalize and mainstream corporate responsibility by providing 'a systematic approach to managing, measuring, and reporting on business impacts in society and on environment'.

Over the past seven years, the CR Index has inspired over 350 companies to continuously improve their impact on society and the environment (see Fig. 6.2). This business-led initiative expects to have more than 100 companies participate publicly and use their tool to both improve their management practices and communicate to stakeholders how seriously they take their CR agenda.

Following the launch of the first index results in March 2003, BITC never looked back. Further modifications are continuously made to the survey to ensure its relevance and usefulness to the business community. The latest development in the evolution of the CR Index is the Platinum Plus Standard (Exhibit 6.2), which was created to challenge companies beyond the boundaries of the CR Index.

EXHIBIT 6.2

The Platinum Plus Standard

The focus of Platinum Plus is to evaluate:
- Connectivity between business strategy and thinking around sustainability
- The commercial impact of having integrated CR initiatives into the business
- How the company is transferring the business model, so as to account for the under-pinning of social and environmental issues

To achieve the Platinum Plus Standard, a three-hour meeting is held during which companies have to give evidence of their performance. Companies have to inform about their commercial activities and provide updates on their appropriate treatment of the social and environmental issues that underpin the business model. This process tests the strategy and tactics deployed to deliver tangible business value through CR.

The Engagement process has five steps:
- The company supplies a pre-agreed list of documents and BITC conducts its research using this as well as other sources.
- BITC holds a teleconference with the relevant CR practitioner, explaining the areas of enquiry that BITC sees as most material to the company, discussing the list of company representatives to be present for the three-hour meeting and fixing a date and location for the meeting.
- That telecon and the conceptual framework form the basis of a 'big conversation' with an inter-disciplinary team from within the company.
- Based on evidence, both public and private, and the outcome of the 'big conversation', Platinum Plus will be evaluated and determined by BITC.
- A one-page written feedback from BITC will be given, detailing the reasons why the Standard was or was not achieved and suggesting areas of future focus. A meeting to explain the result can be set up on request.

Source: www.bitc.org.uk, accessed on 18 April 2010.

The forerunner of the CR Index is the BiE Index and its successor, the 'Environmental Index' (launched in 1996). The BiE Index is incorporated in the CR Index and Environmental Index. The CR Index provides the recipient with a detailed feedback, one concerning the environment and another on the entire CR agenda. This enables the companies to benchmark and compare their management practice across the four areas of community, environment, marketplace, and workplace, as well as their performance in a range of environmental and social impact areas.

STRUCTURE OF BITC'S CR INDEX

The model provides five social impact areas (product safety, health and safety at the workplace, supplier relations, equal opportunities, and community investment).

The three areas that are the most relevant to the company have to be assessed. Additionally, companies are asked to select two core environmental performance areas of global warming (or energy/transport) and solid waste, plus two additional performance areas (which could include biodiversity).

The strategy section of the index represents 10 per cent of the overall score, integration and management receives 22.5 per cent, and the performance and impact section receives 35 per cent (equally split between environment and social). The final 10 per cent of marks are awarded for the level of assurance (5 per cent) provided by participants and their willingness to disclose certain information relating to their survey submission (5 per cent).

'Green America' is a not-for-profit membership organization founded in 1982. It was known as Co-op America till 1 January 2009. Its goal consists of (a) harnessing the strength of consumers, investors, markets, businesses to create socially just and an environmentally sustainable society; (b) making social and ecological improvements possible by enlightenment and supply of strategies, organization strength, and practical assistance for enterprises and

Source: Business in the Community, 2003, Corporate Responsibility Index 2002, accessed on 13 April 2010.

Figure 6.2 Corporate responsibility index model

private people. Green America operates as a worker member cooperative, where staff members seek to achieve consensus through democratic decision-making processes on key strategic issues for the organization.

Green America's programmes strive for four goals: empowering individuals through their purchasing and investing choices demanding an end to corporate irresponsibility through collective economic action, promoting green and fair trade business principles and helping in promoting the market for businesses adhering to these principles and building sustainable communities in the US and abroad.

Green America's programmes include:
- The Living Green Programme gives customers ideas for greener ways of living, purchasing, and investing.
- The WoodWise Programme promotes economic action to end deforestation.
- The Fair Trade Programme is a system of exchange that honours producers, communities, consumers, and the environment (read the opening case of Chapter 7 as an example).
- The Green Energy Programme forwards the distribution of clean, green, and renewable energy.
- The Responsible Shopper Programme reports on the social and environmental performance of some of the largest consumer product companies.
- The Boycotts Programme uses boycotts as a powerful tool for raising awareness about the impact of corporate practices on workers, communities, and the Earth.
- The Sweatshops Programme provides the information needed to help stop sweatshop labour (sweatshops are places of employment, usually a factory or a shop, where employment is commonly characterized by low pay, poor working conditions, safety violations, and generally inhuman treatment of employees) and promote fair treatment of workers everywhere.
- The Shop & Unshop Programme gives information and strategies needed to make green purchasing decisions that work for costumers and their families and gives ideas helping to cut down on purchases that harm people and the planet.
- The Green Business Programme supports small, particularly socially and environmentally responsible companies, and gives an account of their success.
- The Social Investing Programme gives strategies for socially and environmentally responsible investing.

An example of how its programme tracks activities is given in Exhibit 6.3.

> **EXHIBIT 6.3**
>
> **Responsible Shopper**
>
> Provides in-depth profiles of 400 US-based consumer product companies. The information includes:
> - Brands
> - Corporate affiliations
> - News (praise, alerts, and background research items)
> - Contact information (address, phone, fax, e-mail, website, contact form)
> - Contact function (send e-mails to company executives—fax capability coming soon)
>
> Ratings of the company being tracked under their programme are studied under the following heads:
> - Company comparisons by consumer product/industry
> - Industry profiles—key issues, what to look for, what to avoid, etc.
>
> *Source:* www.responsibleshopper.org.

Rating Criteria and Basic Structure of the Rating Process

A stringent process of checks is implemented before a company is listed in the 'Green Pages Online'. The screening team investigates each applying company to determine two items: (1) its familiarity with and commitment to social and environmental responsibility and (2) significant action in terms of this commitment.

To qualify for listing, companies have to demonstrate:
- focus on using business as a tool for positive social change,
- are 'values-driven', as well as 'profit-driven',
- are socially and environmentally responsible, and
- are committed to and employ extraordinary and innovative practices that benefit: (1) workers (2) communities (3) customers, and (4) the environment.

EXPERTS IN RESPONSIBLE INVESTMENT SOLUTIONS

EIRIS or Experts in Responsible Investment Solutions is an independent, not-for-profit organization set up in 1983. It provides research in environmental, social, governance (ESG), and ethical performance of companies. EIRIS is headquartered in London and partners with Centre for Australian Ethical Research (CAER, Australia), Fundacion Ecologia y Desarrollo (EcoDes, Spain), Institut für Markt—Umwelt—Gesellschaft (imug, Germany), EthiFinance (formerly Observatoire de L'Ethique, France), and Avanzi SRI Research (Italy).

Their research is client driven and designed to allow investors to compare company performance. Besides providing research in ESG issues, it also deals with specific ethical concerns such as involvement in arms or tobacco. Today, there is a demand from investors for factoring ESG performance analysis into their investment decisions. Companies cannot ignore reporting on these issues. Thus, the EIRIS surveys give companies an opportunity to provide the most up-to-date and accurate information on their ESG performance to more than 100 investment institutions.

EIRIS claims to be a global market leader as their research is used by a variety of asset owners and asset managers (including pension funds), investment banks, and charities throughout the world. As a not-for-profit organization, EIRIS does not assess companies' financial status but looks at their ESG policies and practices. They provide assessments on over 150 individual criteria for the benefit of the business community to assess their activities. To provide these data, EIRIS works on two basic branches of business:

1. They inquire, evaluate, and provide information of important data relevant to sustainability for companies belonging to the FTSE4Good (Created in 2001, FTSE4GOOD indexes are a range of socially responsible stock exchange indexes included in the British FTSE (*Financial Times* and Stock Exchange) index to create a selected list of qualified companies for the index.
2. EIRIS has also developed a special concept called the Ethical Portfolio Manager (EPM). The EPM, established in spring 2000, is a software tool that allows EIRIS's clients to access research information on the social, environmental, and ethical performance of companies.

In 2005, EIRIS launched a new service called Convention Watch, which looked into labour and human rights issues. Convention Watch also identifies bribery, corruption, military, and environmental concerns. EIRIS analyses companies against 350 environmental and social indicators, including governance issues, environmental issues, social issues, and other issues like animal testing, disclosure, fur, genetic engineering, intensive farming, etc. Their commitment is to handle relationships with companies professionally, independently, and in a timely fashion.

SUSTAINABLE INVESTMENT RESEARCH INTERNATIONAL

SiRi (Sustainable Investment Research International) group was established as an association in 2001. The headquarters of the SiRi Company is in Fribourg, Switzerland. The research is mainly focused on the principle of Sustainable Development, based on the stakeholder model. In 2006, it released the 1900 sustainability ratings and profiles of large-cap companies.

The methodology adopted by SiRi is two-pronged. It first gathers data on sustainability issues, which include transparency, management systems, policies, and strategies, including controversial issues. Second, it collates and analyses the data through an assessment grid. It makes use of web-based application for its processes. SiRi bases its ratings on seven themes, which are divided into four different levels. Each theme has a unique evaluation criterion and for that, specific indicators are chosen. The whole process is analysed on scoring and the analyst provides scores ranging between 100 as best and 0 as worst. Over 140 indicators are scored, then through a weighted matrix, it is consolidated for the criterion and theme levels. SiRi collects data on company information, controversies, stakeholder information, internal quality control, and quality control. It also starts a process of dialogue with the company and submits a draft to the company for feedback.

The screening criteria include business ethics, community, corporate governance, customers, employees, environment, contractors, and human rights.

According to SiRi, they have an excellent client base and acceptance in the market.

INFOSYS SUSTAINABILITY SOLUTION

Infosys—the Indian IT industry icon—also helps in creating a sustainability framework in businesses catering to healthcare, banking, power, energy and utilities, logistics, and retail sector through the Infosys Sustainability Solution, which helps organizations to deploy a sustainability reporting framework (refer to the case in Chapter 7). Like other rating frameworks, this also helps companies to capture data on energy efficiency, water conservation, product performance, economic performance, human resource and labour efficiency, and safety performance.

The above mentioned rating frameworks show the varied components and methodologies followed by various agencies and institutions. Thus, many companies are setting up their own matrix for tracking the CSR activities that are more relevant to their own business practices. Two examples, one of an indigenous Indian company and the other of a multinational company, have been given below to show how intricately the matrixes need to be formulated. This naturally requires a high level of conviction from the management of the companies. Both the featured companies (Tata and Philips) are world renowned brands and enjoy unparalleled trust from stakeholders and therefore have an excellent balance sheet showing sustainable profits.

TATA GROUP'S CSR RATING FRAMEWORK

In keeping with the Tata ideology, this business house took up the challenge to create a measure for corporate social responsibility. The Tata Council for Community Initiative (TCCI) spearheaded this project of creating an index for measuring actual CSR impact and results. TCCI has been the nodal agency of the Tata group that brings together the best practices of the different group companies. These practices are discussed and debated and consensual group practices are evolved. What is of great importance is that the participants in such discussions include heads of human resources, business excellence and strategy, communications, community, and environmental management.

The group has provided eight basic ideas that should drive their social responsibility:

1. Serving the community is the purpose of our business—The Tata group visualizes the community not just as a stakeholder but as central to the purpose of their business.
2. Enhancing human excellence and improving the quality of life is our endeavour—The respect for human excellence and human dignity is captured by the group through this. The effort of the group is not to destroy the traditional means of earning livelihood but enhancing them through change in attitudes, methods, and systems.
3. Conserving the environment, restoring biodiversity, and social development are integrated into one—The Tata group companies 'are committed to conserve the environment while selecting products, location for facilities, finalizing manufacturing and business processes, purchasing equipment and machinery'.
4. Core competence, expertise, and technology reach the common people, especially the underprivileged—Instead of funding social work, the Tata group actually 'enables technologies to work for the poor, by designing and marketing products and services for the underprivileged also as prospective markets'.
5. Tata companies are partners in development—The group works as partners in progress with the government, development agencies, NGOs, media, and other similar actors in the field. Tatas have set up regional groups with full autonomy in major cities to design and deploy developmental activities.
6. The culture of volunteering is pervasive throughout the Tata group—The employees are encouraged to use their unique learnings, skills, and experience to provide services to the community. This effort naturally has made CSR a part of the DNA of the Tata group.

7. Working with people brings organizational and personal learning—Tata employees enthusiastically participate in programmes designed to 'foster learning, creativity, and experimentation'. This promotes an environment of teamwork, innovation, respect among partners, and the spirit of personal learning. Thus, it creates a 'learning organization'.
8. Tata companies and their business process are environmentally and socially sustainable—The commitment and involvement of the Tata management to CSR programmes in every Tata company is visible. 'Every Tata company:
   (a) has a separate policy on protection of the environment and community development
   (b) has a cross-functional team headed by the CEO, consisting of corporate heads of social responsibility, HR, quality, ethics, communications, and facilitators of community development and environmental management to run properly defined programmes, which are aligned to the group level directives provided under the functions of TCCI, group HR, Tata quality management services, and management of business ethics
   (c) has a proper strategy on CSR, encourages initiatives beyond compliance to the regulation and budgets this work as regular cost of development
   (d) institutes schemes to encourage employee participation
   (e) has developed career plans, training and development programmes for its key facilitators
   (f) has processes in place for triple bottom-line reporting as per the Global Reporting Initiatives (GRI) guidelines and the progress of this activity is reviewed periodically by the top management.'

ASSESSMENT PROCESS

The assessment team is selected from the cross-functional team (ideally comprising of members from the community, communications, human resource, business excellence, and the programme officer) and the corporate head—social responsibility is responsible for this assessment and annual review. This team is encouraged to be certified by the internal assessors' certification programme of the Tata business excellence model. This assurance is conducted from a three-level response: systems, people, and programme.

System Response Level 1

The assessment is conducted at the major divisions, locations, and properties by visiting sites and projects, and interviews with people, programme officers, local heads of HR, communications, community and environment and the plant or divisional head. To ensure commitment at the level of employees, training and development is provided to attune them towards the company CSR policies and the performance appraisal process also takes into account CSR efforts of employees. Exhibit 6.4 shows the break-up of the total score (1000) in the three assurance levels.

EXHIBIT 6.4

Scoring Break-up
Assurance Levels Score

Assurance levels	Process (P)	Outcomes (O)	Process and outcomes (P + O)
Systems response	150	125	275
People response	100	75	175
Programme response	300	250	550
Total	550	450	1000

At each level of assurance, the approach innovates ways to combine a process (P) and an outcome (O) for each parameter that finally culminates into an overall performance in human excellence.

Process
Process refers to how the requirements of a parameter are addressed. Processes include values, concepts, perspectives, approaches, work systems, flowcharts, procedures, and intent deployed progressively into mature practices, conventions, arrangements, and information.

Outcomes
Outcomes refer to the specific results of the processes in the same spirit as cause is related to effect. The factors used to evaluate outcomes include current performance relative to appropriate comparisons/benchmarks and the rate and breadth of your performance improvements.

Assignment of scores to response on performance
The following guidelines may be observed in assigning scores to performance on the parameter:
- The assessment programme, module, or unit at a time should be planned in a manner that it comprehensively includes all parameters to the best extent possible, although it should reflect what is important to the programme, module, or unit.
- In assigning a score to a parameter, first decide the scoring band (e.g., 50 to 60 per cent) that best fits the overall parameter response.

- A process item score of 50 to 60 per cent represents an approach that meets the overall objectives of the parameter and that is deployed to the principal activities and work units covered in the parameter. Higher scores reflect maturity, integration, and broader deployment.
- An outcome item score of 50 to 60 per cent represents a clear indication of improvement trends and good levels of performance in the principal outcomes areas covered in the parameter. Higher scores reflect better improvement rates and levels of performance, better comparative performance, broader coverage, and integration with business requirements.

The team then makes a presentation to the top management, along with all the facilitators. The aim of this annual event is to combine a formal assessment to identify opportunities for improvement with the subsequent year's action plan.

The above mentioned scoring procedure is further distributed by assigning of points across the index with a balance between process and outcomes at the three levels with 17 sub-levels and 46 parameters under these levels. (For more details the TCCI can be contacted.)

The company has a process of appointing a director in charge of CSR and assigning a specific role to the CEO and all senior leaders. The company has developed a matrix matching core competence with CSR possibilities and has a long-term, medium-term, and short-term strategy on CSR, based on surveys and impact assessments. At least three times a year, there is a review of CSR programmes. Transparency in the CSR programmes is maintained by reporting CSR activities in monthly and annual reports/directors' annual report sent to the TCCI for group-level reporting, there are specific outcomes in terms of the triple bottom-line reporting. These reports are adequately communicated and available in the public domain. Thus, CSR in the Tata group is process-driven and not person-driven and therefore has very deep roots and is perennial (long-lasting). Eighteen major Tata companies have formed CSR cross-functional teams since June 2002 and five more companies are in the process. Twelve out of these are geared to the triple-bottom-line reporting under GRI and 27 companies are enrolled under the UN global compact.

This framework reflects the core Tata perspectives on CSR decided by 18 Tata Companies to be a part of the Tata Index for Sustainable Human Development to assure that any activity or programme progressively moves towards human excellence:

1. Managing change and assessment of social impact
2. Felt needs of the key community related to core competencies
3. Volunteering process in the community
4. Social concerns addressed through programmes

5. Improving attitudes/government processes
6. Self-reliance and sustenance
7. Learning and innovation transfer
8. Effective management and good governance

IDENTIFYING PARAMETERS FOR INDEXING TATA CSR

The Tata group, through its various interventions, has understood the need to synchronize the socio-cultural aspects while deploying CSR programmes (for further information, read Chapter 5). It also 'listened' to the convergence and developments globally to arrive at a TCCI-UNDP partnership to develop the Tata (corporate) index for sustainable human development (TISHD), guidelines 2003–2004.

Embarking on a Journey towards Human Excellence

Since 2002, efforts to develop various correlations between HR and business model initiatives were undertaken. An assurance process on CSR was developed for the Tata Quality Management Services to deploy it as part of the business process. To give a proper structure and institutionalize the process, the TISHD is being deployed to ensure that the goal of all initiatives is assessed in terms of their human achievement and excellence. The broad concept of the measurement is mentioned below.

Tata Model for Corporate Sustainability

This includes two broad parameters with their indicators for easy and structured assessment.

I. Tata Index for Environmental and Ecological Management
   1. Compliance to regulation
   2. Reduce, reuse, recycle
   3. Green-house gases
   4. Green the supply chain
   5. Lifecycle analysis
   6. Restore biodiversity
   7. Conserve wildlife
   8. Deployment mechanism

II. Tata Index for Sustainable Human Development
   1. Managing change and assessment of social impact
   2. Felt needs of the key community related to core competencies
   3. Efficient management and good governance
   4. Social concerns addressed through programmes
   5. Improving attitudes/government processes

6. Self-reliance and sustenance
7. Learning and innovation transfer
8. Volunteering process and deployment mechanism

A Tata programme is a journey towards human excellence. The distinctions/new perspectives built the way it is positioned/scaled up from the lowest level to the highest. Since scores are allotted at each of the levels (Exhibit 6.4), it is easy for the companies to understand the gaps and evolve relevant processes to scale up. All this, the Tatas have done, not because legal compliance demanded them, but out of their own volition (wish) and dedication to human excellence and sustenance.

Human Consideration
(0–250)

The intervention is the first level dealing with extremely marginalized people who cannot become self-sufficient due to various reasons like a long history of dependence, helplessness, or vulnerability. The lack of any systemic approach to improve the basic living condition is a major concern at this stage. Though people live in groups, they lack any sense of community.

Human Concern
(251–450)

At this level, there may be adherence to traditional modes of work, but people are also open to new ideas. At this level, there is tangible company involvement like the cause of women or children or the disabled. A reciprocal relationship germinates and people respect and respond to such approaches better when based on shared values, and it creates the desired closeness to becoming a community.

Human Achievement
(451–650)

At this level, the focus shifts to mutual learning, leading to greater improvement in the overall quality of life. Now, there develops an urge to create products out of skills and a market for these products and services. This may result in incomes generated and redistributed on mutually agreed terms. Self-help groups begin to emerge now, and trust-building and mutual respect help to provide a better experience of community living. There are open discussions on the conflicting issues and they are resolved mutually.

Human Development
(651–875)

This is a much higher level and goes beyond compliance and rules. Human beings are central to the process and are more significant as ends rather than means to growth. The processes are supported by systems, practices, and key strategies derived from values and are uniformly deployed. Measurable achievement in terms of income generation, leadership, growth of assets, and access to technology is remarkable at this stage. The extent of education and health contributing to longevity is high. The sense of belonging and high-trust are the basis of community and there is consensus on shared values and vision among the people in terms of quality of life.

Human Excellence
(876–1000)

At the level of human excellence, the quality of life enjoyed becomes significant and can be used as a benchmark for others. There is acceptance of the universal claims of life for their own sake. This is the highest level of human existence in terms of human rights. This is a state where all other approaches and levels of achievement flow in the same direction of achieving the needs of the people. There is an overarching need to create human excellence above everything. There are systems of good governance, procedures for maintaining order, and arrangements for revisiting and assessing.

The Tata group purpose statement clearly shows how well business and responsibility have been coincided: 'Our heritage of returning to society what we earn evokes trust among consumers, employees, shareholders, and the community. This heritage will be continuously enriched by formalizing the high standards of behaviour expected from employees and companies.'

Thus, all Tata group companies have developed a process to identify their core competence, expertise, talents, capabilities, and skills that could be useful to common people by way of a matrix. This assessment process that offers a quantifiable framework for measuring CSR interventions has been one of the first in India, and today, many Indian companies have created their own models of measuring, considering the importance of CSR in business.

(The Tata CSR Rating Framework is courtesy Anant Nadkarni, Vice President Group—CSR, Tata Council for Community Initiatives.)

PHILIPS—FRAMEWORK FOR CSR RATING RELATED TO ENVIRONMENTAL REPORTING

The Philips CSR rating framework featured below has special reference to environment accounting and reporting as part of their CSR initiatives. Recognizing that energy efficiency is one essential answer to climate change, Philips has made a serious commitment to develop, promote, and market more energy-efficient solutions. The company has undertaken certain specific measures to ensure that its environmental performance meets the expectation of its vision to be an environment conscious company by promoting environmental accounting.

There has been a concerted effort to meet the challenge of environmental sustainability with green products and green innovations and by inspiring individuals to make simple changes that can have profound results. Philips believes in creating responsible energy practices among all the stakeholders, so that there is awareness among all to face the climate change threats that have emerged, and offer better and easier solutions to tackle them.

The aim is to reduce the ecological footprint of the organization. The ecological footprint is a measure of human demand on the Earth's ecosystems and estimates the area of the Earth's productive land and water that is required to provide the resources that an individual or group needs to support a particular lifestyle, as well as to absorb the wastes that the individual or group produces in the process. To achieve this reduction, the company has decided to maintain its focus on overall environmental performance improvement and has developed two action programmes called EcoVision III and EcoVision4. EcoVision III covered the years 2006–2009, and EcoVision4 runs through 2012. EcoVision III focused primarily on reducing the environmental footprint of the manufacturing processes spanning a broad range of parameters. The EcoVision4 programme is focused on energy and material efficiency over the entire product lifecycle, as well as the daily operations. The aim of the programme is that by 2012, Philips will:

- generate 30 per cent of total revenues from green products
- have doubled investment in green innovations to a cumulative €1 billion
- improve the operational energy efficiency by 25 per cent and reduce carbon dioxide emissions by 25 per cent

(All the above are compared with the base year 2007.)

Philips facilitates new solutions to drive responsible energy practices and have long focused on the energy efficiency of their products and production processes. Some of the striking and significant examples of such efforts can be seen in the activities listed below.

Green Products

In the third year of EcoVision4, green products (carbon-free products) already represent a significant share of the revenues in all the markets that Philip operates in. In fact, green products grew 19 per cent in 2009 (see Exhibit 6.5) and this encouraged Philips to raise the bar and aim for 50 per cent growth in 2015. The Philips green logo helps to identify an increasing number of green products that it produces. To further increase awareness and encourage individuals to make smart daily choices, the website—www.asimpleswitch.com—was relaunched.

Philips is renowned for its lighting products and is the world leader in lighting. Therefore, when a McKinsey report identified energy-efficient lighting as one of the most effective solutions for greenhouse gas reduction, Philips

EXHIBIT 6.5

Philips Landmark Achievements

EcoVision4: Green product sales

Sales from green products increased in 2009 to €7.1 billion, contributing significantly to the total revenue stream. As a percentage of the companies total sales, green product sales rose substantially to 30.6 per cent, up from 22.6 per cent in 2008, exceeding Philips EcoVision4 target for 2012.

Green product sales
(in billions of euros unless otherwise stated)

	2007	2008	2009
Philips Group	5.3	6.0	7.1
as a % of total sales	19.8	22.6	30.6

All sectors contributed to the growth in green product sales.

Consumer lifestyle achieved the highest green product nominal sales growth (30 per cent), followed by healthcare (17 per cent) and lighting (14 per cent).

Consumer lifestyle introduced 81 green products in 2009, healthcare 15, and lighting over 700. Major acquisitions, like Respironics, Consumer Luminaires, and Genlyte, have been included for the first time, causing the decrease in green product sales in 2008 in healthcare and lighting. Prior to joining Philips, these acquisitions did not have a process in place to develop new products with significantly improved environmental performance and it took time to bring new products through the pipeline.

Green product sales per sector
(as a percentage of total sales)

	2007	2008	2009
Healthcare	22	20	23
Consumer lifestyle	8	14	23
Lighting	46	40	52
Philips Group	20	23	31

Overall, improvements are predominantly realized in the energy-efficiency green focal area.

Operational energy efficiency and carbon footprint: 2009 details

The 2009 results can be attributed to several factors:

- Total CO_2 emissions from manufacturing decreased 6 per cent due to lower production volumes as well as continued energy efficiency improvement actions.
- CO_2 emissions from non-industrial operations (offices, warehouses, etc.), which represents 9 per cent of the total, decreased 12 per cent. Despite an increase in the number of office buildings due to new acquisitions, the amount of floor space remained virtually flat, as Philips continued to centralize and re-allocate facilities. Energy consumption per square meter decreased along with the lower number of employees.

- The total CO_2 emissions related to business travel decreased 17 per cent. This significant reduction was achieved by promoting video-conferencing in combination with their strict air travel policy. CO_2 emissions from lease cars decreased 8 per cent compared with 2008 due to their green lease car policy.
- Overall, CO_2 emissions from logistics, representing approximately one-third of the total, decreased 14 per cent. Sea freight fell 24 per cent as a result of lower volumes along with improved container utilization. The same applied to road transport, which decreased 24 per cent as well. CO_2 emissions from air freight remained unchanged.

decided to immediately take up the challenge and innovate better lighting solutions. Thus emerged the green innovations.

Green Innovations

To keep in line with sustainability as a strategic innovation driver for Philips, regular review of the research portfolio is carried out from a sustainability angle. Some examples of such innovation are: the world's first OLED-based (organic light-emitting diode), interactive lighting concepts for consumer and professional use; production of TVs that carry the EU ecolabel; and the famous Philip method of DoseWise radiation management that ensures optimal image quality while protecting people in X-ray environments. Switching currently installed older lighting to the latest technology would save more than euro 100 billion.

Philips integrated operational energy efficiency by reducing emissions of carbon dioxide. In addition to continuing the systematic energy potential scans, green lease car policy and global green IT programme were promoted. Initiatives like green purchasing policy and investigating options to buy and generate renewable energy has helped Philips to keep to its vision of an environment-friendly company.

By signing the statement 'Caring for Climate: The Business Leadership Platform', Philips joined the movement to care for the climate and save the environment. The statement was created in 2007, during the UN Global Compact Leaders Summit convened by UN Secretary General Ban Ki-moon. Business leaders from 153 companies worldwide participated. They all committed to speeding up action on climate change and called on governments to agree as soon as possible on measures to secure workable and inclusive climate market mechanisms after 2012, as the Kyoto Protocol would expire then.

The management of Philips realizes that the significant issues for their kind of company and industry are always in the environmental area. The concerns usually centre around energy efficiency, chemical content of products, and collection and recycling. Philips claims that 'we remain committed to giving our full attention to these challenges despite the economic downturn.'

The highlight of this initiative shows clearly the efforts made by Philips to promote the concept of recycling and reduce carbon footprint or promote eco-friendly products.

Collection and Recycling

In keeping with integrating CSR in the production process (see Chapter 5 for more details about integration of CSR in the production process), Philips employees consider the end-of-life (i.e., understanding disposability of a product) during the EcoDesign process. To achieve success in this, Philips promotes active improvement in the environmental performance of collection and recycling compliance schemes, particularly in the EU. The idea is also expanded by introducing voluntary collection and recycling services started in 2008 in India and Brazil, and also by launching them in Argentina in 2009. An example of practical implementation of such a policy is the cradle-to-cradle (taking care of a product from production level to disposability after usage) inspired product—the Performer Energy Care vacuum cleaner—made partly from recycled and bio-based plastics.

To further its agenda on environment-related issues, Philips also supports the 'EU REACH (registration, evaluation, authorization, and restriction of chemical) compliance, Philips participated in developing the "Bill of Material (BOM) check", an industry platform for suppliers to provide chemical information on the items they sell. BOM-check also facilitates RoHS (restriction of the use of certain hazardous substances in electrical and electronic equipment) compliance. By providing full material declaration, BOM-check also supports EcoDesign and our phase-out of brominated flame retardants (BFRs) and polyvinyl chloride (PVC) in consumer products. Following a pilot in 2009, we plan a full roll-out to suppliers in 2010.'*

Philips supports the development of Waste Electrical and Electronic Equipment (WEEE). This legislation creates a level playing field, based on fair and transparent financing mechanisms, and stimulates maximum collection and responsible recycling.

Since Philips believes in involving all stakeholders in their strategy, it supports the general concept of individual producer responsibility and collaborates with stakeholders to find practical and fair solutions for its implementation. In a meeting that brought together representatives of businesses, corporate technologies, product development, corporate sustainability, and others, the sustainable business strategy was articulated: 'To become the recognized leader in key Philips global market opportunities relevant to society at large, by

* http://www.philips.com/shared/assets/Downloadablefile/Investor/Annual_Report_Full_English_2009.pdf, accessed on 8 August 2010.

applying our company strengths.' Therefore, in addition to energy efficiency, the company is also participating in alleviating social issues by focusing on available and affordable healthcare, and shows a commitment to continue to use their capabilities to make a positive impact on society at large. 'Engaging stakeholders and monitoring customers' satisfaction enable Philips to better understand people's needs. Promoting innovation and research and development (R&D) ensure the creation of unique products. The definition of clear environmental and social policies ensures sound manufacturing practices. Managing brands and a comprehensive code of conduct further support a proper market appearance. In all these areas, Philips achieves a score that is well above its industry's average.'*

Thus, we see that this multinational has put in place policies and processes that help to promote CSR through environmental sustainability, as the products that Philips deals with come under scrutiny because of carbon footprint (i.e., measurement of the amount of carbon dioxide that ones' activities produce). Philips is transforming the global market by participating in a global initiative to accelerate the uptake of low-energy light bulbs and efficient lighting systems by the global environment facility and the United Nations environment programme.

The aim is to reduce the electricity bills of consumers in developing economies, reduce emissions of greenhouse gases, and replace fuel-based lighting systems, such as kerosene, which lead to health-hazards as a result of indoor air pollution. As a conscientious organization, Philips is constantly involved in R&D of better and greener energy and also attends to social issues as a CSR strategy. According to Philips, 'We aim to share expertise and co-create innovative solutions that will make a difference to future generations'.

World leaders from developed and developing countries alike, representing all United Nations member states, have pledged to achieve the eight Millennium Development Goals (MDGs) by the year 2015—to significantly reduce poverty, illiteracy, inequity, and disease in poor countries. The experience of Philips has shown that reaching these markets requires tailor-made solutions, a different approach to marketing and distribution, and multi-sector partnerships (see Chapter 5 to understand the need for country-specific CSR solutions).

CONCLUSION

From the above examples, it is very obvious that the majority of the company evaluation systems are based on stakeholder models. It is observed that the stakeholder model is common in UK and the US. In European countries other than Britain, the tradition of environmentally focused sustainability analysis still continues. The methods presently being used for CSR ratings worldwide are

* http://www.philips.com/shared/assets/Downloadablefile/sustainabilitydownloads/simplerstrongergreener.pdf.

heterogeneous and lack standardization. Conscientious companies are trying to find the best possible fit among the varied frameworks for reporting their CSR and sustainability. Like Infosys, Tata, and Philips, which are portrayed in this chapter, other major companies in India also have their own framework for reporting CSR. Since the corporate governance code in India demands CSR reporting, every listed company is creating its own or following standardized patterns for reporting CSR. The case studies given at the end of the chapter highlight some of the best practices followed in CSR by business enterprises.

SUMMARY

CSR rating tools help in corporate governance processes by providing information and helping in monitoring socially responsible behaviour. To design these tools, management would have to undertake with immense sincerity the designing of processes that provide a holistic picture of the impacts of its business decisions, not only within the corporate as a whole, but also in its departments. The commonly used rating frameworks can be used for developing CSR reporting in an organization. However, most organizations have their unique vision and strategies. Therefore, they try and create their CSR reporting framework in accordance with that (as can be seen in the two examples given in the chapter).

KEY TERMS

Global Reporting Initiative A network-based organization that has pioneered the development of the world's most widely used sustainability reporting framework.

Inter- and intra-generational justice Understanding the interdependence and interconnectivity between and within generations.

Ratings Measurement process.

Tata Business Excellence Model Adapted from the renowned Malcolm Baldrige archetype. The model works under the aegis of Tata Quality Management Services (TQMS). The processes essentially relate to two factors: business excellence and business ethics.

The Philips Environmental Report Follows a structured form of accepted international reporting standard to inform about the impact of their business on environment.

EXERCISES

Concept Review Questions

1. In your opinion, how important is CSR reporting?
2. Trace the development of CSR reporting.
3. Describe the GRI reporting framework.

Critical Thinking Questions

1. Explain why modern organizations are emphasizing CSR reporting. Give examples to support your answer.
2. Is it possible to find a balance between resource exploitation and resource preservation? Give examples to substantiate your argument.

Research Question

Give two examples of CSR reporting frameworks and analyse their strengths and weaknesses.

Project Question

Compare the CSR reporting process of any two companies and analyse the strengths and weaknesses in their process.

REFERENCE

Gladwin, T.N., J.J. Kennelly, and T.S. Krause (1995), 'Shifting Paradigms for sustainable Development—Implications for Management Theory ad Research', *Academy of Management Review*, vol. 20, issue no. 4, pp. 874–907.

Web Resources

http://www.eiris.org/index.html, accessed on 17 April 2010.
http://www.globalreporting.org, accessed 10 April 2010.
http://www.orse.org/, accessed on 17 March 2010.
http://www.philips.com/shared/assets/Downloadablefile/Investor/Annual_Report_Full_English_2009.pdf, accessed on 8 August 2010.
http://www.philips.com/shared/assets/Downloadablefile/sustainabilitydownloads/simplerstrongergreener.pdf, accessed on 8 August 2010.
http://www.responsibleshopper.org, accessed 12 April 2010.
https://www.coopamerica.org/programs/, accessed on 10 April 2010.

ANNEXURE

REPORT ON ENVIRONMENTAL REPORTING
(by Prof. L. Ramakrishnan)

This report on environmental reporting was prepared by Prof. L. Ramakrishnan* and, with his kind permission, has been reproduced here as a contribution to the chapter.

Environmental Accounting and Reporting

The subject is relatively new. Environmental accounting probably started about 30 years ago, in the 1970s, and environmental reporting started in the 1990s. Since the subject is relatively new, there are many things to learn and improve.

Need for Environmental Accounting within the Organization

The need for environmental accounting and reporting has been felt within and outside organizations for quite some time. It is well known that 'what gets measured gets managed'. In the case of an enterprise, the measurement of its environmental performance helps it to manage its environmental impacts successfully. Environmental impacts of an organization arise out of its use of resources, its generation of waste (or emissions), and the characteristics of its products and services. Environmental accounting deals with measurements and reports that are related to the environmental management of an organization, especially those that can affect the financial position of the enterprise, environmental expenditures, risks, and liabilities. Environmental accounting identifies and allocates costs, in order to correctly price the products and helps the organization to take investment decisions based on total costs, including environmental costs, and benefits. In general, environmental accounting information can help the organization to:
- encourage defensive and prudent operations and waste reduction
- improve manufacturing, waste disposal, and shipping practices
- negotiate and settle disputes with insurance carriers
- influence regulators and public policymakers
- determine suitable levels of financial resources
- re-assess corporate strategy and management practices (think green)
- articulate a comprehensive risk-management programme
- improve public citizenship
- identify hidden risks in take-overs and acquisitions

Environmental accounting information can also be used by investors/lenders/bankers for assessing the risk involved in investing in or lending to such enterprises. Customers will be interested in the green credentials of organizations and their products, while selecting a product from a wide variety of available products.

* Prof. L. Ramakrishna, FIEMA, C. Env. has done dual PhD, in Chemistry and also in Environment Management. He was the General Manager and National Coordinator, Environment, in Philips when he developed the report and case study. Presently, he is Distinguished Professor and Head, Indsearch Centre of Sustainability Management (I-COSM), Indian Institute of Cost and Management Studies and Research (an autonomous institute under the University of Pune).

Global Trends that Catalyse Environmental Accounting and Reporting

In the last ten years or so, there has been an increasing interest among various stakeholders on the activities of corporate organizations, especially multinational organizations. This increasing interest has been driven by:

- expanding globalization, resulting in free movement of goods, services, and activities; breaking barriers to trade
- search for new forms of global governance, striving for sustainable future—development with environmental, economic, and social concerns
- reforms of corporate governance, especially after the recent scandals involving Enron, Worldcom, etc.
- emergence of Brazil, Russia, India, and China (BRIC) as significant economies—resulting in shifting of manufacturing and other activities to these emerging economies from developed countries; they also provide a new emerging market for goods and services from developed and developing countries
- development in communication technologies, e.g., Internet, playing its role in making companies more visible and raising the expectation of them from stakeholders; information about companies move across the globe very fast, allowing low response times, i.e., the time taken to respond to a concern or issue is less today because of better connectivity
- desire of companies to measure their progress towards sustainability
- interest of governments in sustainability reporting
- interest shown by financial markets in sustainability reporting
- emergence of alternative principles of next generation accounting

The above trends stimulate discussions within organizations for sustainability management (or environmental management, being a part of sustainability management) and reporting.

Environmental Accounting

As in conventional accounting, environmental accounting has also developed into:
(a) Environmental financial accounting
(b) Environmental management accounting
(c) Natural resources accounting.

Environmental financial accounting deals with *accounting for* and *reporting on* environmental transactions and events that affect or are likely to affect the financial position of business.

Environmental management accounting deals with the identification, collection, estimation, analysis, use and reporting of material, and energy flow information, environmental and other costs information for internal purposes of the organization.

Table 1 provides general information on environmental costs that are normally hidden and can be used profitably in environmental accounting.

TABLE 1 Potentially hidden environmental costs in a business enterprise

Potentially hidden costs		
Regulatory	**Upfront**	**Voluntary (beyond compliance)**
• Notification • Reporting • Monitoring/testing • Studies/modelling • Remediation • Recordkeeping • Plans • Training • Inspections • Manifesting • Labelling • Preparedness • Protective equipment • Medical surveillance • Environmental insurance • Financial assurance • Pollution control • Spill response • Storm-water management • Waste management • Taxes/fees	• Site studies • Site preparation • Permitting • R&D • Engineering and procurement • Installation **Conventional Costs** Capital equipment Materials Labour Supplies Utilities Structures Salvage value **Back-end** • Closure/decommissioning • Disposal of inventory • Post-closure care • Site survey	• Community relations/ outreach • Monitoring/testing • Training • Audits • Qualifying suppliers • Reports (e.g., annual environmental reports) • Insurance • Planning • Feasibility studies • Remediation • Recycling • Environmental studies • R&D • Habitat and wetland protection • Landscaping • Other environmental projects • Financial support to environmental groups and/or researchers
Contingent costs		
• Future compliance cost • Penalties/fines • Response to future releases	• Remediation • Property damage • Personal injury damage	• Legal expenses • Natural resource damage • Economic loss damage
Image and relationship costs		
• Corporate image • Relationship with customers • Relationship with investors • Relationship with insurers	• Relationship with professional staff • Relationship with workers • Relationship with suppliers	• Relationship with lenders • Relationship with host communities • Relationship with regulators

Source: US Environmental Protection Agency, An Introduction to Environmental Accounting as a Business Tool: Key Concepts and Terms, Washington DC, 1996.

Table 2 provides a comparison between conventional accounting and environmental accounting.

TABLE 2 Conventional accounting versus environmental accounting

Accounting types	Conventional accounting	Environmental accounting
Management accounting	Focuses on cost and other information for decision-making within the organization	Focuses on material and energy flow and environmental cost information
Financial accounting	Focuses on reporting financial information to external parties	Focuses on reporting environmental information to stakeholders
National accounting	Focuses on economic and other information to characterize national income and economic health	Focuses on natural resources, stocks and flows, environmental costs, externality costs, etc.

Table 3 shows how conventional accounting and environmental accounting can be integrated to form a unified accounting system.

TABLE 3 Integrated accounting system

	Accounting in monetary units		Accounting in physical units	
Conventional accounting	Environmental accounting			Other assessing tools
	MEMA Monetary EMA	PEMA Physical EMA		
Conventional bookkeeping	Transition of environmental part from bookkeeping and cost accounting	Material flow balances at the corporate level for mass, energy, water, etc.		Production planning and stock accounting systems
Cost accounting	Activity-based material flow costing	Material flow balances on the process/product lines		Other environmental performance measures and tools
Internal use for statistics, indicators, calculating savings, budgetary and investment appraisals	Internal use of statistics, indicators, calculating savings, budgetary and investment appraisals of environmental costs	Actual use of environmental management systems, performance evaluation, and benchmarking		Other internal use of cleaner production projects and ecodesign
External financial reporting	External disclosure of environmental expenditures, investments, and liabilities	External reporting		Other reoperting to government, statutory bodies, etc.

Source: Environmental Management Accounting—Principles and Procedures, United Nations Division for Sustainable Development (2001).

Role of environmental accountants Environmental accountants play important roles in environmental management in organizations. As environmental financial accountants, they ensure that environmental cost and liabilities are accounted for by following relevant accounting standards or, in their absence, generally accepted accounting practices. They also ensure meaningful disclosure of the environmental performance of the business is provided.

As environmental management accountants, they ensure that appropriate management accounting procedures are, where necessary, developed and used; for instance, to cost out pollution controls, to compare alternative materials that can be used in manufacturing, and to investigate recycling alternatives.

Environmental management accountant should take into account the interaction of an enterprise with the environment including material/energy flows. Figure 1 shows the interaction of a manufacturing organization with the environment.

Figure 2 shows a schematic of energy flow within a manufacturing organization.

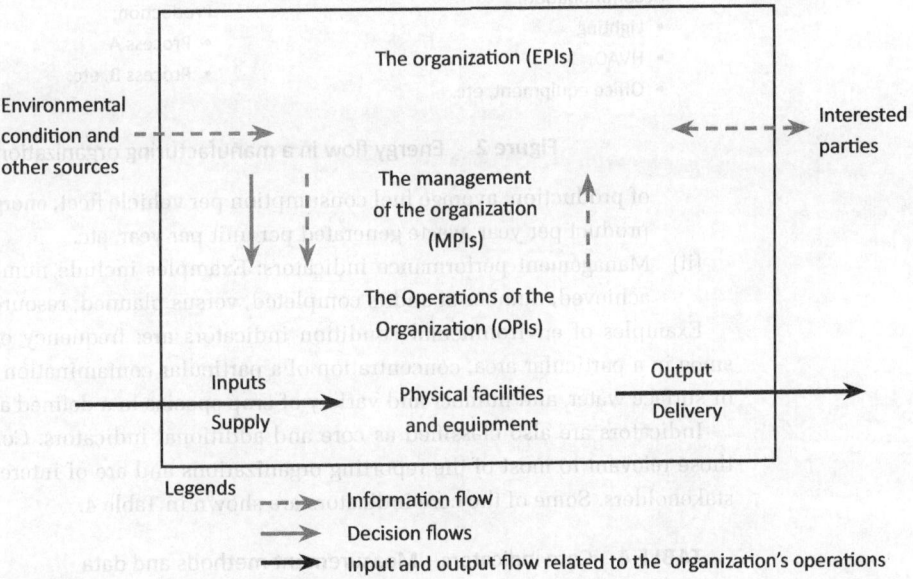

Source: ISO-14031: Environmental Management—Environmental Performance Evaluation—Guidelines (1999).

Figure 1 Inter-relationships of an organization's management and operations, and the condition of the environment

Environmental performance indicators As Fig. 1 suggests, there are different types of environmental performance indicators that can be used in tracking trends and monitoring environmental performance in an organization. These indicators can, generally, be grouped under two headings:
(a) Environmental performance indicator
(b) Environmental condition indicator
Environmental performance indicators are again divided into:
(i) Operational performance indicators: examples include quantity of water per unit

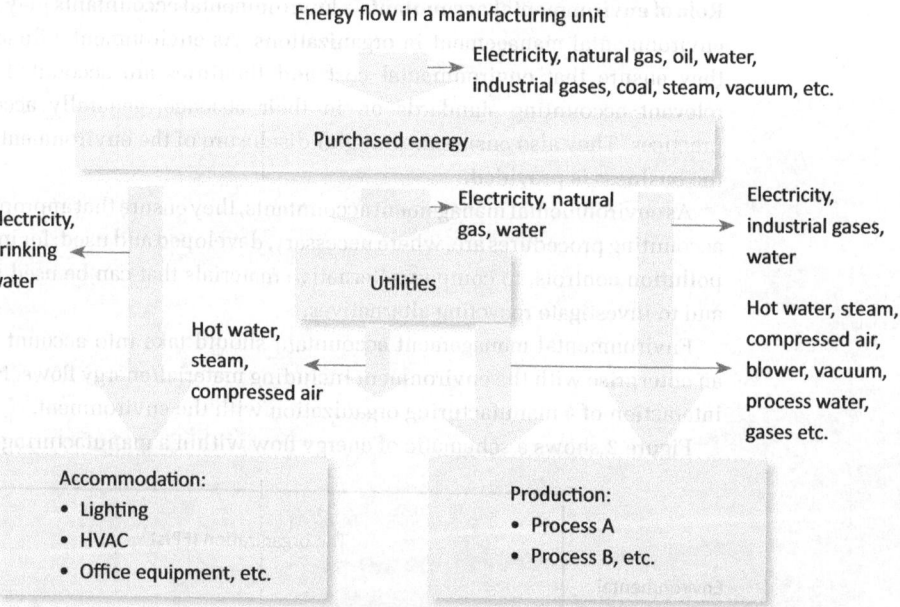

Figure 2 Energy flow in a manufacturing organization

of production, average fuel consumption per vehicle fleet, energy consumed per product per year, waste generated per unit per year, etc.

(ii) Management performance indicators: Examples include number of objectives achieved, number of audits completed, versus planned, resources used, etc.

Examples of environmental condition indicators are: frequency of photochemical smog in a particular area, concentration of a particular contamination in ground water or surface water, and number and variety of crop species in a defined area.

Indicators are also classified as core and additional indicators. Core indicators are those relevant to most of the reporting organizations and are of interest to most of the stakeholders. Some of the core indicators are shown in Table 4.

TABLE 4 Core indicators—Measurement methods and data

Core indicator	Description	Measurement reference	Data source
Unit/number/ mass of product or service made or sold	Number or mass (in metric tons) of final product or services produced or sold to customers (excludes intermediate products/services)		Cost Report and/or production report
Net sales	Sum of net sales (i.e., in Rs) for the entire organization evaluated	International accounting standards	Annual financial report
Energy consumption	Total amount of energy (in giga-joules) including electricity, heat (purchased and on-site non-fossil fuel generated), and energy from fossil fuel combustion	Energy conversion factors for various fuels	Cost report and/or facility management report

Contd

Table 4 *contd*

Core indicator	Description	Measurement reference	Data source
Material consumption	Mass of process and auxiliary material or semi-manufactured goods input (in metric tons) to make final product, including materials to make intermediates and formulate finished product, excluding water (account for at least 90% by weight of inputs)		Cost report and/or procurement report
Water consumption	Amount of water (in cubic meters) purchased and obtained from surface and groundwater sources (account for at least 90% of water use)		Cost report and/or facility management report
Green house gas (GHG) emissions	Amount of GHG emissions (in tons of CO_2 equivalents) from fuel combustion, process reactions and treatment processes (account for at least 90% of GHG)	Kyoto protocol	Cost report and estimation or calculation
Ozone depleting substance (ODS) emissions	Amount of ODS emissions (In tons of CFC11 equivalents) from all sources (account for at least 90% of ODS emissions)	Montreal protocol	Cost report and estimation or calculation

Source: WBCSD, 1999.

Additional indicators are those representing a leading practice, though currently not in use. They provide information of interest to stakeholders who are particularly important to the reporting organization. These indicators are worthy of studying further for their use in the future as core indicators. In practice, most of these indicators are expressed in different ways. Some of them are:

(a) Direct measures or calculations (e.g., tons of materials used)
(b) Relative measures or calculations (e.g., quantity of emissions per year)
(c) Indexed (e.g., quantity of emissions this year as a percentage of emission in the reference year)
(d) Aggregated (e.g., quantity of carbon dioxide emitted in a year from all the manufacturing units this year)
(e) Weighted (e.g., equivalent carbon dioxide emissions per year)

GRI Guidelines of 2002 provides a good number of examples of environmental indicators that one can use for reporting.

Table 5 provides an example of how measuring and monitoring core environmental performance indicators can help an organization track its performance with respect to various environmental parameters.

TABLE 5 Environmental performance of a manufacturing organization—2001–2003

	2001	2002	2003	% change wrt 2001
Energy-GJ	935156	846171	850120	−9.09
Water- KL	489427	360431	321885	−34.23
Emissions Haz. Chem Kg	2004	1198	719	−64.12
Other Chem Kg	6703	5038	897	−86.62
VOC Kg	585501	491704	261738	−55.30
Packaging Kg	8349595	8276415	7500695	−10.16
Waste Kg	4625250	5887885	6963776	+50.55

Example of the use of Environmental Performance Indicator Data in Decision-making

Environmental performance indicator information is of importance to the managers in taking strategic decisions. Table 6 provides information on the energy consumption of three manufacturing units, A, B, and C. The second column provides information on the conventional cost information, cost of energy (US$) for manufacturing 100 pieces of products in each of these units. The third column provides environmental performance indicator information, viz., amount of energy used (in mega joules) for the production of 100 pieces of products. The fourth column provides another environmental performance indicator information on the amount of carbon dioxide emitted for manufacturing 100 pieces of products.

TABLE 6 Energy cost and energy consumption in three manufacturing units

Factory	US$100/pcs	MN/100 pcs	Kf CO_2/100 pcs
A	0.34	73.00	7.09
B	0.43	55.80	11.05
C	0.38	83.00	12.26

The data are taken from three manufacturing units manufacturing the same product. Suppose the manager has to take a decision to close down one of the three factories; he knows that energy efficiency is one of the key factors for his decision. If the manager has to take a decision to close down the most energy inefficient factory and if he depends only on the conventional cost information (US$/100 pieces), he will decide to close down Factory B. If he has access to environmental accounting information (energy consumed in mega joules per 100 pieces), then he will find that B is the most energy efficient and will consider Factory C for closure, i.e., in the absence of the environmental cost information, he would have taken a decision to close down the most energy-efficient factory. His decision to close down Factory C now can be strengthened by more environmental cost information; the more carbon dioxide emitted per 100 pieces may mean more carbon tax in the future.

Table 7 provides another example where environmental performance indicator information can be used in strategic decision-making. Table 6.5 provides information on the waste generated by three manufacturing units A, B, and C. The second column provides information on the cost of waste in terms of US$ as well as percentage of cost of materials. As in the earlier example, a decision taken based only on the conventional cost information need not be the best decision; the decision may be reviewed, if environmental accounting information, such as the total quantity of waste generated (third column), or the quantity of waste being sent to the land-fill (fourth column), in each of the manufacturing units is considered while taking the decision.

TABLE 7 Waste generated—Conventional and environmental accounting information

Factor	Waste K US$ (% of COM)	Total waste (Kg)	Landfill waste (Kg)
A	411 (3.3)	550033	477433
B	214 (3.3)	2088505	8
C	152 (6.8)	82021	0

Environmental Reporting

Once an organization decides to share environmental information with stakeholders, it can plan an environmental report. Environmental reporting is the disclosure by an entity of environmentally related data (verified or not) on environmental risks, impacts, policies, strategies, targets, costs, liabilities, or performance to those who have an interest in such information as an aid to enabling or enriching their relationship with the reporting organization.

The objective of environmental reporting is 'to provide information about the environmental impact and operational performance of the entity that is useful to relevant stakeholders in assessing their relationship with the reporting entity' (FEE).

Compare this with the Objective of Financial Reporting: 'to provide information about the financial position, performance, and changes in financial position of an enterprise that is useful to a wide range of users in making economic decisions' (IASC).

The environmental report is meant, therefore, for a wider audience and the focus is on relationship, rather than on economic performance alone.

Association of Certified Chartered Accountants of UK (ACCA) requires that the environmental report has the following characteristics:
- Completeness (entity and its impacts)
- Credibility (internal and external)
- Communication

GRI Guidelines of 2002 address these requirements systematically. This is elaborated in the GRI guidelines as given in Fig. 3. (Also see GRI reporting in the framework section.)

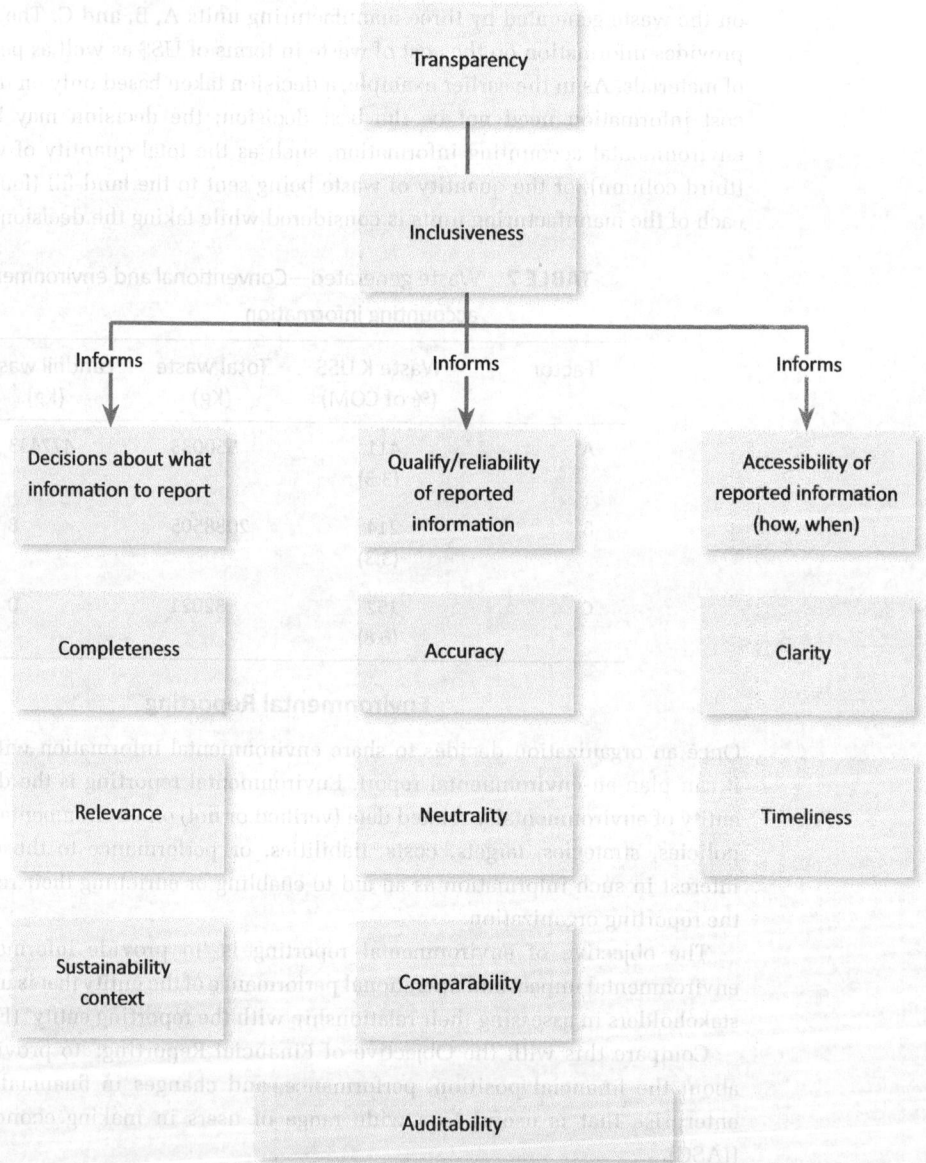

Figure 3 Reporting principles from GRI guidelines 2002

GRI Guidelines require that the report should have the following structure:
(a) Vision and strategy
(b) Profile of the reporting organization
(c) Governance structure and management system
(d) GRI content index
(e) Performance indicators

GRI Guidelines' General Notes provides further information on the Report Structure (Exhibit 1).

EXHIBIT 1

'General Notes' from GRI Guidelines 2002

Boundaries Organizations using the *Guidelines* may have complex internal structures, multiple subsidiaries, joint ventures, and/or foreign operations. Particular care should be taken to match the scope of the report with the economic, environmental, and social 'foot-print' of the organization (i.e., the full extent of its economic, environmental, and social impacts). Any differences should be explained.

Use of technical protocols In reporting on indicators contained within the *Guidelines*, reporters should use GRI technical protocols whenever available. Drafting of protocols for a limited number of GRI indicators began in 2002, and drafts in progress can be found on the GRI website (www.globalreporting.org). GRI recognizes the need for continued development of protocols, and the current set represents the first of many that will follow in coming years. If, for any reason, a reporting organization does not use an existing GRI protocol, it should clearly describe the measurement rules and methodologies used for data compilation. For situations where a formal GRI protocol is not yet available, reporting organizations should use their professional judgement, drawing on international standards and conventions wherever possible.

Metrics Reported data should be presented using generally accepted international metrics (e.g., kilograms, tonnes, litres), calculated using standard conversion factors. When other metrics are used, reports should provide conversion information to enable international users to make conversions.

Time frames and targets Wherever possible, reports should present information for all performance indicators in a manner that enables users to understand current and future trends. At a minimum, reporting organizations should present data for the current reporting period (e.g., one year) and at least two previous periods, as well as future targets where they have been established. This information provides essential context for understanding the significance of a given piece of information. Comparisons with industry averages, where available, can also provide useful context.

Absoluted normalised data As a general principle, reporting organizations should present indicator data in absolute terms and use ratios or normalized data as complementary information. Providing only normalized data may mask absolute figures, which is the information of primary interest to some stakeholders. However, if it absolute data are provided, users will be able to compile their own normalized analysis using information from Section 2 of Part C (Profile). Nevertheless, GRI does recognize the utility of data presented as ratios. Ratio data may be useful in conjunction with absolute data for communicating performance trends or articulating performance across two or more linked dimensions of sustainability. When ratios are included, organizations are asked to make use of normalizing factors from within the report, and from Section 2 of Part C, if appropriate. See Annex 5 for more information on ratios.

Data consolidation and disaggregation Reporting organizations will need to determine the appropriate level of consolidation (aggregation) of indicator data. For example, indicators could be presented in terms of the performance of the organization worldwide or broken down by subsidiaries, countries of operation, or even individual facilities. This decision requires balancing the reporting burden against the potential additional value of data reported on a disaggregated (e.g., country or site) basis. Consolidation of information can result in loss of a significant amount of value to users, and also risks masking particularly strong or poor performance in specific areas of operation. In general, reporting organizations should disaggregate information to an appropriate and useful level as determined through consultation with stakeholders. The appropriate level of consolidation/disaggregation may vary by indicator.

Graphics The use of graphics can enhance the quality of a report. However, care should be taken to ensure that graphics do not inadvertently lead readers to incorrect interpretations of data and results. Care is needed in the selection of axes, scales, and data (including conversion of raw data to ratios and indices for graphic purposes), and the use of colour and different types of graphs and charts. Graphics should be a supplement to—not a substitute for—text and narrative disclosure of information. In general, raw data should accompany graphical presentations, either alongside or in appendices. Graphs should always clearly indicate the source of their data.

Executive summary GRI encourages the inclusion of an executive summary. In keeping with the reporting principles in Part B, the summary should draw only on material from within the report and be materially consistent with the content of the report.

Steps involved in the Environmental Report Preparation

A lot of preparation is required for bringing out an environmental report of an organization. The various steps involved in this process are:

- Collection of data—departments, factories, plants, business units, product divisions, offices
- Collation and review—discussions with the help desk—local approval by the finance manager and the plant manager
- Reporting on-line (before the due date)
- Pre-validation—by the regional environmental office (or the pre-validation officer)
- Validation—by the product division
- Site audits and verification—by the verifier
- Release to editorial staff for preparing the report—by the corporate office
- Release of report

Figure 4 is a schematic of the various stages of data collection and reporting. Each stage is important as there is always a possibility of data corruption at each one of them. Verifiers are particular that the data trail is intact for approving the data.

Framework for Rating Corporate Social Responsibility | 223

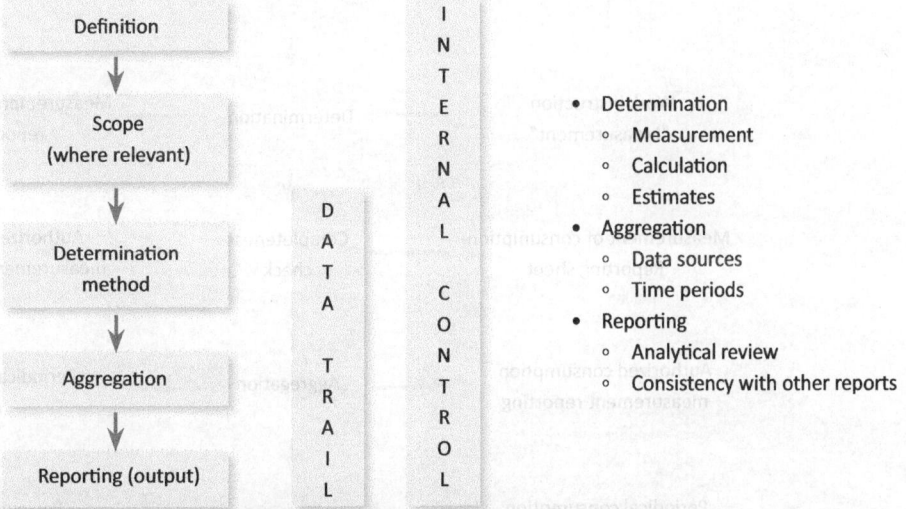

Figure 4 Schematic overview of the data flow

Figure 5 is a schematic of a data trail, e.g., resource. Verifiers will be interested in checking the information collected, collated, reviewed, and reported using such a data trail.

Remarks—Today environmental accounting and reporting are in their infancy. Quite a few drawbacks and opportunities exist in data collection and reporting activities. The following are some of the issues to be addressed in the near future:

- Too many parameters/too many units/PIs (performance Indicators)
- Data collectors are not conversant with various aspects of the requirements
- Knowledge within the organization on environmental issues is limited
- Experience in data collection, collation, reporting, and verification is limited
- No dedicated manpower for reporting within the organization
- Definitions need standardization
- Data collection from different sources—uniformity of approach need to be ensured
- Tendency to put problems under the carpet
- Genuine misses
- Indifferent data collector

If we have to establish an effective and efficient environmental accounting and reporting framework in organizations, we need to:

- Develop data collectors in a formal way
- Develop environmental and sustainability auditors with professional accreditation
- Develop verifiers of environmental data
- Develop competence centres on environment/sustainability in each of the organizations

224 | Corporate Social Responsibility

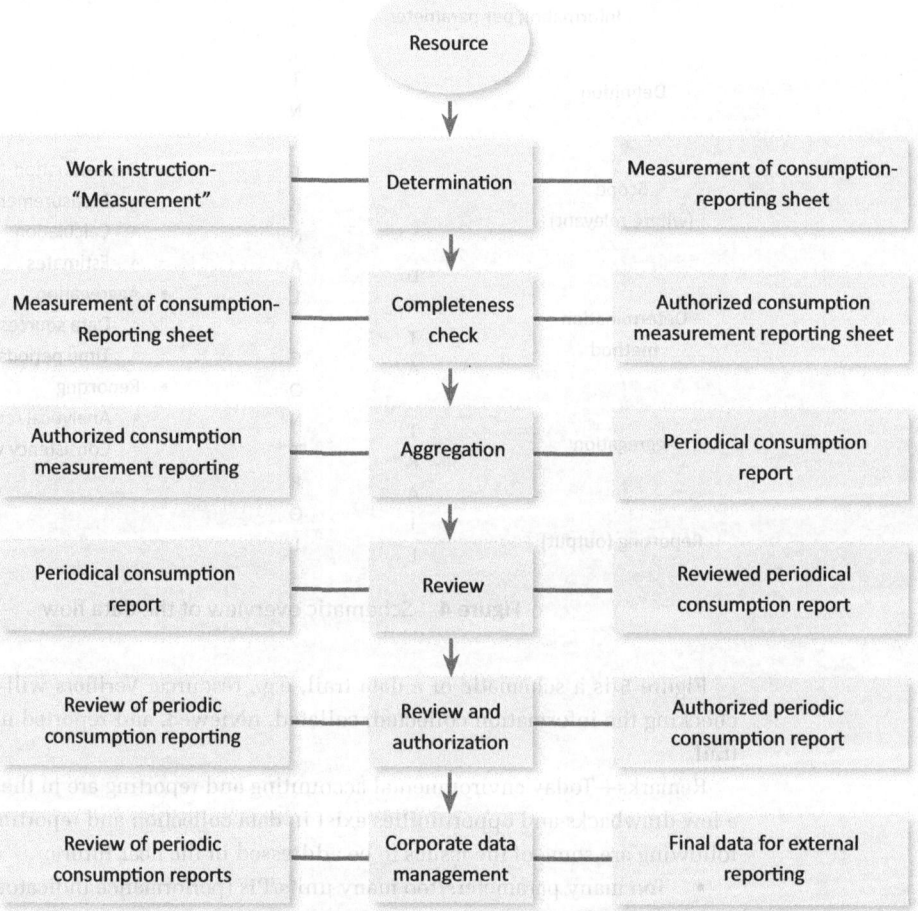

Figure 5 Procedures and records (evidence) in assessing data quality

The hope is that more and more organizations in India will start publishing environmental reports and reach their stakeholders with environmental information about their processes and products in the near future.

Sustainability and Its Challenges

INTRODUCTION

Ben & Jerry's initiatives (see Exhibit 7.1) are excellent examples of how to humanize capitalism or earn profit in a sustainable manner. Their efforts towards waste treatment by setting up a dissolved air flotation unit can be compared to Tata International's efforts of reusing water after removing toxins in their leather unit at Dewas, where there is a scarcity of water (a detailed case is given at the end of Chapter 3). Both companies, though situated in two different socio-economic paradigms, have the same vision of increasing their profits by contributing to the welfare of the societies in which they are located. For the success of globalization steered by capitalism, this vision of sharing profits for the benefit of society is pertinent.

Friedman Thomas (2000) has rightly highlighted that 'globalization is not a phenomenon. It is not just some passing trend.' Today, it is impacting and shaping every aspect in the domestic and foreign relations of virtually every country. Therefore, this understanding should guide every activity that deals with socio-economic factors. This omnipresent globalization is a result of capitalism that promotes the free flow of goods and services and is based on the concept of equal opportunity for all. This concept of capitalism needed responsible businesses as an ally. Unfortunately, lack of stringent rules and regulations in the free market economy could not be appreciated by the untrained minds practising it; therefore, capitalism became exploitative as greed for more and more selfish gain increased. Short-sighted consumerism failed to deliver the promised Utopia. This phenomenon was visible even as early as the year 1800, when Nicolai Gogol (1948) described a landowner's apprehension of the factory culture promoting consumerism when he wrote 'the factories will spring up of their own accord for providing what man needs on the spot … in order to keep going and to sell their wares, (the factories) use every sort of abominable means, depraving and disintegrating the unfortunate people …' The answer to this

LEARNING OBJECTIVES

After studying this chapter, you will be able to
- Understand capitalism and the relationship between capitalism and sustainability
- Understand the efforts to measure sustainability
- Know the difficulties faced in the implementation of measurement frameworks

> **EXHIBIT 7.1**
>
> ## Ben & Jerry's Ice Cream Promotes Sustainable Development
>
> CSR or corporate citizenship entails companies behaving in a socially responsible manner and dealing with other business parties who do the same. With growing public awareness and demand for socially responsible businesses, companies of today are now taking CSR into account when planning future socially responsible business operations. Let us look at an example of CSR exemplified by Ben & Jerry's, which is a manufacturer of one of the best-known super premium ice cream, frozen yoghurt, and sorbet in the US. It is based in Vermont, was founded in 1978, and was subsequently acquired by Unilever. 'Business has a responsibility to the community and the environment' is Ben & Jerry's mantra and it certainly walks the talk when it comes to CSR.
>
> In 2008, celebrating 30 years of success, Walt Freese, the then CEO, identified the following long-term goals in his open letter on their website:
>
> 1. Use our company to further the cause of peace and justice.
> 2. Harmonize our global supply chain and ensure its alignment with our company values.
> 3. Take the lead in promoting global sustainable dairy practices.
>
> **Ben & Jerry's Missions**
>
> The three-part mission of the Ben & Jerry's Foundation is to make the world a better place by empowering Ben & Jerry's employees to use available resources to support and encourage organizations that are working towards eliminating the underlying causes of environmental and social problems.
>
> *Product mission* To make, distribute, and sell the finest quality of all natural ice creams and euphoric concoctions with a continued commitment to incorporating wholesome, natural ingredients, and promoting business practices that respect the earth and the environment.
>
> *Economic mission* To operate the company on a sustainable financial basis of profitable growth, increasing value for our stakeholders, and expanding opportunities for development and career growth for our employees.
>
> *Social mission* To operate the company in a way that actively recognizes the central role that business plays in society by initiating innovative ways to improve the quality of life locally, nationally, and internationally.
>
> True to their statement, Ben & Jerry's launched a companywide environmental programme in the US, which started from looking for reusable waste in their dumpsters. This immediately revealed the amount of trash that any company generates. Normally, the trash is overlooked because it is not visible everyday. Ben & Jerry's targeted three key types of trash—plastic, paper, and cardboard—each with its own unique set of challenges. The company sent all of the plastic ingredients buckets

to Vermont. The goal was to foster environmental awareness, education, and action throughout the company. 'From info-postings and other employee communications to entertaining and often offbeat environmental awareness events, the Green Team (at Ben & Jerry's) creates and facilitates fun ways to keep folks on the upside of the eco-learning curve.' They also facilitate paper recycling by setting up convenient systems of separating white and mixed office paper, newsprint, paper board, and glossy paper. They used to sell their cardboard boxes to ReBox Corporation, which promotes cardboard reuse solutions. Ben & Jerry's decided to reuse cardboard rather than recycle. An interesting and innovative way of promoting the use of solar panels was the Ben & Jerry's Circus Bus with solar panels fitted to power the on-board electronics. In fact, it was a 'community celebration featuring world-class street performers and a message to encourage development of solar energy'. They installed a dissolved air flotation unit (DAF) as a permanent addition to upgrade their waste pre-treatment process. The process uses a natural flocculent (carrageenan, a type of seaweed) to separate the high-strength dairy waste from the wastewater, before the wastewater is further processed through pre-treatment lagoons.

The tangible actions of Ben & Jerry's were efforts like being the first publicly traded company in the US to become a signatory of the CERES Principles (formerly known as the Valdez Principles), in 1992. Under CERES' terms, they have to submit a report of environmental performance each year, which adds yet another set of important tasks to the growing list that they present to their Manager of Natural Resources Use.

Use of Fair Trade Ingredients
Procurement of fair trade ingredients has been adopted by various socially responsible businesses who exemplify corporate citizenship. This is part of its wider framework for CSR. Fair trade products (or Fairtrade as it is known in many countries), such as fair trade coffee, fair trade clothes, and fair trade chocolate, are meant to remedy some of the problems associated with regulating factory and workplace conditions of companies that produce goods and services in foreign countries and import their products into their home countries. Fair trade standards ensure that employees have safe working conditions, work reasonable hours, and get paid a fair amount for their work.

According to Ben & Jerry's website, wherever possible, it sources its ingredients from producers and suppliers who share its values in its supply chain strategy. This can mean anything from purchasing free-range eggs to sustainably produced dairy, to fair trade certified ingredients. Ben & Jerry's began using fair trade certified ingredients in 2005. The ice cream giant announced a plan in February 2010 to go fully fair trade by 2013.

Engaging the Community through Community-based Projects
One approach to engaging in CSR is through community-based development projects. Community-based and community-driven development projects have become

an important form of development assistance among global socially responsible companies. An economic relationship implies a strategy of engaging the wider community into the core business activity of the company, so that communities become embedded in a corporate supply chain strategy to create a sustainable business. In 1999, Ben & Jerry's launched the Vermont Dairy Farm Sustainability Project, which sought to develop practical methods that could be used on typical dairy operations to safeguard water quality from nitrogen and phosphorus run-off, while not sacrificing the economic viability of the farm and making the farm a sustainable business.

According to the Ben & Jerry's social and environmental assessment 2004 report, the result of this three-year study demonstrated that farmers could reduce nutrient levels without decreasing crop size and that improved water quality and cost savings resulting from reductions in the amount of nutrient use on the farm would be beneficial for the environment as well as the farmers' bottom-line. These would thus help the farm become a more sustainable business.

Corporate Philanthropy

Ben & Jerry's also donates a portion of its pre-tax profits to corporate philanthropy as part of its efforts to be more socially responsible. Corporate philanthropy is employee-led through the Ben & Jerry's Foundation and Community Action Teams (CATS) at each site. It is interesting to note that they have created positions like chief euphoria officer and manager of natural resources use. As an organization, they send out the message that euphoria can be experienced in activities related to the well-being of society.

Source: http://www.benjerry.com/company/sear/2008/sear08_2.0.cfm, accessed on 19 February 2010; http://social-corporate-responsibility.suite101.com/article.cfm/corporate-social-responsibility-at-ben--jerrys, accessed on 26 July 2010.

---

is not undiluted socialism because we have seen how that has failed, in Mikhail Gorbachev's lament that communism has failed in Russia. It is very apparent that the middle path between unbridled conspicuous consumption and annihilation of human freedom in the name of equality has to be found for viable and sustainable development. Selfish exploitation of resources for personal gain by an individual or a company would create a very lopsided growth in a society. Similarly, promoting restriction on private freedom for selfish gain by a few powerful entities in the name of fair distribution of goods and opportunities to all also cannot be justified. 'Equality of poverty' should not be the game, instead at all levels, there has to be a culture of hand-holding for the less privileged to move up the chain.

CAPITALISM

Businesses have to realize that they owe a social obligation because it is society that gives them the sanction to do business, helps them in the process of production and promotion, and rewards them through profits. If the social system is destroyed in the rush for economic growth, what would be the use of such growth? Capitalism symbolized freedom from the shackles of an oppressive state-run economy and therefore promised a life that would be self-fulfilling and comfortable. It seemed to answer man's aspiration to move beyond the basic subsistence level of existence or the bare minimum of food, clothing, and shelter, which are needed to survive. To achieve this objective, rationalism explained as self-interest, not selfishness, soon replaced emotions and values. The most favourite question for judging any activity is, 'What am I going to gain out of it?' If this is true rationalism, then we go against our own argument when we eulogize and put those people on a pedestal who look beyond their personal gains to achieve welfare for all.

Capitalism is based on neo-classical economics, which propagates that supply and demand determines price, output, income distribution, etc. in the market. Therefore, utilitarian ethics of the greatest good can be achieved only when individuals are allowed to pursue their own self-interest. This corollary leads to efficient and effective production, personal autonomy, and freedom. Therefore, capitalism has to invest in idealism to ensure the fundamental practice of providing transparent information to all for ensuring equal opportunity to all. Vogel (1991) and March (1992) point out that self-interest and other interests are mutually beneficial in this system. Therefore, duty-based morality is ignored and it accepts restraint from public regarding the path self-interest should take. Lindblom (1977) called this social restraint as 'authority and persuasion'. The danger with this form of unfettered growth of self-interest has been well captured by Hardin (1968) in the 'Tragedy of Commons', where he shows that in a common grazing area of a community if everyone only pursues self-interest and grazes cattle, then the common (the grazing ground), which is the shared limited resource, will disappear. Neither socialism nor capitalism has delivered the good society that they promised. Since freedom of spirit is more important for a human being than a process of hierarchy based on command and control, socialism failed to deliver and thus lost its original enchantment. Hence, capitalism with its free market proposition has to re-invent itself now to cater to the true emancipation of human existence. This requires that everyone should have the freedom to enjoy their life as long as they take care that others also enjoy the same freedom. This would lead to a society that would be free from fear and oppression. Capitalism cannot survive by doing acts of charity that depends on choice. It has to integrate ethical behaviour that makes it mandatory for corporates to maintain sustainable relationships with its internal and external constituents. It has to build a symbiotic give and take relationship based on mutual sharing. This can be achieved when commitment gets reviewed as 'to think of commitments—from marriage and work to political and religious involvement—as enhancements of the sense of individual well-being rather than as moral imperatives' (Bellah et al. 1985).

HUMANIZING CAPITALISM

Capitalism, in its effort to promote individual welfare, forgets that in a knowledge-driven specialized world that is interdependent, one cannot survive solely by advancing personal goals. Even for one's selfish existence, one has to allow others to exist and when all of us are promoting our individual welfare, collaboration is what would sustain it, contrary to the belief that competition would. Competition can never be a win-win situation; its inherent quality is win-lose. Therefore, to make it more endearing, we talk about fair competition by creating a level playing field. The prerequisite of such a field is collaboration and that requires development of the human spirit of sharing. Business needs to have a human face, if it wants to be successful because the web of relationships that it creates is based on trust and that trust needs to be honoured. Therefore, to reap the benefits of a free spirit promoting innovativeness and creativity, freedom has to be used responsibly, as explained lucidly by Rabindranath Tagore (1984): 'It cannot be asserted that man shall have no independence, but that he shall not be selfish. In short, for oneself there must be something of one's own: everything else should be for others'.

This humanizing of capitalism has to be the driving force of globalization. It is promoted as the provider of better jobs, clean water, nutritious food, and uncontaminated environment; in short, improving the quality of life of the common citizens. Unfortunately, the underbelly of globalization is extremely ugly because it has created more disparity between the rich and the poor, greed for more profit has led to indiscriminate use of non-renewable resources, exploitation of workers, violation of human rights, and environment degradation, in the name of development. Therefore, CSR demands that the corporate world embrace globalization to create a more perfect world, which allows a more equal distribution of opportunities through more transparent flow of information, goods and services, and human beings between the geographical borders.

Capitalism and globalization cannot lead to economic and ethical imperialism. This happens when multi-national organizations take advantage of the lack of the host country's stringent government policies and rules resulting from their lack of resources, like availability of finance, skilled people, and regulatory institutions. In such a scenario, the only guiding factor for business is its value foundation. Authors like Donaldson (1989) have offered a list of fundamental rights that corporations must practise as a moral minimum. He also suggests a concept of 'rational empathy test', according to which organizations can judge the validity of their action by putting themselves in the shoes of the host country by creating a 'hypothetical altered social condition' similar to the home country and asking the question 'would their practices be permissible in their home countries that are more developed than the host country?' Here the author would like to add that when we are propagating empathy in terms of being in somebody else's shoes, we must first 'take off our shoes' because otherwise we would not be able to do a true assessment of the situation, as our own perceptions would strongly colour our judgement.

Corporates must understand that CSR is not about creating a charitable trust to do philanthropic work in lieu of incorporating responsible behaviour in all its activities. It cannot work on the 'Robin Hood principle' of justifying stealing by promoting some superficial charitable activity. The legendary Robin Hood at least stole from the rich to distribute the wealth among the poor and the disadvantaged and created his own system of distributive justice. The modern business, in the name of profit for the shareholder, overlooks the human and spiritual aspect considering them as esoteric concepts beyond business. Businesses cheat themselves when they believe that parking part of the 'unethically' earned money in trusts and NGOs exonerates them from all social responsibility because long term sustenance is dependent on understanding the different levels of CSR (as mentioned in Chapter 1). Modern corporate management must realize that they have to distribute the benefits produced by the firms and also allocate the costs imposed by them in a manner that the stakeholders feel it is right and just. If the modern corporate journey believes that profit at any cost should be the mantra and human beings need to be subdued to business instead of business being subdued to humanism, it would not be able to sustain itself.

The case of Arthur Andersen given in Exhibit 7.2 highlights the danger of profit becoming the only driving force in the belief that the market forces would take care as long as business is within the rules. The problem is: who decides the rules and who monitors whether business is within the 'rules of the game'? Therefore, CSR can no longer remain a philanthropic activity and has to be woven into the practices, processes, and concerns of business. Capitalism has to look beyond the materialistic world, towards the human aspect, because what is the value of material wealth if it does not sustain human life and comfort for all.

EXHIBIT 7.2

Arthur Andersen and the Free Market

Arthur Andersen originally built his business by putting reputation over profit. New hires, known as 'green beans', recited the founder's motto, 'Think straight, talk straight'. And they learned Andersen's 'four cornerstones'—provide good service to the client, produce quality audits, manage staff well, and produce profits for the firm.

This philosophy was diluted when the firm decided to not just audit the books but set up the computers clients needed to keep the books. For the first time, the firm admitted partners from outside the US and in 1979, Andersen become the world's largest professional-services firm. It raked in huge profits because of being the pioneer in the field of providing technology practices by an accounting firm. Realizing that business consulting was a very lucrative business, in 1989, Arthur Andersen and Andersen Consulting became separate units of Andersen Worldwide, based in Geneva. Andersen began using its accounting services as a springboard to sign up clients for Andersen Consulting's more lucrative business.

The auditors and the consultants competed fiercely, turning the annual race for profits into a devilish sport. Leonard Spacek—who led the firm from 1947 to 1963—campaigned to clean up the accounting industry. He accused Bethlehem Steel of overstating its profits in 1964 by more than 60 per cent and charged the Securities and Exchange Commission (SEC), the regulatory body, for failing to crack down on companies that cooked their books, saying that at best the regulatory agency has been 'a brake on the rate of retrogression in the quality of accounting'.

As the firm grew from a close-knit partnership to a global firm, pressure to boost profits became intense. Andersen leaders chose the path of selling their services like salesmen. This naturally disturbed the delicate balance that an auditor must perform between pleasing a client and looking out for the public investor. Ethics was being sacrificed in the name of profit and competition to remain on top.

Chinks in the armour of ethicality and values that an audit firm must 'wear' became visible when in 1998 Andersen agreed to pay $75 million to settle shareholder suits arising from an accounting scandal at waste management. In May 2001, Andersen paid $110 million to settle shareholders' claims related to an accounting scandal at Sunbeam.

To enhance their financial situation, Andersen floated the idea of 'integrated audit', which would mingle not only internal and external audits but a whole package of services ranging from tax strategy to advice on corporate finance issues. This left the field open for misuse of auditing powers to earn extraordinary profits. Profit seemed to become the sole motive of this market-driven company. SEC, finding this array of services being offered by audit firms questionable, wanted to limit the amount of consulting work that accounting firms could perform for their audit clients. Samek (the then head of Arthur Andersen) called the SEC proposal 'fatally flawed'. He said it arrived 'just as we need to take an even more active role in making needed changes in the measurement and reporting system in support of better information for decision-making by corporations, investors, and the government'. The Big Four accounting firms (PriceWaterhouse Coopers, Deloitte Touche Tohmatsu, Ernst & Young, and KPMG) defeated the SEC proposal.

It was not long before Andersen was put to shame in its own revolutionary practice of 'integrated audit' at Enron (who were Arthur Anderson's audit client since 1986). Under the scheme of integrated audit, Enron's entire team of 40 internal auditors were hired and added to its own people. An office was opened in Enron's Houston headquarters that was as big as some regional Arthur Andersen offices. Practices and concepts like the '2×' strategy required partners to bring in two times their revenues in work outside their area of practice (that meant that if an auditor brought the firm $2 million by auditing a company's books, he should bring in an additional $4 million in non-audit services, such as tax advice and technology consulting). Practices like judging auditors against '2×' during performance reviews, as well as asking auditors to 'empathize' with clients' books sounded the death knell for this firm. The lure of 'profit-based performance appraisal' made it difficult for auditors to fight back against clients who wanted to test the limits of accepted accounting standards. Thus, it showcased a clear example of market taking over and being in control.

The final straw was the debacle at Enron. Andersen was charged with obstruction of justice in a Houston federal court for shredding papers sought by an SEC investigation, thus resulting in a humiliating end to a company that once stood as the world's largest professional services firm. Andersen's end has also brought to the forefront the question of oligopolies, which develop in a free market economy because the audit world was and is still dominated by the Big Four. This creates fierce competition to procure business from large global corporations, leading to unethical practices in the name of profit.

Source: Report on 'Arthur Andersen's Fall From Grace Is a Sad Tale of Greed and Miscues' by Ken Brown and Ianthe Jeanne Dugan, staff reporters of *The Wall Street Journal*, 7 June 2002, and http://www.corporatenarc.com/anderson.php, accessed on 20 February 2010.

SUSTAINABILITY

Related to the concept of capitalism and the urgent need to create a human face of growth is the theory of sustainability. The notion of sustainability is not easy to analyse because it depends on the different perceptions of sustainability. It often gets lost as it becomes a relative factor with a myriad definition.

The word sustainability is derived from the Latin *sustinere* (*tenere* means to hold, *sus* means up). Let us look at some of the definitions of sustainability.

Sustainable development is 'development that meets the needs of the present without compromising the ability of future generations to meet their own needs' (WCED 1987).

'Finding a balance between economic prosperity, environmental quality, and—the element which business has tended to overlook—social justice, moves organizations in an absolute state of sustainability' Elkington (1999).

'The sustainable society is one that lives within the self-perpetuating limits of its environment' Coomer (1979). Thus, we find that sustainability is measured through the lens of either social development and justice or human welfare and social justice (Fig. 7.1).

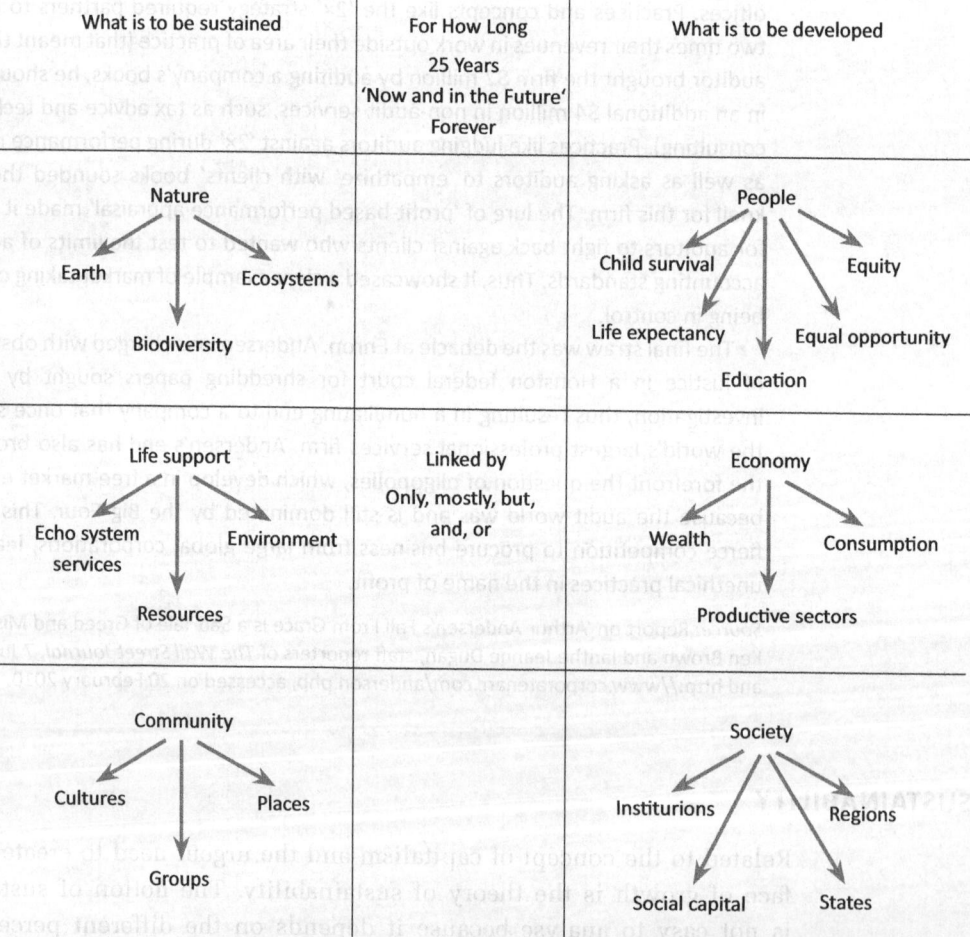

Source: US National Research Council, Policy Division, Board on Sustainable Development, *Our Common Journey: A Transition toward Sustainability* (Washington, DC: National Academy Press, 1999; also from Kates et al., 2005).

Figure 7.1 Sustainable development

This apparent ambiguity of certain parameters of sustainability makes it appear as nothing more than a feel-good buzzword without any true meaning or substance (Dunning 2006) However, in spite of its lack of focus on concrete deliverables, it is considered as important because it highlights concepts like 'liberty' or 'justice' (Blewitt 2008). This intangible aspect is described as a 'dialogue of values that defies consensual definition' (Ratner 2004).

Though it is difficult to define, there is a consensus that it cannot be ignored. Therefore, attempts to explain its importance continues at all levels. Some of the international efforts to define sustainability are given below.

Brundtland Report

WCED (World Commission on Environment and Development), which had been formulated in 1983, published a report entitled Our Common Future, which came to be known as the Brundtland Report after the name of the Chairwoman of the Commission who was also the Prime Minister of Norway, Gro Harlem Brundtland. Sustainability, itself, was first defined by the Brundtland Commission of the United Nations in 1987.

The environment does not exist as a sphere separate from human actions, ambitions, and needs, and attempts to defend it in isolation from human concerns have given the very word 'environment' a connotation of naivety in some political circles. The word 'development' has also been narrowed by some into a very limited focus, along the lines of 'what poor nations should do to become richer,' and thus again is automatically dismissed by many in the international arena as being a concern of specialists, of those involved in questions of 'development assistance.' But the 'environment' is where we live; and 'development' is what we all do in attempting to improve our lot within that abode. The two are inseparable.
– WCED 1987

Various international meetings to pursue the agenda of sustainability were initiated after the WCED report was published. The United Nations Conference on Environment and Development (UNCED) in Rio de Janeiro in 1992 (the so-called 'Earth Summit') issued a declaration of principles, a detailed Agenda 21 of desired actions (see Annexure 1), international agreements on climate change and biodiversity, and a statement of principles on forests (UNCED 1992, Parson and Haas 1992).

In 2002, at the World Summit on Sustainable Development in Johannesburg, South Africa, the commitment to sustainable development was reaffirmed. The 2002 World Summit on Sustainable Development introduced the three pillars of sustainable development: economic, social, and environmental. The Johannesburg Declaration created 'a collective responsibility to advance and strengthen the interdependent and mutually reinforcing pillars of sustainable development—economic development, social development, and environmental protection—at local, national, regional, and global levels' (*The Johannesburg Declaration on Sustainable Development*, 4 September 2002).

In spite of ambiguous and esoteric nature of sustainable development, interest in the subject has continued to grow at different institutional levels and is being researched at countless international organizations, national institutions, corporate enterprises, 'sustainable cities', and locales.

One important study—by the Board on Sustainable Development of the US National Academy of Sciences made an effort to standardize the rather broad and fluid aspect of sustainability (National Research Council, Policy Division, Board on Sustainable Development, *Our Common Journey: A Transition toward Sustainability*, 1999) (see Fig 7.1). In its report, the board focused on the seemingly inherent distinction between what advocates and analysts sought to sustain and what they sought to develop, the relationship between the two, and the time-horizon of the future.

Again, the focus was on people, economy, and society. The earlier thrust on economic development, with productive sectors providing employment, desired consumption, and wealth has shifted to human development, including an emphasis on values and goals, such as increased life expectancy, education, equity, and opportunity. The list has been enhanced by the Board on Sustainable Development to social responsibility by including society that emphasized the values of security and well-being of national states, regions, and institutions as well as the social capital of relationships and community ties (Kates et al. 2005).

Sustainable development needs to set some achievement targets, or goals, within a specific timeframe. Certain illustration of such analysis can be seen in the three sets of goals that use different time-horizons: the short-term goals (2015) of the Millennium Declaration of the United Nations (see Annexure 2); the two-generation goals (2050) of the Sustainability Transition of the Board on Sustainable Development; and the long-term goals (beyond 2050) of the Great Transition of the Global Scenario Group.

The belief that sustainability has to be captured in its various manifestations is the essence of the above initiatives. Corporations have to look beyond the bottom-line if they want significant improvements in their bottom line because long-term profit can be earned only when all the stakeholders see true commitment of the company to ensure a holistic development. The case of Merck and Company (Exhibit 7.3) is an example of such commitment.

EXHIBIT 7.3

Beyond the Bottom-line—Profits can be Earned in spite of being Ethical and Socially Driven

The efforts of Merck and Company is another brave story of professional values. The American drug company helped in eradicating river blindness in the tropical regions of Africa and Latin America. Onchocerciasis, also known as river blindness or Robles' Disease, is the world's second leading infectious cause of blindness. It is caused by a parasitic worm, which is spread in the human bloodstream through bites from blackflies and buffalo gnats found in parts of Africa, South America, and Central America.

Scientist Dr William Campbell discovered the potential of the animal drug Ivermectin to cure river blindness. This was a breakthrough that revolutionized treatment of the dreaded widespread disease, especially in Africa and South America, and brought hope to millions of underprivileged people of the world. Since countries there were economically not so developed, the need for cheap medicine was the priority but there were apprehensions regarding the cost of development, misuse of the cheap drug, logistic problems, and increasing competition in the drug market. However, it was believed by certain visionary value-oriented professionals that the company was morally obligated to proceed, specially in the face of the magnanimity of the problem of river blindness despite the cost and slim chance of economic reward. Unfortunately, there were no buyers, considering the economic situation in the afflicted areas, and that is when Merck took a bold decision, beyond profits, to distribute the drug free.

The chairman of the company, Dr P Roy Vagelos, justified the decision on moral and ethical grounds saying that once the company suspected that one of its animal drugs might cure a severe human disease that was ravaging people, the only ethical choice was to develop it. He further pointed out that from the long-term perspective, people in the Third World 'will remember' that Merck helped them and would respond favourably to the company in future. The positive impact of going beyond self-interest by a company is further endorsed by his comment, 'When I first went to Japan 15 years ago, I was told by Japanese business people that it was Merck that brought streptomycin to Japan after World War II to eliminate tuberculosis, which was eating up society. We did that. We didn't make any money. But it's no accident that Merck is the largest American pharmaceutical company in Japan today.'

Source: Manuel G Velasquez—*Business Ethics Concepts and Cases,* Pearson Education, 2004, p. 3, 4; *Wall Street Journal,* 'Merck & Company to Donate Drugs for River Blindness', 22 October 1987, p. 42; and David Bollier, 'Merck & Company—The Business Enterprise Trust', Stanford, CA, 1991, p. 5 and 16.

INTEGRATING CSR IN ORGANIZATIONS: GUIDELINES TO EFFECTIVE CHANGE

The question that now arises is what standards are available to put CSR into practice. Does the implementation of sustainable behaviour by a company depend solely on the whims and fancies of the management or can a company follow processes that would help it to implement CSR? The three mechanisms—ISO 26000, Triple Bottom Line (TBL), and Triple Loop Learning (TLL)—of incorporating CSR by a company are given below. However, as we analyse them, we will see that each system has its own strengths and weaknesses.

ISO and CSR

ISO is the International Organization for Standardization. It is the world's largest developer and publisher of International Standards. The term 'ISO', is derived from the Greek *isos*, meaning 'equal'. Whatever the country, whatever the language, the short form of the organization's name is always ISO.

One hundred and sixty-three countries are members of ISO. Membership is given to one member per country and the Central Secretariat is located in Geneva, Switzerland, which coordinates the system. ISO is a non-governmental organization that connects the public and private sectors. This is achieved through its public sector and private sector membership: on the one hand, many of its member institutes are part of the governmental structure of their countries, or are mandated by their government. On the other hand, other members have their roots uniquely in the private sector, having been set up by national partnerships of industry associations.

Therefore, ISO is able to build a consensus on solutions that meet both the requirements of business and the broader needs of society. Some of the well-known standards are ISO 9001 that deals with quality, ISO 22000 relates to food safety management systems, ISO 14001 is a standard for the environmental management of businesses, and other similar standards have been created. The international body decided to launch the development of an International Standard providing guidelines for social responsibility (SR) by promoting ISO 26000.

ISO 26000

ISO standardization does not, as a rule, pre-determine which particular type of organization may use its standards or other deliverables. As a result, ISO social responsibility deliverables are referred to without organizational specification. Keeping in mind the inter-relationship between economic, environmental, and social aspects the characteristics and underlying principles of social responsibility according to ISO include the following:

- Assumes compliance with all applicable laws and regulations (as a minimum)

- Includes voluntary commitments that address economic, environmental, and social aspects not addressed in laws and regulations
- Inclusiveness, communication, and engagement with affected or/and interested parties involving dialogue on expectations and activities
- Accountability
- Transparency
- Ethical behaviour
- Flexibility to reflect diversity and needs
- Part of sustainability/Sustainable development

Social responsibility specifically include issues such as:
- Human rights (Universal Declaration of Human Rights, ILO Core Conventions)
- Workplace and employee aspects (including occupational health and safety)
- Unfair business practices including bribery, corruption, and anti-competitive practices (all organizations)
- Organizational governance
- Environmental aspects
- Marketplace and consumer aspects
- Community aspects
- Social development aspects

ISO has decided to launch the development of an international standard providing guidelines for social responsibility. It has chosen Swedish Standards Institute (SIS) and Brazilian Association of Technical Standards (ABNT) to provide joint leadership of the ISO Working Group on Social Responsibility (WG SR). The WG SR has been given the task of drafting an international standard for social responsibility that will be published in 2010 as ISO 26000 and will be voluntary to use. It will not include requirements and will thus not be a certification standard.

ISO 26000 is supposed to provide harmonized, globally relevant guidance, based on international consensus among expert representatives of the main stakeholder groups, and so encourage the implementation of best practice in social responsibility worldwide.

There is a range of many different opinions as to the right approach, ranging from strict legislation at one end to complete freedom at the other. ISO claims that it is looking for a golden middle way that promotes respect and responsibility, based on known reference documents without stifling creativity and development.

The standard will aim to encourage voluntary commitment to social responsibility and will lead to common guidance on concepts, definitions, and methods of evaluation. The need for organizations in both public and private sectors to behave in a socially responsible way is becoming a generalized requirement of society. It is shared by the stakeholder groups that are participating in the WG SR to develop ISO 26000: industry, government, labour, consumers, non-governmental organizations, and others, in addition to geographical and gender-based balance.

About the Standard

According to the new work item proposal, the standard should:
- assist organizations in addressing their social responsibilities while respecting cultural, societal, environmental, and legal differences and economic development conditions;
- provide practical guidance related to operationalizing social responsibility, identifying and engaging with stakeholders, and enhancing credibility of reports and claims made about social responsibility;
- emphasize performance results and improvement;
- increase confidence and satisfaction in organizations among their customers and other stakeholders;
- be consistent with and not in conflict with existing documents, international treaties and conventions, and existing ISO standards;
- not be intended to reduce government's authority to address the social responsibility of organizations;
- promote common terminology in the social responsibility field; and
- broaden awareness of social responsibility.

The ISO 26000 standard* offers a framework through its proposal for CSR but does not provide any incentive for organizations to put the scheme into action. Every ISO standard has a certification process that encourages a company to achieve it as a brand of quality. Unfortunately, the CSR standard is propagated as a voluntary commitment and therefore may not be practised. Thus, though it proposes an international standard for social responsibility, it may only remain a wish list, as organizations can provide various excuses for not putting the standard into practice. The other risk is unscrupulous organizations may use ISO 26000 as a smokescreen to enhance their image without really being accountable for socially responsible activities, since there is no certification process, and therefore checking fraudulent use would be difficult, if not impossible.

Triple Bottom Line

This is another popular mechanism that was considered a practical method for implementing CSR. The phrase was coined by John Elkington in 1994. It

* The source for ISO 2600 is http://isotc.iso.org/livelink/livelink/fetch/2000/2122/8309 49/3934883/3935096/home.html, accessed on 8 August 2010.

was later expanded and articulated in his 1998 book, *Cannibals with Forks: The Triple Bottom Line of 21st Century Business*. Elkington was the co-founder and chairperson of SustainAbility Limited, which was founded in 1987 and is headquartered in London, with offices in US and Europe, and also has a number of partnership networks in other parts of the world, especially in emerging economies like China, India, Brazil, and South Africa. It is an international business consultancy dealing with principles of sustainable development or what is called 'performance with purpose'. TBL accounting attempts to describe the social and environmental impact of an organization's activities, in a measurable way, to its economic performance in order to show improvement or to make evaluation more in-depth. TBL is a form of reporting that takes into account the impact a business has in terms of social and environmental values, along with financial returns. TBL has its own synonyms in Triple-E (economy, environment, equity) or 3P (people, planet, profit), which are penetrating the traditional language of business. The 3P is explained below.

People

The concept looks at the human aspect of business not just as a human resource but as human capital. This is not only about fair employment opportunities but also about giving back to society in the form of social investment. Therefore, it goes beyond providing just a fair day's pay for a fair day's work; it entails returning to the community through sponsorships, donations, and investments for common good and welfare. This reinvestment can usually be factored in business operating expenses, as it would give long-term benefits to the organization by building a strong reputation and trust in society.

Planet

This is natural capital or the environmental issues that need immediate attention if long-term sustainability is the aim. A business will strive to minimize its ecological impact in all areas—from sourcing raw materials to production processes including administration, to marketing of its products and services. It is a 'cradle-to-grave' approach and in some cases 'cradle-to-cradle' approach i.e., taking some responsibility for goods after they have been sold—for example, offering a recycling or take-back programme. A TBL business will also refrain from the production of toxic items, even as effluents or waste products.

Profit

This brings to the forefront the ways and methods of earning profit and not just making profit. The argument is that the means are as important as the ends. Profit should be earned honestly in harmony with the other two principles of people and planet. In today's global and virtual business perspectives, the supply chain and outsourcing processes also need to be scrutinized under the TBL principle.

Importance

There are currently few standards for measuring these other impacts. However, the importance of the concept lies in the fact that at least it raises the issue that an organization cannot accomplish economic growth responsibly and holistically without embracing the vast multitude of non-financial impacts of its activities.

Considering the growing influence of the business world and the wide spread of its tentacles, one cannot remain immune to the responsibility of business in all spheres of business activities. TBL tries to capture the myriad of influences of business through three parameters and that is where it faces problems in the eyes of critics, which are discussed next. Read the Key Findings of Corp Watch (Exhibit 7.4) to understand the extraordinary growth of business.

EXHIBIT 7.4

Key Findings of Corp Watch

1. Of the 100 largest economies in the world, 51 are corporations; only 49 are countries (based on a comparison of corporate sales and country GDPs).
2. The Top 200 corporations' sales are growing at a faster rate than overall global economic activity. Between 1983 and 1999, their combined sales grew from the equivalent of 25.0 per cent to 27.5 per cent of World GDP.
3. The Top 200 corporations' combined sales are bigger than the combined economies of all countries minus the biggest 10.
4. The Top 200s' combined sales are 18 times the size of the combined annual income of the 1.2 billion people (24 per cent of the total world population) living in 'severe' poverty.
5. While the sales of the Top 200 are the equivalent of 27.5 per cent of world economic activity, they employ only 0.78 per cent of the world's workforce.
6. Between 1983 and 1999, the profits of the Top 200 firms grew 362.4 per cent, while the number of people they employ grew by only 14.4 per cent.
7. A full 5 per cent of the Top 200s' combined workforce is employed by Wal-Mart, a company notorious for union-busting and widespread use of part-time workers to avoid paying benefits. The discount retail giant is the top private employer in the world, with 1,140,000 workers, more than twice as many as No. 2, DaimlerChrysler, which employs 466,938.
8. US corporations dominate the Top 200, with 82 slots (41 per cent of the total). Japanese firms are second, with only 41 slots.
9. Of the US corporations on the list, 44 did not pay the full standard 35 per cent federal corporate tax rate during the period 1996–1998. Seven of the firms actually paid less than zero in federal income taxes in 1998 (because

of rebates). These include: Texaco, Chevron, PepsiCo, Enron, Worldcom, McKesson, and the world's biggest corporation, General Motors.
10. Between 1983 and 1999, the share of total sales of the Top 200 made up by service sector corporations increased from 33.8 per cent to 46.7 per cent. Gains were particularly evident in financial services and telecommunications sectors, in which most countries have pursued deregulation.

Source: *Top 200—The Rise of Corporate Global Power*, Sarah Anderson and John Cavanagh, Institute for Policy Studies, 4 December 2000.

It is also worth noting that the TBL provides a framework within which corporate economic performance and social responsibility are measured. Therefore, it is not an accreditation or certification process. It is just a measurement process that a corporate may adhere to voluntarily and be transparent about their agenda of common good. This would endear the public to such businesses. TBL is 'a valuable management tool—that is, an early warning tool that allows you to react faster to changes in stakeholders' behaviour, and incorporate the changes into the strategy before they hit the [real?] bottom line' (Jorgensen 2000).

Some of the support for the TBL concept can be seen when MacGillivan (2004, 121) states that the 'economic, environmental, and social balance sheets must all be in the black for a business to be sustainable' and Wright et al. (2002) promote the TBL by exhorting decision-makers to look to the 'triple bottom line from which trade-offs can be more clearly defined and simultaneous social, economic, and ecological benefits can be achieved and maintained over time'.

Critique

Critics point out that ever since the TBL concept was first introduced, it has amounted to little more than a metaphor for corporate sustainability management. The criticism has largely centred around the inadequacy of quantifying and measuring multiple, and competing objectives of organizations. That is, how can one talk about a bottom line without an agreed-upon methodology that allows, at least in principle, to add and subtract various data until the net sum is achieved (Norman and MacDonald 2003). Like the ISO, critics feel that the TBL is no more than a means for enhancing the organization's public image (Schilizzi 2002). The difficulties of reporting formats are the biggest challenge in operationalizing TBL. Certain suggestions like providing a 'dashboard' of measures (Epstein and Weiser 1997), attempts to monetize all three bottom lines (Richardson 2004) have been offered but not with much acceptance in the organizational world. In fact, Schilizzi (2002) provides an alternative method to quantify the environmental and social dimensions of organizational performance by recommending 'real options' valuation techniques.

Thus, the tools and methods for operationalizing the TBL have been elusive. The concept of sustainability entails dyadic relations. The success of this dyadic relation is dependent on the creation of a symbiotic environment where no parasitic behaviour can operate. As long as symbiosis prevails, the system remains sustainable. Thus, in reality a multi-bottom line (MBL) reporting needs to be done, as there are number of actors in each of the three areas that TBL defines. The non-financial impacts of an organization on its stakeholders need to be understood and calculated to put CSR into practice.

Norman and MacDonald (2004) describe the TBL as a 'good old-fashioned single bottom line plus vague commitments to social and environmental concerns'. These ideas are corroborated when we see that there are multiple relationships among and within the three paradigms (PPP) of sustainability. The organization affects and is affected by these systems, and changes in one system lead to changes in the other, creating a matrix of change, which has different goals, objectives, and performance criteria.

The argument that the TBL pioneered the concept of measurement and reporting is challenged by the fact that larger movements with similar initiatives were already present. For example, movement identified by the acronym SEAAR: (Gray 2001) social and ethical accounting, auditing, and reporting, has produced a variety of competing standards and standard-setting bodies, including the Global Reporting Initiative (GRI), the SA 8000 from Social Accountability International, the AA 1000 from AccountAbility, as well as parts of various ISO standards.

One of the major practical difficulties of trying to analyse the social and environmental propositions in financial terms lies in the fact, 'What are the ethical/social equivalents or analogues of, say, revenue, expenses, gains, losses, assets, liabilities, equity, and so on? The kinds of raw data that TBL and other SEAAR advocates propose to collect as indications of social performance do not seem to fit into general categories, analogous to these, that will allow for a straightforward subtraction of "bads" from "goods" in order to get some kind of net social sum' (Norman and MacDonald 2003).

It is believed that as a society becomes richer, its citizens develop an increasing aspiration for a better life. The quality of this life is defined in terms of clean environment, protection of life and property, saving resources and wildlife, and contributing towards the well-being of others. This is considered as a measurement of progress. However, there is a darker side of progress as well, where GDP does not reflect the health of a nation and material well-being does not equal to happiness. Moral progress has to underpin both economic and scientific progress of the modern century if we want to reap the benefits of development.

Triple Loop Learning

The third parameter that can be used for incorporating CSR is TLL. TLL is concerned with the concept of transformational changes in the domain of knowledge, organization, and the individual. It goes beyond the domain of secular rational knowledge and merges with wisdom and mystical spiritual understanding. As mentioned above, TLL answers the question of moral progress, which needs to be understood for implementing CSR. Francisco Varela (Varela 2000) plays one of the key roles in this process, which has been developed further by many others (Gregory Bateson, and extended by Chris Argyris and Peter Senge).

With the arrival of the concept of knowledge, society, and its unique challenges, more focus is now on knowledge and knowledge creation. This entails cultivation of the individual and his/her intellectual, as well as personal, ethical values. This is explained by Hargrove (2007) as 'empowering people to transform who they are and reinvent themselves by helping them to see how their frames of reference, thinking, and behaviour produce unintended consequences ... to surface and question the way they have framed their points of view about themselves, others, or their circumstances with the idea of creating a fundamental shift.'

Since knowledge is gained through actively perceiving, acting, and interacting with the environmental structures, it is achieved through a process of incremental learning. This forms a feedback loop between the realm of knowledge and of the environment. This is commonly referred to as the single-loop learning or Kolblearning (Kolb 1984). Peschl (2006) highlights the limitation of this learning as it does not allow for the construction of paradigmatically new knowledge and radical innovation. Therefore, a second loop of learning is introduced and is referred to as double-loop learning or reframing. This second feedback loop takes into consideration that any kind of knowledge is always based on assumptions, premises, or a paradigm (Kuhn 1970). A person becomes an observer of his/her behaviour. The triple loop goes even beyond this cognitive level and touches the very existence of the human being, as expressed by Peschl (2007): 'It goes beyond the level of personal skills, competencies, personality, etc., because it transcends the domain of personality traits, behavioural and cognitive patterns, solely quantifiable data, etc. It touches the person on his/her fundamental level of being and, in many cases, concerns the domain of wisdom ...' This is the most difficult stage of learning because it questions the most fondly held views and unmasks us, shows how one has to move beyond oneself, if we want permanent positive change. Obviously, this process is resisted because no one likes to challenge their self-image.

The question that now arises is how this process of learning can be implemented. Theoretical models have been developed by various authors like Scharmer (2000, 2001) and Senge et al. (2004). The theoretical model that tries to explain triple loop learning is referred to as the 'U-Theory' or 'presencing'. The process can be viewed as a U-shaped curve that is realized in a series of states: the left branch going down the U focuses on issues of observation, perception, sensing, discovery of patterns of thought, and cognition, and on how to leave these patterns behind oneself in order to be cognitively and emotionally 'prepared' for profound change. At the bottom, one finds oneself in the state of presencing: it can be characterized as stepping into a corresponding state, where one is able to evaluate one's gifts and dysfunctional motivations and behaviours. This opens up a path for an upward journey on the right side

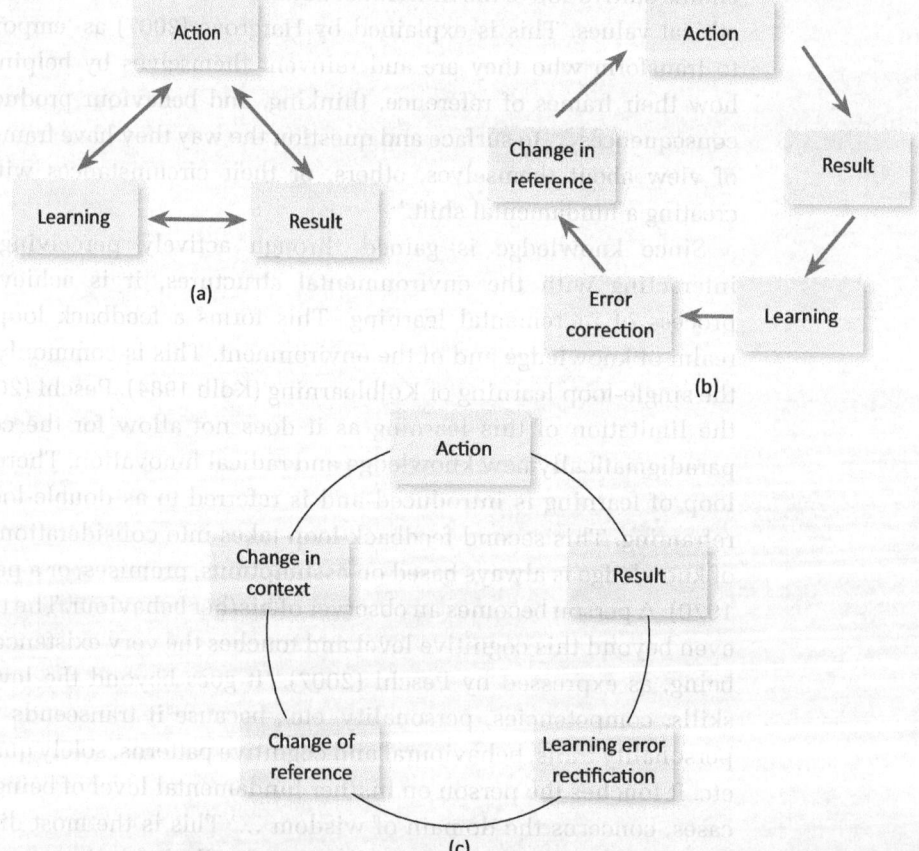

Figure 7.2 (a) Single loop learning (b) Double loop learning—Change in perspective, doing things differently (c) Triple loop learning—Fundamental change, questioning the context, enhancement of knowledge and self

of the U by creating a condition of high receptivity and openness, leading to enhanced knowledge and acceptance of change. The upward branch deals with issues concerning the realization, prototyping, and embodying these changes in the (external or internal) environment (Peschl 2007).

The TLL strategy as well as the presencing approach provides a framework in which these processes of profound change can emerge (Fig. 7.2). However, rigorous efforts are required to find a balance between the practical goal-oriented learning and this deeper all-embracing learning. Both are complementary to each other and have to be pursued in that manner for achieving success at various contexts levels. These contexts comprise both the individual (e.g., individual's self-development, vision, etc.) and the collective domain (e.g., organizational change, radical innovation, etc.).

The case of Infosys (Exhibit 7.3) is a good example of how to integrate accountability and integrity into business processes, a prerequisite for integrating TLL into the business process. The practices at Infosys reflects TLL practices because a combination of practical goal-oriented learning and deeper idealism is visible in their effort to earn profit and create an exclusive brand for itself. Infosys's success is its own certificate verifying that good governance and transparency helps the bottom line to grow.

EXHIBIT 7.3

Infosys Technologies and Its Values

Infosys Technologies of India has shown the path towards transformational change by becoming the victor of the environment rather than the victim. When the rest of Indian entrepreneurs were complaining of red tape, poor infrastructure, lack of support, and other constraints in the Indian political and socio-economic environment, Narayan Murthy, the visionary, conceived Infosys in 1981 and today it is a world-renowned company. He believed in sharing the wealth earned by the company with all the stakeholders and it is visible in their activities, ranging from the employee stock ownership plan (ESOP), facilities provided to employees, customer service, sheltering of schools, and other support for education of the underprivileged, etc., thus covering CSR at all levels—inner, intermediate, and outer. It was voted as India's best-managed company for six years in a row, between 1996 and 2001, by the Asia Money Poll. In 2003, Infosys Technologies co-founder and chairman, N.R. Narayana Murthy, won the Ernst & Young World Entrepreneur of the year award. Judges of the award praised his 'intellectually, philosophically, ethically and spiritually-driven entrepreneurship' and his company's 'outstanding financial performance and global impact in a dynamic and volatile industry'. Infosys won the prestigious 'Global Most-Admired Knowledge Enterprises (MAKE)' Award in 2004. It won the award for the second time in a row, and remains the only Indian company ever to have been named for this award. Many more such awards have substantiated its value-orientation. The employee challenges are addressed through what it terms 'PRIDE' (Process Repository @ Infosys for Driving Excellence), an online resource that segues into the company's fancied knowledge management system termed Kshop (Knowledge Shop) at one end and the actual development environment at another. As a result of this, 'Infosys will reap the benefit of an army of employees that works the same way, gains in process efficiency and productivity, and higher quality.'

Ingrained in the soul of Infosys is a drive to awaken in our employees, customers, investors and other stakeholders, as well as the larger society, a spirit of responsibility—to ourselves, the environment, our civic systems, the governments in the regions where we work and contribute, and to the future of the generations to come.

The efforts of Infosys to continuously add value to the business environment can be seen when in July 2007, Infosys co-chairman Nandan Nilekani co-chaired a report, *Tomorrow's Global Company*, along with John Manzoni—Group Managing Director and Chief Executive, Refining and Marketing, British Petroleum, to identify three specific ways in which global companies can fulfill this role through 'expanding the space' in which they operate. The report clearly points out that that the market economy has been the driver of unprecedented growth and should not be replaced but working of the market economy certainly needs a revisit to embrace a more holistic growth. Today, the market economy has to address the unsustainable outcomes like climate change, persistent poverty, and abuse of human rights that have emerged as a result of earlier business practices. The report stresses that the purpose of tomorrow's global company is 'to provide ever better goods and services in a way that is profitable, ethical and respects the environment, individuals, and the communities in which it operates'.

Sources: Fernando 2006; http://www.infosys.com/sustainability/pages/index.aspx, accessed on 21 February 2010; http://www.infosys.com/sustainability/tomorrows-global-company/Documents/global-company-tomorrow.pdf, accessed on 21 February 2010.

CONCLUSION

Here again we return to the same problem of inherent flexibility in the definition of social responsibility. Many critics believe that asking business to be socially responsible actually curtails their freedom while others assert that it is only a facade that pays lip service to social justice and the protection of nature. In reality, big businesses and multinational companies continue their aggrandizing and rapacious behaviour in the search for more and more profit (Clark 1995).

However, in spite of these warnings, there appears to be a silver lining, for according to a recent survey by the International Council for Local Environment

Initiatives, '6,416 local authorities in 113 countries have either made a formal commitment to Local Agenda 21 or are actively undertaking the process', and the number of such processes has been growing dramatically (Second Local Agenda 21 Survey, 2001).

The history of management shows that man has continuously searched to make the world a better place. Progress has been perceived and measured in various ways. There has been a conscientious effort to use commerce and science and technology to contribute to sustainable development. This can achieve success only when the idea of moral progress is used to restrain the misuse of commerce and science and technology. Both need to be governed with an eye on social good. Business has to join hands with the community and undertake developmental activities.

Certain visible and measurable dimensions of corporate responsibility may be grouped as:

(a) Various campaigns by NGOs to change corporate environmental and social behaviour ICCR or CorpWatch, and many other NGO efforts like Green Peace, OXFAM, etc., including local NGOs and NPOs in various countries).

(b) Corporations are taking initiatives by mandatory reporting of their efforts to contribute to sustainable development goals and to reduce their negative environmental and social impacts. For example, adhering to the sustainability-reporting guidelines in their corporate reports as part of the Global Reporting Initiative.

(c) International initiatives such as the UN Global Compact, which aims to bring companies together with UN agencies and labour and civil society to support 10 principles in the areas of human rights, labour, environment, and anti-corruption or the World Business Council for Sustainable Development that seeks to harness the knowledge, energies, and activities of corporations to better serve nature and society. The efforts of this body are to ensure commitment to sustainable development via the three pillars of economic growth, ecological balance, and social progress. Already, 170 international companies have shown their commitment to this mandate.

There is a growing body of thought that propagates simple living by advocating that beyond certain thresholds, ever-increasing consumption does not increase subjective levels of happiness, satisfaction, or health (Inglehart 1990; Chakraborty 2006; Nearing and Nearing 1990; Elgin 1993). In today's consumer-driven affluent societies, consumerism and immediate satisfaction of wants visible in the mantra of Anything Anywhere Anytime may lead to crash hedonism, which is a major concern because our resources are not perennial.

SUMMARY

Sustainable development is development that meets the needs of the present without compromising the ability of future generations to meet their own needs. The three pillars of sustainable development finds a wide variety of environmental, economic, and social pillars with differences most pronounced in characterizing the social pillar. For the apparent ambiguity of certain parameters of sustainability, it is perceived, at one extreme, as nothing more than a feel-good buzzword with little meaning or substance but, at the other, as an important but unfocused concept like 'liberty' or 'justice'. It has also been described as a 'dialogue of values that defies consensual definition'. Various efforts have been made at international levels to define sustainability. Examples being, the Brundtland Report, Agenda 21, World Summit on Sustainable Development, UN Millennium Declaration, etc.

ISO 26000, TBL, and TLL help organizations to incorporate the concept of sustainability. ISO 26000 is a standardization tool offered to apply CSR.

TBL accounting attempts to describe the social and environmental impact of an organization's activities, in a measurable way, to its economic performance, in order to show improvement or to make evaluation more in-depth. TBL has its own synonyms in triple-E (economy, environment, equity) or 3P (people, planet, profit), which are penetrating the traditional language of business. Tools and methods for operationalizing the TBL have been elusive, and the promise of an actual accounting system for measuring and reporting the TBL does not have a universal consensus among business organizations.

TLL is concerned with the concept of transformational changes in the domain of knowledge, organization, and the individual. It goes beyond the domain of secular rational knowledge and merges with wisdom and mystical spiritual understanding.

Rigorous efforts are required to find a balance between the practical goal-oriented learning and this deeper all-embracing learning. Both are complementary to each other and have to be pursued in that manner for achieving success at various contexts levels.

KEY TERMS

Agenda 21 A programme of the United Nations (UN) related to sustainable development and was the first summit to discuss global warming related issues. It is a comprehensive action plan that should be followed globally, nationally, and locally by organizations of the UN, governments, and major groups in every area in which humans directly affect the environment.

Brundtland report Brundtland Commission, originally World Commission on Environment and Development (WCED), was convened by the United Nations in 1983 to address growing concern 'about the accelerating deterioration of the human environment and natural resources and the consequences of that deterioration for economic and social development'.

Esoteric concepts Concepts that are highly theoretical and without obvious practical application, usually understood by a select group.

Sustainability Integrating economic, environmental, and social considerations into decision-making to ensure that future generations can enjoy a good quality life.

Triple bottom line (TBL) Also known as 'people, planet, profit'. It is a reporting framework that takes into account ecological and social performance in addition to financial performance. It was coined by John Elkington in 1994.

Triple loop learning Involves 'learning how to learn'. This form of learning helps us to understand a great deal more about ourselves and others regarding beliefs and perceptions.

UN millennium declaration The Millennium Summit ratified the United Nations Millennium Declaration in September 2000. This meeting was the largest gathering of world leaders, wherein 189 member states of the United Nations agreed to help citizens in the world's poorest countries to achieve a better life by the year 2015.

EXERCISES

Concept Review Questions

1. Explain the concept of sustainability.
2. What are the complexities faced in implementation of the sustainability concept?
3. Analyse the effectiveness of 'triple bottom line' as a CSR measurement framework.
4. Describe 'triple loop learning'. How do you think this can be implemented to promote CSR?

Critical Thinking Questions

1. 'Without humanizing capitalism, productivity may not make economic sense.' Discuss.
2. Is the concept of sustainability a myth or a reality? Discuss.
3. What is the relationship between CSR and sustainability?

Research Question

Compare the strengths and weaknesses of both capitalism and socialism with relation to sustainability.

Project Question

Choose a company where you think transformational changes are being practised and define those practices.

REFERENCES

Amalric, F. (2004), 'The Relevance of Selected Social Movements for the Great Transition Initiative', October 2004, University of Zurich (mimeo), and forthcoming as a Great Transition Initiative report, http://www.gtinitiative.org, accessed on 3 June 2010.

Argyris, C. and D.A. Schön (1996), *Organizational learning II—Theory, method, and practice*, Addison–Wesley, Redwood City, CA.

Blewitt, J. (2008) *Understanding Sustainable Development*, Earthscan, London, pp. 21–24.

Brecher, J., T. Costello, and B. Smith (2000), *Globalization from Below—The Power of Solidarity*, South End Press, Boston.

Centre for Innovation in Corporate Responsibility (2004), *The triple bottom line*, CICR at http://www.cicr.net/tblbasics.html, accessed on 3 June 2010.

Chakraborty, S.K. (2006), *Ethics in Management, Vedantic Perspective*, Oxford University Press, Delhi.

Cheney, G. (2004), 'The Corporate Conscience and Triple Bottom Line', *Accounting Today*, July 12.

Clark, J.G. (1995), 'Economic Development vs. Sustainable Societies—Reflections on the Players in a Crucial Contest', *Annual Review of Ecology and Systematics*, vol. 26, pp. 225–48.

Coomer C. James (ed.) (1979), 'Quest for a Sustainable Society', 'The management of sustainable growth', *Woodlands Conference on Growth Policy*, published in 1981, Pergamon Press, New York.

Denison, Daniel R. and Aneil K. Mishra (1995), 'Toward a Theory of Organizational Culture and Effectiveness', *Organization Science*, vol. 6, issue no. 2, March–April, pp. 204–223.

Diller, J. (1999), 'A Social conscience in the Global Marketplace? Labour Dimensions of Codes of Conduct, Social Labelling and Investor Initiatives', *International Labour Review*, 138, 2, 99–129.

Donaldson, Thomas (1989), *The Ethics of International Business*, Oxford University Press, New York, pp. 81, 124.

Dunning, B. (2006), 'Sustainable Sustainability', *Skeptoid—Critical Analysis of pop Phenomena*, No. 5, Skeptoid Media Incorporation, retrieved on 16 February 2009.

Earth Charter International Secretariat, *The Earth Charter Handbook*, http://www.earthcharter.org/files/resources/Handbook.pdf, page 4, accessed on 16 February 2009.

Earth Charter International Secretariat, *The Earth Charter—Values and Principles for a Sustainable Future*, http://www.earthcharter.org/files/resources/Earth%20Charter%20-%20Brochure%20ENG.pdf, page 1, accessed on 24 May 2020.

Elgin, D. (1993), *Voluntary Simplicity*, William Morrow, New York.

Elkington, J. (1994), 'Towards the sustainable corporation—Win-win-win business strategies for sustainable development', *California Management Review*, vol. 36, issue no. 2, pp. 90–100.

———— (1998), *Cannibals With Forks—The Triple Bottom Line of 21st Century Business*, New Society Publishers, Stony Creek, CT.

———— (1999), 'Triple bottom line reporting—Looking for a balance', Australian CPA, vol. 69, issue no. 2, pp. 18–21.

Epstein, M. and P. Wisner (2001), 'Good Neighbors—Implementing social and environmental strategies with the BSC', *Balanced Scorecard Report*, May/June, 4p.

Fernando, A.C. (2006), *Corporate Governance, Principles, Policies and Practices*, Pearson Education, India pp. 34–35.

Freedom 21 Santa Cruz, *Understanding Sustainable Development (Agenda 21)—A Guide for Public Officials*, http://www.freedom21santacruz.net/guide.pdf, accessed on 24 May 2010.

Friedman, L. Thomas (2000), *The Lexus and the Olive Tree*, Anchor Books, New York.

Gogol, N. (1948), *Dead Souls*, Pantheon Books, New York, p. 394.

Gray, Rob (2001), 'Thirty Years of Social Accounting, Reporting and Auditing—What (if anything) have we learnt?' *Business Ethics, A European Review*, January, vol. 10, issue no. 1, pp. 9–15.

Hargrove, Robert (2007), *Masterful Coaching*, John Wiley and Sons, San Francisco, CA.

Inglehart, R. (2000), 'Globalization and Postmodern Values', *Washington Quarterly*, vol. 23, issue no. 1, pp. 215–28.

International Council for Science, Initiative on Science and Technology for Sustainability, and Third World Academy of Sciences, *Science and Technology for Sustainable Development*, ICSU Series on Science for Sustainable Development, no. 9 (Paris, ICSU, 2002), http://www.icsu.org/Gestion/img/ICSU_DOC_DOWNLOAD/70_DD_FILE_Vol9.pdf, accessed on 19 May 2010.

Kates, R.W. (2003), 'Sustainability Science', in *Transition to Sustainability in the 21st Century—The Contribution of Science and Technology*, National Academies Press, Washington, DC, pp. 140–45. Also see statement of the World Academy of Sciences, http://www4.nationalacademies.org/iap/iaphome.nsf/weblinks/SAIN-4XVLCT?OpenDocument.

Kates, W. Robert., Parris M. Thomas, and A. Anthony Leiserowitz (2005), 'What is Sustainable Development? Goals, Indicators, Values, and Practice', *Environment—Science and Policy for Sustainable Development*, vol. 47, issue no. 3, pp. 8–21, April 2005. Also see http://www.heldref.org/env.php, accessed 12 December 2009.

Kolb, D.A. (1984), *Experiential learning—Experience as the source of learning and development*, Prentice Hall, Englewood Cliffs, NJ.

Leiserowitz, A., R.W. Kates, and T.M. Parris (2004), 'Sustainability Values, Attitudes and Behaviors—A Review of Multi-National and Global Trends', Center for International Development Working Paper No. 112, Harvard University, Cambridge, MA.

Lindblom, C.E. (1977), *Politics and Markets*, Basic Books, New York.

Mabogunje, A.L., and R.W. Kates (2004), 'Sustainable Development in Ijebu-Ode, Nigeria—The Role of Social Capital, Participation, and Science and Technology',

Center for International Development Working Paper No. 102, Harvard University, Cambridge, MA.

MacGillivan (2004) in Adrian Henriques and Julie Richardson (eds), *The Triple Bottom Line—Does it All Add Up,* EarthScan, London, UK.

March, G. James (1992), 'The war is over and the victors have lost', *The Journal of Socio-Economics,* vol. 21, issue no. 3, pp. 261–267.

Markus, J., M.K. Milne, K. Kearins, and S. Walton (2006), 'Creating Adventures in Wonderland—The Journey Metaphor and Environmental Sustainability', *Organization,* vol. 13, issue no. 6, pp. 801–839.

Marshall, J.D. and M.W. Toffel (2005), 'Framing the Elusive Concept of Sustainability—A Sustainability Hierarchy', *Environmental and Scientific Technology,* vol. 39, issue no. 3, pp. 673–682.

National Research Council, Policy Division, Board on Sustainable Development (1999), *Our Common Journey—A Transition toward Sustainability,* National Academy Press, Washington, DC, p. 22.

Nearing, H. and S. Nearing (1990), *The Good Life,* Schocken, New York.

Parris, T.M. and R.W. Kates (2003), 'Characterizing and Measuring Sustainable Development', *Annual Reviews of Environment and Resources,* vol. 28, pp. 559–86.

Peschl, M.F. (2006), 'Modes of knowing and modes of coming to know. Knowledge creation and knowledge co–construction as socio–epistemological engineering in educational processes', *Constructivist Foundations,* vol. 1, issue no. 3, pp. 111–123.

—— (2007), 'Triple–loop learning as foundation for profound change, individual cultivation, and radical innovation. Construction processes beyond scientific and rational knowledge', *Constructivist Foundations,* vol. 2, issue no. 2–3, pp. 136–145.

Raskin, P.T. Banuri, G. Gallopin, P. Gutman, A. Hammond, R.W. Kates, and R. Swart (2002), *Great Transition—The Promise and Lure of the Times Ahead,* Stockholm Environment Institute, Boston.

Ratner, B.D. (2004), 'Sustainability as a Dialogue of Values—Challenges to the Sociology of Development', *Sociological Inquiry,* vol. 74, issue no. 1, pp. 50–69.

Recasting the Triple Bottom Line Introducing the *Quotients Approach* to Sustainability Reporting and the *Social Footprint* A Working Proposal Prepared by Center for Sustainable Innovation, June 2007, DRAFT 10.2.

Richardson, J. (2004), 'Accounting for Sustainability' in Adrian Henriques and Julie Richardson (eds) *The Triple Bottom Line—Does it all add up,* EarthScan, London, UK.

Sawarjuwono, T. (1997), 'The Chinese Indonesians and Business', in Goodfellow, op. cit., p. 77.

Scharmer, C.O. (2000), Presencing—Learning from the future as it emerges. On the tacit dimension of leading revolutionary change. Retrieved from http://www.dialogonleadership.org/Presencing-TOC.html.

―――― (2001) 'Self–transcending knowledge. Sensing and organizing around emerging opportunities', *Journal of Knowledge Management,* vol. 5, issue no. 2, pp. 137–150.

Schilizzi, S. (2002), Triple Bottom Line Accounting—How serious is it? *Connections.* Online publication of Agribusiness Association of Australia, at http://www.agrifood.info/10pub_conn_Win2002.htm, accessed 7 June 2010.

Senge, P., C.O. Scharmer, J. Jaworski, and B.S. Flowers (2004), *Presence—Human purpose and the field of the future,* Society for Organizational Learning, Cambridge, Massachusetts.

Senge, P.M. (1990), *The fifth discipline—The art and practice of the learning organization,* Doubleday, New York.

Tagore, Rabindranath (1984), *Letters from Russia,* Viswabharati, Kolkata, p. 35.

The International Council for Local Environmental Initiatives, 'Second Local Agenda 21 Survey,' UN Department of Economic and Social Affairs Background Paper No. 15 (2001), http://www.iclei.org/rioplusten/final_document.pdf, accessed 7 June 2010.

The Johannesburg Declaration on Sustainable Development, 4 September 2002, http://www.housing.gov.za/content/legislation_policies/johannesburg.htm, accessed on 5 May 2010.

The United Nations Conference on Environment and Development (UNCED), http://www.un.org/geninfo/bp/enviro.html; (accessed 5 May 2010) and EA Parson and PM Haas, 'A Summary of the Major Documents Signed at the Earth Summit and the Global Forum', *Environment,* October 1992, 12–18.

UN Millennium Project (2005), *Investing in Development—A Practical Plan to Achieve the Millennium Development Goals, Overview,* United Nations Development Program, New York.

United Nations General Assembly (2000), 'United Nations Millennium Declaration', Resolution 55/2, United Nations A/RES/55/2, 18 September.

Varela, F. (2000), 'Three gestures of becoming aware', http://www.dialogonleadership.org/Varela-2000.pdf, accessed 12 November 2009.

Varela, F.J., E. Thompson, and E. Rosch (1991), *The embodied mind—Cognitive science and human experience,* MIT Press, Cambridge, Massachusetts.

Vogel, D. (1991), 'The ethical roots of business ethics', *Business Ethics Quarterly,* vol. 1, issue no. 1, pp. 101–120.

Wayne Norman, and Chris MacDonald (2004), 'Getting to the bottom of the 'triple bottom line'', *Business Ethics Quarterly,* vol. 14, issue no. 2, pp. 243–262.

WCED, United Nations General Assembly (1987), *Report of the World Commission on Environment and Development—Our Common Future,* Annex to document A/42/427, Development and International Co–operation: Environment, UN General Assembly.

Wright, P.A., G. Alward, J.L. Colby, T.W. Hoekstra, B. Tegler, and M. Turner (2002), 'Monitoring for forest management unit scale sustainability—The local unit criteria and indicators development (LUCID) test', USDA Forest Service Inventory and Monitoring Report No. 5, Fort Collins, CO, p. 54.

Zadek, Simon, Peter Pruzan, and Richard Evans (1997), *Building Corporate Accountability—Emerging Practices in Social and Ethical Accounting, Auditing and Reporting*, Earthscan Publications, London.

Web Resources

http://millenniumindicators.un.org/unsd/mi/mi_goals.asp; http://www.developmentgoals.org/, accessed 7 June 2010.
Ibid., p. 43, http://www.gtinitiative.org/, accessed on 2 January 2009.
www.pwcglobal.com.
www.sustainableinnovation.org.

CASE STUDY

GLAXOSMITHKLINE—CSR THROUGH INNOVATION AND RESEARCH

Established in the year 1924 in India, GlaxoSmithKline Pharmaceuticals Ltd. (GSK Rx India) is one of the oldest pharmaceuticals companies in the country. The mission of the company is to improve the quality of life by enabling people to achieve more, feel better, and live longer. This mission drives it to strive to make a difference to the lives of millions of people with its commitment to effective healthcare solutions. GSK believes that strong values are central to business success. It places great importance not only on what it achieves but also on how it achieves it.

To GSK, being a responsible business conglomerate means operating in a way that reflects its core values, treating stakeholders with respect, and connecting business decisions to society's healthcare needs. It seeks to minimize negative impacts and maximize benefits of its business. Also, its approach is guided by its unique corporate responsibility principles. The spirit of GSK is a framework that enables it to achieve its mission. It is focused around its company values:

- Respect for people
- Patient-focused
- Transparency
- Integrity

GSK aims at promoting CSR by the following initiatives for various sectors:

For communities

By focusing on projects that are relevant to its business and the skills of its people, it helps communities prevent disease and improve health. It wants to do more to support the delivery of healthcare to those who need it most. Therefore, research is constantly undertaken to find new methods of treatments that address the needs of patients and healthcare payers. The effort is to make the products as widely available as possible. This is what GSK believes is at the heart of what responsibility means and leads to its commercial success. GSK's contributions range from:

- Investing in the research and development (R&D) of new medicines and vaccines
- Treating diseases such as diabetes and cancer
- Preventing disease through vaccines and consumer healthcare products.
- GSK also invests in long-term programmes and focuses on preventing disease, building healthcare capacity of communities, and promoting education

In its concern for the community, GSK contributes money, time, medicines, and equipment to support communities around the world. To integrate CSR into the organization structure, GSK encourages employees to actively support causes they care about and run volunteering programmes to make it easier for them to get involved. This creates a feeling of ownership of CSR among the employees, who are the most important asset for any organization. To encourage ethicality, the following agenda is implemented:

- All GSK employees and contractors must comply with its code of conduct (which sets out fundamental ethical standards) and follow the guidance and policies in its employee guide to business conduct.
- Its regional marketing codes ensure that they demonstrate high ethical conduct when marketing their products to doctors, hospitals, and governments.

To promote responsible behaviour among the suppliers who form an important group of stakeholders, GSK only works with suppliers that score above a minimum health, safety, and environment standard. Since the organization deals with important and sensitive products like life-saving drugs and healthcare medicines, extreme care is taken to monitor the performance of the suppliers, so that nothing unethical is practiced. The supplier contracts include human rights clauses, so that there is no violation of human rights. The quality of materials bought is vigorously checked and every effort is made to stop counterfeiting of GSK products.

For the environment
GSK is increasing its efforts for environmental sustainability. It needs to optimize efficiency and increase its use of renewable materials and energy. It has prioritized reducing its impact on climate change and is lowering its water use.

Human rights
Promoting and protecting human rights is considered by GSK as central to CSR practices. It works hard to protect human rights within its sphere of influence, which includes employees, suppliers, communities, and society.

Like any conscientious organization, GSK is a signatory to the UN Global Compact, a voluntary global standard on human rights, labour, environment, and anti-corruption.

Commitment to transparency
Being open and transparent about how it does business helps it build trust with its stakeholders. This is part of some of the commitments it made in 2009.

GSK believes that to build unhindered trust with stakeholders, it has to go beyond R&D and improving access to medicines and vaccines. Therefore, it has put in place an elaborate plan to disclose all its business activities. The details can be seen in the declaration given below:

- We have set new standards for funding medical education in the US for healthcare professionals, ensuring we support programmes that bring the greatest improvements to patient health
- Speaking and consulting fees paid to US healthcare professionals have been published, and data for Europe and other countries will be published during 2010
- We will disclose research payments to healthcare professionals and their institutions. This will start with payments in the US for research studies that begin in 2010
- The results of clinical studies published on our Clinical Study Register now include observational studies and meta-analyses which evaluate our medicines and vaccines
- We have committed to seeking publication of the results of all clinical studies as full scientific papers in peer-reviewed journals. We believe we are the only company to make this commitment. If the paper is not published we will include additional information to support interpretation on our Clinical Study Register
- The names of the principal investigators participating in GSK-sponsored clinical studies, together with their research institutions, are included on our Clinical Study Register
- We have stopped all corporate political contributions

GSK's corporate responsibility principles identify its key responsibility issues and provide guidance for employees on the standards to which GSK is committed. GSK stands for:

Corporate Responsibility Principles

Employment practices

We will treat our employees with respect and dignity, encourage diversity and ensure fair treatment through all phases of employment. We will provide a safe and healthy working environment, support employees to perform to their full potential, and take responsibility for the performance and reputation of the business.

Human rights

We are committed to upholding the UN Universal Declaration of Human Rights, the OECD guidelines for multi-national enterprises and the core labour standards set out by the International Labor Organization. We expect the same standards of our suppliers, contractors, and business partners working on GSK's behalf.

Sustainability and Its Challenges | 259

Access to medicines
We will continue to research and develop medicines to treat diseases of the developing world. We will find sustainable ways to improve access to medicines for disadvantaged people and will seek partnerships to support this activity.

Leadership and advocacy
We will establish our own challenging standards in corporate responsibility, appropriate to the complexities and specific needs of our business, building on external guidelines and experience. We will share best practice and seek to influence others, while remaining competitive in order to sustain our business.

Community investment
We will make a positive contribution to the communities in which we operate, and will invest in health and education programmes and partnerships that aim to bring sustainable improvements to under-served people in the developed and developing world.

Standards of ethical conduct
We expect employees to meet high ethical standards in all aspects of our business, by conducting our activities with honesty and integrity, adhering to our CR principles, and complying with applicable laws and regulations.

GSK is changing
GSK has a real opportunity to make a difference to patients and to society and it is committed to making the changes needed to achieve this. GSK is ensuring that it creates the reputation of being a responsible organization by

- increasing greater trust in GSK products
- attracting, retaining, and motivating talented people as fewer people are pursuing science-based careers
- engendering constructive engagement with stakeholders to prevent avoidable conflict and identify innovative approaches that benefit GSK and wider society
- promoting greater access to markets and the ability to influence healthcare policy through improved relationships with regulators and healthcare payers
- helping governments to increase access to medicines and resolve healthcare challenges is particularly significant
- anticipating and preparing for legislative changes and maintaining a competitive advantage
- helping maintain support for the intellectual property system by finding innovative ways to increase access to medicines
- increasing environmental efficiency by reducing costs and by ensuring efficient use of resources

GSK is a large and, by default, complex organization; therefore the challenge is to be able to successfully transform the operational model to reduce complexities, improve

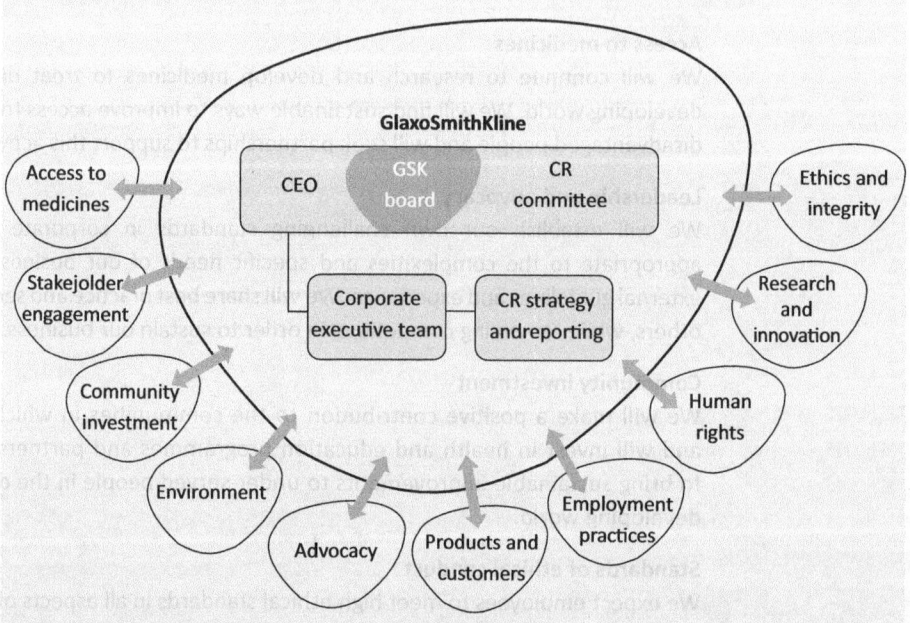

Source: GSK Corporate Responsibility Report, 2009.

Figure 1 Management of corporate social responsibility

efficiency, and reduce costs. Figure 1 gives an idea of the number of stakeholders that GSK is catering to successfully, and thus achieving sustainability in the long run.

Thus, it can be concluded that GSK maintains its standards of being extremely sensitive towards the needs of its people and the environment, and continues to be one of the most active companies in the pharmaceutical industry towards the noble cause of social responsibility. This, in turn, assists the company to gain a tremendous amount of goodwill in the associated industry and brings about phenomenal business success.

[The source for this case has been taken from the official website of GSK, www.gsk.com (accessed 6.8.10) and their Corporate Responsibility Report, 2009. Inputs for the case has been provided by Anindita Banerjee, PGDM student at IFIM Business School, Bangalore].

Discussion Questions
1. Discuss GSK's values as a company focused towards CSR?
2. Do you think 'commitment to transparency' is one of the key reasons for GSK's success?
3. Do you think GSK is taking the correct initiatives to promote its CSR objectives?

Sources: http://www.gsk.com/responsibility/downloads/GSK-CR-Highlights-2009.pdf, accessed on 10 August 2010; http://www.gsk.com/responsibility/cr-at-gsk/our-corporate-responsibility-principles.htm, accessed on 10 August 2010.

ANNEXURE 1

Agenda 21

Agenda 21 consisted of issues related to:
1. Combating poverty
2. Changing consumption patterns
3. Demographics and sustainability
4. Protection of human health
5. Human settlements
6. Integration of the environment and development in decision-making
7. Protection of the atmosphere
8. Planning and management of land resources
9. Combating of deforestation
10. Desertification and drought
11. Sustainable mountain development
12. Sustainable agriculture
13. Conservation of biological diversity
14. Management of biotechnology
15. Protection of the oceans
16. Management and use of water resources
17. Management of toxic chemicals
18. Management of hazardous wastes
19. Management of solid wastes
20. Management of radioactive wastes
21. Global action for women
22. Role of children and youth in sustainable development
23. Role of NGO partners
24. Strengthening of workers and trade unions
25. Role of business and industry
26. Role of farmers

The above plan was based on the following macro acceptances:
(a) Humans depend on the earth to sustain life
(b) There are linkages between human activity and environmental issues
(c) Global concern requires local action
(d) People have to be involved in planning developments of their own communities if such developments are to be sustainable

ANNEXURE 2

UN Millennium Declaration

To mark the millennium, heads of state gathered in New York at the United Nations in September 2000. During the meet, the UN General Assembly adopted some 60 goals regarding peace; development; environment; human rights; the vulnerable, hungry, and poor; Africa; and the United Nations (18 September 2000). Many of these contained specific targets, such as cutting poverty in half or insuring universal primary school education by 2015. It was decided that international agencies should be entrusted the task of monitoring the progress of eight major goals: 'careful monitoring is under way for 8 goals with 18 targets and 48 indicators to measure progress by experts from the United Nations Secretariat, International Monetary Fund, Organization for Economic Co-operation and Development, and the World Bank' (ST/ESA/STAT/ MILLENNIUMINDICATORS2003/WWW, unofficial working paper 23 March 2004). The findings of these agencies revealed the glaring gap in the progress and assessed that the achievement of goals would fall short of the target, particularly in Africa. Yet it was felt that the goals were attainable by collective action of the world community and national governments. Therefore, the Millennium Project, commissioned by the UN Secretary-General, provided a financial estimate of the requirements to meet the millennium development goals: $135 billion in 2006, rising to $195 billion in 2015. This would require the doubling of official aid flows and it would still fall below the UN goal of aid flows from industrialized to developing countries of 0.7 per cent of the gross national product for industrialized countries (United Nations Development Programme, New York, 2005).

Board on Sustainable Development

In 1995, the Board on Sustainable Development of the U.S. National Academy of Sciences created a platform for analysing sustainable development in a more meaningful scientific process (National Research Council 1999).

The methodology consisted of a two-generation time horizon to address the needs of a global population with half as many more people as there are today—needs that, if met successfully, are not likely to be repeated within the next century or two because of the demographic transition. Hence, according to the members of the board, a minimal sustainability transition would be one in which the world provides the energy, materials, and information to feed, nurture, house, educate, and employment to the many more people of 2050. Consecutively, efforts should be put in place to reduce hunger and poverty and preserve the basic life support systems of the planet. To create an implementable process that would meet human needs, reduce hunger and poverty, and preserve basic life support systems of the planet, the board analysed the text and statements from recent global conferences, world summits, international environmental treaties, and assessments. Less optimistic than the UN, the board concluded that it would take a generation to reach the 2015 goals of the Millennium Declaration and another generation to achieve the board's goals of meeting human needs for a 2050 population.

Global Scenario Group

The Global Scenario Group, as the name suggests, assisted the Board on Sustainable Development to conduct a scenario analysis of a proposed 'Sustainability Transition', focusing specifically on hunger and the emission of greenhouse gasses. The Global Scenario Group was convened in 1995 by the Stockholm Environment Institute to engage a diverse international group in an examination of the prospects for world development in the twenty-first century. This initial analysis served as the subsequent basis of the Policy Reform Scenario of the Global Scenario Group (Raskin et al. 2002). Raskin states that a Great Transition Initiative has been launched to help crystallize a global citizens' movement to advance the vision of the scenario leading to 'a rich quality of life, strong human ties, and a resonant connection to nature' (Raskin et al. 2002) and concluded that a sustainability transition is possible without positing either a social revolution or a technological miracle. But it is 'just' possible, and the technological and social requirements to move from business as usual—without changing lifestyles, values, or the economic system—is daunting. Most daunting of all is the governmental commitment required to achieve it and the political will to do so.

Finally, the Global Scenario Group also prepared a more idealistic Great Transition Scenario, which not only achieved the goals of the sustainability transition outlined by the Board on Sustainable Development, but went further to achieve for all humankind 'a rich quality of life, strong human ties, and a resonant connection to nature'. In such a world, it would be the quality of human knowledge, creativity, and self-realization that represents development, not the quantity of goods and services. A key to such a future is the rejection of material consumption beyond what is needed for fulfilment or for a 'good life'. Beyond these goals, however, the details of this good life are poorly described. Numerous studies at global, regional, and national levels have relied on the group's scenario framework and quantitative analysis (Kates et al. 2005).

Some of the studies (Parris and Kates 2003) that have used the global scenario framework for assessing sustainability include global coverage, using country or regional data like the UN Commission on Sustainable Development, Consultative Group on Sustainable Development Indicators, Well-being Index, Environmental Sustainability Index, Global Scenario Group, and the Ecological Footprint. Others either relate to country studies, e.g., in the US, the Genuine Progress Indicator and the Interagency Working Group on Sustainable Development Indicators, and in Costa Rica, the System of Indicators for Sustainable Development; or describe a city study, viz., the Boston Indicators Project.

These studies reveal and confirm the intangible aspect of the term sustainability at the implementation level. This occurs because of the extraordinarily broad list of items that need to be sustained and developed. The inherent flexibility of 'sustainable development' often results in internal politics of the measurement, as the initiatives are often undertaken by diverse sets of stakeholders, with varied aspirations. Therefore, arriving at a consensus on sustainability raises the issue of 'trade-off', justice, and fairness (see Parris, 'Toward a Sustainability Transition: The International Consensus', *Environment*, January/February 2003, 12).

Values Underlying the Millennium Declaration

The Millennium Declaration—which outlines 60 goals for peace; development; the environment; human rights; the vulnerable, the hungry and the poor; Africa; and the United Nations—is founded on a core set of values described as follows:

'We consider certain fundamental values to be essential to international relations in the twenty-first century. These include:

Freedom Men and women have the right to live their lives and raise their children in dignity, free from hunger and from the fear of violence, oppression, or injustice. Democratic and participatory governance based on the will of the people best assures these rights.

Equality No individual and no nation must be denied the opportunity to benefit from development. The equal rights and opportunities of women and men must be assured.

Solidarity Global challenges must be managed in a way that distributes the costs and burdens fairly in accordance with basic principles of equity and social justice. Those who suffer or who benefit least, deserve help from those who benefit most.

Tolerance Human beings must respect one other, in all their diversity of belief, culture, and language. Differences within and between societies should be neither feared nor repressed, but cherished as a precious asset of humanity. A culture of peace and dialogue among all civilizations should be actively promoted.

Respect for nature Prudence must be shown in the management of all living species and natural resources, in accordance with the precepts of sustainable development. Only in this way can the immeasurable riches provided to us by nature be preserved and passed on to our descendants. The current unsustainable patterns of production and consumption must be changed in the interest of our future welfare and that of our descendants.

Shared responsibility Responsibility for managing worldwide economic and social development, as well as threats to international peace and security, must be shared among the nations of the world and should be exercised multi-laterally. As the most universal and most representative organization in the world, the United Nations must play the central role'.

Sources: United Nations General Assembly, 'United Nations Millennium Declaration', Resolution 55/2, United Nations A/RES/55/2, 18 September 2000; http://gsg.org/.

The Indian Saga

INTRODUCTION

Mature and well-developed economic ideas of financial systems and institutions existed in ancient India. The basic elements of economics—land, labour, capital, and organization—is visible in
(a) Land as the basis of production of wealth.
(b) Slavery as the chief source and supply of labour.
(c) Trade, commerce, and production and distribution of goods, which were usually controlled by the state. State also intervened and acquired monopoly over certain items of trade, mostly luxury items.
(d) State expenditure on public works and welfare activities, which is also recorded.

The backbone of the ancient Indian economy was agriculture. Therefore, the social pattern was also based on the ownership of land. Almost all ancient societies show traces of some kind of social division, similar to the caste system in India. Priests, warriors, and landowners have been the revered groups in most of these societies, be it among the Aztecs of Mexico, the Europeans, the Japanese societies, or the African agricultural communities. Stories relating to the respect given to samurais or knights in armour and to the clergy and rich land barons bear out this social division.

Early Indian history reveals that the king met his expenses primarily through incomes from royal holdings and from bounty and donations. The three most important sources of taxation for the king were land revenue, tax on traders, and tax on artisans. The guild system was a very important economic development of ancient Indian economic structure. In early times, currency and exchange was usually based on barter. There is also mention of *nishka*, probably a form of gold coin used as a medium of exchange. It is interesting to note that in that era also the concept of social responsibility was well-established, as can be seen from a quote in Mahabharata (XII.87.13-21): 'A realm is like a cow, it must not be over milked.' Buying and selling were carried out in open markets

LEARNING OBJECTIVES

After studying this chapter, you will be able to
- Understand a brief historical perspective of economic development in India
- Understand the challenges that a corporate faces in implementing CSR
- Get an overview of the Government of India's initiatives to promote CSR
- Learn to create the framework for CSR by understanding present practices

transparently and secret bargains were not encouraged. Cost of production and normal profits were taken into account while fixing the price of products. Thus, the theory of producers' surplus was a practice followed even in ancient India. This shows that profit was considered a proactive part of business and not a sin. Examples of professional tax and income tax are also available in ancient India, showing that the seeds of modern economy were sown as early as Vedic times.

The idea of a welfare state germinated in ancient India when it was pronounced that justice was the first duty of the king and that he should be dedicated to duty. Family burden was shared by the state, in the form of providing welfare measures like assistance to neglected or orphaned people, protecting minors and abandoned wives and children, and providing medical relief and employment to the unemployed. The state actively participated in building roads, highways, and rest houses. During natural calamities, the state machinery ensured relief. The gift system as an institution flourished in ancient India, probably denoting a redistribution of wealth in the macro level by inculcating a sense of social awareness among individuals.

As time passed, the economy opened up and the private sector became important. As old ruling dynasties were overthrown, previously existing social equations and hierarchies were also challenged and modified. India experienced the usual socio-economic challenges of foreign invasion and rule under the Muslim hegemony and British colonial structure. During periods of urban expansion and accelerating trade, opportunities for social mobility, particularly horizontal mobility, opened up for the artisan classes, and mercantile classes enjoyed special benefits. The fortunes of India swayed between moderate advantages to the common population and severe economic exploitation. Differential access to modern education and other amenities increased the distance between the haves and the have-nots.

POST-INDEPENDENT INDIA

Amid the commotion of having experienced colonial anguish and the agony of a very painful partition, the post-independence Indian government decided to establish a democratic and secular structure to tackle the issues pertaining to its society, economy, security, foreign relations, and overall development to emerge as a respectable nation in the world. To deal with its unique problems of diversity—the gap between the haves and have-nots in society—and to set up the basic industries and build the infrastructure, various models were chosen.

Models Chosen to Revive the Economy

India emerged out of its colonial status with a destroyed economy, and the major challenge before the leaders was to reconstruct the country's economy. India started with the 'license-permit raj', which was intended to protect the nascent Indian industries against competition from the mature industries of the developed world. Unfortunately, the Indian industry failed to take advantage and the regulatory processes bred nepotism and bureaucratic corruption. The 'mixed economy' model, based on public ownership of all necessary and infrastructural amenities and private ownership of the other sectors, was chosen as the economic structure. Both the innovations did not deliver the required results and India suffered from major fiscal imbalance, inflationary pressure, and also balance of payment crisis. It was in 1991, when the government decided to open up the economy, that India entered an era of liberalization, privatization, and globalization (LPG).

Emergence of the Private Sector

State intervention and control over economic activities have reduced markedly and this has given a boost to the private sector in India. The services sector has recorded maximum benefit from this liberal face of economic reforms. Information technology (IT) and information technology enabled services (ITES), communication, and banking and insurance have reaped enormous profits. GDP has increased from a meager 1.4 per cent for the period after independence till 1991, when the economy liberalized, to almost 7.5–8 per cent at present.

However, this growth has not been an inclusive growth and the disparity in the socio-economic sphere is still glaring. The infrastructure sector is a major impediment to investment. The restrictive labour- and product-related laws hamper the proper utilization of the strength of our economy. India has a sizeable population of well-educated youth who can actually add to the economic growth process but they need to be employed efficiently and effectively. The public sector in India has been administered on a socialistic pattern to ensure sharing of wealth. However, the regulatory and governance processes have led to their stagnation and they have become symbols of loss and misappropriation of public money. In contrast, the private sector has emerged as a better-governed entity using resources well.

Reforms and Their Impacts

The tax structure of India also needs to be reviewed to attract foreign direct investment (FDI). Finding the fine balance between the capitalist model versus the socialist model is the only way to the expected economic prosperity.

Obviously, this needs a sound base of regulation related to governance issues. The Government of India has tried to address this issue through de-regulation of the market. India has consciously moved towards a market economy. Direct taxes have been reduced and the financial markets have been revived with major growth-oriented changes in the banking sector.

As explained in the section on corporate governance in Chapter 2, this was the time when bodies like the Securities and Exchange Board of India (SEBI), the Confederation of Indian Industry (CII), and the Company Law Board provided the necessary impetus to better supervision and regulation. Entry barriers of foreign investments were reduced and there were also currency reforms, which encouraged economic growth. According to the OECD report, all these reforms led to a rise of 24 per cent in exports and imports in the GDP. Inflows of FDI increased to 2 per cent of GDP from less than 0.1 per cent of GDP in 1990. There was a massive increase in output, with the potential growth rate of the economy estimated to be around 8.5 per cent per year in 2006. GDP per capita is now rising by 7.5 per cent annually in spite of the worldwide economic recession. India is today recognized as the third largest economy in the world (after the US and China, and just ahead of Japan) The current expansion, which started in 2003, has not led to an imbalance between supply and demand, despite annual GDP growth reaching 9 per cent in 2006 (Organization for Economic Co-operation and Development, Policy Brief, Economic Survey of India, 2007).

The sectors that have contributed to India's economic development have been manufacturing, communications, trade, agriculture, and construction. In the period 2003–04 to 2007–08, the annual growth rate of agriculture was more than 4 per cent. India became self-sufficient in food because of the record increase in foodgrain production. In fact, the production of foodgrains increased by about 10 million tonnes each year to reach an all-time high of over 230 million tonnes in 2007–08. Even manufacturing registered a growth of 9.5 per cent at the rate of 27 per cent and 13.5 per cent per annum, respectively, in the period 2004–05 to 2007–08. The manufacturing sector experienced an increase in investment growth of around 30 per cent per annum. Exponential growth in capital stock and efficiency measured by the capital output ratio in construction, manufacturing, and in trade, hotels and restaurants can be gauged from the fact that it increased one-and-a-half times more from 2002–03 to 2007–08. All this was a result of free competition and technological upgradations. Per annum GDP growth rate moved from 5.6 per cent to 8.9 per cent between 2001 and 2008. Almost all the states recorded growth. The key factors behind this growth have been the liberalization policy, supported by a robust banking system and a large domestic market (see Exhibit 8.1).

EXHIBIT 8.1

India—Macro-economic Indicators

	2007	2008	2009	2010	2011
Real GDP growth	9.1	6.1	6.1	7.3	7.6
Inflation[1]	4.9	6.3	2.6	5.4	5.7
Consumer price index[2]	6.2	9.1	7.8	7.1	6.2
Wholesale price index (WPI)[3]	4.7	8.4	3.5	7.0	6.2
Short-term interest rate[4]	8.9	9.6	4.8	6.9	7.9
Long-term interest rate[5]	7.9	7.6	7.1	7.8	8.1
Fiscal balance (per cent of GDP)[6]	–4.2	–8.8	–10.1	–9.0	–8.1
Current account balance (per cent of GDP)	–1.4	–2.5	–1.9	–2.0	–1.8
Memorandum: calendar year basis					
Real GDP growth	9.4	6.9	5.6	7.2	7.6
Fiscal balance (per cent of GDP)[6]	–4.4	–7.3	–10.3	–9.3	–8.2

Note: Data refer to fiscal years starting in April.
[1] Percentage change in GDP deflator from previous period.
[2] Consumer price index for industrial workers.
[3] All commodities.
[4] Mumbai three-month offered rate.
[5] 10-year government bond.
[6] Gross fiscal balance for central and state governments.

Sources: OECD Economic Outlook 86 database; http://www.oecd.org/dataoecd/52/11/36761627.pdf.

THE GRIM REALITY

In spite of the optimistic projections, the reality is quite grim. Growth and development need to be more inclusive. Corporates have to play a proactive part to achieve this inclusive growth by ensuring the prosperity of the poorer section of the population. Government reforms have to be complemented with corporate social responsibility activities. Businesses have to ensure more transparency and accountability in their activities, which have to encompass their core business as well as community development projects. More lives have to receive the healing touch through sharing the fruits of growth.

The scenario is like this because in any society, social stratification decides how power status and resources are distributed. It does not need much imagination to understand that the distribution of wealth and opportunities in any society is skewed by the power and status enjoyed by the different groups and their levels in society. This skewed distribution often gets manifest in not only lack of resources but also lack of basic human necessities. Another important result of this differentiation in society is the psychological impact that it has on individuals belonging to the 'un-included' group in society. Therefore, efforts at mobilizing them need an understanding of the different levels of interaction—individual, inter-personal, inter-group, and socio-cultural. There is a time lapse between the individual acquiring self-esteem and self-efficacy from ascribed identities of caste, creed, class, and family. Developing community activism needs patience and tenacity expressed through long-term sustainable intervention. This is an area the corporate world is not very committed to because it requires long-term investment of capital and human resource investment, which may not generate quick returns.

GOVERNMENT INITIATIVES

As mentioned above, the public sector undertakings (PSUs) in India are based on a socialistic model and therefore have a high level of public accountability attached to them. This obviously requires socially responsible reporting by PSUs. To facilitate this process, the Committee of Public Undertakings (COPU) was entrusted in 1992 to review the issue relating to social obligation of Central Public Sector Enterprises. It reported that 'being part of the "State", every Public Sector Enterprise (PSE) has a moral responsibility to play an active role in discharging the social obligations endowed on a welfare state, subject to the financial health of the enterprise.'

In keeping with the recommendation of the COPU, the Department of Public Enterprises (DPE) issued general guidelines in November 1994. These guidelines relied entirely on the board of directors of the PSEs to devise socially responsible business practices in accordance with their articles of association, under the general guidance of their respective administrative ministry/department.

In an effort to create a synergy in the socio-economic scenario, the government is aware that CSR has to play a very significant role. The government understands that 'CSR is at heart a process of managing the costs and benefits of business activity to both internal (employees, shareholders, investors) and external (institution of public governance, community members, civil society groups, other enterprises) stakeholders.'

To understand the enormity of the issues and concerns, the Government of India conducted a limited review of selected sectors and their CSR initiatives. The main focus of the review was on the following aspects:

- CSR policy
- System of planning for CSR activities
- System of fixation of targets for CSR activities
- Budget allocation and budget utilization for CSR activities
- Monitoring mechanism for implementation of CSR activities

To further enhance the implementation of CSR processes to fill the time-gap between the growth and distribution, the government has created a framework for delivering CSR initiatives. The preamble revolves around the crux that with the unprecedented growth in economic activities worldwide, a number of challenges and opportunities has emerged. This approach also 'reaffirms the view that businesses are an integral part of society, and have a critical and active role to play in the sustenance and improvement of healthy ecosystems, in fostering social inclusiveness and equity, and in upholding the essentials of ethical practices and good governance'. Government has expressed a strong belief in the ancient wisdom of India promoting welfare for all. Therefore, the government is confident that these sound and all-encompassing values are even more relevant in the globalized world of today as 'organizations grapple with the challenges of modern-day enterprise, the aspirations of stakeholders and of citizens eager to be active participants in economic growth and development'. To provide companies with guidance in dealing with the above-mentioned expectations, while working closely within the framework of national aspirations and policies, the Voluntary Guidelines for CSR have been developed. Though the guidelines basically relate to the Indian context, even multi-national and trans-national enterprises can benefit from using these guidelines for their overseas operations. Since the guidelines are voluntary and not prepared in the nature of a prescriptive road map, they are not intended for regulatory or contractual use.

The government has faith that more and more companies would make a sincere effort to adhere as closely as possible to the guidelines. It is hoped that 'India Inc.' would respond to these guidelines with keen interest. The voluntary guidelines promulgated by the government are given in Exhibit 8.2.

EXHIBIT 8.2

Voluntary Guidelines

Ministry of Corporate Affairs

Fundamental Principle

Each business entity should formulate a CSR policy to guide its strategic planning and provide a roadmap for its CSR initiatives, which should be an integral part of the overall business policy and aligned with its business goals. The policy should be framed with the participation of various level executives and should be approved by the Board.

The CSR policy should normally cover the following core elements.

Core Elements

1. **Care for all Stakeholders**

The companies should respect the interests of, and be responsive towards all stakeholders, including shareholders, employees, customers, suppliers, project-affected people, society at large, etc., and create value for all of them. They should develop a mechanism to actively engage with all stakeholders, inform them of inherent risks, and mitigate them where they occur.

2. Ethical functioning

Their governance systems should be underpinned by ethics, transparency, and accountability. They should not engage in business practices that are abusive, unfair, corrupt, or anti-competitive.

3. Respect for workers' rights and welfare

Companies should provide a workplace environment that is safe, hygienic, and humane, and which upholds the dignity of the employees. They should provide all employees with access to training and development of necessary skills for career advancement, on an equal and non-discriminatory basis. They should uphold the freedom of association and effective recognition of the right to collective bargaining of labour, have an effective grievance redressal system, should not employ child or forced labour, and provide and maintain equality of opportunities without any discrimination on any grounds in recruitment and during employment.

4. Respect for human rights

Companies should respect human rights for all and avoid complicity with human rights abuses by them or by a third party.

5. Respect for environment

Companies should take measures to check and prevent pollution; recycle, manage and reduce waste, should manage natural resources in a sustainable manner, and ensure optimal use of resources like land and water, should proactively respond to the challenges of climate change by adopting cleaner production methods, promoting efficient use of energy, and environment-friendly technologies.

6. Activities for social and inclusive development

Depending upon their core competency and business interest, companies should undertake activities for economic and social development of communities and geographical areas, particularly in the vicinity of their operations. These could include: education, skill-building for livelihood of people, health, cultural and social welfare, etc., particularly targeting the disadvantaged sections of society.

Implementation Guidance

1. The CSR policy of the business entity should provide for an implementation strategy, which should include identification of projects/activities, setting measurable physical targets with timeframes, organizational mechanism and responsibilities, time schedules, and monitoring. Companies may partner with local authorities, business associations, and civil society/non-government organizations. They may influence the supply chain for CSR initiative and motivate employees for voluntary effort for social development. They may evolve a system of need assessment and impact assessment while undertaking CSR activities in a particular area. Independent evaluation may also be undertaken for selected projects/activities from time to time.

2. Companies should allocate specific amount in their budgets for CSR activities. This amount may be related to profits after tax, cost of planned CSR activities, or any other suitable parameter.
3. To share experiences and network with other organizations, the company should engage with well established and recognized programmes/platforms, which encourage responsible business practices and CSR activities. This would help companies to improve on their CSR strategies and effectively project the image of being socially responsible.
4. The companies should disseminate information on CSR policy, activities, and progress in a structured manner to all their stakeholders and the public at large through their website, annual reports, and other communication media.

Source: Corporate Social Responsibility Voluntary Guidelines 2009, published by the Ministry of Corporate Affairs, Government of India, New Delhi.

However, this is a non-mandatory requirement and is issued as the voluntary code. The code encourages business to contribute to society in an effort to bring about inclusive growth.

The business world has tried to emulate the code through efforts aimed at the grassroots level. The efforts can be grouped broadly into

1. Creating community-based organizations, which primarily aim at empowering the participants.
2. Delivering social learnings to break the barriers of social systems like caste, gender discrimination, religious segregation, etc., to encourage people to participate in grassroots level business models.
3. Designing specific projects catering to the need of the region or area that needs immediate and/urgent attention.

The government in its wisdom has also promulgated various regulations related to sustainability in the triple bottom line—social, economical, and environmental. Compliance to these multifarious laws is aimed at driving the CSR agenda in the right direction. A review of some of the laws and regulations indicates the importance that sustainability as a component of CSR is gaining in India and also worldwide (see Exhibit 8.3).

EXHIBIT 8.3

Sustainability-related Acts and Rules of the Government of India

Some of the Acts and Rules of the Government of India (sustainability-related) are listed below for ready reference and understanding the spread and depth of the CSR concept.

(a) Environment (Protection) Act (1986) (amended in 1991) & Environment (Protection) Rules
(b) Environment (Siting for Industrial Projects) Rules, 1999
(c) Coastal Regulation Zone Notification (1991, as amended)
(d) The Scheme on Labelling of Environment-friendly Products (1991)
(e) Eco-sensitive Zones Notifications (especially the notifications on Matheran, Mahabaleshwar-Panchgani, Dhahanu Taluka, Murud-Janjira, and in general about other notifications)
(f) Environment Impact Assessment Notification (2006, as amended)
(g) Hazardous Waste (Management & Handling) Rules 1989 and amendments
(h) The Batteries (Management & Handling) Rules (2001)
(i) The Recycled Plastics Manufacture and Usage Rules
(j) Prohibition of Azo Dyes
(k) The Chemical Accidents (Emergency Planning, Preparedness and Response) Rules 1996
(l) The Manufacture, Storage, and Import of Hazardous Chemicals Rules 1989 (amended in 2000)
(m) The Municipal Solid Waste (Management & Handling) Rules 2000
(n) The Bio-medical Waste (Management & Handling) Rules, 1998 (amended in 2003)
(o) The Rules for the Manufacture, Use, Import, Export, and Storage of Hazardous Micro-organism, Genetically Engineered Organisms or Cells (1989)
(p) Noise Pollution (Regulation and Control) Rules (2000), as amended
(q) The Ozone Depleting Substances (Regulation and Control) Rules, 2000
(h) The Water (Prevention and Control of Pollution) Act, 1974 (amended in 1988) & Rules under the Act
(i) The Water (Prevention and Control of Pollution) Cess Act, 1974 (amended in 2003) & Rules under the Act
(j) The Air (Prevention and Control of Pollution) Act, 1981 (amended in 1987), Rules under the Act and important notifications under the Act
(k) The Public Liability Insurance Act, 1991, The Public Liability Insurance Rules, 1991, and notifications under the Act
(l) National Environment Apellate Authority Act, 1997 (National Green Tribunal Bill, 2009)
(m) National Environment Tribunal Act, 1995
(n) The Prevention of Cruelty to Animals Act, 1960, Rules and notifications under the Act
(o) The Wildlife (Protection) Act, 1960 (amended in 2002); The Indian Wildlife (Protection) Act 1972, amended in 1993. Rules and notifications under these Acts
(p) The Indian Forest Act, 1927, The Forest (Conservation) Act, 1980 (amended in 1988), Scheduled Tribes and Other Traditional Forest Dwellers (Recognition of Forest Rights) Act, 2006, Rules and notifications under the above Acts

(r) Biological Diversity Act, 2002 and Biological Diversity Rules, 2004
(s) The Factories Act and the Factories Rules of Various States
(t) The Explosives Act and the Explosives Rules
(u) The Petroleum Act and the Petroleum Rules
(v) Static and Mobile Pressure Vessels Rules
(w) Gas Cylinders Rules
(x) Inflammable Substances Rules
(y) Companies Act, etc.

Source: The list has been compiled by Prof. L. Ramakrishnan—Distinguished Professor and Head, Indsearch Centre of Sustainability Management (I-COSM).

CHALLENGES

We need to understand here the challenges that the business world can face while trying to implement these processes. Sociologists have shown that creation of any community organization is either based on conflict or consensus. Here, the concept of conflict goes beyond the common understanding of the word—it relates to direct action that people resort to by expressing their grievances due to the disadvantages that they suffer as a result of their socio-economic status. The hope is that their 'agitation' would lead to a change in the policies and programmes so far in place. Since these people believe that they may not be in a capacity to judge the situation or enforce change, they look up to corporates to solve all their problems. They look upon the process as a lifetime opportunity to remedy and rectify all the disadvantages that they are suffering from. It also stems from the belief that though a corporate is a powerful opponent, it can be used against other dominant entities like the government and bureaucracy. Therefore, the business world has to create an environment where a rapport with the 'have-not' group is built to help it become a powerful force and not use the power of the corporate world for short-term selfish gains.

Community Development and Empowerment

This brings in the concept of empowerment through community development. The prerequisite for this process is 'capacity building'. As the name suggests, community relates to a web of relationships that need to be nurtured and shared because it is an interdependent world. Each member in the community is an expert in their skill sets and owns some resource. These have to be mutually exchanged to reap benefits for all. Everyone has to feel wanted, so that a 'we feeling' develops in the community to leverage the diversity of knowledge, skills, and experience. Once this capacity building happens, then leaders would emerge in the community, leaders who would be able to drive the self-help groups that can be formed based on requirements and interest. Thus, this needs a long-term commitment from the corporate world to really enjoy the benefits of increased purchasing power, trained workforce, healthy environment, and the immortal brand built on faith and loyalty.

The process of empowerment includes not only socio-economic upliftment or political freedom but also goes much deeper into the deep recesses of the human psychology, which gives the confidence of belief in one's own capabilities. This gets translated into the disadvantaged finding their voice and engaging in dialogue, which makes them feel that they are the masters of their destiny. They become the change agents in society and their collective effort leads to positive socio-economic development. Thus, the CSR initiatives of the corporate world can be focused either on individual empowerment or community/collective empowerment and the journey entails movement from dependency to independence to interdependency. Figure 8.1 explains the process and contingencies required to achieve success in this passage, from reliance on outside agencies for help and support to self-esteem and self-reliance by mutual acceptance.

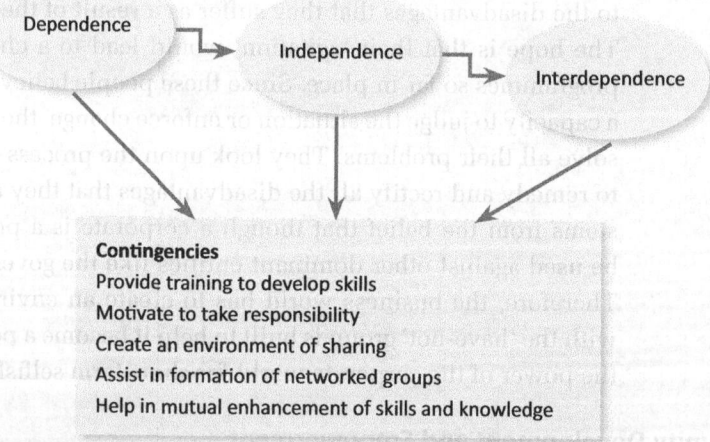

Figure. 8.1 Community development and empowerment

CONCLUSION

Once the above process is complete, the CSR process owners should create the framework for implementation. If in-depth understanding of the socio-cultural issues are not available, then even the most sincere efforts of deploying socially relevant and responsive activities would not take root. The framework design, therefore, should factor in historical and cultural aspects of the ecosystem, within which the corporate is performing. The community-based challenge relates to the outer level or macro level of CSR intervention. Within this, the intermediate or the meso-level and the inner, i.e., the micro-level of CSR interventions have to be ensured (see Chapter 2). For successful CSR implementation, ownership of the processes has to be created among the members of the inner and intermediate circles within the corporate. This is termed as inclusive growth, which should be the aim of any modern society. In India, these challenges have been met by various homegrown business houses in their unique programmes. The foremost among them is of course the house of Tatas. The Tata Council of Community Initiatives (TCCI) provides an excellent example of how CSR has progressed from being in the level of personal charity and philanthropy to the levels of strategy design in the board rooms of the corporate world. Through this initiative, the Tatas have mitigated the Robin Hood syndrome of earning profits through any means—ethical or unethical—and then distributing a meagre amount of it in charity to justify profiteering. This syndrome has been followed and promoted by many business houses. TCCI has shown the path for integrating CSR in the corporate process to create socio-economic advantages.

SUMMARY

India has a very rich historical past that has witnessed the development of various political and economic institutions of significance. Concepts like the producers' surplus and welfare state are not new to India. As a consequence of its mature and structured systems, India boasted of a developed economy, which attracted the attention of imperialist countries like England. The colonial rule took its toll on the political and socio-economic structure and India had to struggle to re-establish its systems and institutions. The great divide between the rich and the poor is, till date, a major concern for India. Therefore, in spite of a good GDP growth, India still has to create more just and fair distribution of its growth. The struggle to ensure inclusive growth and development is compounded by diverse socio-cultural factors. This is where the corporate in India can play a proactive role by participating in nation-building through CSR. The business community has to realize that it is only through well-structured deployment of CSR programmes that community development and empowerment can be achieved. This grassroot-level development is the backbone of the sustainable future of a nation.

KEY TERMS

Community development Is about empowering individuals and groups by providing them with the skills they need to affect change in their own communities.
Eco-system Here it refers to the various components of the economic community and environment that supports growth of business.

Empowerment Increasing the strength of individuals in social and economic spheres so that they gain confidence to voice their opinion and enjoy their rights and privileges.

Guild system Is an association of persons of the same trade, craft, or pursuits. It is formed to protect mutual interests and maintain standards for better business returns.

Inclusive growth Refers to equitable allocation of resources and benefits that accrue to every section of society.

Liberalization, privatization, globalization (LPG) Liberalization is the loosening and easing the control of government, thus making it easier to pursue business activities. Privatization means that the government does not control every activity in the world of business and allows citizens to own their own factories and businesses. Globalization means crossing borders to share resources and do business.

License-permit Raj The system of licenses, regulations adopted by the Indian government to allow setting up and running of any business. This led to corruption and accompanying red tape because of the stringent government control.

PSU Public sector undertakings are those business enterprises that are run and controlled by the government.

Stewardship In general terms, refers to responsibility to take care especially of something owned by someone else.

EXERCISES

Concept Review Questions

1. Briefly trace the history of CSR in the Indian corporates.
2. What was the model adopted in India to encourage economic growth? Discuss its strengths and weaknesses.
3. Describe the CSR-related initiatives undertaken by the Government of India.

Critical Thinking Questions

1. What is the relationship between CSR and empowerment of a community?
2. Analyse the specific challenges that the Indian corporations face in terms of CSR.
3. Define inclusive growth and suggest certain measures that the corporates need to take to achieve it.

Research Question

Analyse the challenges of community development and empowerment of the 'un-included' sectors in society.

Project Question

Visit an NGO or NPO and prepare a report on the activities pursued by them.

REFERENCES

Bellah R., R. Madsen, W. Sullivan, A. Swindler, and S. Tipton (1985), *Habits of the heart—Individualism and community in American Life*, Berkeley, University of California Press.

Ganguly, K.M. (trs) (2003), *Mahabharata* (XII.87.13–21), 12 vols., Munshiram Manoharlal, New Delhi.

Hardin G. (1968), 'The Tragedy of the Commons', *Science*, vol. 162, no. 3859, pp. 1243–1248.

Inglehart, R. (1990), 'Globalization and Postmodern Values', *Washington Quarterly* 23, no. 1: 215–28.

Norman, W. and C. MacDonald (2004), 'Getting to the bottom of the "triple bottom line"', *Business Ethics Quarterly*, 14(2): 243–262.

Organisation for Economic Co–operation and Development, Policy Brief, Economic Survey of India, 2007.

Web Resources

http://www.cag.gov.in/html/reports/commercial/2009_22CA/chap_3.pdf, accessed 5 June 2010.

http://www.oecd.org/dataoecd/52/11/36761627.pdf, accessed 5 June 2010.

CASE STUDY

CASE OF TCCI—DEVELOPING THE CSR FRAMEWORK

The Tata Council of Community Initiatives (TCCI) was created in 1996 as a response to requests from the Confederation of Indian Industry (CII) and the Prince of Wales Business Leaders' Forum to the group, first to Mr J.R.D. Tata (1992) then to Mr R.N. Tata (1995) for solutions in corporate sustainability. The context of their reference was to see how Indian business would respond to its new responsibilities as a consequence of embarking on socio-economic reforms.

Following the Tata tradition, the management of the group decided to set up a mechanism to undertake this important task. The Tatas were of the strong belief that first they need to look inside their own conglomerate of companies and draw up a framework in the relevant perspective. The significance of the project can be visualized from the fact that the board of Tata Sons resolved to create the TCCI with two of its senior Directors in charge of the initiative. TCCI provided three main thought processes:

1. As mentioned earlier, that CSR is not about setting up a foundation or a trust to pursue certain philanthropic activities is well-exemplified by the TCCI initiative of the Tatas. It was decided to go away from the 'norm' and embed TCCI into business. TCCI has been conceived as a 'department' of Tata

Services with a Secretariat and one of the 'group services' to Tata companies under the brand.
2. This new possibility has actually put the macro-perspective of CSR in action. The theoretical conceptualization that CSR needs to be integrated into the day-to-day working of the business world, is facilitated by such institutions. Now the companies in the group focus more on those aspects that would come from the domain of typical business-outreach programmes rather than pure social work-related delivery. This has helped the group companies to evolve from mere economic entities, serving only the economic purpose, to becoming engines of overall socio-economic development. Business within the group has been encouraged to innovate and fit into the new role of extending professional expertise and competencies for the betterment of society and also mitigate the issues related to social or environmental disruption caused by business processes.
3. TCCI also helps in exploring strategies that can lead to community development (the requirements of which have already been discussed). Hence, the new initiative of Tata is continuing the vision of the founders dedicated to nation building by touching the lives of large sections of humanity.

The methodology adopted was not of forceful pushing down of norms but building a consensus among the group companies and creating a passion for inclusive growth. Therefore, it was never about finding solutions to all ills but about creating sensitivity about them and sharing ideas and expertise to find the most feasible solution. 'Over 28,088 registered volunteers resonate this commitment to "community as the purpose of our existence", thus setting off something like a virtuous cycle of goodwill and reputation around all our companies and facilities'. Some of the key changes brought about are:

Charity to development This is being institutionalized through setting goals and indicators of human development, thus bridging the gap between everyday activity and overall growth. The main thrust is to improve quality of life for all. All the efforts and stories are documented for future reference and learning aids so that there is continuity of processes and consolidation of efforts.

Evolving guidelines Like many firsts that the Tata group has given to India, even this is one of its special offerings. 'TCCI put together key perspectives and some common threads amidst our enormous diversity and brought out guidelines of sorts—perhaps the first of their kind in India, and globally. Companies 'processed' their work in this light and enlisted core competencies to find imaginative and creative ways to apply technology to meet society's needs. For instance, TCS led this movement with the Adult Literacy Programme, where a person can read newspaper headlines in 40 hours of training. TCCI took this up at a group level. Recently, it helped to take it across nine Indian states, benefiting 1,11,265 people'. Similar examples of community service known by the special name 'Innovations for the Community' have been brought to the fore by other group companies. In fact, the MBBS course of the Maharashtra Government has included a course on learning disability as a result of the efforts of the Tata interactive initiative of helping children with learning disability.

Integrating environmental management In keeping with the original mandate of creating an all-inclusive framework on environmental management, biodiversity, and wildlife conservation initiatives, TCCI first studied the skewed method of or gap in fulfilling this mandate by the group companies. To rectify this imbalance, 'all major companies were encouraged through TCCI to uniformly adopt environmental management systems such as the ISO 14000 series, the Global Reporting Initiatives, sign the UN Global Compact and the SA 8000—in all impacting over 85 % of group-turnover and 90% employee base!' More than 15 cases were brought out showing the Tata groups' commitment to environment sustainability. Now businesses are encouraged to factor in environment risk, along with business risk in their business models.

Creating the global development index As we have seen, very often the question that arises in CSR is how does one report on value-addition to social indicators. Reporting on economic or environmental indicators is much easier because the factors are tangible and easily quantifiable. Judging socio-psycho paradigm changes is not easy because it is very subtle and spreads over a long timeframe, and often is not even uniform. However, the entire concept of CSR relates to the quality of human life and existence, therefore, it becomes imperative on business to assess this important yet ambiguous aspect. The Tata group has succeeded in creating an index that would address the ambiguity about 'social' indicators in most of the national and global frameworks, including the GRI. The TCCI joined hands with the UNDP and created the Tata Index for Sustainable Human Development. This is now simplified into an assessment process of the Tata Business Excellence Model (TBEM) and is recognized by the UN as perhaps the only contribution made by a corporate to address human development through a business process.

Building sustainable livelihoods This reinforces the belief that CSR is about building sustainable livelihoods through capacity-building and creating self-help groups. TCCI helped to reorient programmes 'to encourage the creation of artisans, micro-enterprises, self-employment, and in a small way promote social entrepreneurship, so that we measure impact, not so much of the eye operations conducted, or children going to school, but more so in what we did to form self-help groups (SHGs), income levels raised, skills provided, and finally, communities we built as a measurable base to 'improving the quality of life'. In recent years, 15 major companies have consistently deployed this process with scores 261 to 620, out of 1000 points on our CS Assessment model in 12 major companies. As on 1 August 2009, our companies have helped communities to form 57,445 SHGs in different contexts with a membership of 5,10,304 people, mostly women! This is done directly and through social intermediaries'.

Aligned aspirations
It is noteworthy that the TCCI programme is not a project that required extraordinary capital or human investment. It just used the synergy of its own group and

created a wonderful ambience of self-motivation and brand value. It has given valuable direction and helped to create world-class benchmarking in sustainable inventiveness. In fact, as suggested by writers on CSR that it should move to corporate social responsiveness to corporate sustainability (CS), TCCI has been able to achieve it in practice. Now the membership has increased from 12 to 40 companies and they have all endorsed the move 'From CSR to CS'. 'The companies recently adopted the term corporate sustainability to 'brand' all these rather unsettling changes and strengthened our conviction on the concept that ultimately the business of business is sustainable value creation'. This has changed the aspirations of the companies to look beyond the bottom line. The effort is more holistic and aims at developing a variety of multiple interdependencies: human, social, natural, and other goals. Thus, important changes have been envisaged in the processes for building strategic alliances with government, civil society institutions, and other social sector partners. 'The "five thousand and odd" diversities in our (Tata Group) companies are now held by a more cohesive meaning.' The involvement is so deep that exclusive CS leadership profile has been developed to handle the nature of change. TCCI has now evolved the group corporate sustainability policy and assessment protocol, serving as guidance to all Tata companies.

Deployment methods

To achieve success in such a noble yet extremely difficult cause, TCCI has put in place processes that can be easily emulated by other business entities. First and foremost, it has decentralized and taken it beyond the company platform by setting up regional groups. They are spread over in six regional groups and now there is also one in London. Clustering in cities where Tata companies had a major presence has provided the opportunities for bigger and smaller companies to assemble on the same platform, to engage in dialogue and share common concerns and create an array of opportunities to serve the common people. An example of such proactive activity is the Hyderabad group whose programmes on vocational training suggested the view TCCI takes on affirmative action. 'What 11 Tata companies did there is influencing the group level initiative! The recall we leave behind on citizens, local authority, media, or opinion makers is amazing!' TCCI regional groups function in Bangalore, New Delhi, Kolkata, Mumbai, and London.

To institutionalize and provide a structure to the multifarious demands on time and resources to achieve excellence, TCCI operates through the processes developed for the Tata Business Excellence Model. Normally, companies are encouraged to focus on customers and related stakeholders, and therefore sometimes revenue decisions take priority above all else. To resolve this dilemma between profit and CSR, CS focuses on stakeholders more as the end rather than the means; so, the process-owners are trained to keep a vigilant eye on those in the community negatively affected by the business or those who could benefit from our competencies. The allocation of resource is usually balanced by processes, budgeting, and other strategic programmes and even through supply chains wherever possible.

There is a practical problem in involving employees on a day-to-day basis in CS activities; therefore, volunteering is increasingly recognized as a way of life in Tata companies. However, sensitivity about social issues is created and employees are also encouraged to see how their own competencies and expertise can be imaginatively deployed to help solve society's enormous problems. This brings greater convergence between CS and professional initiatives, which has been suggested in Chapter 2 under the 'professional' concept.

Impact and influence
It certainly is not surprising that TCCI is recognized as a pioneer in the field of practical corporate sustainability. The Tata group continues to influence the CSR and CS issues through representations on boards and committees of national and global CS-related institutions; and also the attention of student and media communities in India and abroad.

Some examples of such representation are: TCCI was invited to help develop the Social Code for Business in India by the UNDP-CII Partnership Forum; TCCI chaired the Panel to develop IS 16001 Standard, 'Social Accountability at the Workplace' under the Bureau of Indian Standards; TCCI representatives are invited on the Advisory Boards of the Global Reporting Initiatives, UN Global Compact; SA 8000, and the World Economic Forum.

Eleven countries invited 17 TCCI Facilitators to make over 60 presentations so far, covering nearly ten thousand eminent persons from development, civil society, the media, and business sectors, including the UN Secretary General in 2003.

Every business school by default teaches Tata cases for students to understand the amorphous concept of CSR and CS. Tata processes are a favourite with researchers not only because of their innovativeness but also because of the simplicity in delivering mechanisms. Above all, the warmth of the Tata culture attracts everyone.

Value foundation
'TCCI is driven on motivation and persuasion to find unique ways to achieve CS performance when there is really no top-down mandate.' This is a unique feature in the Tata group where no coercion is necessary for creating an environment of 'giving back' to society. From its inception the House of Tatas has created processes and institutions that have added to the development of India. In fact, government of India has borrowed Tata practices while framing labour laws and other industry regulations.

TCCI is no exception and 'operates on principles of participatory-networking'. Therefore, there is seamless integration across the group. The entire process is based on dialogue and sharing of best practices in group-level goals like innovation, globalization, and so on, with emerging contexts in 'development', 'market economics', 'environmental management,' and different systematic and organic elements by different Tata companies in annual forums.

TCCI recognizes and helps in evolving a kind of leadership profile for CS stewardship. The corporate sustainability programme needs to be driven by leaders possessing a specialized skill that inculcates a concept of stewardship, i.e., taking care of and being accountable for the activities. The special training also helps leaders in designing processes as well as measuring the impacts of business activities in the community. These skills are consciously developed by TCCI among its members.

TCCI has also been extremely proactive in developing unique tools and methods in CS. One such important tool being an outstanding combine between the Tata business excellence model (business process) and the UNDP's Human Development Work (indexing development).

The most important contribution has been the creation of new ways to move from concept to sustainable value-creation through designing doable templates that the entire Tata group endorses and follows.

Discussion questions
1. What role does TCCI play in the Tata group of industries?
2. Describe the processes that have helped to transfer concepts to implementable programmes.
3. Is TCCI a public relations tool for the Tata group? Justify your answer.

Source: The information about TCCI is courtesy Mr Anant G. Nadkarni, Vice President – Group Corporate Sustainability, Tata Council for Community Initiatives, tcci@tata.com.

Global CSR

INTRODUCTION

If we analyse the three words in CSR, i.e., corporate, social, and responsibility, it would be easier for us to evaluate whether a common CSR formula can be created. When we look at the word corporate, we find it easy to define because there is a global consensus on which institutions can be grouped under the term 'corporate' or 'company'.

The term 'social' has been debated by various authors to include the wide concept of a national social system to narrow the vision of the surrounding community around a company. Society involves a number of actors and therefore a number of relationships have to be sensitively and delicately handled. Dealing with social concerns like basic sanitation, housing, water and electricity supply, and transport facilities are much easier than macro issues related to freedom, human rights, justice, fair distribution of facilities, and governance. These factors have a close relationship with the history and culture of a nation. The perception about these macro factors differ from one country to another, depending on the ethos of the country.

'Responsibility' deals with intangible emotions like accountability and integrity. Measuring responsibility is not easy and requires a longer time to assess. While assessing responsible behaviour, it may become difficult to segregate the impact of policies when a number of organizations work at the same time and in the same place. Responsibility requires that a fair trade-off between various stakeholders is achieved to ensure least dissatisfaction among the stakeholders. Effective and efficient usage of limited resources can bring to the forefront the question of sustainability, i.e., ensuring that future generations have enough resources at their disposal to enjoy quality life. The 'cause and effect' relationship becomes complex as major social problems have to be tackled to ensure value-added development that leads to inclusive growth of all sections in society.

LEARNING OBJECTIVES

After studying this chapter, you will be able to
- Understand if there is a commonality in CSR practice
- Showcase four countries from four different continents and at different levels of economic development and ethical practices to understand CSR in more depth

Thus, we see that designing a 'one fit for all' CSR model is not easy. In fact, the universal ethical concepts can only serve as the base for the design and the corporate should ensure compliance to basic human rights and dignity. When it comes to implementation of CSR efforts, every nation would have to take their unique socio-economic and political structure into account and build around the basic human rights. The better an organization understands social needs, the easier and more effective is the CSR programme design and implementation.

Working towards bringing changes in a society or community requires long-term intervention moving through different levels (see Chapters 5 and 6). Thus, trying to imitate the CSR practices either of a country or of an organization would never yield positive results. Responses to these challenges differ from nation to nation, reflecting different national business, economic, political, and cultural environments. Specific and focused study of problems that need urgent remedy needs professional training to arrive at near-accurate solutions. The solutions are near accurate because in a dynamic world, where change in one area impacts the other, long-term intervention would require constant monitoring and upgradation. This diversity of CSR practices can best be understood when we look at the approach of multinational companies (MNC) to CSR and country-specific CSR practices. CSR practices in four countries (the US, UK, Indonesia, and New Zealand) are showcased below to highlight differences in perception and practices of CSR. All these national patterns are historically modern ones and appeared around the mid-19th century. They deal with the coming of the modern business enterprises—those that employed a number of full-time salaried managers.

MULTINATIONAL COMPANIES

As is obvious from the term 'multinational', multinational companies are those that have subsidiaries or operations in several different countries. They usually operate by setting up branch offices in multiple locations across the globe. These companies are also known as transnational companies, multinational enterprises, or are sometimes referred to as international corporations. These companies came into greater prominence with the growth of globalization. The phenomenon of globalization has been surrounded by both concurrence and controversies about its impact on the socio-economic structure of different countries. The general concern has been whether the MNCs have used their wider reach, better knowledge, and technologies to exploit vulnerable workforces and degrade the environment because of lax environment protection laws and regulations. To abate these fears and project an image of being responsible, most multinationals use CSR practices to highlight their ethical intentions. The CSR code has been used in portraying different aspects by different companies. For example, according to Diller (1999), the codes are used to establish a company's legitimacy in the eyes of those who are not directly involved with the organization. A similar thought was expressed by Crouch (2006), who described the adoption of a CSR code as the approach 'by firms that voluntarily take account of the externalities produced by their market behaviour'. Thus, multinational companies have used the concept of CSR to promote their business and earn profit among diverse communities and countries by projecting the image of a well-wisher and not an exploiter. However, we find that these companies have pursued CSR in varied ways as explained below.

Differences in CSR Practice

A study conducted by Welford (2005) of 15 countries' CSR practices showed that there is a link between the economic development of a country and the development of its CSR practices. This idea is further explored in the writings of Baughn, Bodie et al. (2007) who conclude that a country that boasts of a high level of wealth and development can provide technology resources that are applicable to social and environmental practices. There is also some evidence that CSR codes are more common in some nationalities of MNCs than others and that the country of origin also affects the character of the codes (Bondy et al. 2004). We have already seen in the course of this book that there is no one definition of CSR or one 'fit for all' strategy; yet there is a common thread of welfare that overlaps in an organization's duty towards its various stakeholders. Thus, if we want to look at the multinational view, then it can be seen as an advocacy of development of products in a country or region to help improve policies and practices, only if justified by the cultural context and preferences (Chaudhri 2006).

CSR codes have also been distinguished in terms of their application, i.e., whether they are 'internal' or 'external'. The internal code deals with the management and employees of the firm itself, while the 'external' targets the outside groups, such as suppliers, or both (Bondy et al. 2004). Connected to the same idea is the distinction that relates to the nature and implementation of the codes. This means one has to understand whether the codes are mandatory or advisory in nature because that would indicate the implementation mechanism. If the codes are laid down by the management, then there are chances that they may not cover all the necessary areas and suffer from the deficiency of unilateral authoritarian decisions. Monitoring would also not be proper as there would be no say of stakeholders in the implementation process. However, if the codes are negotiated with stakeholder representatives like trade unions, environmentalists, government regulators, and others, then the chances are that they would cover issues more extensively and in greater depth. The monitoring in this case would include stakeholder representatives and therefore the accountability would be higher, which would ensure that the provisions of the codes are put in practice.

Challenges of Multinationals

Globalization is 'a complex, accelerating, integrating process of global connectivity' (Tomlinson 2007) and therefore MNCs would always have to be alert to the demands of the values and norms of their home and host country (Chapple and Moon 2005). Thus, the prerequisite for any organization, small or big, that is operating in the global arena is to capture the new and upcoming CSR practices in the 'global framework', so that it is responsive to diverse cultures, norms, values, and communication practices (Stohl et al., 2007, p. 34). This challenge of integrating global and local practices is further highlighted by Chaudhri (2006, p. 41), who explains that both global and local concerns are likely to determine factors within the multinational 'business model, global citizenship mission/vision, scope of operation, and availability of monetary and non-monetary resources'.

This trend of combining the local and global components of business is termed as glocalization and relates to global or international business practices having the ability to target the local consumers or markets. MNCs have to use multiple formats to influence and push the local people to identify with their cultural or national background through the global products or services a company offers (see Maynard and Tian, 2004). The challenge is to earn goodwill in the local community because very often MNCs are looked upon with suspicion because of their overwhelming capacity to influence the political, social, and economic fabric of a country.

To address these factors, MNCs are using various means to promote social interaction and work towards a sustainable future. With the spread and penetration of information technology (IT), organizations are increasingly using the Internet to publicize their CSR activities. According to Chapple and Moon (2005), companies functioning internationally are more likely to report their CSR practices than those only functioning domestically. Therefore, we can see how CSR practices are spreading beyond the perimeters of nations and achieving a global consensus and commonality of practices at the macro level.

COUNTRY-SPECIFIC CSR INITIATIVES

The brief country-specific CSR initiatives given below further corroborate the fact that there is a concerted move in the world today towards CSR.

The US

A Brief History

We can trace the seeds of modern corporation in the US to the railroad and the telegraph. Since the railroad required managing vast geographical areas and demanded precision in delivery, it brought in the management concepts of control and strategy. Managers faced absolutely new challenges while constructing the network of railways and operating them. Thus, the railroads led to the development of the modern concepts of organization as an institution and theories of production and operations management. Since the railroads required a large amount of capital for financing, their construction and operation led to the development of the modern capital market. The Wall Street came into existence and financial instruments were traded in the national exchange. The Wall Street is a street in Lower Manhattan, and the New York Stock Exchange is located here. It represents the American financial markets, financial institutions as a whole, or by extension, big-business interests. The railways also ushered in an era of competition among small groups of business entrepreneurs leading to the development of oligopolies. To regulate these business groups, the government stepped in with its own system of control. With the quick growth of transportation and distribution, which was more regular than the earlier ways, transporting goods, the wholesale, and retail business got a tremendous boost in the US. 'The mass retailer—the department stores, mail-order houses, and chain stores—whose profits were based on low price and high 'stock-turn' that is, the number of times stock inventory was sold and replaced within a specified time period. The higher the stock-turn with the same working force and equipment, the lower the unit costs, the higher the output per worker, the greater the profit' (Chandler 1977, p. 223). Soon, there was a surge of technological innovations and the old industries such as food processing and metal-making were transformed.

Industrialists now competed for more market share and profits. They improved their functional effectiveness (improved manufacturing, research and development, marketing and distribution, and labour relations) and strategically began to move more quickly into new markets and out of old ones (Chandler 1977, pp. 34–36). These large enterprises continued to dominate the industries of the 1880s and 1890s, which transformed the economies of their day. The significance of this extraordinary growth can be measured from the statement made by US President Rutherford Hayes in 1884: 'This is a government of the people, by the people, and for the people no longer. It is a government of corporations, by corporations, and for corporations.' Corporations have continued to play a similar role in transforming industries, such as motor vehicles in the 1920s and the 1930s and computers after World War II.

Emergence of Modern Industries

In the US, modern industrial enterprises grew in four ways:
  (a) They merged with competitors in the same market (horizontal combination).
  (b) They obtained suppliers or distributors (vertical integration).
  (c) Those companies whose organizational capabilities were learned by exploiting the economies of scale tended to move into new, more distant geographical markets and became increasingly multinational.
  (d) Those whose capabilities were based on economies of scope tended to enter related product markets and became multiindustrial.

With this kind of extraordinary growth and competition, naturally, earning profit was the main purpose. However, the potential of largescale industrial growth needed expansion in facilities of infrastructure and quicker means of transportations, which increased pressure on the government to provide for them. A result of such pressure on the US government led the government to encourage a revolution in Colombia to ensure that American companies could proceed with the construction of the Panama Canal, which was vital for trade and military interests. The lure of profits was so high that large conglomerates began to appear on the scene.

One famous example is Andrew Carnegi (a Scotsman by origin and the founder of the US Steel) who is considered one of America's hard-core capitalist businessmen and also one of the most renowned philanthropists. The Standard Oil Company is another such organization, which showed such exponential growth and became a monopoly that was so big that in 1911, the US Supreme Court ordered that Standard Oil be broken up into 33 parts. The Chief Justice stated: 'The nation has been rid of a human-slavery ... slavery that results from the aggregations of capital in the hands of a few individuals and corporations controlling, for their own profit and advantage exclusively, the entire business of the country, including the production and sale of the necessities of life.' Exxon/Esso, Mobil, and Chevron grew out of the pieces.

This trend towards earning more and more profit is also exemplified in the growth of the Ford Motor Company, which pioneered the concept of mass production in 1913, and Model T was mass produced in the US. Henry Ford increased the pay of his employees to $5 a day. This helped create a legion of workers prosperous enough to buy one of his cars. However, three years later, two shareholders sued Ford for breach of fiduciary responsibility, complaining the money he was putting into plant expansion should be going into dividends to them. They won the case, which shows the acceptance of profit as the main outlook for business. Shareholders were considered the most important stakeholder and even employees were ignored in the process. There was, thus, a consensus among many that there was an urgent need to control industry and remind capitalists of their social responsibilities.

Measures to Control the Rapid Growth

This economic growth could not be sustained and the Roaring Twenties, as the era was called, because it had ushered in mass consumption as a socio-economic trend, came to an end with the crash of the Wall Street in 1929. This led to the government passing various laws to check uncontrolled growth. The Glass-Steagall Act was passed in 1933 to separate ownership of banks and investment firms, so as to separate bank profits and lending patterns from the stock market, controlled growth (depending on the market forces based on demand and supply). The Act was repelled in 1999 to allow mergers and acquisitions in the upbeat economic scenario. In 1934, the US government brought into existence the Securities Exchange Commission (SEC) to restore investor confidence in the markets. It created public disclosure and enforcement mechanisms to protect investors and promote the dissemination of reliable corporate information to the marketplace.

In spite of the efforts of the government to rein in business, there were still no serious efforts on the part of business to look beyond profits. During this time, famous global brand names like Coca Cola came into existence. It was the American military that carried the drink to Asia, Europe, and Africa. In the natural resources sector, oil was a coveted investment and Aramco was created in Saudi Arabia. The company has been aptly described by one investor as 'by far the greatest, most important, and most dramatic overseas American enterprise, which has ever existed. Aramco, the largest oil concession in the Middle East, is a guiding hand in the politics of the region for the next few decades ...'

Growth of Business Management Ideologies

The extraordinarily quick growth of business led to the emergence of two conflicting ideologies in business management thinking. One highlighted that business should share social responsibility and the second promoted that the only purpose of business is to earn profit. The most famous author of the second vision was Milton Friedman. In his famous work, *Capitalism and Freedom* published in 1962, he stated that 'the business of business is business' and corporations have neither the legitimacy nor the interest to consider wider questions of social responsibility. These contradictory thoughts and visions are not new and have been seen in all civilizations and have always moved hand in hand. It was no different in the US.

This trend was captured by management guru—Peter Drucker—in 1945 in the book entitled *The Concept of the Corporation*. It was the first full-length study of one corporation. He had studied General Motors, which till date is one of the major corporations of the US. Drucker highlighted the conflict between industrial efficiency and social harmony. He accused GM of introspection and inward-oriented behaviour. According to him, such myopic vision was going to impact GM's growing business. This was obviously not heeded by the then legendary CEO, Arthur Sloan. GM's inability to read wider social changes where the other stakeholders operated led to loss of market share, and in the 1970s, on the back of the oil crisis, Japanese car manufacturers, with their focus on the primacy of the consumer, overtook GM in the US market.

Appearance of CSR

The first glimpse of CSR is seen in the Quaker movement, which was founded in 1652 by George Fox, who rebelled against the established political and religious practices and promoted what he believed was genuine Christianity. Quakers are credited with being the first group of investors to use social criteria to investing standards, based on their belief in human equality and nonviolence.

The first significant judgement came in 1819 in the *Dartmouth College* versus *Woodward*, 17 U.S. (4 Wheat.) 518 (1819), case. The judgement declared the role of the state was no longer that of a sovereign over the corporate, but that of a partner in a private contract. In 1886, the US Supreme Court declared that a corporation is considered a 'natural person'.

The social awareness was first reflected in the creation of the Pioneer Fund in 1928 to take care of the needs of the church group investors, who did not want to invest in 'sin' such as gambling, tobacco, and alcohol. The beginning of using shareholder activism to create social awareness can be traced to 1970, when Ralph Nader launched a campaign against General Motors. He submitted nine shareholder resolutions on consumer rights, minority hiring, and representation on GM's board. In the same year, the Interfaith Centre on Corporate Responsibility (ICCR) was formed. It is a coalition of almost 300 groups of religious investors who sponsor shareholder resolutions on social issues in order to affect corporate policies and practices.

Some examples of early initiatives by organizations Examples of some early initiatives by organizations that began to take active steps towards CSR are discussed here. The Pax World Fund was the first mutual fund to adopt social responsibility standards for its investments. It promoted the idea of a mutual fund with conscience and included companies with fair employment practices and sound environmental policies. South Shore Bank is the country's oldest bank that is involved in the largest community development activities. It promotes and focuses on improving the economic health of neighbourhoods and also caters to individual financial concerns of consumers, businesses, religious, and community organizations. The bank is also the first bank to offer bank accounts to social investors with development deposit options, for funds to go directly towards rebuilding urban communities.

The promulgation of the Sullivan Principle, which was drafted by Rev. Leon Howard Sullivan to promote social, economic, and political justice through corporate codes of conduct, encouraged the business world to get involved in ethical and human rights concern (see Chapter 4). It is interesting to note that Rev. Sullivan was the first black member in the board of the General Motors Corporation, and he secured GM's support in development of the Sullivan Principles, which began as a code of conduct for American businesses operating in South Africa. The principles were later widened for universal application.

Similarly, the Coalition for Environmentally Responsible Economies established voluntary Corporate Codes of Conduct (CERES Principle) regarding waste reduction, energy conservation, and public safety (see Chapter 6). This is also known as the Valdez Principle. Organizations like the Body Shop, Ben & Jerry's (see Chapter 7), Seventh Generation, and Aveda were the first to endorse the principle and were willing to report on their environmental activities.

Another interesting index that took shape around the same time, i.e., 1990, was the Kinder, Lyndenberg, Domini and Co. Inc (KLD), which created the Domini 400 Social Index (DSI). The main purpose behind this was to track the performance of a number of companies that pass multiple broad-based social screens. DSI attempts to reflect the market as it exists for most socially responsible investors. This means that it further attempted to reflect the behaviour of stocks of companies that socially responsible investors might purchase. The famous Dow Jones Global Sustainability Index is the first index to incorporate social, environmental, and financial analysis into a comprehensive rating system (see Chapter 6). The evaluation is based on the company's ability to compete in a global economy and focus on sustainability. A movement by students called Students for Responsible Business, now called Net Impact, has a membership of about 1500 graduates who together work to foster socially responsible businesses.

Exposure of unethical dealings, some of which are given below, further strengthened the argument favouring CSR.

The NGO sector plays an important role in promoting CSR activities by proactive activism against unethical issues. Environmental pressure groups like Greenpeace and Friends of the Earth have campaigned against pollution and waste by corporations. After the Bhopal Gas tragedy, which occurred as a result of negligence on the part of the company to ensure high standards of safety, Greenpeace protested against the then head of Union Carbide, Warren Anderson, for shirking responsibility of the disaster on flimsy grounds. When Shell tried to sink the disused Brent Spar oil platform into the North Sea, it was stopped by Greenpeace direct action protests. Shell temporarily lost the confidence of investors and the public. These activities played a significant role in bringing civil society actions against corporations to the forefront.

Corporations woke up to the fact that public relations and their reputations matter more than ever. Public campaign, especially by children, against McDonald's styrofoam packaging forced the company to change to recyclable packaging material. The American mining giant Freeport McMoran admitted to have paid huge money to the Indonesian military, who were notorious for their record in torture and extra-judicial murder, to protect their operations in West Papua, a troubled Indonesian province. The Iraq War exposed links between politicians, business organizations, and the military for mutual benefit at the cost of the common citizens. Some other examples include:

(a) The nexus between the political leaders and the business world was exposed by the incident of Richard Perle. Perle resigned as chairman of an influential Pentagon advisory board after disclosures that he was involved in payment of bribe to persuade the government to allow US telecommunications infrastructure belonging to the collapsed Global Crossing Corporation to be sold to Chinese investors.

(b) The US government's Agency for International Development announced that Halliburton, an oil services company chaired by US Vice-President Dick Cheney for five years until 2000, was not in the running for a $600m (£381m) US government contract to rebuild Iraq; but Halliburton's subsidiary Kellogg Brown and Root secured some business.

(c) Becthel, the famous engineering, construction, and project management company, on whose board sat a former Republican Secretary of Defense and Secretary of State, secured the $600m reconstruction contract instead.

(d) And, as war continued, TotalFinaElf (a leading oil, gas, and chemicals company) looked set to seal the deal it secured to exploit the 20 billion barrel oilfield at Majnoon in southern Iraq. Thus, the public declarations of providing equal rights to bid for exploring oil in Iraq were farcical.

All these naturally created a need to concentrate on the concept of CSR more deeply.

CSR in the US Today

Today, in the US, there is widespread awareness about CSR. There is a distinctive emphasis on the stakeholder theory (Chapter 3), sustainability (Chapter 7), corporate citizenship (Chapter 4), systemic risks of business, business integrity, accountable corporate governance, and ethical and responsible leadership. Thus, it is apparent from the emphases that the focus has widened to every field of business, including ethical challenges in technological innovation, human rights, equality in distribution of benefits, and sustainable environment practices. Compliance and responsible behaviour beyond compliance is the present requirement. According to Ibrahim and Parsa (2005), almost every aspect of American business' revolve around laws and regulations. Businesses in the US usually encouraged volunteerism, while giving communities resources with philanthropic programmes, and compared to Europe and Asia, in the US philanthropic practices were most established (Baughn et al. 2007).

Many business organizations are putting in place ethical business processes and codes of ethics. There is a closer understanding of how to manage ethical risks in organizations. Compliance to government laws and adherence to corporate governance are being encouraged at the organization level. At the business leadership level, ethics training is receiving much attention. Training in areas of ethical decision-making, ethical leadership development, which also includes how to use power, is becoming extremely popular. Ensuring integrity in all activities and conduct of the leader is being endorsed by all. American companies are promoting ethical business practices because American consumers like to identify with companies that practise ethical behaviours beyond legal requirements. The modern awakened consumers feel satisfied when they believe that they are connecting with a brand due to its moral and ethical make-up and buying quality products. This encourages the American companies to reveal and publicize a general strategy of CSR practices and strategies, which include consumer safety, equal opportunity employment practices, non-exploitative supply chain processes, and environment-friendly technologies. An example of business contributing to society is Carnegie (the steel tycoon), who gave away most of his money to establish many libraries, schools, and universities in the US, the UK, and other countries, as well as established a pension fund for former employees.

To inculcate ideas about ethics and responsibility among managers, business ethics and social responsibility have become important themes in research and teaching. There has been a sustained effort to promote social responsibility among business organizations since 1995. Business scams centreing around accounting frauds like Enron, World Com (at one time, the second largest long-distance phone company grew rapidly by acquiring other telecommunications companies), Tyco (a major US company that produced a variety of products, from electronic components to healthcare products and operated in more than a 100 countries), and environment as well as human disasters like the Bhopal gas tragedy have increased the need to review responsibility as a requirement for future sustainability. American companies today are trying to position themselves as promoters of honest and reliable business practices so that consumers will purchase their product assuming it is high quality (McWilliams and Seigel, 2001). Various actions based on mandatory regulations and codes have been taken to ensure more transparent CSR.

The Sarbanes–Oxley Act (see Chapter 3 for details) was passed in 2002 as a safeguard against frauds like Enron. The Act is meant to accomplish quality and transparency in financial reporting, independent audits, and accounting services for public companies. The Child Labour Deterrence Act (the Harkin Bill) was passed through US Congress to safeguard children against unfair exploitation. However, this kind of regulation led to tens of thousands of children in Bangladesh and elsewhere to lose their jobs and be impoverished, showing how interconnected business is and one has to be careful in designing the strategy of CSR. However, still there is a gap in the sharing of best practices among industry and among regions. The trend to emphasize contextual dimension of corporate responsibility is more common among the industries. The challenges that need to be attended to are global sustainability, which analyses the issues of corruption and poverty that create a gap between the privileged and the under-privileged sections of a society. There is an urgent need to promote thought leadership among business managers, so that a holistic growth is encouraged, more than just earning profit for shareholders. Businesses have to realize that because of their widespread impact, they can no longer avoid issues related to morality and good governance. A broad understanding of the risks involved in the business world, whether related to technological innovation or human rights have to be weighed with much consideration, so that the least harm is caused.*

The UK

A Brief Background

The UK has always played a pioneering role in shaping international understanding on how to address issues associated with both the positive and negative impacts of business on society. The growth of commercial ventures, as we know them today, can be traced to as early as 1553, when Sir Richard Willoughby created the first English joint stock company called The Mysterie and Compagnie of the Merchant Adventurers for the Discoverie of Regions, Dominions, Islands, and Places Unknown. He raised money to finance his voyage to the East by selling stocks to merchants. The merchants who took this bold risk made a fortune when he returned from Moscow laden with treasures. Britain's supremacy as a commercial power became entrenched when around 1718, France suffered an economic crash, which almost led to the bankruptcy of the French state known in history as the Mississippi Bubble. This was an early example of how unbridled speculation around a corporate entity that does not deliver can lead to disastrous results.

The rise of Britain as a colonial power added steam to its commercial growth. In the coveted colony India, after the battle of Plassey in 1757, the

---

* Adapted from information available on http://www.opendemocracy.net/theme_7-corporations/article_1035.jsp and http://www.socialfunds.com/media/timeline.cgi, accessed on 27 July 2010.

fortunes of the East India Company changed to make it one of the most eminent commercial companies. The East India Company was an early English joint stock company (see Chapter 3). The company traded cotton, silk, indigo dye, saltpetre, tea, and opium. The company brought under its control large parts of India and exercised military and administrative control over the areas. This extraordinary growth of the company led to the passing of the India Act in 1784, which transferred executive management of East India Company's Indian affairs to a board of control, answerable to the British Parliament. From then on, there was no looking back for England in its meteoric rise as a world power.

The growth of factories had led to a change in the socio-economic framework of common English people. However, attempts at mechanization led to the famous Luddites movement in 1811–13, which protested against what they called the 'labour saving' (mechanization of processes) devices, and looted and destroyed the new machines. The movement was ruthlessly put down by the passage of the Frame Breaking Act, which enabled people convicted of machine-breaking to be sentenced to death. Extra security was provided in areas where factories were being vandalized and slowly the uprising died. Labour suffered when wheat prices rose and sufficient incomes were not there to support families. Thus, this was an era of growth as well as discontent in the UK.

In 1833, the government tried to resolve the discontent by passing The Factory Act, which defined the legal limit to the working day as 15 hours, starting at 5.30 a.m. Children aged 9–13 were not to work more than 10 hours a day in a factory. Today, such an Act would be considered ridiculous, when evaluated on the basis of human rights. Popular pressure continued against injustice of every kind and the government had to abolish slavery within the British Empire in 1834. The legendary Royal Navy of Britain actively got involved in stopping slave trade. There was no systematic effort to rein in business or deal with social issues. In fact, after the British victory in the Opium War in China, imports of massive amount of drugs into China was allowed and trading companies emerged to manage the lucrative business. One such company was the Jardine Matheson, which was founded as a trading company in China in 1832. Jardine Matheson is today a diversified business group, focused principally on Asia. Its businesses comprise a combination of cash-generating activities and long-term property assets.

Beginning of Modern Corporations

The first attempt to define a joint stock company came with the UK Joint Stock Companies Act. This was passed in 1844 and defined the corporation as a charter granted by the state to a group of investors to gather private funds for a specific purpose. The same year also saw the birth of the cooperative society movement, which is a form of ownership of the means of production, distribution, and exchange, and is often created as an alternative to the equity corporation. In the UK, the first such society was The Rochdale Equitable Pioneers Society. It was founded by working men in Yorkshire, England, and was later renamed as the Co-operative Society. The seeds of the modern concept of limited liability companies can be seen in the UK Limited Liability Act. The Act helped to curtail risks for investors. It allowed companies to limit the liability of their individual investors to the value of their shares. Prior to this, investors could go bankrupt if a company went out of business, as the investor was totally liable and all the wealth of the investor would be lost. The government was getting more and more involved in economic activities. In fact, after the 1857 Sepoy Mutiny in India, the East India Company was dissolved and the Crown brought the colony under its direct administration.

With the advent of the Labour Party in 1899, the economic strategy changed. There was nationalization of major industries like coal and railways. It was as early as 1914 that Britain's First Lord of the Admiralty, Winston Churchill, ordered government purchase of a controlling stake in the Anglo-Persian Oil Company (later BP) to ensure strategic security of oil supplies for the Royal Navy. It was in 1980 that another landmark industry made its presence felt in the UK—Rupert Murdoch's News Corporation. He broke the print union and made available cheaper affordable news to everyone. Today, it is a $40 billion global empire that dominates much of US, UK, and Australian media and plays an important role in China, India, and elsewhere. In 2001, the London Principle came into existence to help in assessing risk of the ongoing environmental and social balance of business activity. Thus, we see that small steps towards a more structured business processes were taking root in the UK.

Movement towards CSR

England is one of the first countries to debate the question of corporate governance and put forth codes to implement them. Most of UK's largest companies follow a dual strategic leadership pattern. This implies that the role of the CEO and the chairman of the company board are separated. The first code of governance was the Cadbury Code of 1992 (see Chapter 3), which suggested such a split. This was the first time that the social impact of business was highlighted and a need for responsible behaviour was promoted.

UK and Europe underwent a huge shock when corporate frauds came to light: AOL Time Warner reported an overall loss of $98.7 billion for the year 2002, one of the largest corporate losses in history. Ahold, the world's third largest retailer, became 'Europe's Enron' when it was discovered that it had overstated its profits by $500 million. Deutsche Telekom reported $28 billion loss—the largest corporate loss in Europe since the Second World War. Since most of the investors in these businesses were institutional investors, their control of the equity market as a whole has grown rapidly in the last 20 years and institutional investors controlled about 80 per cent of the UK equity market as of 31 December 2003 (Mallin et al. 2005, quoted in Aguilera et al. 2006). There was much unrest in this sector of the economy and some landmark decisions came into existence.

In 2002, and again in 2005, the Institutional Shareholders' Committee (ISC), which represents over 80 per cent of institutional investment in the UK, issued revised Statements of Principles for institutional shareholders and agents. These principles set out guidelines for institutions' engagement with and monitoring of portfolio companies and the important aspect was that each indicated the importance of CSR by making it a basis for engaging in a discussion with companies (Aguilera et al. 2006).

Similar attention to social responsibility can be seen when the Association of British Insurers (ABI) issued its Disclosure Guidelines on Socially Responsible Investment (ABI 2001). These guidelines 'focus on the need to identify and manage risks to the long and short-term value of the business from social, environmental, and ethical matters'. Williams and Conley (2005) point out that institutional investors' coalitions in the UK have emphasized significant social issues such as climate change, extractive industry revenue transparency, HIV/AIDS, environmental and social issues in project finance, and supply chain labour conditions. Investors realized the advantage that they can derive from handling social issues well and this has encouraged them to view social concerns with acceptance (Solomon et al. 2004; Armour et al. 2003).

An example of this involvement is how institutional investors in the UK have became involved in the Extractive Industry Transparency Initiative, which encourages oil, gas, and mining companies to publish what they pay to host countries for licences to extract natural resources. The idea is that this would reduce corruption and therefore would become safe investment havens, especially for long-term infrastructure investments (Williams 2004). Climate change is also an important agenda of institutional investors. They have expressed concerns about the long-term financial implications in a wide range of industries from the physical changes that climate change is bringing about, and about the short-term costs of greenhouse gas emissions under the European Union's (EU) Emissions Trading Scheme to some particularly vulnerable industries such as insurance, re-insurance, and energy (Institutional Investors' Group on Climate Change, 2003). To many investors, the social, environmental, and ethical responsible behaviour of a company indicates its quality of management and therefore they may decide to invest or not depending on these parameters (Solomon et al. 2004). The interest can be measured from the fact that 20 of the largest fund managers for the UK pension industry are members of the UK Social Investment Forum, as are seven of the top fund managers in the UK charity sector (Williams and Conley 2005). It has been pointed out by Bansal and Roth (2000) that geographical and social proximity is one of the major reasons for cohesion and consequent pressure to conform to CSR among the institutional investors.

A few years ago, companies were mostly sceptical or cynical about CSR, whereas there is a genuine consensus and effort today to consider CSR as a mainstream activity. There is a conscious effort on the part of organizations to analyse the issues of CSR under various heads that include internal actions to external, social, and environment-related actions. There is a movement towards developing company-specific CSR focus to emerge as a preferred company in the market through a deeper comparative understanding of the investment goals and engagement practices.

However, there has to be constant monitoring of CSR activities to ensure that companies are not misusing their power, by engaging in superficial philanthropic activity, while continuing with the fundamental harmful core activities that they were practising to earn profits. By the middle of 2006, CSR had become a much debated term in the UK, ranging from whether there was too much emphasis on the social issues and not enough emphasis on the environmental concerns, whether CSR was being used more as a publicity and public relations activity and no real contribution to the social sector was visible. This has led to frustration among many committed practitioners, as no consensus appears to be emerging in these debates and there is a trend to rename CSR as 'corporate responsibility' or 'business and sustainable development' or 'corporate accountability'. Therefore, there is a need to create a better understanding of the range of perspectives and markers of success, both locally and globally for CSR.

Requirements to Perpetuate CSR

This raises issues about the nature of UK's commitment to CSR. If the UK government is to play a stronger, more active role in promoting CSR, it needs to intervene in the marketplace for the benefit of society. It should lead the way to greater sustainable development in the UK and the world because of the respect that UK has earned for itself as a nation. The UK is home to some of the world's leading thinkers, practitioners, and campaigners in the field. Progressive coalitions are already emerging on an issue-specific basis—for example, the Business Leaders Initiative on Climate Change and the Business Leaders Initiative on Human Rights. The emergence of a group of business stakeholders expressing their collective concern following Chancellor Gordon Brown's decision in November 2005 to drop the Operating and Financial Review is another example. But to sustain the good work of these thought leaders, there has to be true commitment by the leaders themselves.

CSR is a dynamic idea and would be under continuous flux. Therefore, constant updation of CSR initiatives has to happen from all the partners in growth. These partners include all the stakeholders of business and each of them needs to create their own credibility. One cannot doubt that the UK companies—from British East India Company to the 19th-century Lever Brothers and Cadbury, to contemporary oil behemoths BP and Shell—have played a key role in shaping international understanding on how to address issues associated with both the positive and negative impacts of business on society. There is a strong presence of CSR-training related to social and environmental issues in the management of the firm. Integrity training concentrates on ethical decision-making and leadership in management. There is a trend towards quality research in the area of CSR and social sciences. There is significant presence of CSR, sustainability issues, compliance issues, anti-corruption issues, and human rights concerns in the management of large organizations, but integration in the small and medium enterprise (SME) sector is still not strong. The future trends include the increasing demand for inclusion of business ethics in the curriculum of business schools and universities. The search is on for a process of global governance and development of a social market economy and methods to integrate sustainable ethics in large and small organizations.

Indonesia

A Brief History

Geographically, Indonesia is situated in South East Asia, which is one of the most populated areas of the world. For almost 250 years, Indonesia was ruled by least socially responsible colonial trading companies. Such companies can be called the transnational companies of the past. The legacy left by the colonial regime and the Dutch East India Company in Indonesia was a complex mixture of patronage and monopolies. Sukarno (1901–1970) was the leader of his country's struggle for independence from the Dutch and became the first president of Indonesia. He was a nationalist leader, who was strongly influenced by Marxism and Islam. He emerged as a dictator and a demagogue. He was the founder of the Republic of Indonesia and was a dominant figure throughout its history until his death. Between 1958 and 1965, Sukarno's Indonesia was positively hostile to foreign investment (Hill 1996). Nationalism was the mantra and it was practised in every sphere from politics to trade. It was during Sukarno's rule that the Non-Aligned Movement (NAM) in repudiation of Western colonialism was promoted. Virtually, no foreign direct investment (FDI) was allowed between the end of the colonial era and 1966. By 1966, any remaining Dutch capital had either been repatriated (restored back to Netherlands) or expropriated (taken away from the Dutch) (Hill 1996). Sukarno's government was not universally accepted in Indonesia and he was overthrown in a coup headed by Suharto.

Indonesia experienced the much-needed political and economic stability when Suharto took over the reins of the government. Suharto was an army officer and political leader and was president of Indonesia from 1967 to 1998.

He was a dictator and his authoritarian regime finally fell victim to an economic downturn and its own internal corruption.

The economic scenario of Indonesia was dominated by monopolistic companies. It included Suharto and his family-owned as well as military-owned monopolistic companies, which are commonly known as conglomerates in Indonesia. Conglomerates are well-connected groups of businesses linked to Indonesian political elites and large state-owned enterprises (SOEs), which are bureaucratic corporations protected by the power of government and patronage. Increasingly, they operate as limited companies (Perseroan Terbatas or PT) and possess the same flexibility as private enterprises. Such companies helped to create concentration of wealth and power in Indonesia. Wibisono (1991) writes that as a result of this early history, capitalism is inextricably linked with colonialism and imperialism in the Indonesian consciousness. The Indonesian military runs a parallel economy through SOEs. Since many SOEs are managed by civilians of Chinese descent, locals in Indonesia express anger against the Chinese instead of the real owners. The Chinese in Indonesia are very much the *kambing hitam* (scapegoats) and targets of sporadic violence. For example, the ultimate control of the military-owned Tri Usaha Bakti group lay with the Department of Defence, but Sofyan Wanadi, a well-known Chinese tycoon, was the front person for it. Yala Trading (logging, i.e., cutting trees for timber trade) and Admiral Shipping (transport) are both owned by the navy, while Mandala Airlines, which went bankrupt during the Indonesian economic crisis, was owned by Kostrad, the strategic reserve command of the army, along with Suharto's youngest son, popularly known as Tommy. These bureaucratic companies have resisted any attempts to put them under government control or make them publicly accountable (Yoon 1989, p. 129).

Modern Business Ventures and their Practices

However, there has been a marked strengthening of economic ties with Japan and other Asian economies, such as the Taiwan Province of China and the Republic of Korea, and has continued until the present time. Between 1998 and 1999, for example, exports to Japan rose by 14 per cent. The Republic of Korea increased its exports to Indonesia by 29 per cent over the same period. It is believed that this domination by East Asian nations is important, as the culture of these countries have a strong influence on the pattern of corporate responsibility in the manufacturing sector in Indonesia. Both the Taiwan Province of China and the Republic of Korea are reported to have poor records in relation to labour rights.*

---

* Report on Taiwan by the Committee on Foreign Relations, US Senate, and Committee on International Relations, US House of Representatives, Country Report on Human Rights Practices for 1999, www.tahr.org.tw/english/taiwan1999.html, www.decheros.org/human-rights/nasia/skorea.html and Amnesty International AI-Index: ASA 25/018/1999 22/04 1999, 'Trade unionists under threat of arrest', accessed 24 June 2008.

The new Manpower Protection and Development Act (2000) was thought to provide the beginnings of a fairer labour management and industrial relations system, which was to be strengthened by a project of the International Labour Organization (ILO) aimed at providing a more 'trustworthy system for workers and employers alike'.*

Ishiwitari et al., (1998) point out that most Asian nations lack the powerful, well-orchestrated consumer lobbies that have sparked the CSR initiatives in the West. It is significant to find that even Japanese transnational corporations (TNCs) do not have formal codes of conduct that they follow while operating in Indonesia (there are no Japanese or Asian Codes of Conduct listed by the ILO or the Asia Monitor Resource Center).** CAUX Round Table Principles for Business meeting Conference Board surveys of 1987 and 1991 have indicated that US-based firms are more likely to have codes of conduct and European firms were more likely to place emphasis on workplace safety.§

On the environmental front, ASEAN-based transnational logging and palm oil companies that operate as joint ventures with Indonesian business and political figures are supposed to have caused the worst irreversible forest and biodiversity losses in the archipelago. Timber from Indonesia's primary forest are used to feed pulp and paper industries, which along with timber products find major markets in China, Europe, the US, and Australia.

The fall of Suharto in 1998 brought some temporary relief from the practice of deliberate intervention in order to generate rents through licenses and franchizes but did not change the system. Indonesia appeared to outside observers to flourish under Suharto's rule. In spite of being named as one of the most corrupt countries on earth (Transparency International 1999) and the most uncompetitive in a group of 49 countries by Institute of Management Development in 2001,# Indonesia was praised by Western nations for its practice of capitalism and carefully managed markets. Over a decade ago, Kunio (1987) wrote that capitalism in Indonesia was actually 'ersatz' (sham) in nature, by virtue of its reliance on patronage and corruption. Similar sentiments were expressed by McLeod (2000, p. 19) when he pointed out that the deep-rooted corruption in Indonesia was cemented by the fact that like Suharto and his franchizees, many of those in enforcement agencies, like the police, Manpower and Public Works, and Judiciary also held franchizes or were too afraid to act. Senior executives of TNCs could participate in similar illegal activities if they went along with 'the system'.

* Personal communication, C. Noriel, CTA on ILO project INS/00/51M/USA.
** www.itcilo.it/english/actrav/telearn/global/ilo/code/main.htm and www.amrc.org.hk/arch.
§ Corporate Ethics Practice Report, 1992, www.itcilo.it/englsih/actrav.telearn/global/ilo/code/main.htm.
# http://www.imd.ch.wcy/criteria/criteria.cfm, posted April 2001.

The legacy of dictatorship created a very weak system of fair governance, and even when Indonesia emerged from the shackles of dictatorship, it plunged into further chaos as various forces vied for power. Jusuf Wanandi, Director of the Center for International and Strategic Studies (CSIS), explained that 'Today's anarchy is a result of 50 years of dictatorship' (*Newsweek*, 9 July 2001). Some even argued that in essence Indonesia moved from organized crime to disorganized crime. Levels of poverty, unemployment, theft, extortion, sectarian violence, and summary justice (trial and punishment of the offender without providing any recourse to formal trial under the legal system) began to escalate.

Emergence of CSR

The prerequisite for CSR is commitment, long-term thinking, and vision from business managers. Faulkner (1995, p. 9) reported that there are too few trained managers in Indonesia, and even among those available, promotions and appointments are often accorded to those with political or family connections. Large companies continue to flout legislation and certifications like ISO. An example is the Barito Pacific, which is a locally owned logging conglomerate, notorious for its destructive logging, unsafe working conditions, noncompliance with minimum wage requirements, and openly polluting practices. Such practices naturally marginalize and compromise voluntary initiatives that aim to promote corporate environmental responsibility, and increase the distrust of citizens and investors in the processes of law.

Socio-religious factors, like resignation to one's fate for all happenings and total dependence on income from work in the absence of any social security, force labourers to accept inhumane working conditions to avoid starvation and death. Vocal activists, a minority in Indonesia, are trying to bring about reform but are limited to urban industrial zones, and even there it is not easy to fight the tradition of feudalistic attitudes. Rossouw (1998) gives an interesting analysis, when he points out that in a society like Indonesia, where corruption is endemic, a tendency to kleptocracy (a ruler who uses power to steal the country's resources/a government characterized by rampant greed and corruption), fed by contemporary insecurity, also exists.

However, the growing influence of Islam, which emphasizes honesty and integrity in business, constitutes a ray of hope that CSR may gain a foothold in Indonesia. The Sharia laws specify that fruits of productivity should benefit the community and that Muslims, as individuals, cannot own public utilities such as roads, schools, or hospitals, or production facilities where cost of the good far exceeds the cost of production. According to some, this concept extends to ownership of gold mines and oil producing or refining as well (Adnan and Goodfellow 1997, p. 57).

The large Chinese-owned businesses, which comprise an important part of the Indonesian economy, are believed to be implementing better standards of accountability. Sawarjuwono and Goodfellow (1997, p. 77) feel that the patriarchal structure is still followed, as most Chinese-owned businesses are set up as limited companies, to minimize outside interference. Their insular style of management is highly personal, encompassing only family members or those known to the family. Unfortunately, this does not auger well for CSR, as it aims to incorporate the needs of multiple stakeholders and Indonesian/Chinese management styles deliberately keeps out any interests external to those of the core management group.

Most multinational organizations want to reap the benefits of availability of cheap raw materials with massive oil reserves and valuable natural resources, such as timber and minerals, and a large domestic market combined with export-oriented strategies. There is an urgent need in Indonesia to capture the spirit of CSR and not just look at it as philanthropy. It is interesting to note that countries like Indonesia suffer a dilemma when they have to choose between foreign investment and following the strict norms of social and environmental responsibilities. This is because many investors search for countries where norms are not very strict and therefore it is cheaper to do business there. In addition, Indonesia enjoyed the patronage of wealthy foreign governments who encouraged efforts by Indonesia to crush communism by assisting with defence, trade, and investment. Thus, until recently, ethical reform was never a condition of foreign support. This two-faced approach led to complacency, particularly among domestically owned firms producing for the huge local market rather than for export, as there were no stringent regulations against exploitation. These practices slowly led to growing political instability and economic downturn, as such a corrupt system is not sustainable. Now, the situation has provided at least some impetus for broader changes which, when coupled with Islam, may give rise to some positive change in terms of CSR.

Examples like the revelation by the owner of a factory that produces shoes for Reebok show the rot in the system. He told reporters that the $2 million he had to spend to meet compliance standards, after an independent monitoring team had made its recommendations, would be repaid in productivity and efficiency gains over three years (*Business Week*, 6 November 2000). Indonesia never really developed any forums like trade unions through which to share information, methods, or models. For many in Indonesia, the basic concept that CSR includes integrating social and environmental issues in their business operations is known but not practised. The interaction with stakeholders, which include employees, suppliers, customers, community, government, and NGOs is still limited to a more voluntary than a structured approach. Since the root of CSR in Indonesia is philanthropy, here the CSR activities are undertaken more as a public relations initiative than true integration of CSR in business processes. This naturally breeds cynicism and scepticism among the public.

There is a feeble prevalence of the concept of accountability of business and punishment mechanisms against those organizations that are not complying available in law. Normally, the NGO sector adopts this route to promote CSR among organizations. The human rights aspect of CSR is still extremely weak in Indonesia. Few companies try to comply by getting outside agencies to audit their human rights records. Such an audit evaluates the level of commitment to the policy and mechanisms of human rights. A weak beginning has also been seen to bring to book errant companies, e.g., Exxon Mobile was tried in a US court for its corrupt practices.

One can see various degrees of CSR reporting in Indonesia, both in terms of quantitative and qualitative reporting. In recent years, seminars and conferences have been held by multilateral agencies on corporate governance. It is clear that the driving force for social responsibility comes from outside Indonesia. The first major campaign to have an effect in Indonesia was started in 1992–93 when the then head of the AFLI CIO (American Free Labor Institute and Council of Industrial Organizations, now superseded by ACILS, American Center for International Labor Solidarity) office in Jakarta, working with the Jakarta Urban Mission, made contact with Nike workers. Suziani (1999, p. 3) has shown that the subsequent campaign pointed out that while Nike's profit rose to over $180 million per year and their advertising budget for Michael Jordan alone was $20 million, a Nike worker in Indonesia earned less than 90 cents per day or $270 per year. Nike was under constant pressure to improve its standards. Nike believed it had taken care to ensure that the system was as fair as it could be. It is often felt that the attention focused on Nike is more due to their high profile and large market share than actual ethical concern. PriceWaterhouseCoopers and Ernst & Young are among the internationally recognized companies that monitored Nike establishments. Another multinational that was embroiled in a human rights case was Levi Strauss. In 1992, the company's manufacturing plant in Indonesia was the subject of a human rights report, which alleged that workers were slapped and abused if their pace did not meet production targets. Adverse publicity forced Levi Strauss to take stern measures to ensure compliance to the company's code of conduct, known as the Terms of Engagement. Since then, the international consumer and anti-sweatshop movements have orchestrated continuing campaigns.

This is creating excitement and interest among various stakeholders. Investors and owners are critically viewing the accountability exercises and using it as a benchmark for evaluating companies. The measurement includes mainly six categories: corporate governance, performance management, stakeholder involvement, strategic intent, public disclosure, and assurance.

However, there is a subtle consensus among many Indonesian leaders that if extra pressure to follow CSR is put on investors, then the foreign investors may shy away as it would no longer be advantageous for them to invest in Indonesia. In today's business climate, this argument may not be absolutely correct because multinationals are aware of the risk of loss of reputation as a result of noncompliance to global norms of social and environmental sustainability.

CSR Practices

In spite of this attitude, there is a trend to move towards CSR among Indonesian organizations, but certainly it is not at par with the developed countries. It is interesting that a study by Credit Lyonnais Securities Asia and Asia Corporate Governance Association showed that in the Jakarta Stock Exchange, shares of companies with good corporate governance traded at almost 200 per cent above other companies. A similar study of trying to evaluate the importance of CSR in building public goodwill was conducted by Transparency Indonesia. Besides including the common CSR factors of sustainability, the study tried to find out about typical Indonesian issues like bribery, creation of educational facilities, jobs, etc. Indonesians voted for a sustainable future built on the production of safe and environment-friendly products. They expect that the companies would not indulge in corruption and bribery and provide community-oriented services like creation of jobs and better educational facilities. Ethical behaviour that promotes fairness and respect for local culture, add value to companies in the eyes of the public. There is still not much awareness to include producing recyclable products and reducing emission as important CSR criteria.

Some other examples of tangible efforts to promote CSR is visible in activities undertaken by the US-based Global Exchange, Fair Labor Association, and Students Against Sweatshops movement with their allies, the more radical Workers Rights Campaign. The Global Alliance, which represents World Bank and corporate interests, has also set up an office in Indonesia. The Fair Labor Association, with funding from the MacArthur Foundation, has developed training for indigenous labour monitors, so that it can monitor codes of conduct and build awareness among labour groups. Several major TNCs operating in Indonesia like Ericsson, Nike, Unilever, BP, and Deutsche Bank have agreed to become part of the UN-sponsored Global Compact, the aim of which is to promote labour, human rights, and environmental principles. Indonesia Business Links, sponsored by the Prince's Trust, represents a British-led informal group of 50 foreign businesses interested in 'generating a new era in Indonesian private enterprise'. Their activities to date have been oriented toward social safety net activities and assisting with small business development, but they are becoming increasingly active in the identification of specific activities to support CSR, such as social accounting and monitoring. Social safety net are programmes run by the government, NGOs, private companies, charities, etc. to prevent the poor or those vulnerable to shocks and poverty from falling below a certain poverty level. The World Bank has overseen the establishment of a body called the National Committee on Corporate Governance, made up of former ministers of finance, the securities commissioner, and various state enterprise leaders in Indonesia. It now hopes that this initiative will provide the groundwork for corporate ethics and CSR. Their task is to compose and recommend a national policy that includes:

- a code for good corporate governance as a frame of reference for the Indonesian business world, including a programme for its promulgation
- detailed improvement of legislative structures to support the code
- attention to institutional structures that support the application of the code

The development of the code has been driven by IMF's insistence on the privatization of state-owned enterprises (SOE), and the need to attract foreign investment to help the ailing Indonesian economy. The code includes the following stated objectives:

> '[to ensure that] the corporations take into account the varying interests of diverse stakeholders, the company shall minimize burden of the cost of mediating the differing interests of the stakeholders; this must be achieved through rational and fair means to strengthen the company's competitiveness ... for the corporation's long-term development and benefit, its shareholders should make every effort to decide and otherwise act upon corporate matters with a strict sense of morality and under principles of good corporate citizenship and social responsibility'.

According to certain promoters of CSR, the code is imprecise and too much oriented to banking and finance.

It is now understood that the biodiversity of the Indonesian archipelago comes close to that of the Amazon Basin (Barber 1997). To protect the biodiversity of Indonesia, Warhurst (undated) has characterized the facets of CSR in mining as being related to:

- The *biophysical sphere*, which includes the effects of mining on the health of the ecosystem, biodiversity, conservation, air, and water; and the physical base of the community's other livelihoods, such as preservation of marine resources, minerals, forests, and agricultural soils
- The *economic sphere*, which includes economic benefits to communities, wages, and distribution of natural resource-based commodity rents (taxes, royalties, etc.) between state and national agencies
- The *social sphere*, which encompasses the rights of individuals and groups, their capacity to organize, health and working conditions, respect for cultural and religious heritage, and the attitudes of the community to its environment and education

It is estimated that the destruction of one million hectares of peat swamp forest in Kalimantan, and the subsequent fires in peat seams, have set back by 10 years the carbon-fixing capacity of pristine peat bogs and added 0.5 parts per million of carbon dioxide to the global atmosphere (Reiley 2001, p. 3). The UK threatened to boycott palm oil produced in Indonesia unless some attempts were made to stop the burning (*Bloomberg News*, 4 August 2000).*

However, there is still a huge gap in areas of financial support for CSR as well as in creation of community awareness and well-being supported by corporations. Besides, the foreign multinational companies often follow a policy of excluding indigenous Indonesian regulators in favour of their home country regulatory codes or international codes. This often leads to discrepancy, as the local culture and history is not taken into account while providing CSR solutions (see Chapters 5 and 6). Eddington (2000) has rightly pointed out, unless the whole organization supports CSR initiatives, they are not sustainable.

The need for commitment from nations whose industries are exploiting the wealth of Indonesia is a crying need. Aditjondro (2001) has clearly shown that powerful interests in Malaysia and Singapore do not believe in CSR above private gain. Malaysia uses Indonesian land and considerably cheaper labour to further its own economic interests.

Certain institutions in Indonesia have taken some tentative steps to promote corporate environmental responsibility with support from several donors. One such initiative is the PROKASIH (the Clean River Programme) that was launched in June 1989. These programmes aimed to reduce water pollution from manufacturing industries. One of the declared aims was to apply pressure on firms to reduce pollution discharges by engaging other stakeholders, such as local communities directly affected by pollution as well as the wider market. PROPER (Program for Pollution Control, Evaluation and Rating) began in June 1995 as a joint initiative between BAPEDAL (Environmental Impact and Management Agency, Regional Environmental Agency) and the World Bank, and was a follow-on activity to PROKASIH. This programme introduced a colour-coded rating system for grading the environmental performance of firms, the results of which were publicly disclosed. The objectives were to (i) promote compliance with existing environmental regulations and (ii) reward firms whose performance exceeded regulatory standards.

Under Indonesian law, new companies are supposed to complete an ANDAL (Analysia Dampak Lingkungan, which is an environmental impact assessment) with the assistance of a private consultant. In 1994, however, the World Bank admitted that the results were disappointing (World Bank 1994, pp. 270, 273).

* Adapted from 'Corporate Social Responsibility in Indonesia, Quixotic Dream or Confident Expectation?' *Technology, Business and Society Programme Paper*, No. 6, December 2001, United Nations Research Institute for Social Development.

Private consultants now have a booming business in preparing what are often reassuring and inaccurate environment impact reports.

The reason for lack of integration and impact of CSR appears to be that any programmes requiring accountability or audits were based on codes rather than actual CSR. If we analyse the reasons for such codes, three important factors can be seen: government sensitivity to World Bank and international pressure; concern over sea pollution that might damage the national interest; and the negative impact of pollution on the lifestyles of the influential Jakarta elite (Cribb 1994). This can be clearly seen from the fact that some of the world's largest transnational oil and mining corporations operate in Indonesia: Caltex, Mobil, BP, Freeport-McMoRan, Agip, Newmont, Shell, Rio Tinto, Oppenheimer, Sun Oil, Total, Petromer, and Conoco. All oil and gas operations have to enter into partnership with Pertamina, the state-owned corporation possessing the monopoly for national fuel supply and sales. There are allegations that there are financial anomalies in such monopolistic ventures. The *Jakarta Post* (24 June 2000) carried a report showing the audit report findings of PriceWaterhouseCoopers, which pointed out an unaccounted-for loss of $16 million. The battle for huge profits in this lucrative industry has been the cause of very many environmental disasters around the world. The recent oil spill (20 April 2010) at the BP undertaking near the Gulf of Mexico shows that profiteering has to be controlled if we want CSR to be truly established as a mechanism for inclusive growth and good in developed or developing countries.

Another example of misuse of codes is the code developed by the Minerals Council of Australia called a Code for Environmental Management, to which some 40 major mining companies are signatory. As is common with most codes, this code is also voluntary and the precepts are vague and general. It deals more with environmental issues and ignores the social and economic concerns that stem from industries such as mining. The preparation of annual performance reports is also not monitored and is left to the companies to declare the reports. There are no sanctions against noncompliance and therefore most of the smaller companies, for whom it is an added cost to show compliance, have not joined this initiative. The larger companies have become partners more to showcase their activity and actually the code has no teeth (Atkinson 2001, p. 5).

Examples of CSR Initiatives

However, there are also conscientious firms that have taken a lead in environmentally responsible initiatives. Some examples are given below.

Ciba Geigy, which owns a large dye fabrication plant on the outskirts of Jakarta, initiated measures to stop contamination by their plant water being discharged into the Candra River. Chemically, the constituents that made the colour of the dye fast was not bio-degradable. Therefore, a recycling process was devised to ensure that the toxic waste did not flow into natural water bodies. A team of engineers created a system by which wastewater was held in specific colour-coded tanks, to enable a recycling process. The plant started reusing the previously colour-saturated water, thus saving on production costs, as less dye was needed. This production process adheres to the most stringent European standard and at the same time has been endorsed by both the mother country (Switzerland) and the local country (Indonesia) where it is operating. According to Ciba Geigy, any TNC could benefit from pursuing the same environmental objectives at all their plants regardless of local regulatory requirements (Schmidheiny 1992, pp. 278, 280) (compare with Tata initiative in leather plant, given in Chapter 3).

Semex, the international cement company, acquired the Indonesian PT Gresik's interests and realized the urgency to rectify environment pollution issues. It immediately began to study and create methods that would ameliorate the worst of the environmental problems such as dust fallout. It also began to get involved in community-based projects by instituting a community development programme, working with local village members to identify priority issues in health and education. This was aimed at gaining the trust of the local community, which is extremely important for any foreign collaboration to function smoothly.

In spite of all the pros and cons mentioned above, there is a trend to move towards CSR among Indonesian organizations but certainly it is not at par with the developed countries. It is interesting that a study by Credit Lyonnais Securities Asia and Asia Corporate Governance Association showed that in the Jakarta Stock Exchange shares of companies with good corporate governance traded at almost 200 per cent above other companies. A similar study of trying to evaluate the importance of CSR in building public goodwill was conducted by Transparency Indonesia (see p. 304). One can see the beginning, however slow, among investors and owners critically viewing the accountability exercises and using it as a benchmark for evaluating companies. Politically, Indonesia's effort to move away from the controlled system that was the legacy of the Suharto regime was not very successful because of widespread corruption. The civil society was not strong enough to fill the gap. Today, the civil society bodies are playing a very successful role in delivering benefits to the grassroots level.

New Zealand

A Brief Background

Over the past decade, the concept of CSR has increasingly attracted attention as an alternative business model to address social and environmental concerns. In the international context, the declining legitimacy of government to provide basic services has resulted in increasing pressure on not-for-profit organizations

(NPOs) and the market to address social demands. Recognition of the potential value of a CSR-based model has led businesses to isolate ways in which CSR can be instituted within the values system and structures of corporations. This 'search' has resulted in an increased understanding of various ways in which CSR can be implemented. Global leaders in the development field are promoting collaboration between NPOs and business as a significant new strategy for promoting sustainable development and reducing poverty. The benefit of such strategic partnerships between NPOs and business is one area of the broader CSR domain that has subsequently been explored in greater depth.

Concurrently, the perceived role of the business sector in development has also changed significantly. For example, in the US and Europe, distrust in corporations is at an all-time high (Berger et al. 2004). Recent events such as the financial downturn have not improved the situation. In the past, a number of accounting scandals, exorbitant CEO compensation packages, and concerns about the role of globalization in contributing to income disparities meant that business was often seen as part of the problem, rather than as having a role in enhancing social development. Indeed, globalization has increased calls for corporations to use firms' resources to help alleviate a wide range of social problems (Hillman and Keim 2001). Thus, we now see a new paradigm where business and the social sector work together while simultaneously retaining the integrity of their core functions.

Though business and NPOs have long formed alliances within their own sectors as a strategy to address specific needs, increasingly they are turning to cross-sector partnerships that provide benefit to both parties, while serving a common good (Sagawa 2001). Collaborative processes, particularly those that involve business-NPO partnerships and public-private partnerships have become a predominant means for addressing social issues and social problem-solving (Blockson 2003).

This new paradigm pairs far-sighted companies that recognize how the social context in which they operate influences their bottom line and highlights how business principles can enable them to fulfil their social missions more effectively (Sagawa and Segal 2000). According to Steurer et al. (2005), companies are actively advocating their CSR strategies as a response to an assortment of social, environmental, and economic pressures.

Despite their numerous obstacles, partnership between business and NPOs shows promise in solving societal problems and improving social development. The increase in such collaboration leaves many unanswered questions for both the academic and the practitioner. Do collaborations between business and NPOs contribute to community development in New Zealand? What is the value and long-term benefits of such collaborations? Were the objectives of the partnership achieved?

Interestingly, in the New Zealand context, socially responsible behaviour within the business community is by no means a new or unusual phenomenon. Positive relationships with stakeholders and an involvement in philanthropic activities have been witnessed for many years. Contributions to local schools and churches are commonplace and it has been found that almost two-thirds of New Zealand businesses contribute to charity (Collins et al. 2007; Lawrence et al. 2006). However, intense competition and globalization is further spurring public demand for greater involvement from business. It has been shown that there are market benefits and competitive advantages for those businesses whose policies and relationships can effectively incorporate CSR (Eweje 2007).

While CSR is not a dominant management concept in the New Zealand business environment, its importance in recent years is growing rapidly. According to Roper (2004, p. 23), the terms 'social responsibility or business responsibility were not even publicly considered prior to 1998. This fact was a reflection of the almost complete dominance of neo-liberal free-market ideology at that time.' However, many businesses have had to reconsider their role in society due to the election of the Labour-led government in 1999, demands from the public, and the historical shift from free-market ideology. One might almost suggest that New Zealand managers may in fact be reticent about using the term 'CSR'. Despite this, business social activities reflect CSR concepts or initiatives and they do in fact have CSR strategies/policies in their businesses.

Examples in the New Zealand Scenario

Some examples of CSR-focused activities are given below.

Example 1—Genesis Energy—Huntly Energy Efficiency Trust (HEET)
The participants in this relationship are a major energy supplier and a NPO dedicated to the promotion of energy efficiency. Genesis Energy is acutely aware of the fact that population growth has resulted in power generation moving closer to communities. For this reason, they have strong environmental values that guide business operations within the community: 'We have teams of people just managing community relations ... we have environmental values and policies that [dictate] how we want to operate ... our aim is 100% compliance with our resource consent conditions.'

Genesis Energy and HEET have been loosely working together for a number of years to promote healthy homes and energy efficiency. In this new partnership, the organizations came together to provide curtains to low-income families within a socio-economically depressed area in the Waikato Region in an initiative called The Curtain Bank. This programme functions in an area of high-level power generation facilities. Genesis Energy has provided key marketing expertise in promoting the programme and encouraging curtain donations. They provided the marketing collateral, including an innovative advertising campaign, posters, and billboard installations. HEET has been responsible for ensuring that the donated curtains are suitable for use prior to their redistribution. HEET liaises with key social service agencies to identify candidates for the curtain bank programme.

Both organizations showed a long-term commitment to the relationship and highlighted the level of donations as a key objective. HEET showed a clear understanding of the fact that any partnership had to satisfy the needs of both partners. An understanding of the corporate partner's objective provides an important starting point for a successful relationship.

While cross-promotion and a willingness to support other programmes was an objective of the NPO, the direct benefit of this programme, in particular, was not discussed as an objective of the relationship for Genesis Energy. For Genesis Energy, the main imperative in aligning with HEET was to further its objective to 'act as a good corporate citizen [and] put investments back into the community'. The recent focus on climate change has merely strengthened the resolve to support such programmes. For HEET, the main impetus to partner was the ability that it provided to influence the lives of people and make a difference in that community and the wider community of New Zealand. Of note is the importance of both a level of organizational and individual commitment to the 'cause'.

Example 2—Meridian Energy—Royal New Zealand Ballet (RNZB)

This relationship is between one of New Zealand's largest energy generators and the RNZB. The two organizations have a relationship that dates back to the year 2000. The association with the ballet provides Meridian with a new means of interacting with key stakeholders. For Meridian, the partnership is all about 'building relationships with the community that they interact with'. This view is taken very seriously by both organizations. The RNZB recognizes the importance of providing their partner with suitable opportunities to interact with key clients. This is fulfilled through careful discussions regarding invitations to opening night and post-performance functions. Meridian has a strong understanding of RNZB's relationship with New Zealand audiences. Their involvement in this regard is based on knowledge of audience development.

Such partnerships provide the opportunity to interact with stakeholders—a key outcome that is used to assess the success of this partnership. This is an important aspect of partnership strategy for an organization relying on the natural resources of a community.

The agreement provides the RNZB with funding and support, and allows Meridian naming rights to three productions each year. The collaboration functions well beyond the basic naming rights—each organization considers this to be an important partnership that requires constant support and interaction.

It has been a 'win-win' situation for both organizations, but by all accounts this success is hard to measure. Meridian conducts surveys and tries to measure net benefits of brand exposure and communication with key stakeholder groups. Part of the success is attributable to the fact that both organizations interact from the outset of a joint project. This was clearly demonstrated in a recent production 'The Wedding', which was an exclusively New Zealand production. Meridian worked with RNZB in planning and marketing from day one. This ensured that both organizations met key objectives and started with a mutual understanding of what the partnership needed to achieve.

For the RNZB, key objectives in this partnership were the ability to work together, maintaining clear communication, showing a generosity of spirit, and the ability to share knowledge. The firms demonstrated an understanding and connection that extended beyond a mere working agreement to collaborate. All of these outcomes were successfully achieved.

A key objective for Meridian was the ability to interact with stakeholders. This was achieved through the partnership. Meridian also has clear procedures in place to assess the uptake of special events designed within the scope of the partnership, and conducts regular reputation surveys with stakeholders. In their view, the relationship has also been a success. They have done lots of things together. Meridian is basically engineers and RNZB is basically ballet dancers. One would have thought that the two would not mix, but when Meridian asked RNZB to send a troupe and do a little production in a town called Twizel, where they controlled their hydro-dams and the community had built a community centre, RNZB delivered a benefit to a community and also got to understand Meridian's business a lot more.

Example 3—DHL—Surf Life Saving New Zealand

The participants in this partnership are a leading international courier company and the foremost water safety organization in New Zealand. This partnership was formed in 2003 between DHL, owned by Deutsche Post World Net, an international business specializing in the rapid delivery of documents and products by air, and Surf Life Saving New Zealand (SLSNZ), a national surf lifesaving association, providing surf lifesaving services to New Zealand communities. In New Zealand, DHL has been in operation since 1973 and employs more than 500 people. The company cites its attention to the individual needs of customers and its ability to work as partners in creating a competitive edge as key reasons for its growth.

From DHL's perspective, the relationship provided an opportunity to make a connection with a broader target audience, the general public, and the media. This was a clear aim that was recognized by both partners: 'we wanted something that would make us seem to be a local company, keep us in touch with our local audiences and with the community, so as not to become this big global company that only looks after certain [large] customers.'

According to SLSNZ:, 'DHL were looking to establish their new corporate brand around the values that they support. So, they were looking for the whole concept of safety, security, and of convincing people of their security. So swimming between the flags gives us that ... you are safe if you swim between the flags. In terms of handling over the property, your goods to us, it is quite similar.. so their corporate values were the important thing they wanted to achieve, but also they were trying to give their brands a bit of a jump start.'

DHL's investment enabled SLSNZ to consistently brand all its clubhouses and to update its facilities and equipment. In addition, the agreement provided for a reasonable level of funding towards the beach education programme launched as a result of this social partnership. This programme works with approximately 450 schools nationwide, each year. DHL also uses the programme to communicate internally with employees' children. Joint advertising efforts on radio, television, and billboards are also a key aspect of the partnership. The level of collaboration has evolved to a point where both organizations have a degree of representation at the key events of each organization, which provides additional opportunities for communicating with stakeholders. Opportunities to showcase the partner brand are passed on freely.

There is evidence to suggest that the public perception of both brands is high, and that the relationship has not been detrimental to either. Since the partnership began, an unexpected bonus has come to DHL in the form of a reality television programme called 'Piha Rescue'. Television New Zealand (the major state-funded television network) has now produced over six seasons of the programme about Piha, the busiest surf beach in New Zealand. Further, the long-term nature of the partnership indicates that it is intended as a strategic contribution to the development of both organizations.

Learnings from the Examples

These examples offer certain interesting learnings about the perception of CSR in New Zealand. We have identified some key findings from the data on these New Zealand collaborations.

First, social partnerships between business and NPOs in New Zealand demonstrate that such collaborations have added value in terms of resources, but more importantly, benefit various stakeholders truly contributing to the CSR efforts of the business. While the business partners made references to CSR and 'license to operate' as some of the major reasons for their involvement in social partnership, NPOs in New Zealand, on the other hand, referred to the need to extend their resource base in order to tackle new challenges (Eweje and

Palakshappa 2009). Thus, NPOs have welcomed corporate involvement as a source of additional funding.

Second, evidence from New Zealand reveals that business participation is seen to increase efficiency and introduce new sources of finance, helping to provide a better solution to pressing social problems. Companies enter into collaboration in the hope of improving societal perception of their activities and legitimacy to operate as well as accessing resources, skills, or markets.

The existence of social partnerships connecting business and NPOs was seen as essential to increasing social benefits, while providing a source of competitive advantage for the businesses concerned. These partnerships bring new skills and human resources to NPOs and, thereby, strengthen them by ensuring services are more efficient and effective (Jørgensen 2006). For example, the relationship between BP and SLSNZ (enduring over 40 years), and DHL and SLSNZ, have made it possible for SLSNZ to continue to provide health and safety duties in all New Zealand beaches. It has also enabled the organization to purchase the necessary equipment needed for their operation as well as continue to train their staff and volunteers, as well as visiting schools to teach water/beach health and safety issues.

Third, Wood and Gray (1991) have argued that successful outcomes of collaborations include finding solutions to problems, learning from partners, distributing risks, a greater level of collective understanding, greater efficiency, and organizational survival.

Fourth, the examples demonstrate that partners entering collaborations intend to retain organizational autonomy while joining forces to tackle a shared social problem (Selsky and Parker 2005). In the collaborations outlined, partners find a 'strategic fit' between their organizations to use skills and resources available between them and work for community projects initiated in the collaboration without affecting their distinct identity, primary function, and crowding out each other.

Finally, we repeatedly found phrases such as 'they trust us', 'we trust them', 'they trust our judgement', 'we cannot have this relationship without trust' being used. Hence, we sense that trust is at the heart of a successful social partnership; without it, the partnerships cannot function and key projects/initiatives cannot be executed. Trust appears to be a key aspect of the structural relationship between two social entities (Bachman 2001; Das and Teng 2001).

Findings from the Examples

Thus, it appears that the drive for legitimacy appears a motivator for many businesses to 'focus on contributing back into the community' (as is the case with the collaborations we studied), and be involved in the development of a socio-economically 'underdeveloped' region (i.e., Genesis and HEET). There is also interaction with key stakeholders to ensure the 'organization is just and worth of support' (i.e., DHL and SLSNZ). Indeed, businesses strive to be considered 'meaningful predictable, and trustworthy'. Further, they want to 'localize' and create a meaningful local community perception. For example, they all agreed that having relationships with NPOs gives them visibility in the locations in which they operate.

It could be argued that business partners enter into these relationships to achieve more focused results to truly make a difference in terms of CSR; businesses are reaching into the community through their relationships with NPOs to form a significant and enduring relationship. The businesses mentioned above are clearly sensitive to their stakeholders and believe that having social relationships with NPOs improved their image and gave exposure to the social activities of their companies. Managers are increasingly aware of the role their businesses play in the wider social community. Accordingly, they are forming social partnerships with NPOs in order to reach out to society and demonstrate their social responsibility and legitimacy to operate. Social partnership in New Zealand is seen as an integral part of corporate strategy and companies' social responsibility to society. Based on the cases outlined, it appears that CSR is employed as a significant strategy when corporations in New Zealand partner with NPOs. Thus, we conclude that business enters into this relationship to improve societal perception of their activities and acquire legitimacy to operate as well as for accessing resources, skills, and markets.*

CONCLUSION

The brief backgrounds of the multinational companies and the four countries given as examples clearly indicate that there is no global standardization as yet of CSR practices. Though it is universally accepted that sustainability is a major concern, with the extraordinary growth that has happened in every sphere, there is no one solution to the concerns. This is because CSR goes beyond just compliance to rules and codes and includes moral values as well. The descriptions of countries show that even in developed countries, the involvement of the leaders in management is crucial for the success of CSR.

The challenges of developed countries like the US and UK are to manage the free market economy to ensure fair distribution of wealth in an economy. Creating a balance between government control and freedom to pursue a market economy is the biggest challenge. In developing countries like Indonesia, the challenge is at the level of eradicating poverty and providing the basic necessities

---

* The country profile of New Zealand is courtesy Dr Nitha Palakshappa and Dr Gabriel Eweje.

to the deprived masses. There is still a lack of awareness and sensitivity to CSR practices. Among the countries showcased in the chapter, New Zealand ranks extremely high on parameters of ethics and honesty and it is not surprising that it gets reflected in the effort of the corporate world to contribute to society. This shows how important it is to promote values, along with skills at the education level as well in a country. However, there is also a need for constant vigil to ensure that greed and profiteering does not take over.

Thus, we can conclude that there is an urgent need to increase awareness of CSR and enforcement of rules to build trust among all stakeholders of business. The deteriorating political and social values need to be arrested. A conscious effort has to be made by all the process owners like the government, corporate, social institutions, academia, and the media to create a receptive environment. The short-term focus of individuals and organizations need to change to include long-term sustainable and viable processes. There should be a multi-disciplinary approach to teach, train, and practice CSR.

SUMMARY

The global flavour captured by the practices of multinational corporations and four countries from different continents and at different levels of socio-economic levels provides a clear indication of the need to push CSR concept and practice with commitment. Though each country faces its own challenges, there has to be a global consensus to help each other to promote well-being and not take advantage of the weaknesses of countries. The immediate answer has to offer both a global and a local viewpoint to CSR processes and practices.

KEY TERMS

Demagogue Political agitator who appeals to the basest instincts of the mob.
Economies of scale Cost advantages that a business obtains by expanding the size of facilities and usage increase of other inputs.
Economies of scope The total cost of production decreases as a result of increasing the number of differentiated goods produced.
Horizontal combination Merging with competitors in the same market.
Infrastructure Basic physical and organizational structures needed for the operation of a society or enterprise.
Institutional investors Investments made by institutions, e.g., banks.
Multinational or transnational companies Companies that have operations in countries outside their home country.
Railroad The railway network.

Trading companies Companies that obtain permission to trade with other countries to earn profit or companies that do not produce goods but earn profit by trading the goods.

Vertical integration Obtain suppliers and/or distributors.

EXERCISES

Concept Review Questions

1. Why is it necessary to understand the global perspective of CSR?
2. Briefly trace the history of CSR in a developed and a developing country and compare them.
3. Do you think in practising CSR, multinational corporations face a bigger challenge than domestic corporations?

Critical Thinking Questions

1. How does economic development impact CSR activities in a country?
2. Create a multi-dimensional approach that would create the appropriate environment for CSR practices.
3. According to you, why are managers in New Zealand more receptive to CSR issues?

Research Question

Why was UK one of the first countries to introduce codes promoting CSR?

Project Question

Choose any oil-exploring or mining company and trace the CSR record of the company.

REFERENCES

Aditjondro, G. (2001), 'Suharto's fires', *Inside Indonesia*, No. 65, January–March, pp. 14–15.

Adnan, M. and R. Goodfellow (1997), in R. Goodfellow, *Indonesian Business Culture—An Insiders Guide*, Reed Academic Publishing Asia, p. 57.

Aguilera, V. Ruth, Cynthia A. Williams, John M. Conley and Deborah E. Rupp (2006), 'Corporate Governance and Social Responsibility—A comparative analysis of the UK and the US', *Corporate Governance Journal*, vol. 14, issue no. 3, p. 147–158.

Armour, J., S. Deakin, and S. Konzelmann (2003), 'Shareholder Primacy and the Trajectory of UK Corporate Governance', *British Journal of Industrial Relations*, 41 (3) pp. 531–555.

Atkinson, J. (2001) 'Mind thy neighbor', and 'Get your act together Aussie!' *Inside Indonesia*, No. 65, January–March, pp. 4–7.

Bachman, R. (2001), 'Trust, power, and control in trans–organisational relations', *Organisation Studies*, vol. 22, issue no. 2, pp. 337–365.

Bansal, P. and K. Roth (2000), 'Why Companies Go Green—A Model of Ecological Responsiveness', *Academy of Management Journal*, vol. 43, issue no. 4, pp. 717–736.

Barber, C.V. (1997), 'The Case Study of Indonesia, (summary)', *World Resources Institute*, www.library.utoronto.ca/pcs/state/indon.indonsum.html.

Berger, I., P. Cunningham, and M. Drumwright (2004), 'Social alliances—Company/nonprofit collaboration', *California Management Review*, vol. 47, issue no. 1, pp. 58–90.

Blockson, L.C. (2003), 'Multisector approaches to societal issues management', *Business and Society*, vol. 42, issue no. 3, pp. 381–390.

Chandler, D. Alfred Jr. (1977), 'The Visible Hand—The Managerial Revolution in American Business', Belknap Press/Harvard University Press, Cambridge, p. 223.

Collins, E., S. Lawrence, K. Pavlovich, and C. Ryan (2007), 'Business networks and the uptake of sustainability practices—The case of New Zealand', *Journal of Cleaner Production*, vol. 15, issue nos 8–9, pp. 729–40.

Cribb, R. (1994), in Carol Warren and Kylie Elston, *Environmental Regulation in Indonesia*, University of WA Press, Perth.

Das, T.K. and B.S. Teng (2001), 'Trust, control, and risk in strategic alliances—An integrated framework', *Organisation Studies*, vol. 22, issue no. 2, pp. 251–283, 2001.

Eddington, R. (2000), 'Corporate Social Responsibility—Current and Emerging Trends, Briefing Paper No. 21', Corporate Responsibility Series, *E3 Consulting*, Brisbane.

Eweje, G. (2007), 'Strategic partnerships between MNEs and civil society—The post WSSD perspectives', *Sustainable Development Journal*, vol. 15, issue no. 1, pp. 15–27, 2007.

Eweje, G. and N. Palakshappa (2009), 'Business partnerships with nonprofits—Working to solve mutual problems in New Zealand', *Corporate Social Responsibility and Environmental Management Journal*, vol. 16, issue no. 6, pp. 337–351.

Faulkner, George (1995), *Business Indonesia*, Business and Professional Publishing, Sydney, p. 9.

Hill, H. (1996), *The Indonesian Economy Since 1986—South East Asia's Emerging Giant*, Cambridge University Press, Cambridge.

Hillman, A.J. and G. Keim (2001), 'Shareholder value, stakeholder management, and social issues—What's the bottom line', *Strategic Management Journal*, 125–139.

Ishiwitari, M. (1998), *Behind the Words of Just Do It, Japan's Nike Boom Contributes to Violations of Indonesian Workers Rights*, ICCR, Vienna.

Jørgensen, M. (2006), 'Evaluating cross-sector partnerships', Working paper presented at the conference on *Public–private partnerships in the post WSSD context*, Copenhagen Business School, Denmark.

Kuniyo, Y. (1987), *The Rise of Ersatz Capitalism in SE Asia*, Curzon Press, Manila.

Lawrence, S.R., E. Collins, K. Pavlovich, and M. Arunachalam (2006), 'Sustainability practices of SMEs—The case of New Zealand', *Business Strategy and the Environment*, vol. 15, issue no. 4, pp. 242–57.

McLeod, R. (2000), 'Soeharto's Indonesia—A better class of corruption', *The Indonesian Quarterly*, vol. XXVIII, issue no. 1, First Quarter pp. 16–27.

Reiley, J. (2001), 'Kalimantans disaster', *Inside Indonesia*, No. 65, January–March 2001, pp. 12–13.

Roper, J. (2004), 'Corporate responsibility in New Zealand', *Journal of Corporate Citizenship*, vol. 14, pp. 22–25.

Rossouw, G. (1998), 'Establishing moral business culture in newly formed democracies', *Journal of Business Ethics*, vol. 17, issue no. 14, pp. 1563–1571.

Sagawa, S. (2001), 'New value partnerships—The lessons of Denny's/Save the children partnership for building high-yielding cross-sector alliances', *International Journal of Voluntary Sector Marketing*, vol. 6, issue no. 3, pp. 199–214.

Sagawa, S. and E. Segal (2000), 'Common interest, common good—Creating value through business and social sector partnerships', *California Management Review*, vol. 42, issue no. 2, pp. 105–122.

Sawarjuno, T. (1997), 'The Chinese Indonesians and Business', in Goodfellow, op. cit., p. 77.

Schimidheiny, S. (1992), *Changing Course—A Global Business Perspective on Development and the Environment*, MIT Press, Cambridge, Massachusetts.

Selsky, J.W. and B. Parker (2005), 'Cross-sector partnerships to address social issues—Challenges to theory and practice', *Journal of Management*, vol. 31, issue no. 6, pp. 849–73.

Solomon, A., J. Solomon, and M. Suto (2004), 'Can the UK Experience Provide Lessons for the Evolution of SRI in Japan?' *Corporate Governance—An International Review*, vol. 12, issue no. 4, pp. 552–566.

Steurer, R., M.E. Langer, A. Konrad, and A. Martinuzzi (2005), 'Corporations, Stakeholders and Sustainable Development 1—A Theoretical Exploration of Business–Society Relations', *Journal of Business Ethics*, vol. 61, issue no. 3, pp. 263–81.

Suziani (1999), *Kasus Nike di Indonesia—Meneropong Kondisi Kerja Buruh Perusahaan Sepatu Olahraga*, published by Yakoma–PGI and the Indonesian Sports Shoe Monitoring Network, (ISMN) p. 3.

Warhurst, A. (undated), 'Corporate Social Responsibility and the Mining Industry, a presentation to the Euromines Conference', Brussels, http://www.mineralresourcesforum.org/docs/pdfs/merncsr.pdf, accessed 10 August 2010.

Wibisono, C. (1991), *Proceedings of an International Seminar on Issues of Development*, Institute Teknologi Bandung and Goethe Institute, Bandung, 20–22 August.

Williams, C. (2004), 'Civil Society Initiatives and 'Soft Law' in the Oil and Gas Industry', *New York University Journal of International Law and Politics*, vol. 36, pp. 457–502.

Williams, C. and J. Conley (2005), 'An Emerging Third Way? The Erosion of the Anglo–American Shareholder Value Construct', *Cornell International Law Journal*, vol. 38, issue no. 2, pp. 493–551.

Wood, D.J., and B. Gray (1991), 'Towards a comprehensive theory of collaboration', *Journal of Applied Behavioural Science*, vol. 27, issue no. 2, pp. 139–162.

Yoon, Hwan Shin (1989), 'Demystifying the Capitalist State—Political Patronage Bureaucratic Interests and Capitalists in Formation in Soeharto's Indonesia', unpublished PhD Thesis, Yale University, New Haven, Connecticut.

CASE STUDY

SUZLON FOUNDATION

This case study is courtesy Mr R. Ravikularaman of Suzlon CSR team. Case inputs have been prepared by Mr Bidish Chatterjee, student of IFIM Business School, Bangalore.

Introduction and Approach

Suzlon is a leading wind power company spread across America, Australia, Europe, Denmark, Netherlands, and India. Headquartered in Pune, it has several manufacturing sites in India as well as in mainland China, Germany, and Belgium. Together with its subsidiary REpower, Suzlon has grown to be the third largest wind turbine supplier in the world and is the largest wind turbine manufacturer in Asia. The company is listed on the National Stock Exchange of India and on the Bombay Stock Exchange.

The vision of the Suzlon Group of Companies is Engage Empower Sustain. They assume that a business and its environment are interdependent, and focus on strengthening the intrinsic and organic link between them. At Suzlon, CSR is not merely charity and philanthropy. Its CSR framework is strategically designed to strengthen all the resources around business environment—financial, natural, social, human, and physical—in order to achieve a higher degree of sustainability in business by balancing growth in all aspects of development. Its CSR mission statement is aligned with its vision of Powering a Greener Tomorrow.

At Suzlon, CSR encompasses corporate values with the goals of

- Having minimal impact on the natural environment
- Enabling local communities to develop their potential and empowering them to deal with livelihood, health, civic amenities, and education issues
- Empowering employees to ensure their own safety and be responsible civil society members
- Committing to ethical business practices that are fair to all the stakeholders and in empowering them to make informed choices that integrate business imperatives with development objectives

CSR is thus helping to boost the economy in an extremely responsible manner.

Strategy and Structure

Suzlon established an independent organization called Suzlon Foundation to lead CSR initiatives across all functional domains. The clear mandate of the foundation is to take care of the community and environment by considering them as important stakeholders of the company, to ensure that these are not negatively impacted, and to contribute towards their sustainability wherever possible. The foundation has a multi-disciplinary team, which facilitates identification of key stakeholders and the impacts of business on them, and evolves interventions to minimize negative impact and optimize positive impacts. The council selects projects and implementing partners towards this goal of collectively contributing towards creating a better world for all. The foundation team monitors the project outcomes and continually gives feedback to business units. A democratic and transparent system is developed to facilitate CSR decision-making and reporting.

Suzlon Foundation plans to work wherever Suzlon Energy Limited has its operations. In each business unit location—be it a manufacturing unit or wind park—a CSR council is constituted to govern the CSR processes. To begin with, the foundation worked only in India but has now initiated the process in Australia, China, and the US. In the next five years, it will reach out to almost all the countries where Suzlon operates.

Programmes
CSR programmes initiated by the foundation fall under three broad categories: transformative, responsive, and proactive CSR.

Transformative programmes work towards preparing Suzlon employees (internal environment) to be responsible members of the civil society. This includes reviewing business policies from a sustainable perspective and integrating CSR along the supply chain and its management.

Responsive programmes address the impact of the business on communities, their culture, ecology, economy, and infrastructure of the regions they occupy. These programmes focus on areas such as livelihood, education, health, and the provision of civic amenities among others.

Proactive programmes focus on combating national and international issues such as climate change and global warming. For a responsible energy major, it is imperative that the unprecedented global natural resource crunch be recognized and therein the cause of renewable energy globally be championed.

Collaborations and Partnerships
Suzlon Foundation supports partners who come forward to provide resources and execute strategies with maximum impact. After a stringent selection process, partnerships are chosen based on the alignment to the foundation's mission, vision, and relevance based on programme objectives. Partners are selected based on the work they conduct in the particular region and the bandwidth they can provide there.

Suzlon Foundation has been associated with several reputed organizations, such as Chaitanya, Isha Foundation, Grameen Vikas Trust, CONCEPT Society, Ekoventure, Project Concern International, Nehru Yuva Kendra Sangathan, Centre for Environment Education (CEE), government departments of health, animal husbandry, education, forestry, and agriculture.

Some key initiatives and noteworthy outcomes have been highlighted vindicating the growing consensus that sustainable business and CSR are inextricably linked. These initiatives include

- Over 3000 hectares of land treated with conservation measures such as rainwater harvesting, tree plantation, grazing lands development

- Over 50,000 families receive livelihood support, most of whom are from disadvantaged groups like women living with HIV/AIDS, pastoralists, landless, women-headed families, traditional artisans, etc.
- Over 20,000 women organized in self-help groups who feel empowered to participate in various decision-making forums like village development committees and gram panchayats
- Over the last three years, Suzlon Foundation has engaged over 50 partners in 8 states and 2 union territories, in over 400 villages through more than 100 land development initiatives

Two specific CSR project details are given below to demonstrate the commitment of the Suzlon team to the community at large. The long-term vision of the organization is illustrated in their efforts to promote sustainable and value-added growth.

Upgradation of the Quality of Education in Anandshala, Gujarat
Goals
- Initiate the process of upgradation of the quality of education imparted in schools
- Develop a demonstrative model of Anandshala in order to co-relate formal education with life-skill activities
- Strengthen the existing educational institutions in the region
- Enhance relations among institutes, individuals, and other stakeholders for future development

Anandshala project in Gujarat aspires to upgrade the quality of education. This is a replication of a successful model implemented in some other districts of Gujarat. Suzlon Infrastructure Limited is partnering with Suzlon Foundation and CEE for this initiative. CEE has established a network among institutes, students, and other stakeholders to impart quality education in 11 selected government schools. It has involved villagers in the initiative by conducting participatory rural appraisals in all the villages of these schools. Students of these schools are benefiting from this project by accessing quality education.

Rural Electrification through Solar Lanterns in Rajasthan and Madhya Pradesh
Goals
- Distribute solar lanterns to attend to the need of lighting in the rural areas of Rajasthan and Madhya Pradesh
- Build a better rapport with the villagers in order to collectively plan a way forward for village development

Lighting was the prime need in the potential development of the people in Jaisalmer. Suzlon Foundation initiated solar lanterns at Jaisalmer and Jodhpur districts to accomplish this need. This has increased the scope of activities that can now take place later in the evenings due to the availability of light in the area. Working potential of people has increased due to the use solar lanterns. Students can study in the evenings with the availability of adequate light. Travelling at night for the villagers is a lot safer. Suzlon Foundation teams in Rajasthan and Madhya Pradesh are independently handling this project. Currently, the foundation has implemented the pilot phase of the project and has distributed 123 solar lanterns in Rajasthan and 212 solar lanterns in Palsodi, Madhya Pradesh. It is looking at more number of lanterns to be distributed in the coming year.

Discussion Questions
1. Discuss the CSR strategy and structure followed at the Suzlon Foundation and analyse whether the strategy facilitates sustainable business.
2. What are the three broad categories of CSR programmes followed at the Suzlon Foundation?
3. 'CSR is merely philanthropy'. Discuss in the context of the Suzlon case study.

The Road Ahead

INTRODUCTION

Having looked at the various aspects of CSR, it becomes amply clear that CSR has been around in various forms since ancient times, depending on one's view of history. The eight goals proposed by the United Nations Millennium Declaration clearly indicate the need to add a social dimension to the business activities of corporates. Today, it has achieved the status of being recognized as a profession with corporates hiring CSR managers and every country debating various methods of finding the best fit. It is being discussed on the world stage in every forum that is looking at sustainable development. Human rights, dealing with freedom and corresponding responsibilities, are a matrix of self-interest and needs (see Chapter 3).

Figure 10.1 is a simplified explanation of the stages of human existence. First is the freedom to survive by selfishly utilizing limited resources available to an individual. Secondly, as wants and needs increase, self-interest makes individuals search for security, so that they can exist peacefully. This peaceful existence cannot last long if individuals take care of only their self-interest. Therefore, in the third stage, one has to learn to behave more responsibly towards other people's wants and needs by creating a culture of sharing (learning to be selfless) by promoting values and the concept of human rights. Therefore, to understand the behaviour of a nation, of a group, or an individual, and their stand and attitude on social and cultural values, the study of the historical background of CSR becomes imperative. The dynamics of the modern business world is trying to constantly understand the human journey (as depicted in Fig. 10.1).

With the advance in globalization and technology, good and bad happenings are impacting everyone, as specialization has created an interdependent world. Today, nothing is limited by distances or geographical proximity. The socio-economic fallout of issues like HIV AIDS, recession, BP oil spill, Enron or Satyam frauds have created an urgent need to review responsibility of all the

LEARNING OBJECTIVES

After studying this chapter, you will be able to
- Understand how CSR will evolve in the future
- Analyse the importance of shared growth through different models
- Understand that CSR has to be integrated in the business process for sustainable development

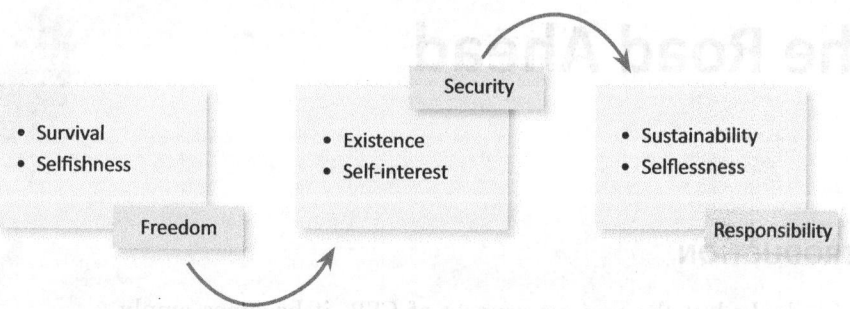

Figure 10.1 The journey of human rights

stakeholders of business. Two research examples, given below, show that CSR is becoming important in the business world.

The European Council that met in Lisbon in 2000 made a formal proposal for stimulating CSR across European firms. This proposal stated best practices for lifelong learning, work organization, equal opportunities, social inclusion, and sustainable development. This European orientation is based on a long-term strategic objective, which is, 'to become the most competitive and dynamic knowledge-based economy in the world capable of maintaining sustainable economic growth with more and better jobs and greater social cohesion' (Lisbon European Council 2000, p. 2). The European Commission also recognized in their final report that 'much progress has been made on CSR since the stimulating proposal presented at the Lisbon Council' (European Commission Report 2006, p. 6).

Lane (2004) published the results of his study on socially responsible investing (SRI). Unlike other studies that employ a negative process of excluding investments from a portfolio of certain socially or environmentally undesirable industries (tobacco, alcohol, gambling, defence, chemicals, mining, timber, and energy), this study followed an approach of positive screening for certain desirable behaviours. The behaviours ranked were in the areas of environmental practices and social justice (including diversity/employee relations, and human rights). A definite positive correlation was established between share value and market perception of the ethical conduct of public corporations. This perception is not only based on the honesty of leaders, but also on the company's overall social responsibility.

CSR has been elevated to the international arena but every stakeholder is aware of the need to keep the local aspect alive for true integration and implementation of CSR. The possible ways of achieving this symbiosis between the global and local paradigms requires us to understand the modern business world.

EXHIBIT 10.1

Eight Goals Proposed by the United Nations Millennium Declaration

In September 2000, 189 nations signed the United Nations Millennium Declaration, committing to halving the number of people in the world who live on less than one US dollar a day by 2015. The eight Millennium Development Goals (MDGs) provide a framework for achieving this aim, and set out time-bound targets by which progress can be measured. These goals are given below.

Goal 1 Eradicate extreme poverty and hunger

Latest estimates from the World Bank show that 1.4 billion people in developing countries were living in extreme poverty in 2005. Recent increases in food prices are expected to push a further 100 million people into extreme poverty. After financial aid, the greatest impact towards this goal will come from support focused on helping people in developing nations to generate sustainable income, especially women and young people, protect themselves from the effects of economic and climate fluctuations, and access safe water and nutrition, especially in Southern Asia and Africa.

Goal 2 Achieve universal primary education

Education is the foundation for economic development. By receiving a good basic education, children will have a stronger chance of earning a decent income in the future and positively contributing to their community. While much progress has been made towards this goal, there are still tens of millions of children who do not go to school on a regular basis, the majority of whom are girls, and those living in rural areas.

Goal 3 Promote gender equality and empower women

Enabling women to generate income on a level equal with their male counterparts will have a significant impact on world poverty. While in many areas women have greater access to education and income-generating activities than ever before, specific issues prevent them from achieving parity with men. The gender gap remains wide in many countries, most notably in Southern Asia and sub-Saharan Africa.

Goal 4 Reduce child mortality

While worldwide deaths of children under five years of age have declined between 1990 and 2006, there is still much to be done in developing countries, where a child is 13 times more likely to die before its fifth birthday than a child born in an industrialized country. Most of these young deaths are from entirely preventable causes such as pneumonia, diarrhoea, malaria, and measles, largely as a result of malnutrition, lack of primary health care, and lack of access to basic infrastructure such as water and sanitation.

Goal 5 Improve maternal health

Every minute a woman dies of complications related to pregnancy and childbirth, according to 2005 estimates. Almost all of these women are from developing countries. The children these women leave behind are up to 10 times more likely to die prematurely than those whose mothers survive childbirth. The majority of these deaths are preventable. Giving women access to better nutrition, sanitation, protection from violence, contraceptives and sex education, and maternal health care would save millions of lives.

Goal 6   Combat HIV/AIDS, malaria, and other diseases
These diseases continue to claim the lives of millions of people in the developing world, particularly in sub-Saharan Africa. Most of these deaths can be prevented through increased aid, better nutrition, access to basic healthcare and health education, and vaccination, and control interventions.

Goal 7   Ensure environmental sustainability
As well as giving vulnerable regions the support needed to protect themselves against the effects of climate change, it is vital that the root cause is tackled by promoting environmental sustainability. Achieving this goal will also require developing countries to cultivate and strengthen their economies, diversify the income of their population, strengthen their natural defences, and become better prepared for future disasters.

Goal 8   Develop a global partnership for development
To achieve global enhancement, emerging economies need financial aid and access to the technology and knowledge required to develop and grow adequately. Doing so will enable them to invest in the basic infrastructure and systems people in these regions need, particularly in healthcare and education, and to put in place effective policies for social and economic development.

Source: http://www.undp.org/mdg/, www.community.nestle.com.

DYNAMICS OF THE MODERN BUSINESS WORLD

With the growth in science and technology, there has been tremendous growth in both human well-being as well as human exploitation. As business has grown, it has continued to use the resources to produce goods and services to fulfill personal and societal wants by creating a market for sharing products and services at a price. The significant impact of the business world is visible in every sphere of life, especially in a market-oriented economic structure. The corporate sector is the prime mover of economic growth. Market borders are blurring, and acquisitions, mergers, and alliances are obscuring the nationality of companies and of the people living in this plural social environment. Such companies are throwing up big challenges, both internally and externally.

Internally, different levels of managers have to be empowered to take multiple decisions on resource allocation, production processes, human resource management, and on marketing strategies across products and services, and across countries. This obviously creates a big challenge to set up the right channel for an information flow that would decrease information loss if the correct decision needs to be taken. With the rise in competition between firms, there is always a time constraint that needs to be kept in mind to take the right decisions because the firm that reaches the market quicker than the others has the advantages of being the first provider of goods and services to the customers to reap in the highest profits before similar products and services enter the market and reduce profits. There is a constant pressure from shareholders, who are keener to earn money in a short duration of the company's operation. Thus, very often, there can be decisions that are taken without proper understanding and analysis of the risk involved in a situation.

Externally, the firm has to create and sustain various relationships with the ever-growing number of stakeholders, each of whom demands his or her share of benefits from the business. The level of awareness among stakeholders is increasing as more information is available within their reach. The awakened stakeholder puts pressure on the organization to deliver with responsibility. This leads to the question of CSR. The moral and ethical dimensions of business become central with rising public expectation, a constant demand for innovation in quality of products and delivery, and increasing social and environment concerns resulting from business processes. This dynamic and complex business environment requires an in-depth study of how to chart the future course of CSR by looking at optimistic and pessimistic views on the subject.

Optimistic View of CSR

- It would become imperative for companies to come forward and share the responsibilities for distributive justice and inclusive growth.
- The crisis of trust in modern industrial capitalism would drive industries towards creating a better branding in society by defining the role business should play in society.
- Industrial crises would vindicate (prove correct) that the only guarantee against such exploitative behaviour is the practice of CSR. However, different levels and framework of CSR would evolve to cater to the unique local needs of the region where the firm would be operating.
- Businesses would increasingly realize the advantages of promoting CSR for their own long-term existence.
- A favourable environment would come into force, which would create more openness towards the concept and practice of CSR.
- With the increase of knowledge workers in society, the acceptance of CSR would increase. The value of intangible assets like trust, loyalty, and honesty would increase.

- The change would happen at a slow pace, as sweeping changes cannot be sustained by the economy, since dismantling earlier processes would require time.
- CSR ideas and tools would become more aligned to business and CSR would get integrated into the strategy of the companies.

Pessimistic View of CSR

- CSR would continue to be used more as a public relations tool. Companies would use it as a façade to hide behind and to conceal their actual performance.
- CSR would not be used to address any real issues or as a change agent.
- Businesses would continue to argue that there is no consensus on the business case for CSR to be integrated in the strategy and therefore, it defeats its own purpose.
- The practice of CSR would become either government regulated or incentive dependent, and therefore, it would never achieve the inclusive growth that it is supposed to.
- Businesses would view CSR as an extra financial burden and therefore, find excuses for not adhering to it.
- Since aligning the interest of the different stakeholders of business is actually a myth, CSR would remain at the superficial level. This would lead to public disillusion and the movement would lose its glamour.
- The initial excitement of firms that would embrace CSR would get eroded when other firms around them would not be practising CSR.
- Thus, CSR would always remain at the periphery of business practice and never receive the importance of a core practice.

In spite of the difference in views about the social impact and the degree of corporate commitment, the majority viewpoint is that CSR is here to stay and would slowly evolve into a mainstream business practice. As mentioned earlier in the book, the integration of CSR would happen at different levels, moving from marginal commitment to compliance to norms and to the final level of integration in the strategy of an organization. To some extent, this continuum would follow the lifecycle of a firm from inception to maturity. The stakeholder model would be the most acceptable model of development in the economic sphere. Thus, a look at the future trends in CSR would help us to visualize the importance of this concept in the socio-economic development of a nation.

FUTURE TRENDS IN CSR

With increasing influence of industrialization and globalization, the business world is becoming more visible in society. Society is expecting that the professionals running industries would honour the trust that society reposes on them to make life more comfortable and improve the quality of existence. Therefore, efforts will continue to move beyond weak endorsements of CSR to in-depth understanding of how it affects corporate business practices. The dilemma of whether the business should cater to the interest of shareholders or all stakeholders will resolve itself as the gains from a stakeholder approach would become more tangible and measurable. In the present scenario, progress in the environment segment would be quicker than that the social segment because there is a general consensus about the environment degradation and an urgent need to rectify it. Besides, the impact of environment exploitation is impacting every country, big or small, developing or developed, and it is probably a little easier to achieve acceptance in this sphere than in the social sphere, as the unique history and culture of each nation plays a major role in social factors. For example, certain very sensitive issues related to the ethos of a community or religious beliefs would require patience and understanding, whereas if a nation is not economically advanced, then prioritization of CSR practices based on urgency and importance would be required. Thus, glocalization (see Chapter 9) would play an important role in implementing CSR in the social sector.

In keeping with the above observation, we find that sustainability reporting is emerging as a key component of CSR implementation, measurement, and reporting in organizations. Of course, there is a rising trend to broaden the scope of sustainability reporting to include socio-economic aspects, but still more needs to be achieved in this area. Many companies are now joining the international reporting initiatives and are either developing in-house or hiring specialized services to measure and report on sustainability.

With the increasing promotion and popularity of the stakeholder concept, there is a very conscious move among business entities to involve stakeholders more closely in business affairs. There is a proactive move to engage stakeholders in issues of mutual concern. A process of give and take is being established, based on shared dialogue. Very often, stakeholders are able to provide more innovative solutions to social issues, as they have better insight into their issues and concerns. Actually, this kind of participation would reduce the feeling of hurt when a business has to do a trade-off between the demands of various stakeholders, as decisions are more transparent and shared. Companies can reap the benefits of establishing trust of their brands among the future consumers by helping to increase the purchasing power of a community and creating a space in the minds of young consumers, who later would become loyal customers or what today is defined as 'brand junkies' (diehard fans of a brand) by marketing professionals. This kind of collaboration would create team efforts, which would result in more useful products and services with enhanced environmental and social properties.

Just as the collective bargaining power of employees is represented in the trade union movement and consumer grievances are addressed by consumer forums and courts, so also we may soon see the emergence of stakeholder councils and similar associations to voice their opinion at the decision-making level of an industry. This would require the development of specific tools and processes to resolve conflicts among the different demands that the growing number of stakeholders would put forth. During such happenings, a company may feel helpless, but the engagement of all stakeholders would show what is right and the practice of this right would become a part of the company's strategy. According to some critics, this kind of close association may reduce the effectiveness of stakeholder engagement as check and balance on the company activities. Therefore, a constant vigil must be kept.

The demand of the stakeholders for timely, comprehensive, and accurate information would become a right of the stakeholders and they would have to be treated fairly and honourably if the business community wants to earn their profits from the community. The spread of modern technology and information would become the strength of the future stakeholders as they would be able to gather more information, and disseminate the same among a larger audience much more effectively and quickly. Thus, the impact of their voice would be more far-reaching. This idea that CSR is related to the core business would lead companies to evaluate their own competencies more seriously. CSR would become the mandate of the entire organization. Therefore, the evaluation process would have to measure resource utilization, methodologies adopted, and short- and long-term impacts of a corporation. This will become a source of market research and risk reduction and will help to build a company's reputation and brand.

As technology continues to make the world conceptually smaller, the actions and decisions of leaders are becoming immediately available for evaluation. This increases the importance of an effective field of educational practice to develop the life-long learning of leaders. Similarly, the elements of social responsibility, access, and human rights have never been so closely aligned between education and business as they are today. The successful multinational company of the future will not only depend upon a level of knowledge development, skills, and education among their employees, but also on accepting cultural diversity and creating a homogeneous recognized set of social and human values. This latter factor is necessary to ensure the dedication and loyalty of the employee and consumer toward optimizing future innovation and success.

To sum up the future trends, the following factors would play a very major role:

- For the future world of business, CSR would lead to increasing focus on priorities. It will impact the nature of decision-making related to

- competition, the development of sustainability-related innovations, and the emergence of new, more successful, business models.
- CSR would emerge as a lucrative investment from which returns are expected. The return on investment (ROI) of CSR would become an important measure for business practices.
- To implement sustainability, optimizing available resources would require closer scrutiny. Therefore, not duplicating but strengthening and supplementing existing services would be the future trend. Sourcing activities will integrate environmental concerns more rigorously.
- There will be more involvement of various institutions like the government, NGOs, and the media in monitoring activities to ensure that initiatives really deliver the desired outcomes.
- CSR would become an important and inseparable part of corporate governance. Reporting performance in an open and transparent way, so that all members of a community can enjoy progress and identify areas for further action will be demanded from future corporations. Thus, new corporate governance structures to develop new models of economic sustainability would be used to deliver CSR. Pressure from a new breed of socially responsible stakeholders will increase the pressure on businesses to behave in an ethical way.
- Organizations have to design a long-term perspective, which encompasses their commitment to both internal and external stakeholders. This would have to reflect in a new emphasis on decent working conditions in a context of protecting human rights, safe and just supply chain rationalization, reduction in carbon footprint, better work–life balance of employees, and innovative methods of developing holistic growth patterns.
- There will be a new emphasis on social and community development initiatives. Contributing to poverty alleviation and poverty-related concerns like community health initiatives, hygiene, nutrition, and education will be seen as an important part of the wider agenda for business entities who will increasingly have to measure their community impacts.
- The role and status of CSR managers will be better recognized by the corporate world. The need is the development of and an increase in professional courses on CSR. Better quality education on CSR will help to increase the understanding and dissemination of what CSR is and the value of having a CSR function within the organization. A growth in certification and qualifications around CSR will help to enhance both the professionalism and the credibility of CSR managers.
- In a customer-driven economy, companies would have to reinvent themselves. CSR can help in the process by managing risks, help to avoid scandals, and help companies to gain a unique selling position.

- In short, the journey has begun and it is not a short-term bubble that would lose its attractiveness. In fact, with every passing day, CSR will receive higher prominence and would become mandatory for companies with a long-term vision of earning profit in a sustainable manner. CSR has become a global phenomenon that makes use of innovative approaches for solving social, environmental, and economic problems with the aim to increase the benefits for society, in general, and for the stakeholders of organizations, in particular.

The above factors clearly bring out the ideology of a shared growth. Human development has to take into account availability of equal opportunities for all. This would have to include the demands of all sections of society and the use of knowledge, skills, and expertise of the different sections to find solutions to the demands. Examples of two models of such shared growth are mentioned below: the stakeholder model and the private-public partnership (PPP) model.

THE AWAKENED STAKEHOLDER

If we look at the stakeholders of today, there is an agreement that sustainable growth is dependent on the satisfaction of this group. This is because the partnership that business and government created in a market economy became obsessive about pursuing shareholder value without any serious concern of the social, economic, and environmental impact. Increasingly, stakeholders are going to have a very significant influence in the market. Stakeholders are looking at their access to accurate information about companies as a right. There is a demand emerging from this group to be treated fairly and honourably. With growth in information technology, it is much easier now for stakeholders to participate in opinion building. One of the important stakeholders is the customer, or consumer, who will play a very significant role in the future development of CSR. However, it is interesting to note certain specific trends among the ethical consumers: it is still very nascent and does not reflect an even trend and usually fluctuates with the changes in the economy and corporate crises.

Consumers will be an important constraint on companies to behave in favour of society and community. The learned and aware consumer would question exploitative practices like environmental degradation, child labour, bribery, and corruption, and therefore firms would have to ensure that they avoid these if they want to remain as a brand among consumers.

It is evident that consumers would organize into groups to put pressure on the companies to integrate ethical practices in their day-to-day activities. It would be difficult for the mainstream consumer to participate in boycotts of goods but they will come forward to create consumer protection institutions.

Employees are the other group of stakeholders who can exert extreme pressure on companies to align their work to CSR practices. Today, employees are well-educated and can take independent decisions based on their value system and refuse to tread the path of unethical practices just because they are drawing a salary. It is the ethical employee who would help companies integrate CSR at the internal, intermediate, and outer levels. Those organizations where CSR practices would be integrated would attract the best talent in the market and create the brand of being the choice of every employee. The branding of an organization as a responsible citizen of society would, to a large extent, depend on the employee rating of the organization.

Socially responsible investment (SRI) will impact the future of CSR in a very positive manner. Stocks that can positively impact environment, labour conditions, and human rights would be the coveted stocks in the market. Shareholder action and pressure from institutional investors will have a significant impact in the future of CSR in the marketplace. There would be increase in the number of institutional investors whose target would be long-term earning at the cost of short-term gains from the market. CSR would be used as a differentiator between firms for investors to choose from. Following CSR practices would ensure that a company is compliant to rules and regulations prescribed both locally and internationally. CSR would ensure that social and environmental issues have been incorporated into business management processes. Increasingly, 'sustainability' or the long-term view will become an important component in the risk benefit analysis. The age-old practice of catering to shareholders would certainly not be the only guiding force in a business entity of the future. For more details on stakeholders and the stakeholder model, please refer to Chapter 3.

To facilitate the integration of CSR in the future of business, a commonly used model is the public-private partnership (PPP) model. It is believed that this would help to garner the strength of both the government and the private business sector to create long-term social and community welfare. This partnership would also help to take care of the major stakeholders in business.

THE PUBLIC-PRIVATE PARTNERSHIP

A PPP is a contractual agreement formed between public and private sector partners, which allow more private sector participation than is traditional. The agreements usually involve a government agency contracting with a private company to renovate, construct, operate, maintain, and/or manage a facility or system. While the public sector usually retains ownership in the facility or system, the private party will be given additional decision rights in determining how the project or task will be completed. The term 'public-private partnership' defines an expansive set of relationships from relatively simple contracts, e.g., A+B contracting, i.e., two parties coming together on mutual convenience, to development agreements that can be very complicated and technical, e.g., contract dealing with decisions regarding which partner will share the responsibility of the project's design, building, financing, operating, and maintaining. In the context of United States Department of Transportation Report to Congress on Public-Private Partnerships December 2004, the term 'public-private partnership' is used for any scenario under which the private sector would be more of a partner than they are under the traditional method of procurement. Further, this broad definition of PPPs includes many elements that are being utilized on a more routine basis (adapted from http://www.fhwa.dot.gov/reports/pppdec2004/).

Government of India's defines a PPP project as a project based on a contract or concession agreement, between a government or statutory entity on the one side and a private sector company on the other side, for delivering an infrastructure service on payment of user charges. A private sector company means a company in which 51 per cent or more of the subscribed and paid-up equity is owned and controlled by a private entity.

There is no universal standardized definition of the PPP model, but it usually relates to contractual agreement between the government or public sector and the private sector, based on sharing responsibility of financing, designing, implementing, and operating the infrastructural facilities that traditionally were in the domain of public sector responsibilities. The contract ensures a fair and mutually agreed sharing of resources, risks, and returns.

PPPs can generate substantial benefits by encouraging innovation and saving time and money on projects. This happens because there is a clear division of the role and responsibilities, based on the expertise of both the agencies. Government continues to own the onus for the quality of service, price certainty, and cost effectiveness. As the well-wisher of the citizens of a country, the government continues to be responsible and accountable for these mega projects and becomes the enabler and facilitator in the partnership. The private sector provides the necessary operational support by helping with the finance, designing, and building, as well as operating the service or facility.

Governments have to play a dual role: first, encouraging risk-averse and less experienced private players to improve and participate in nation-building activities, and second, ensuring that contracts are formalized after due diligence. Due diligence requires developing processes for soliciting participation, ensuring fair competition, and then allocating resources as well as risks. Often, such systems deter the private sector, which finds the government processes restrictive and limiting private sector flexibility. These tangible (actual money spent in developing a process) and intangible costs (creating an aversion to participate as a result of cumbersome processes) associated with developing a PPP can diminish the potential value PPPs can offer.

PPPs generally fall into one of the categories given below, based on the reasons for their creation. The key PPP categories are:

1. Partnerships designed to accelerate implementation of high-priority projects by seeking new ways.
2. Partnerships that turn to the private sector to provide specialized management capacity for large and complex programmes.
3. Partnerships focused on arrangements to facilitate the delivery of new technology in design, construction, and service delivery developed by private entities.
4. Partnerships that draw on the private sector expertise in accessing and organizing the financial resources.
5. Partnerships to allow and encourage private entrepreneurial development, ownership, and operation of infrastructural facilities.

Some partnership arrangements may involve several or all of these functions. Regardless of the specific functions involved, partnership arrangements are intended to provide greater flexibility.

Therefore, PPP is different from privatization. In privatization, there is an outright sale of government-owned services and facilities. In a PPP, even when the private sector has a high level of participation, the government will continue to play a role in granting permits, ensuring safety, verifying fulfilment of environmental requirements, or even exercising its power of eminent domain to obtain land for rights-of-way.*

The private partners in a PPP may include private company, a consortium, or a non-governmental organization. The PPP is operationalized through a contractual relationship between a public body (the conceding authority) and a private company (the concessionaire). This partnership could take many contractual forms, which progressively vary with increasing risk, responsibility, and financing for the private sector. However, the most common partnership options are (i) service contract, (ii) management contract/lease, (iii) build operate transfer (BOT), (iv) concession, (v) joint venture (JV), and (vi) community-based provision.**

* Adapted from Congressional Budget Office, *Innovative Financing of Highways: An Analysis of Proposals*, January 1998, p. 2, http://www.cbo.gov/showdoc.cfm?index=320& sequence=0. Also, National Council for Public Private Partnerships, AECOM CONSULT, and Parsons Brinckerhoff, Ltd. 'Partnerships in Transportation Workshops, Final Report' prepared at the request of the Federal Highway Administration, 17 March 2004, p. 2.

** Facilitating Public-Private Partnership for Accelerated Infrastructure Development in India Regional Workshops of Chief Secretaries on Public-Private Partnership Workshop Report, December 2006, Department of Economic Affairs (DEA), Ministry of Finance, Government of India, and Asian Development Bank (ADB).

The reasons for adopting the PPP model are almost similar in both the developed and developing countries. With rapid economic development, there is an increase in the trend of urbanization. There is a steady inflow of people from the rural sector to the urban sector, especially in developing countries. This has increased the pressure on the existing infrastructural facilities and increased the demand–supply gap in these developing countries. The developed world also needs to meet the constraints faced by the government in mobilizing financial and technical resources, as well as adding value by garnering innovations and cost-effective methods of the private sector.

The private sector brings in efficiency and effectiveness in the projects because the incentives to limit costs in the private sector are much higher. Since the private sector assumes the risk of non-performance of assets and realizes the returns if the assets perform, the PPP process involves a full-scale risk appraisal and that helps in streamlining the processes. In a PPP, the responsibility of implementation rests with one entity, which is not possible in a bidding method followed traditionally.

The possibility of innovative means of financing through better restructuring of finances, using borrowed funds, and by raising finance for high-priority public infrastructure projects reduces delays due to lack of funds, and using better project management methods help to achieve results quicker. Therefore, PPPs help reduce the time it takes to build a project. It has been observed that PPPs deliver better results in areas of quality, innovation, and environmental sustainability.

Despite the benefits of PPPs, there has been criticism from the civil society and the media. There has been a lack of trust in the private sector with public service. Complaints of tariff increases, increasing layoffs, and poor stakeholder management have contributed to these concerns. The detractors also accuse PPPs of high procurement costs, which deter small companies and curtail competition. They also point out that obstacles in the form of legal, financial, political, and cultural hurdles are often encountered in the formation of these partnerships. However, many PPP experts attribute the failure of some of these projects to hurried judgements made to favour vested interests. It is pointed out that non-competitive and non-transparent application of the PPP principles are often the cause of failure. Often, local-level resistance from the state government and local populace are also a cause for delay, if not failure.

CONCLUSION

As we come to the end of the book, it becomes evident that CSR is here to stay. Concerns about the environment, social exclusion—particularly poverty and access to bare necessities—and governance and accountability, including issues of transparency and integrity, would remain the urgent issues raised by CSR.

Historical evidence is crucial to exploring the causal relationship between social and economic symbiosis, which is at the core of CSR. A historical perspective in this would provide important lessons from the past to deliver and contribute in modern times. An understanding of the historical role of culture and values on CSR behaviour emphasizes the difference in perception of CSR by different individuals and organizations.

The understanding of the core values of CSR will create increased attention on issues of democracy and capitalism, both in the economy and in the political arena—locally, nationally, and globally. There was much interest in how corporate accountability and transparency will evolve over the next decade along with the related issues of corporate governance and integrity. The feeling that the private sector has not contributed enough to the social system and that there is a greater need for responsibility, accountability, and transparency will only increase.

The trend towards compliance and reporting on the global dimensions like the UN global compact, the UN Millennium Declaration, or the triple bottom line will be visible in the economic sphere worldwide. Innovative CSR tools and technique creation would be a challenge that the corporates would undertake to ensure better governance reporting.

The future of CSR appears extremely bright. There is already a trend in place to create more consensuses on preparing acceptable codes of CSR conduct. Consolidation of the various standards of measuring CSR would be undertaken at a global level. There will be clarity in distinguishing between actual and real CSR from pseudo and cosmetic CSR. The future generations would be able to follow CSR much more easily, as there would be standardizations of processes and practices. The evolution of CSR will continue to create better means of managing human existence. The standardization would be the starting point but there will always be flexibility and freedom that need to be available for organizations to create their unique programmes to address the specific CSR issues they would encounter in their journey of growth. History is witness to the fact that decay in socio-economic sphere has always been arrested by society and CSR is one such tool developed by society to answer the concerns on unsustainable behaviour.

SUMMARY

CSR is not a new concept but has received tremendous attention in the present century due to the unbridled growth of businesses that did not take into account the concern of sustainable development. On the one hand, such development has brought comfort to the common people and on the other, much deprivity to the 'un-included' sections of the people. There has been a constant search to create ways and means to rectify the situation. Some of the models used are the stakeholder model and the PPP model. The concept of CSR would continue to evolve as long as industry and business would continue to participate in the economic growth, nationally and globally.

KEY TERMS

Continuum Having a continuous structure.
Myth Widely held but false notion.
Optimistic A tendency to expect the best, or at least, a favourable outcome.
Pessimistic A general disposition to look on the dark side and to expect the worst in all things.
PPP model Public-private partnership based on a contract between the public and private sector in a country.
Socially responsible investing Any investment that is based on social, environmental, and ethical criteria, while maximizing financial performance.
Stakeholder model Relates to including any party that can affect or be affected by the actions of the business as a whole.
Urbanization A process in which an increasing proportion of an entire population lives in cities or suburbs of cities as a result of global change.

EXERCISES

Concept Review Questions
1. Give a brief description of the future trends in CSR.
2. Explain the PPP model with a few examples.

Critical Thinking Questions
1. If you were heading a business or company, would you implement CSR? Justify your answer.
2. Take any two PPP initiatives in India and analyse the reasons for their success or failure.

Research Question

Find out any new initiative that may be used to deliver CSR.

Project Question

Visit an NGO and see whether the modern trends of CSR are applicable.

REFERENCE

Lane, M.J. (2004), *Corporate Behavioral Screening—A New Perspective for Social Investors*, Marc J. Lane, Esq, Chicago, Illinois.

Web Resources

'Public-Private Partnerships—Terms Related to Building and Facility Partnerships' GAO/GDD–.

99–71, April 1999, http://www.gao.gov/special/pubs/Gg99071.pdf accessed 15 August 2010.

www.corostrandberg.com/pdfs/Future_of_CSR.pdf, accessed 15 August 2010.

www.in.kpmg.com/pdf/CSR_Whitepaper.pdf, accessed 15 August 2010.

CASE STUDY

THE CSR PRACTICES OF NESTLÉ

Nestlé is a renowned multinational that is involved in cross-border CSR activities. They have realized that poor diet and lack of opportunity have given rise to many of the societal issues that need to be addressed. Nestlé has taken the initiative to support the attainment of the millennium declaration goals by making safe and nutritious food products accessible to consumers in poor regions and by continuing their presence in rural and developing communities, providing important sources of investment, knowledge, and opportunity. Nestlé has developed a unique CSR programme called creating shared value (CSV), which is the perfect driver for CSR within the business as it ensures responsible operation and creation of sustainable value for shareholders, whilst simultaneously creating value for society. After analysis of the value chain, Nestlé has chosen areas of greatest potential both for their business and for society as nutrition, water, and rural development. These three focus areas are also incorporated into Nestlé's key performance indicators, placing them at the heart of the organization.

According to reports on the website each year, Nestlé spends approximately CHF 20.4 billion (Swiss francs) on agricultural raw materials. About half of their factories are in the developing world, primarily in rural areas. Thus, they provide the vital and sustainable sources of income to these deprived regions. About 540,000 farmers in total, approximately 5000 agricultural extension workers, and about

1000 agronomists are impacted by Nestlé's projects. The core practice of Nestlé has been to transfer technical knowledge combined with ability to operate in diverse and complex environments. This has enabled people in emerging economies to increase and protect their income, now and for the future. An area showcasing such exemplary work is the dairy sector.

Supporting dairy farmers

Nestlé is the world's largest dairy company. The company supports a number of farmers in the developing world by procuring 12 million tonnes of milk each year and injecting millions of US dollars into rural communities. Nestlé does not depend upon middlemen but utilizes its considerable experience and expertise to deal directly with farmers. They support farmers by helping them to improve the quality of their produce, the productivity of their herds, and the sustainability of their activities by giving them access to financial support and providing them with free technical advice and training. This business model helps in achieving multifarious benefits for Nestlé because it safeguards long-term supply of quality milk, improves the livelihoods of rural communities, protects the environment, and secures access to affordable nutritious food products for people in developing regions. This is a clear example of how their creating shared value concept creates important mutually beneficial situations that have lasting positive effects. Examples of effects of CSV in action in different countries are given below.

India

India has a very fragmented milk-supply chain and to manage this effectively, Nestlé Agricultural Services used experience gained in other parts of the world to establish a system of direct and efficient contact with farmers in Moga, Punjab. To make the system robust, the company employs veterinarians and agronomists to supervise milk routes and provide farmers with advice on various issues. This service is provided to all farmers irrespective of whether or not they are Nestlé suppliers. The veterinary services are offered free of charge and medicines are provided at wholesale cost. Even this wholesale costs are adjusted against subsequent milk payments to the farmers, thus, providing enough time to make the payments, and hence affordable. Nestlé also supports farmers in other growth areas like artificial insemination programmes for their cattle, subsidize the purchase of milking machines and help them to procure loans. During the past few years, approximately INR 500 million (USD 10.8 million) has been invested in Moga to: install cooling tanks and chilling centres to preserve the quality and nutritional value of milk; provide veterinary aid; promote breed improvement; assist in dairy development projects, and other related activities. Investment of nearly INR 300 million (USD 6.5 million) has been undertaken in procuring goods on behalf of farmers, to be supplied at wholesale prices. The system used in Moga enables Nestlé to purchase more and better quality milk directly from hundreds of thousands of farmers. This has helped them to earn better profits, by providing improved nutritional value-added products to customers, and also helped the suppliers of milk to enhance the quality of milk. This has improved the region, and brought increased income to the area's dairy-farming communities. In addition to their direct support for farmers, Nestlé is continuously implementing initiatives to improve quality of life in the communities around their factories in India, including the provision of clean water sources at village schools and nutrition education for teenage girls.

China
In China, Nestlé's Shuangcheng milk production facility is the fourth largest in terms of annual dairy production. A unique milk-collection programme called 'Factory and Farmers', which provides farmers with technical assistance while eliminating the need for middlemen is practiced here. This has improved traceability and accountability across the supply chain. Through the programme, more than 300 free training sessions for dairy farmers in the region is undertaken by the company. These programmes are anchored by agricultural extension experts, who introduce farmers to best practices and new tools, and offer continuous skills development. Farmers are also given access to new technologies to improve cow selection and to ensure feed quality. The introduction of biogas digesters has reduced effluents contaminating local water resources. Thus, here also Nestlé is able to fulfil the sustainability requirements of CSR.

East Africa
In East Africa, Nestlé is partnering with the East African Dairy Development Board (EADD) to help secure and increase sustainable milk production in Kenya and Uganda over the next two years. Here, the programme focuses on training, advice, and assistance based on the world class Nestlé experience. The programme, financed by the EADD and the Bill and Melinda Gates Foundation, offers technical assistance to dairy farmers in all aspects of feeding, breeding, and milking practices. Nestlé very closely monitors safety and quality standards of the products. This is achieved by implementing the food safety management across the entire value chain—from farm to processor. Regular audits are conducted to ensure quality of production and delivery. Nestlé also provides technical assistance to two EADD factories involved, on quality control and food safety management. It is estimated that 155,000 families in Kenya and Uganda will be able to emerge from extreme poverty over the next ten years and the real income of dairy farmers in the region will double. This, in fact, meets the UN millennium goal requirements excellently.

Discussion Questions
1. Do you think the CSR practices of Nestlé help it to meet the UN millennium goals?
2. What is the driving factor behind the dairy project undertaken by Nestlé?
3. How do you think Nestlé is combining profit earning and social responsibility? Do you think Nestlé is gaining any advantage by practicing this?

Source: Adapted from www.community.Nestle.com

Index

Business 1, 3, 89, 124, 147, 186
   categories 4
   customers 1
   demand–supply 3
   development 4
   dilemmas 89
   free market 152
   functional areas 1
   impacts 89
   Indian Companies Act 4
   industrial corporations 25
   marketplace 4, 95
   profit 147
   sectors 4
   stockholders 1
   system engineer 6
   trading companies 4
   utility 3

Capitalism 229
   humanizing 230
Child labour 130
Company 4, 5, 37
   bonds and shares 40
   confraternity 38
   corporation 37
   development 39
   early corporations 38
   incorporation 5, 41
Company/corporation
   mission 149
Companies 163
Consumerism 3, 83
Corporate governance 40, 42, 50, 186
   agency 44
   board of directors 43
   fiduciary 46
   fiduciary duties 43
   governance 43
   management 43
   sociological theory 49
   stewardship 46

theories 44
transaction cost 49
Corporate Social Responsibility (CSR)
   accountability 14
   analysis 8
   common good 10
   continuum 10
   corporate social performance 11, 55
   definitions 8
   dimensions 5
   economic perspective 9
   guilds 21
   history 13, 18
   ill-defined concept 7
   importance 5
   inclusive growth 277
   inequality 135
   merchant class 21
   modern 24
   philanthropy 22, 24, 38
   religion 19
   responsibility 12, 50
   return on investment (ROI) 58
   role of the state 18
   social cohesion 150
   social contract 16
   social impact 54
   social responsibility 135, 138
   stakeholders 149, 330
   sustainability 150, 186
   trade-off 149
   welfare state 164
   understanding 12
   viewpoints 8
CSR framework 147
   apprehensions 154
   corporate culture 156
   corporate ideology 152
   creating 156
   culture 148, 152, 155
   global ideology 166
   history 150

Index | 347

history and culture 147
implementation 157
implementation framework 166
Indian tradition 169
integration 159
national ideology 163
operation and process 160
risk analysis 149
statutory regulations 163
stereotyping 164
strategy 148, 154, 155
CSR model 285
CSR reporting 189

Distributive justice 122

Educational institutions 134
 stakeholders 134
Emotional quotient 92

Framework
 business in the community 190
 EIRIS 194
 environmental reporting 211
 global reporting initiative 186
 Green America 192
 Infosys 196
 Philips 203
 regulatory bodies 189
 securities indexes 188
 SiRi 195
 stock exchanges 189
 Tata group 197
Free market 3, 7, 83
 cartelling 3
 niche marketing 3

Global CSR 284
 CERES principle 292
 CSR codes 286
 CSR practice 286
 DSI 292
 multinational companies 285
 Sullivan principle 292
 the Harkin bill 295
 Valdez principle 292
Globalization 2, 153, 163, 225, 230, 287
 consumerism 225
 global crises 135
 glocalization 287

liberalization 7
modern economy 6
nationalism 155
Governance 154
Government initiatives 270
 public sector undertakings (PSUs) 270
 voluntary guidelines for CSR 271

Indian economy 265
 guild system 265
Indian saga 265
 challenges 275
 community development 275
 gift system 266
 LPG 267
 post-independent 266
 private sector 267
 reforms 267
 rest houses 266
 society 269
Indonesia 300
 AFLI CIO 305
 conglomerates 301
 emergence of CSR 303
 examples of CSR 309
 global compact 306
 history 300
 Indonesia business links 306
 modern business 301
 national committee on corporate
  governance 307
 PROKASIH 308
 PROPER 308
 Suharto 300
 Sukarno 300

Leadership 52

Markets 118
 capital market 118
 consumer market 119
 labour market 119
Media 138
 conscience-keeper 138
 social awareness 139

New Zealand 310
 background 310
 examples 312
NGOs and not-for-profit organizations 128

donors   130
registration   129
traditional professions   130
NPO   129
NPOs and NGOs   130

Poverty   132
Professionals   90, 94

Rating   185
   global reporting initiative   186
   history   185
Road ahead
   future trends   333
   optimistic view   330
   pessimistic view   331
   public-private partnership   336
   stakeholder model   335

Society   284
Stakeholder(s)   12, 17, 41, 82
   competitors   88
   customers/consumers   87
   employees   86
   government   88
   intangible aspects   92
   relationship   85
   society and community   89
   stockholder   85
   suppliers   86
   taxonomy   84
Stakeholder theory   48
   shareholder   48
Sullivan principle   126
Sustainability   15, 244, 225, 233, 332
   Brundtland Report   235
   effective change   238
   ISO 26000   238
   stakeholder   332
   triple bottom line   240
   triple loop learning   245
Sustainable   6

The Club of Rome   185
The UK   295
   Association of British Insurers   298
   background   295
   Cadbury code   297
   cooperative society movement   296
   East India Company   296
   London principle   297
   Luddites movement   296
   Mississippi Bubble   295
   Opium war   296
   transparency initiative   298
   UK Joint Stock Companies Act   296
   UK Limited Liability Act   297
Trusteeship   25

United Nations   136
United Nations Organization   129
UNO
   World Bank, IMF   154
   World Trade Organization   154
Utilitarian   122, 129
   business   229, 231
   concept   126

Values   5, 7, 17, 53, 93
   business ethics   136
   corruption   152
   duty, rights, and justice   9
   ethical   138
   ethical standards   16
   ethics   93
   holistic growth   95
   tax havens   152
   transfer price   156
   trust   150, 230, 332
   virtue   138

Women empowerment   132
World Economic Forum   149